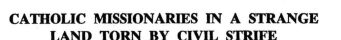

CATHOLIC MISSIONARIES IN A STRANGE LAND TORN BY CIVIL STRIFE

This, the 40th day of the siege of Wuchang, peace negotiations have been concluded. The City has surrendered to the South, the Cantonese. We now realize that all the information at our disposal during the past weeks has been misleading. Hupeh and the neighboring provinces are already subject to the new regime. In this city many thousands have died of starvation. The sights witnessed daily are revolting and deplorable. The helpless and the hopeless, the women with faces wan and haggard, the younger people with hands pressed against their stomachs, shouting with hunger, all like walking corpses, moving about, heedless of bombs or bullets. Within the city there is no burial ground and the supply of coffins has long been exhausted. Along the street, corpses lie around any old place . . .

Avon Books by WILLIAM E. BARRETT

THE SHADOWS OF THE IMAGES

THE SUDDEN STRANGERS

THE WINE AND THE MUSIC

THE EMPTY SHRINE

THE FOOLS OF TIME

A WOMAN IN THE HOUSE

THE LEFT HAND OF GOD

THE SHAPE OF ILLUSION

The Red Lacquered Gate

William E. Barrett

Authors Choice Press
New York   Lincoln   Shanghai

The Red Lacquered Gate
*The stirring story of the early days of the Columban Fathers' Catholic mission
and the courage and faith of its founder, Father Edward Galvin.*

Authors Choice Press
an imprint of iUniverse, Inc.

For information address:
iUniverse
2021 Pine Lake Road, Suite 100
Lincoln, NE 68512
www.iuniverse.com

Originally published by Sheed and Ward: New York

ISBN: 0-595-26232-5

Printed in the United States of America

DEDICATED TO ALL COLUMBANS
PAST, PRESENT AND TO BE

CONTENTS

ACKNOWLEDGMENTS

The debts which I incurred in the research and writing of *The Red Lacquered Gate* are many. I cannot acknowledge them all, nor adequately repay any.

Father Donal O'Mahony, nephew of Bishop Edward J. Galvin and erstwhile editor of *The Far East,* American edition, inspired and fanned my interest in the subject and, after my commitment to the book, offered encouragement, much solid fact and occasional conjecture. He was the indispensable element.

Very Rev. Timothy Connolly, who was superior general of the Columban Society when I started on a long project, contributed greatly to my understanding of the society and its men. His successor, Very Rev. James A. Kielt, was no less generous, offering many valuable suggestions.

I owe deep gratitude to Father John Blowick, who shared with my wife and me his rich memories. The Most Rev. Patrick Cleary also shared with me his many recollections of Bishop Galvin; he and his diocese in China deserve a book of their own.

Dr. Michael O'Dwyer illumined the achievements of the society for me in terms of human beings. Father Timothy Leahy was a great source of information, particularly about the Chinese parish, its organization and its people. Father Edmund Lane, to whom I am indebted for one of the richest interviews about Bishop Galvin, was a source, too, of odd facts about a priest's life in China. Father Paul Hughes provided valuable answers to questions, and Father Seamus X. O'Reilly supplied me with marvelous material on the bishop's friends in Brooklyn.

Father Daniel P. Fitzgerald gave me more anecdotes

9

than any other single source. Father Gerard Marinan threw open to me the archives of Navan. Father Daniel Conneely, editor of the Irish edition of *The Far East*, was most informative, as were Fathers Denis McAlindon, Joseph A. Whelan and Charles O'Brien.

I owe much to the Very Rev. Daniel Boland, pro-director at Omaha, and Father Fintan Keegan, vice pro-director; to Fathers Abraham Shackleton; Thomas Murphy; Edward McManus; Joseph Mullen—archivist at Omaha, who answered letters and phone calls with all manner of detail and much good humor—and my neighbor from Colorado Springs, Father John F. Cowhig.

Among the many happy experiences during the research for *The Red Lacquered Gate* was a luncheon with The Most Rev. Cornelius Lucey, Bishop of Cork, as well as an interview with Canon Edward Fitzgerald, who knew Bishop Galvin as a boy. Another boyhood friend who told me many anecdotes was Maurice O'Connell, of Cork.

The family, of course, provided primary sources on the life of Edward J. Galvin. To all of them I am grateful for hospitality, for information and for warm, friendly interest.

John Gavin, who provided for Bishop Galvin's needs after his expulsion from China, shared his memories with me. Frank Hall, news director of the National Catholic Welfare Conference in Washington, D.C., gave me access to his library and back files, as did his successor, Floyd Anderson. Patrick F. Scanlon, managing editor of *The Brooklyn Tablet*, aided me in solving a few riddles of the Brooklyn era.

One has difficulty in expressing gratitude to letters but, to any reader of this book, my obligation to letters is obvious. I am grateful, too, that the following unpublished books were written: *The History of the Society*, by Rev. John Blowick; *The Trumpet Call*, by Rev. E. J. Galvin; *The History of Hanyang*, by Rev. Abraham Shackleton, and *Father John Henaghan*, by Rev. E. J. McCarthy. *Lorettine Education in China*, by Sister Antonella Marie Gutteres, S.L., which was published, was also a most helpful volume.

The only work prior to *The Red Lacquered Gate* on the life of Bishop Galvin was a pamphlet by Robert T. Reilly, titled "Christ's Exile."

10

One last note of gratitude belongs to *The Far East,* the monthly magazine of The Society of St. Columban. I consulted, with profit, the files of the Irish and American editions, regretting that I could not also see the edition from Australia.

To all of those who helped and who have not been thanked, my apologies.

WILLIAM E. BARRETT

Denver, Colorado
January 15, 1966

Behind the red lacquered gates,
wine is left to sour, meat to rot.
Outside these gates lie the bones of
the frozen and the starved.
The flourishing and the withered are
Just a foot apart—
It rends my heart to ponder on it.

—TU FU
Circa 700 A.D.

PART ONE

Everyone
Was
Young

1 : : PEOPLE NAMED GALVIN

The tall, gaunt man faced the press in Hong Kong. He was shabby and his clothes did not fit. He was obviously weary but his eyes were patient and he spoke with soft courtesy. He was one of the great men, by any human measurement; a hero, a builder, a commander, a man who had sailed all the seas and who spoke many languages fluently; a man who knew the cities of the world and many of the world leaders; a man who had known song and laughter, who had lived long months with death.

"I do not know what you want with me," he said, "nor how much of my story will interest you. I was born in Cork, Ireland, in 1882, near a small place called Newcestown. I went to Brooklyn, New York, when I was a young man. I learned everything that I had to know in Brooklyn, everything that I needed later...."

* * * * *

There were many people arriving on earth, or leaving it, in 1882. Among the departures were Henry Wadsworth Longfellow, Giuseppe Garibaldi, Mrs. Abraham Lincoln, Anthony Trollope, and Jesse James. The arrivals were a more interesting lot, including in their number such people as Franklin Delano Roosevelt, John Barrymore, Geraldine Farrar, Leopold Stokowski, Igor Stravinsky, Sigrid Undset, James Joyce, George Jean Nathan, Rockwell Kent, Felix Frankfurter, Jacques Maritain, Fiorello La Guardia, Eamon De Valera—and Edward J. Galvin.

All of the newcomers were babies, of course, and of little interest to anyone outside of the family circle; few of them had as little promise of world attention as the Galvin child, who arrived on November 23 and who was promptly christened Edward. His birthday was the feast of Saint Columban but neither relatives nor neighbors laid any emphasis on that. It was much more interesting

15

to Irish people that the day was the anniversary of the Manchester Martyrs, a grievance day against Britain that dated back to 1867.

Newcestown was a village of no great size and of little renown. It derived its name from a British Captain Newce who had failed in an attempt to become the local Oliver Cromwell and who existed in the regional folklore as a rather ridiculous character. The people of the village were people of the soil who sent their share of young people abroad as emigrants and who, in their own remaining, settled firmly in one place and put down immovable roots. They were not compromisers in either religion or politics.

There had been Galvins in the Newcestown area, under various spellings of the name, since 1663, and there was a firm record of O'Galvins at the Battle of Corcomroe Abbey in 1317. One of the Galvins was said to have traced the family origin to Melesius, king of Spain, and to have established it in Ireland through Cormac Cas, king of Munster, in A.D. 483. Both claims were regarded with reserve and a pursing of the lips. In 1882 John Galvin, a tall, strong, handsome young farmer, who had changed the spelling of his name from his father's "Gallivan," sought a wife. He found her in Mary Lordan.

The Lordans had impressed their name upon the records in West Cork as early as 1200. Mary Lordan was a farmer's daughter, taller than most women at five feet seven; light-brown hair and blonde coloration, oval-faced and possessed of the Lordan nose, long and prominent. She was the seventh child of her mother and the fact was always to possess significance for her. She believed in signs and wonders and she read miracles into small commonplaces. Repeatedly she saw herself as the central figure of supernatural manifestation, as a person of exceptional vision, if not second sight. She was ten years younger than John Galvin. They were married on the fourth of February, 1882.

The ownership of land by those who lived on it was a new thing in Ireland. For centuries, absentee landlords lived in England on rents from land that the majority of them had never seen. In 1881 procedures for the purchase of land by the Irish were clarified and John Galvin was one of the young men who longed for possession of the soil he worked, who was not afraid to go into debt in

16

acquiring it. He owned a threshing mill, and his decision to farm lengthened a working day that was already long, but he still found time for local politics. He was one of the active, progressive young men of the region, and highly respected.

On the 23rd of November, 1882, John Galvin rode his horse to the forge three miles from his rented farm outside Newcestown. He left his wife with her mother who had come down from the Lordan place to stay with her. It was a cold, gray day and the dark came early. When John rode over the crest of the hill on his return journey he saw a banner of flame above the roof of his house. Believing that his home was on fire, he whipped his horse to a gallop. As he neared home the crimson column disappeared. He entered his door to discover that his first child had been born during his absence and that it was a boy.

Such is the legend, which may have been born many years later than the baby. Perhaps not. It is suspect because it is a tale related almost exclusively by women. The story told by men features the exuberance of the normally quiet and undemonstrative John Galvin; his pride in his first-born son, climaxed immediately after the child's baptism when he carried the youngster in his arms to the high altar of the church. "Accept him, Lord," he said, "and make of him whatever you want him to be. To thy honor and glory, Amen."

John Galvin ultimately became the father of nine children; but he never repeated that exultant proclamation of his fatherhood nor the solemn dedication before the altar. His son, Edward, growing up, had no sense of being the preferred child or his father's favorite. John Galvin had little time to spend on small children and there was a new small child nearly every year. The man's strength was drawn upon to its limit as he struggled to acquire land and animals; the woman, bringing a family into the world and raising a group of lively boys, had a house to keep and a garden to maintain and many roles in the affairs of her husband. The Galvin children were not spoiled; they had a sense of community, of family loyalty, of each individual serving in his own place and according to his capacity.

In his family, Edward Galvin was known as "Ned." He looked like his mother and he had the Lordan nose. His mother, lacking a daughter and realistic in the facing of her needs and her necessities, sought an aide and an assistant in him. She taught him the skills that she would have taught a girl. He learned early to cook and to sew and to darn, to take care of the children younger than himself. When his mother decided to open a provision shop, the family moved in to the village and he assumed the responsibility of a full-time baby sitter for John (Seano), Richard, Denis and Patrick, the children immediately after him.

Ned Galvin became a solemn child, a loner, with no close friend among his contemporaries and no time for their sports. In the adult world of imagination and of eloquent storytellers, when the work was done and the dark came down, he stepped into the background and was accepted as a quiet listener from whom naught but listening was expected.

There was tradition and an accepted form to conversation and storytelling in a country house. The neighbors knew one another well and had grown up together. They were dwellers in one small part of a small island with no adjacent mainland from which to draw fresh material, so the figures in the stories were familiar figures and the stories themselves were oft-told tales. Among those who assembled there was always a strong percentage of literal folk who did not tolerate radical changes in the stories which they knew well. These people acted as a check on the imaginative who, confronted by them, developed great ingenuity and skill in the making of small changes, the adding of a new detail, the elimination of a minor character or the changing of a background. Ultimately, as the many twists and adjustments were absorbed, a new story emerged from the old. Such a new story was accepted, however; like the people, it had grown in the community and was part of it; it was not alien, not imposed from the outside.

The long evenings when he listened before a peat fire were part of Ned Galvin's education, part of his experience. He was imaginative and his mind did not stop with acceptance of a storyteller's tale; it moved beyond the story to the area of supposing, to the seeing of the different story that would have developed if a different character had been involved in a tale, if a different decision had been made at a critical moment. Stories moved in his

18

mind; but he listened to the elders, to those who commanded attention when they spoke. It was a magical world of learning for a boy, that place of listening.

Ned Galvin's mother always played a leading role in the gatherings at her own hearth. She prided herself that she was welcome where men gathered, and she had small regard for women. She was a great reader, as readers were rated in Newcestown. Books were few, but she read the newspaper from Cork City and she discussed the news, arguing her points with any man if her opinion was challenged. She was Mrs. John Galvin, but no one ever referred to her as Mrs. Galvin. She was forever Mary Lordan to those who knew her; in talks around a fire, in the village, or on the road.

John Galvin, in the political arena of the area, had a reputation as a shrewd debater, but in small family gatherings he was content to leave the platform to his wife, smoking quietly, following the conversation with his ears and his eyes, saying little. He loved music and was at his best in the song sessions which often took up the entire evening. In this his son Ned followed him. Ned learned songs from the time that he learned to talk. He haunted anyone who could play any musical instrument and he learned to play, after his fashion, the harmonica, the jew's-harp and, ultimately, the violin.

Ned Galvin, in the years of his growing, absorbed a sense of family and of family names that he never lost. He knew, too, that he was Irish and, above all, that he was a Cork man. Later in his life he would hear the opinion expressed that the people of Cork are defensive in their exaggerated expression of county identity, that a sense of inferiority underlies it; but he never believed that. As a boy, with no personal knowledge of any other county, he gloried in his identification with Cork. It was the largest county in Ireland, ranging in scenery from the mountains to the sea, and one would find anything within it if one looked diligently. The men of Cork were braver, the women fairer, its land more abundant in the harvests. There was nothing grandiloquent in all of this. He actually believed in the Corkonian superiority, as the men and women from whom he absorbed his faith believed in it.

He was a Roman Catholic. This was unquestioning faith of another order. Here there was no alternative, no necessity to assert or to prove, no one to question or to challenge. God had created the world and all within it. There was a sublime mystery of one God and three Divine Persons. Jesus Christ, Second Person of the Holy Trinity, became man and died to redeem mankind. The Mass was the perpetual offering of that sacrifice, and at the Mass Jesus Christ became flesh and blood under the semblance of bread and wine. Sinners confessed their sins to the priest and received absolution. At death one went to heaven for the reward of a virtuous life, or to hell for the eternal punishment of unrepented mortal sin, or to purgatory for penance and for purification. One prayed for the welfare of the living and for the salvation of the dead.

As he grew older, Ned Galvin learned more of Catholicism, the profundity of its philosophy and the depth of its sacred mysteries, as he learned, too, more of Ireland beyond the boundaries of County Cork; but the simplicities remained always with him and were part of him, beyond outside challenge. It was as natural as breathing to say "God bless all here" when entering a house, to stop and say the Angelus when the bell rang, to speak to God and the Blessed Virgin and the saints in prayer as one spoke to friends and neighbors. One did not consciously think or reason about all this; it was.

Ned Galvin was a tall boy when he was very young and he maintained an advantage in height over his contemporaries through the growing years. He was straight and swift and exceptionally strong, but shy and withdrawn. He attended the Newcestown National School as did the other youngsters of the area; one hundred and fifty of them, equally divided between girls and boys. The girls were taught by a woman team and were strictly separated from the boys, even to the extent of a different time for recreation. The school itself was a long, narrow stuccoed building located on high ground. From the front of it one could look across the wide fields to the south and see the Protestant church of Farran Thomas. Ned Galvin saw the church every day of his life but he had no curiosity about it. It was alien, of a different world, the symbol of an incomprehensible way of life.

This Newcestown region was soft and lovely, lacking in spectacular beauty and unknown to tourists; a series of low hills separating the Valley of the Bride from the Valley of the Bandon. The hills marched from east to west and the rivers, flowing between them, flowed eastward. Fuchsia grew along the roads, and this was remarked as an unusual thing since the roads were thirty miles from the sea.

In 1891 Mary Lordan Galvin was pregnant again, as she had been in 1882, '85, '86, '87, '88 and '90. All of her children were boys, and she had never been given the daughter that she wanted. This time she was calmly, quietly certain. "It is the seventh child. It will be a girl," she said.

The baby was born and it was a girl. She was christened Katherine but everyone in the family called her "Kate." She was the seventh child of a seventh child of a seventh child and much was made of that. Oddly enough, Kate actually did seem to have extraordinary qualities and became the strong point of reference in the family; the one human being close to her mother in years of stress, the contact point for all of the others.

When Ned Galvin was eleven years old, his father decided that the boy needed to get away, to break with a home environment that was, apparently, shutting out contemporaries. He enrolled him in the Classics School of Professor Fitzsimmons in Bandon. The school fee was five pounds a year and board had to be arranged for five days a week. Such expense loomed large to John Galvin; but he managed it as quietly as he managed most of the decisions of his life, and the decision was wisely made.

The Fitzsimmons school was an important chapter in the life of Ned Galvin. He was released suddenly from responsibility for children younger than himself and thrown into direct competition with boys of his own age. Bandon was a large town of more than three thousand inhabitants. Ned lived with the O'Driscoll family on North Main Street and roomed with his cousin, James O'Callaghan, who was also from Newcestown parish. On weekends the two boys pedaled home on their bikes, about eight miles as the road wound. They rode back on Sunday evening, accepting the weather that they found.

The trips held much of adventure in terms of old castle and priory ruins to be explored, old battlefields to be traversed. Here the MacCarthys and the O'Mahonys had fought each other, and the lesser families of MacSwineys, O'Keefes, Murphys and Barretts. Many of the events related around the fire had happened on these roads and in these fields; a man's ancestors had died here. All this was heady thought for a boy of eleven or twelve, running his hand over the worn stone of an ancient tower or taking refuge from a sudden shower under the arch of an old abbey. Yet the hero whom Ned Galvin discovered in Bandon did not belong in the place and was not even Irish.

He discovered Buffalo Bill.

Colonel Prentiss Ingraham's nickel novels of the great scout and buffalo hunter, Colonel William F. Cody, were enjoying great popularity with young readers in Ireland where they sold for tuppence; but Ned Galvin had never seen the books until he attended the Fitzsimmons school. Buffalo Bill was, of course, strictly a hideaway item in the Classics School, but traffic in the books was brisk. Ned purchased copies, traded copies and sold copies. The world of the prairies, of the American west, of Indians and outlaws and U. S. Cavalry and Scouts was the world into which he escaped from all that was dull and commonplace. He was enthralled and enchanted. He found places where he could hide from adults who had work for him to do, places where he could read without interruption, touching in imagination a far frontier of great shaggy beasts, of painted savages, of covered wagons, fast horses and brave men. In the summer when he was home from school and working on his father's farm, he shared the books with Seano, his brother, a year younger than he, and together they fashioned lariats, roping their father's colts and riding them bareback.

John Galvin had thirty cows which Ned herded during the summer, but he did not like caring for or slaughtering animals. He liked to plant things and watch them grow. Flowers responded to him where they would not grow at all for his mother, who loved flowers and wanted them around her. Ned found this seemingly irrational fact fascinating, but he did not find an explanation. He compromised the problem by planting flower beds for his mother and finding time to tend them.

The Galvin family had grown for his mother if the flowers would not. In 1899, following Ned, there were Seano, Richard, Denis, Patrick, Michael, Kate, James and Mary. Denis was confirmed that year. He was, reputedly, the brightest of the boys, the best scholar, but he had

22

suffered a birth injury and he was unable to walk normally. On Den's confirmation day, his father cried when the boy hobbled down the church aisle on his crutches. The boy's mother, who had a reputation for never crying, clicked her tongue impatiently.

"Instead of weeping," she said, "you ought to be thanking God that he's confirmed."

Ned Galvin was sixteen in the summer of 1899. He served the Masses of Father Dan Cummins, a particularly well-loved priest, and rode sick calls with him. Always devout, he spent more time in church that summer and often he would lie quietly on his back in the field, looking up at the sky. Finally he went to his father.

"I'd like to be a priest," he said.

"Are you sure?" John Galvin asked.

"I've thought about it."

"May God bless you in the thinking, then. We'll send you to Farranferris, please God."

It was as simple as that; not a subject to be talked to death between a father and his son.

Farranferris was the seminary of Saint Finbarr in Cork City. It was located high on a hill overlooking the town. From the playground a boy could look toward the red sandstone side of the pepperbox steeple of St. Ann's in which the famous bells of Shandon hung. There was a clock in the tower and a salmon weathervane on the top. Behind St. Ann's there were roofs and domes and steeples. To the left, on a bleak hill, were the Victoria Barracks in which the British garrison of Cork was quartered.

Ned Galvin adjusted uneasily to the junior seminary. He disliked and distrusted cities and he resisted regimentation. He did, however, have an awe of the priesthood, and the priests who guided him were shrewd psychologists. He moved into a pattern that was stronger than he was; when he ceased to fight it, the days went easily, almost magically, despite his problems as a scholar. He was, his teachers said, weak on fundamentals and he had to do extra work to make up for his deficiencies. At the year's end he stood in the middle of his class, neither scholar nor dunce, saint nor sinner.

The vacation period was release, a return to home and long free days guided, at least theoretically, by his own will. The farm work was heavy and his father expected him to help. He worked and his muscles hardened, and occasionally he escaped from work to light, lazy loafing with his brother, Seano. On one such escapade he met disaster.

He found his lariat in the barn and carried it with him when he went across the fields accompanied by his brother and a boy named Maurice O'Connell. There was a small abandoned house behind the town and, as they neared it, a cat started up from the grass and some dogs pursued it. Blessed with a long start, the cat scampered up to the sloping roof of the house which was a low structure but a safe platform from which to look down on barking enemies.

The three boys ran after the dogs and Ned Galvin, who had had no practice in roping for a year, uncoiled his lariat. The rope spun high in a circle, glistened in the sunlight, then flowed toward the roof top. The loop dropped on the cat and he leaped to escape it, spinning from the roof edge into the space below. The dogs killed him in seconds.

The cat belonged to the curate of Newcestown parish, Father Francis O'Connor, who held the boys, Ned Galvin in particular, strictly accountable for its death. The priest swore out a complaint and the boys were brought to court.

"I'll never be a priest now," Ned Galvin said desperately. "They won't keep me at Farranferris after this."

He was wrong, but it was months before he could be certain of that. His father paid his fine and he returned to the seminary in the fall, positive that there would be a letter at Farranferris before him, reporting on the cat's death and his own court experience. While nothing was said to indicate that he was in disgrace, he moved with a suspended sword over his head. Any day the letter might arrive and he would be told to leave the seminary. He was young and the worry dominated his days and he failed in his studies. As a consequence, he spent an extra year in Farranferris, which was the fact that changed the direction of his life, the fact which involved his life with countless thousands of human beings two oceans away from Cork.

2 : : ROSALEEN DHU

The ghost of the curate's cat, having slowed Edward Galvin's march to the priesthood by a full year, vanished into the mists of the regretted and the deplored. The student who had Farranferris behind him when he came home for the summer of 1902 was no longer a boy. He was a determined young man of strong convictions, stubborn opinions and a vision of the role he had been created to play. He walked on the road with his father during the first week of his return.

"I've been thinking on what I can do," he said. "I want to be a missionary. I would like to go to a missionary college."

John Galvin absorbed the shock slowly. "Being a priest in Ireland is enough for any man," he said gruffly. "There's work here for you to do."

"I'm not the man to be a priest in Ireland. I have a feeling about myself. I'd do well in the missions."

"The blacks in Africa will get along without you. Your place is here."

"It's them I was thinking of."

"And the same thing it is. I'll give no consent to it. The best priests in the world come out of Maynooth. You'll go there or you'll go to farming."

The younger man's mouth set tightly. "I'll go to farming," he said.

As far as he was concerned, the issue was sharply drawn. He had completed his courses at the junior seminary and his vocation had taken shape and form in his mind. He was not content to minister to souls already in the fold of the faith; he wanted to go among the pagans and bring the words of Christ to them. He had read a small pamphlet on the work of missionaries in China and it had excited him, but, China or Africa or anywhere at all, he wanted to be a missionary. That was the priesthood as he felt called to priesthood. If he could not be the priest whom he could see in his mind, he would not compromise; he would go to the land.

His parents were disturbed at his decision. His mother believed as his father did about the missions. In Ireland at that time, a boy whose parents could afford to pay for his education did not prepare for a career in some distant and heathen country. It was taken for granted that a boy who entered a missionary order was either unable to meet the standards of the regular seminary or was in need of a missionary burse to finance his education. Ireland was self-contained, provincial, without missionary spirit, blessed in its own priests and in the priests that it sent to America and to Australia. The Galvins were sincere people, willing to make deep sacrifices for the blessing of a priest in the family but secure in their sense of a right decision which any neighbor or relative would unhesitantly endorse; the place for Ned Galvin was Maynooth, the greatest seminary in Ireland and, perhaps, the greatest seminary in the world.

Ned did not in the least agree with them, but an Irish boy with a vision of the altar in his mind could not stand in defiance of his parents. They had been fair to him. They had offered him an alternative to the course which they advised. He accepted the alternative.

John Galvin still worked his farm to the left of the road as one came out of Newcestown, but he had purchased a farm at Clodagh, about seven miles away, within a mile of Crookstown and Kilmurry. It was a property of seventy-two acres; hay, grain and pasture land. John Galvin planned to build a new home on it but, in the interim, he had a housekeeper named Kit Sullivan living in the thatched-roof cottage. He sent Ned down to take care of the land and the cattle, assisted occasionally by Seano. Denis was living in the cottage and he had worked out his own compromise with the problem of a working day; he was passionately interested in beekeeping.

Ned worked with the animals and with the hay and the corn, but he had a greater interest in building and he made excuses to build new buildings or to repair the old. He attended the market days and the fairs in Macroom and Bandon when he could, usually with Seano. He had studied the native tongue at Farranferris but he was not fluent in it as his parents were, and he was fascinated by the people from the Gaeltacht, the Irish-speaking district west of Macroom, who spoke nothing else. He often danced far into the night and the word that he had abandoned the seminary made him more interesting to the girls.

Ned Galvin was not a handsome young man, but he was a compelling one. That summer he was nineteen, nearly six feet tall, a quick, alert youth who appeared slow and awkward, a careless dresser who would wear anything that he found without giving a thought to it. He had the prominent Lordan nose and his hair never looked brushed. His smile broke slowly, starting in his eyes; when he laughed, he laughed heartily. He loved to sing and he would play, or attempt to play, any instrument. He remembered every folk tale and every ghost story that he had ever heard and he had his own variants of many of them. He was popular with men and he liked girls.

The summer passed swiftly; the work and the evading of work, the fairs and the music, the dancing and the seeing of oneself in a girl's eyes, the hot weather and the chill weather and the quick rains. At the end of August, Ned Galvin went back to his father.

"I want to be a priest. There's no avoiding it," he said. "I'll go to Maynooth but I'd rather go to All Hallows."

He went to Maynooth. Seven boys from County Cork made the journey together, new students on the longest trip that any of them had ever taken. They traveled on the Great Southern and Western Railway to Hazelhatch, seven miles from Maynooth. Jarveys with sidecars called to the boys invitingly.

"How much?" Ned Galvin asked.

"Ten shillings each man and we carry your baggage."

"Too much," Galvin said.

He had assumed leadership of the small party in the course of the journey, although seemingly making no effort to lead. Several of his companions saw no alternative to paying the ten shillings now, but they were not organized in opposition.

"The walking of a few miles never killed a man," Ned Galvin said.

He drew a jew's-harp from his pocket and started to play:

Oh, from Bantry Bay up to Derry Quay
And from Galway to Dublin town

No maid I've seen like the brown colleen
That I met in the County Down.

Seven young men divided up the bags and boxes, including Ned Galvin's. Galvin walked ahead of them and the young men walked seven miles on the road to Maynooth. At the end of the miles there would be seven years of study awaiting them before they could be priests. They came within sight of the single, tall spire which looked grim in the deepening twilight. At the stern gate they paused. The couchant stone sphinxes on either side of the gate seemed to be staring at them with cold contempt. Ned Galvin put his jew's-harp away.

"Well, we are here," he said, "and devil a ten shillings did we pay."

"Yes," said a voice from the rear, "and witness who carried no burden but a nice mouth harp."

Ned Galvin did not turn his head. "If I hadn't played, you wouldn't have marched," he said.

He was staring at the Georgian Stoyte House in front of him. He was awed, perhaps suddenly aware of what Maynooth would demand of him, of what it would offer.

In 1176 Maurice Fitzgerald had built a castle here and there had been a seminary before the time of Henry VIII. In 1795 the present seminary had come into being, largely through the efforts of Edmund Burke. The British Government, committed to ruthless suppression of Roman Catholicism in Ireland, had been confronted with the terrible reality of the French Revolution which had spilled the royal heads of France into the dirty baskets of the guillotine. Ireland, because her priests could not be educated at home, had been sending boys with vocations to the seminaries of France. Against the danger that French revolutionary doctrine or other radical continental ideas might be brought to the British Isles by these young men, the education of Irish priests in Ireland seemed not only acceptable but desirable.

The British parliament appropriated money for buildings and for the support of "An Act for the Better Education of Persons Professing the Popish or Roman Catholic Religion." The foundation stone of the seminary was laid on April 20, 1796, and Catholic scholars accepted the sacrifices demanded of them as the first faculty.

28

They were, some of them said facetiously, dedicated to "plain living and high thinking" and to "living spaciously on a tidy income."

There were six hundred students studying in Maynooth when Ned Galvin entered it. As a "chub" he fared no better than did a freshman anyplace else. He moved into a world of long monastic silences, intense study, frequent prayer and the discipline of the Clock; there was a time for everything. Years later the writer of a magazine article stated solemnly: "Maynooth moulded him along the traditional pattern of the Irish clergy; solid piety, plain theology, unquestioned loyalty to Pope and Bishop." Probably so, but there was more than that, so much more.

In the course of seven years there are engaging pictures. One tree on the campus was known as the Cork tree and Ned Galvin was the leader of many discussions there. No other county had a special tree for the simple reason that no other county sent to Maynooth such passionate talkers. "Look at those Cork men," a Cavan seminarian said one day. "Plotting how to blow up the place, no doubt, while still remaining in the state of grace."

There were plots concocted under the Cork tree and ideas, some of them grandiose. Ned Galvin was one of the most prolific producers of ideas and schemes in the seminary. A dead-level, middle-of-the-class student, he had an imagination which leaped beyond the books. One of the ideas which he did not originate but which he supported ardently was "Buy Irish." He made speeches on the subject and wrote letters, insisting that employment in Ireland would rise, and emigration drop, if the Irish themselves created a demand for Irish-made products. He followed friends and foes into stores to check on their purchases.

"Most of the things that he insists we should buy Irish," a classmate plaintively said, "aren't even made in Ireland."

He was a strong young man with easy-flowing muscles; one of the fastest men in Maynooth on the sprints; but either through indifference or a lack of coordination, he was never a man of note in hurling or football. He had a gift for verse writing of all kinds, even in Latin.

Summers meant home, Newcestown and Clodagh, and work on the farm. The local coursing club was in need of funds one summer and seeking for a means of raising money. Ned Galvin volunteered to train and direct actors

29

and actresses from the region, cast them in a play and present the play for the benefit of the coursers. His family laughed at him but he recruited a group of young people, including his own relatives, and surprised them with his air of authority and no-nonsense attitude.

"This is a serious project," he said. "I won't tolerate anyone in it who does not take it seriously."

The play he had chosen was titled *Rosaleen Dhu* and not one member of the cast he had chosen had ever seen a play of any kind. The play was produced in a tent at Crookstown and at Macroom. It drew four hundred people and was considered a great success. Only one scene went wrong.

The play concerned an eviction, and one bit of action called for the firing of two shots. On opening night it was assumed that the gun was loaded with blanks and nobody checked the assumption. When Jack Manning pressed the trigger twice, he missed the whole cast with two live bullets.

"My brother, the sometime priest, had his angels with him," Pat Galvin said.

Ned Galvin had a definite place in the community after the success of the play. He was no longer a mere local boy studying for the priesthood; he was someone linked to a definite accomplishment, to something that was to be discussed for years. He was aware of his new place in public and it amused him. He had done something which he had wanted to do and he had enjoyed himself. Many other people had a good time. He had no desire to stretch or to prolong his small fame, and he made no attempt to direct another play, although there were many requests for a repeat offering.

The younger Galvins were becoming human beings with personalities and wants and doubts and desires. Ned was a hero to the younger ones, a comrade to Seano, a favorite companion of the crippled Denis. One afternoon, Mary Lordan Galvin made a visit to Clodagh without advance warning. Her two sons were in the area of the beehives and Ned was playing his violin. There was a moving, shifting, intricate pattern of bees in the air above and about him. The bees climbed and dived and changed positions with the precision of ballet dancers. Mary stared at them.

"What is it they're doing?" she said.

30

Ned did not glance at her. He seemed absorbed in the music that he was drawing from the violin. Den hobbled over on his crutches.

"He does it whenever he's in the mood," he said, "and the bees like his violin music. They understand it."

At one time or another various members of the family and a few neighbors witnessed the dance of the bees and they commented on it; but Ned never discussed it. It was something he did. If anyone asked him questions about it, he walked away.

The older Galvins and Lordans found Ned interesting, as he found his brothers and sisters interesting. He was drawn into the unending discussions of events and from those discussions, and the earlier listening in silence before the fire, he drew most of his knowledge of the contemporary world. Neither Farranferris nor Maynooth had permitted the reading of newspapers. During his ten years at the two seminaries, the Boer War had been fought, with Irish sympathy strongly pitched to the Boer cause; Queen Victoria had visited Ireland; the Boxer Uprising had taken place in distant China; the Wright brothers had made man's first flight in a heavier-than-air machine; the first Irish-speaking college had been established in Ballingeary, County Cork; Japan had, astonishingly, beaten Russia in a war; there was a great Irish tenor named John McCormack who was charming audiences in London and in America. A man did not learn of such matters when he was studying for the priesthood; he absorbed the knowledge of them when he was with his own people.

There was other knowledge. One of Ned Galvin's uncles was fond of whisky. When Ned was home and his uncle was wandering, Ned took care of the situation, sometimes seeking the wanderer as far away as Cork City. There was a strong bond of sympathy between the older man and the younger, the drunkard and the seminarian who was pledged to abstain from alcoholic beverages. Ned took his uncle home, ministered to his needs as one man to another, got him to bed and, more importantly perhaps, listened to him.

"He's given me more than I've ever given him," Ned said one night. "I've learned from him and that is my gain."

He did not elaborate on what he had learned. He was

inclined to be aloof from human beings, but he was interested in them, curious about them, a good listener and a good reader. He knew the history and the folklore of his own area of Ireland, of Kilmurry, Kilmichael, Newcestown, and Macroom as few young people did, and he knew the land, the people who lived on it and the ghosts of people who had died on it. There was a spot on the Geataban road that appealed strongly to him. He would walk on it and stand, looking down on the widely separated farm houses, the cultivated land, the stand of trees; ash, elm, sycamore, hawthorn, a few poplars.

"It's the loveliest view in Ireland," he said.

It wasn't that; but the elements were so blended in the picture as he saw it that it was forever memorable to him. He would stand motionless, staring across the Valley of the Bride to the Ridge of Rathlenn where colors and symbols blended: the misty grey of Clodagh Castle and the dull white of Crookstown Mill, the grey again of Castlemore of the MacCarthys and a smoky glimpse of Kilcrea Abbey. At the rim of the horizon, when the light was flat on the valley, he could see the green and the red, the limestone and brick of Cork City, shimmering a little and not quite a solid place.

"He loved Cork, or at least a part of it," a classmate said, "and one wondered why he was driven in himself to leave it, as indeed he was."

The summer was short and Maynooth dominated the balance of his year. It sheltered many types of human beings, faculty and student, but in itself it was big, impersonal, almost inhuman. "The place was no respecter of persons," a priest-graduate wrote. "I might say it had no interest in persons."

Maynooth tended to its own reasons for being. The business of Maynooth was to train young men for the priesthood, to shape and to develop them. It had well-staffed faculties in arts, science, philosophy and theology. Maynooth took seven years out of a man's life and left none of that time unemployed.

Ned Galvin paid to solemnity the solemn attention which was its due, but he found ways, as others did, to move joyfully through the intricate pattern of study and prayer. There is a story, probably apocryphal, that in his last year at the seminary he was master of ceremonies for

32

the solemn High Mass of an archbishop. Many high ranking prelates participated, adding their colorful presence before the altar, adding their voices to the singing of the Mass. The archbishop curled his fingers into a beckoning gesture and Ned Galvin moved behind the grouped priests, pausing at the celebrant's right. Without looking at his master of ceremonies and still seeming to be singing with the others, the archbishop said:

"Tell Murphy to stop that bellowing."

Ned Galvin glided away. Moving easily as though in the service of ceremony, he paused again beside Monsignor Murphy, a bulky, red-faced man of great vocal energy. "The archbishop says to sing up," Ned Galvin said.

On March 21, 1909, when his son was within a few months of the priesthood, John Galvin died suddenly. He had reached most of the goals that he had set for himself. He had a good family, he was esteemed by his neighbors and he had acquired land that would provide farms for his sons. Only the one fond desire had been thwarted. "It will be a great day when we go to Ned's first Mass," he said to the table on Christmas Day. He did not have that.

Mary Lordan Galvin did not cry when her husband died. Her children were to say of her that they never saw her cry. She did, however, lean heavily on the arm of her eldest son.

"Ned, lad," she said, "I'll need you now more than ever I did."

"I'll be here—somewhere."

He believed that, as he had every reason to believe it. It was as certain as the coming of light and darkness, as the rising at 6:00 A.M. at Maynooth, as the regular ringing of Maynooth's many bells. At the end of study there was ordination and the seminary turned its finished product back to his bishop who, in the course of time, assigned him to a parish in his own county. Ned Galvin might well anticipate the spending of his life in the one parish, as so many priests did. He would be within reasonable distance of his home, his family, his relatives and the neighbors through all the years of his life.

In the spring months of 1909, however, a rumor was seriously discussed under the Cork tree at Maynooth. There were, as had never happened before, no vacancies in the parishes of Cork. The bishop had new priests coming

33

from the seminary and nowhere to place them; no parishes, convents or hospitals with room for another priest. By May first a member of the faculty semi-officially confirmed the rumor to the Cork men due to be ordained.

"I'd advise you to seek a parish in America or Australia," he said. "Preferably in America. You can come back in three years and be all the better for the experience."

Ned Galvin had no friends in the ranks of the American or Australian clergy and no idea of how to seek a parish. A classmate of his, Ulick Buckley, was corresponding with a pastor in Brooklyn.

"He'll find a place for me, I believe," Buckley said. "He's most encouraging. That may be because I plan to stay in Brooklyn, although I'm saying nothing of that here. He might not like it if you have only three years in mind."

"Three years is all I want."

Ned Galvin looked at the address which the other man wrote on a strip of paper: Rev. J. J. Flood, St. Saviour's, Sixth Street and Eighth Avenue, Brooklyn, New York. It proved to be the only link he needed. Before he was ordained, Ned Galvin had received and accepted an invitation to be a priest to the diocese of Brooklyn.

There was a moment of anticlimax when a most embarrassed bishop formally told his new priests from Cork that he could not use any of them. The Most Reverend Thomas O'Callaghan had 190 priests serving in his diocese. The Archbishop of Dublin, and only the Archbishop of Dublin, had more; but there were no vacancies. "God has been good to us," the bishop said. "Our priests have remained in good health. Go with my blessing where you find a parish and an opportunity, but come back to me in three years."

Ordination day was June 20, 1909. The young men filing into the college chapel at St. Patrick's, Maynooth, were many, and ten of them were from Cork. Ned Galvin, for all of his years of study, for all of his qualities of leadership which implied sophistication, was oddly innocent as he approached the altar for the solemn sacrament that would make him a priest forever. He wanted sincerely to serve others, to bring Christ into places where He was

34

unknown, to administer and to console and to convert He asked little for himself and he wanted little.

On June 21 he said his first Mass at the convent of the French Sisters of Charity at Cabra. Not until he had said his Mass in his home church, St. John's of Newcestown, did young Father Galvin tell his mother that he was going to America.

She took it better than he had expected. It was, after all, unlike the missions; a civilized land with a great many Irish people in it. Three years was not a very great time and a priest could not dictate to a bishop. If there was no room for Ned in Cork, one had to accept the fact of the matter.

Father Edward Galvin sailed from Queenstown on the White Star liner *Oceanic* on July 22, 1909, for New York. He traveled second-class at a cost of ten pounds, ten shillings, and he was accompanied by a young priest, a classmate named Joe Devane, with whom he had very little in common outside of the Roman collar. He walked the deck and he sought solitude and he fought the seas of loneliness and homesickness which built up in him as the ship steamed westward. He did not want to leave Ireland for America. The United States, as he thought of it, duplicated the situation that he was leaving; it was not mission country, it was a settled land where one played the priest to people who already possessed the faith. The United States had no glamour for him. Ireland was *Rosaleen Dhu* and he, ordained for Cork, had been evicted, banished from her presence.

Ned Galvin was young and emotional and romantic, more than a little frightened. He was twenty-seven years old.

3 : : BROOKLYN—
    IN REGARD TO IT

Father Edward J. Galvin's problems with customs were minor. He owned little and none of the little was frivolous

35

save, perhaps, his violin. His traveling companion, Father Devane, was swooped upon by a large welcoming committee and Father Galvin stood alone—a tall, thin young man in an unpressed suit, a Roman collar two sizes too large for him, and a large flat hat that was safely anchored to the lapel of his coat by a length of button-bearing cord. A short, dapper priest approached him, slowed and cocked his head to one side.

"You've got to be Galvin," he said.

"I am—but why do I have to be?"

"You're here and you're certainly from Ireland. Nowhere else in this big world! Where did you get that hat?"

"In Cork. Is there anything wrong with it?"

"I never saw anything like it." The short priest extended his hand. "I'm Father Barrett from St. Saviour's. Bob Barrett, that is. You get a lot of first names over here."

Ned Galvin shook the extended hand. "I expected Father Ulick Buckley. He was a classmate of mine. We've been exchanging letters."

"I know. He had some terribly important thing to do, something very American. I never saw anyone become American so fast." Father Barrett turned his head to one side, looking up out of the corners of his eyes at the taller priest. "Did you know that he is Reverend Ulick O'Sullivan Buckley now?"

"No, but it doesn't surprise me."

"It surprised me. It exudes elegance and he is not an elegant type. How about helping you with the bag or the fiddle? We'll get going."

Father Ned Galvin had his first vision of New York in the company of Father Robert Barrett. The other priest had been a year ahead of Galvin at Maynooth and was from Tralee in Kerry. They had not known each other at the seminary. The Barrett voice had a constant quality; it flowed on and on. He was, he said, an amiable man who was forever being burdened with jobs that no one else wanted to do. He did not know what would ultimately happen to Galvin, and that was not his affair, but, temporarily, by invitation of Father Flood, the rector, Galvin was welcome at St. Saviour's. It had a large rectory and there was no problem to putting him up. He would be placed in a parish, too. No problem about that, either.

"Brooklyn is better than Manhattan," Father Barrett said.

36

"You'll like it. Father Flood won't remember you from one minute till the next, but he's a good pastor."

Manhattan was large, tightly packed, noisy and confusing; Brooklyn was quieter, with a greater sense of space, a slower timing. There were no priests at home in St. Saviour's rectory, a fact that did not seem to surprise Father Barrett. He led the way to a large room on the second floor and laid the violin, which he was carrying, on the bed.

"Guest room," he said. "Yours for a while. I suppose you'd like to see the church."

"I would."

It was an attractive church and more money had been spent on it than on churches that Father Galvin knew in Ireland. He looked curiously at the confessionals. "You know," he said, "I've never heard a confession."

"Not one?"

"Never."

"Lord! They did send you out barely hatched, didn't they?" Father Barrett tapped the back of a pew with his fingernails. "Look here. You've got to start some time. The first confession is the difficult one. There's a chapel in the basement and a confessional down there. I'll let you hear mine."

He led the way to a dark stairway without waiting for assent, pausing for a moment at the head of it. "If we started hearing a confession upstairs," he said, "we'd have a dozen of the faithful popping in on us in five minutes They're pious folk and they've nothing else to do, the most of them."

Father Galvin followed him down the stairs, more embarrassed than he was willing to admit. In the sombre quiet of the chapel confessional he heard his first penitent. Father Barrett laughed aloud as they returned to the rectory.

"I like you," he said. "You'll never go American as I do, or as the eminent Ulick O'Sullivan Buckley emphatically does. You were a damned fool to leave Ireland."

"Why?"

"Because I've a sound notion that you belong there and nowhere else."

"My mother has the same notion."

"And she's right."

They re-entered the rectory and the other priests were

37

home. For all of his light touch and his seemingly frivolous attitude toward people, Father Barrett's estimates of his contemporaries were sound. Father Flood was absent-mindedly hospitable, seemingly more interested in his extending of a welcome than in the man he welcomed. Father Buckley, in clothing, speech and attitude, was emphatically American. Father Galvin was amused at the Buckley vocabulary of American slang. Late that night, in the guest room that was temporarily his, he wrote to another Maynooth man who would not misunderstand him: "You should see old Ulick. He is going through an ecclesiastical adolescence."

There was a period of four days when nothing was required of the visitor save a reasonable amount of orientation and sightseeing. Father Buckley took him to Manhattan and up Riverside Drive to Grant's Tomb. Father Barrett conducted a tour of Brooklyn neighborhoods and explained the intricate transportation system which supported simultaneously the elevated railway and the horse-car. There were four bridges across the East River and two of them, the Manhattan and the Queensboro, were new, opened to the public in the summer and spring of 1909.

They were coming home to the rectory on the day that they visited the bridges when Ned Galvin said suddenly: "Bob, I've been thinking. There are stores here in great quantity, big stores and small ones. If we went to them and made a strong point of it, we could have them buying Irish goods instead of whatever they're buying."

"Not me, laddie. I haven't time to change the world," Father Barrett said.

His side step did not operate as well when Father Flood asked him, referring to Father Galvin: "Has this fellow any place to go? We can't keep him here indefinitely, you know."

"Oh, no. That is, I think not. He wouldn't confide in me, of course. I was a year ahead of him at Maynooth and I'm from Kerry. He's a Cork man, a classmate of Buckley's."

Father Flood ignored the obvious attempt to escape involvement. "I think you should see to him," he said. "The bishop is in Rome and this man could be here a long time waiting for him to return. Take him up to the V.G. and get him settled in a parish. It will be best for him and for us."

38

The vicar general was Father P. J. McNamara, an impressive-looking man with gray hair and smooth, florid skin that looked buffed and polished.

"Ah, yes, Father Galvin," he said. "I have a report on you here from Maynooth. I have an opening for you in Holy Rosary parish. Monsignor McEnroe, the pastor, is one of our fine old priests. He may be a bit difficult or cranky at times, but that's an old pastor's prerogative, Father. You'll do well to remember that he was a priest here in Brooklyn before you were born. . . . Wait! I'll give you a note for him."

Father Galvin carried the note and Father Barrett walked beside him, quiet for once and without comment. Holy Rosary rectory was at Chauncey Street near Reid Avenue, an old frame house with bay windows upstairs and down. It was set back from the macadamized street and it had rose bushes in front of it. The pastor himself opened the door. He was a man of medium height, with no apparent excess weight. He had a full crop of white hair and a large face. His eyes were of faded gray. He seemed vague about the identity of Father Barrett who was introducing another strange young priest to him, but when Father Flood was mentioned, he nodded his head. He invited the two young man into his parlor but it quickly became obvious that he did not understand the purpose of the visit.

"Monsignor McEnroe," Ned Galvin said, "I was sent here by Father McNamara to be your assistant. He wrote you a note."

The old pastor accepted the note but he did not look at it. "My assistant," he whispered. His whole body straightened as he turned to Father Barrett.

"This young Irishman, in regard to him," he said, "which of my assistants is he replacing?"

"Father O'Carroll."

Monsignor McEnroe rose with the agility of a young man. He crossed the room and opened a door into the hallway. "Father O'Carroll, with regard to it," he called out loudly, "there's a young priest here that's sent by the vicar general to take your place. You can leave this house as soon as ever you like and, in regard to it, the sooner the better I'll like it."

A voice as loud as his own made answer to him. "I'll be

happy to leave this house if there's any truth in what you're saying; but I'll leave when I get good and ready, and not one minute before."

Father Barrett looked appalled. He rose swiftly, one hand touching Ned Galvin's shoulder. "Well, Old Man," he said, "there's nothing more that I can do for you. You've got a parish."

Father Galvin had a parish. His pastor came back from the hall door, rubbing his hands together. "What's your name again? Galvin, is it? Well, you'll have to sleep in the guest room till that fellow upstairs gets out. In regard to that, I'll show you where it is."

Monsignor McEnroe seemed amiable and cheerful, but it was a question, of course, whether he was pleased at securing a new assistant or losing the old. He led the way to a small room in the back of the house. The month was August and the room was very hot.

"In regard to it," the pastor said, "it will do till we have a better. Look now! I want you to remember this. In regard to it, the house is lighted by gas. This is how we turn it off. You must not blow it out. Under no circumstances, blow it out. Never!"

He demonstrated the turning of the control valve, turning it slowly. Ned Galvin smiled at the solemnity of it and Monsignor McEnroe addressed himself to the smile. "Ah, maybe they have come to gas in Maynooth these days," he said. "Have they now?"

"No," Ned Galvin said. "They have electricity."

"Electricity! Have they now? Think of it!" The pastor, momentarily taken off balance, shook his shoulders impatiently. "In regard to it, Father Galvin, remember what I told you and don't go blowing out a gas light."

He left the room abruptly without a goodnight. Ned Galvin was to learn that the use of "in regard to it" and variations of the phrase was characteristic of McEnroe in conversation or sermon; that young people of the parish made bets on the number of times he would say it in the course of a single sermon. He had been clocked once at 112 times.

Ned Galvin had brought his bag with him. As he was unpacking, the door opened without a preliminary warning knock. A lean, dark-haired man stood in the doorway.

40

He was wearing trousers and undershirt. He looked angry.

"I'm Father O'Carroll," he said. "And you're taking my place?"

"I am. At least, that's how I understand it."

"Well, you're welcome to it. It's the worst parish for a priest that there is in Brooklyn. There are things that no man should be expected to endure."

Father O'Carroll leveled a long, thin finger like a pistol. "McEnroe's got the biggest, ugliest set of false teeth this side of the cemetery. They fit him badly and he takes them out halfway through a meal and he sets them on the tablecloth beside his dinner plate. How do you like that?"

Ned Galvin met the other man's angry eyes. "I'll get along with him," he said.

Father O'Carroll turned and walked away, leaving the door open. He stayed in the house four more days and he did not speak another word to Ned Galvin, who was to learn that Monsignor McEnroe was not so easily described as the other priest had described him. There were depths and contradictions in his nature; he could not be measured in obvious terms.

On his first morning in the house, after his breakfast, Ned Galvin was alone at the table with his pastor. "What's your name again?" Monsignor McEnroe said. "Galvin, is it? Well, in regard to it, Father Galvin, the monthly salary of an assistant in the parish is fifty dollars. It is payable at the end of the month but, in regard to that, you're a young man and just here from Ireland. You're probably needing money."

He counted out fifty dollars on the tabletop. "In regard to it," he said, "it's your first month's salary and there's work to do and it's up to you to find it."

He walked away then, making no attempt to explain about duties or responsibilities, offering no information about people in his parish or parish societies; no caution, no instruction, no advice. His assistant went to the small guest room he was occupying and, when he was alone, counted the money. It was more money than he had ever possessed, more money than he had ever held in his hand at one time. He had paid for his steamship ticket in two installments and the total of them had been a little less than this.

There was a knock on his door and when he opened it, Mary Stritch, the housekeeper, was standing in the hall. "Excuse me, Father," she said, "but there's a girl downstairs who says her mother is dying. Father O'Carroll has been taking care of sick calls, but he says that I should tell you about it."

"Thank you, Mary. I'll be right down."

Father Galvin hurried to the pastor's room and borrowed a stole, pyx and oil stock. Monsignor McEnroe asked no questions. He seemed detached entirely from the problem of a young priest facing his first appointment with death at the bedside of a penitent.

The penitent's daughter was waiting in the parlor and when Father Galvin saw her he was startled, hesitating momentarily before he spoke to her. The girl was a Negro, of deep black skin, full lips and wide eyes. Ned Galvin had never seen a Negro until he came on his journey to America. There had been Negroes working on the *Oceanic* and he had seen a few in Brooklyn, but he had never spoken to one until he asked this girl her name. He walked with her to her home in a poor area close to downtown. When he entered the bedroom in which the ill woman lay, he expected to encounter someone as black as the girl who accompanied him; the woman on the bed was as white as he was.

Father Galvin sat and talked to her. Her eyes were wide, fixed intently on his face. She had little strength but she wanted to make her confession. She had been away from the Church for many years. He heard her and he absolved her and she said the Act of Contrition falteringly.

"Father," she said, "are you an Irish priest?"

"I am. My name is Galvin, Edward Galvin, and I'm from County Cork."

"Praise be to God for it," she said. "I've asked Him all my life to send me an Irish priest when I came to die. God is good to me. Father, I'm Irish, too. I'm from County Mayo. I married a colored man when I came out here and he has been very good to me. My poor children."

Her voice trailed off. There was sweat on her face and Father Galvin wiped it off gently with his handkerchief. Two smaller children, boys, had crept into the room with the girl who had come to the rectory. He addressed himself to the girl.

"Do you know where to reach your father?" he said.

She shook her head. "He works on the railroad. He's away."

"Is there a friend, a neighbor?"

She nodded her head, looked anxiously at her mother, then hurried from the room. She returned with two women, Negroes. The woman who had come from County Mayo had slipped into unconsciousness. One of the women leaned over her and spoke, but there was no reply. The two little boys began to cry.

Father Edward Galvin stayed in the room until the woman died. He walked back to the rectory through city streets on which houses and small apartments stood. There were open spaces of land, too, which were called vacant lots. Boys played in these lots. There were many children and their voices were loud with the excitement of being young. Brooklyn was a good place to be. There was work for a man to do, even missionary work if a man wanted that. That poor woman from Mayo did not know a single priest by name and her children had no religion at all. There would be other such people if one looked for them.

He entered his church and he prayed for the soul of the Mayo woman and he was oddly content.

4 : : THE EAST SIDE OF
THE RIVER

The social standing of Holy Rosary parish was never high. There were fine people on the parish roster and some impressive homes within the boundaries but there was a downtown area, too, and the fringe of downtown, which was semi-slum. The next parish, Our Lady of Victory, only seven blocks away if one measured from church to church, was considered the fashionable parish of the area; Our Lady of Good Counsel, a few blocks more distant in the other direction, was considered more pretentious. At Good Counsel the ushers wore cutaway coats and striped trousers on Sundays. Father Galvin mentioned this odd fact to Monsignor McEnroe. The old man grunted.

"And a sight to behold they are!" he said.

Father Ned Galvin placed no premium on social standing or morning coats; he liked Holy Rosary as he found it. He liked the medley, the many kinds of people who entered the church. He liked the sense of struggle, the knowledge that people worked industriously for their money and that there was never too much; no waste or sham or show. Needs were real in Holy Rosary when needs arose.

It was a peaceful parish on the whole. He liked to walk its streets in the twilight and watch the lamplighter at work. The street lights were gas burners and a stocky man with a slight limp tended them. He had a short bayonet on the end of the pole which carried his torch. The bayonet opened an aperture in the base of the lamp and the torch lighted the burner. It was a deft performance and there was poetry, if one looked for it, in the man's hurried charge down the long blocks as he pursued the darkness, banishing it with his fragile weapon. A small dog accompanied him, standing till a lamp was lighted, then racing to the next dark standard and waiting for light to overtake him.

There weren't three automobiles in the parish. Several well-to-do families had horses and carriages and so did the two doctors. Girls came to the church in carriages to be married, and the departed left the church in horse-drawn hearses for the cemetery. There were two electric trolley lines and a horsecar line within easy walking distance of the rectory. People took walking for granted. The priests had no other means of covering ground, not even a bicycle. There were, however, many parishioner bicycles.

The rectory did not have a telephone because the pastor did not like telephones. Parishioners in need of a priest sent a member of the family to the rectory or phoned the Daltons, one block away, who would have one of their young girls deliver the message. Father Galvin, when he settled in, received his calls from the priests he knew through Mr. Joyce, the undertaker. There were ways of doing anything that had to be done and life was compounded of many simplicities which wise people never magnified to profundity.

44

Father Ned Galvin sought to keep himself employed in the service of the parish and when he needed help he appointed assistants. His first problem was that of the boys' Sunday school. Holy Rosary did not have a school, so the two hundred boys who attended each Sunday in the basement of the church were public school students. They considered Sunday a holiday, not a school day. They ran, played leapfrog, fought and even tossed baseballs around in the church.

Monsignor McEnroe did not give any time, thought or attention to the Sunday school and Father O'Carroll, whose responsibility it had been, had given little aid to the few devoted women who tried, courageously, to hold it together. Father Galvin met the boys and was not impressed by their swagger or the obvious challenge in their attitudes; he had grown up as the eldest in a family of brothers. In his first few minutes, facing the boys, he identified the leaders of the group. The quality of leadership in another man was a quality which he always recognized. His attention focused on the one boy who had trouble-maker written plainly on his face, the boy whom the others would follow either through fear or ineffectuality. The Galvin finger leveled.

"You are my assistant," he said. "You are the captain. I'll want five lieutenants. We have to reorganize this Sunday school. It is an important activity."

His finger moved over the group, selecting lieutenants, while the newly-appointed "captain" wavered between a liking for rank and a habit of opposition. Lieutenants stepped out of the crowd and Father Galvin knew that he would have no trouble with this troublesome Sunday school.

"There will be promotions as we see fit," he said, "and demotions, if necessary, although that is unlikely."

He divided the boys, then, into easily commanded groups and brought in twenty women teachers, with each teacher instructed to recognize the rank of boy leaders and to consult with them when problems arose. He lent his own presence to the classes; a strong, fit, athletic presence which did not tolerate any serious challenge to its authority. Once he was in firm command, he invited friendly overtures and the boys became his personal army. He listened to their problems and when a problem was beyond

45

a boy's own solving, he provided aid. He bought shoes and clothing with his own small amount of money for boys who were in need, and he found jobs for boys who wanted to work after school.

Father Galvin reorganized the altar boys, too. He trained new servers himself and set strict schedules, barring from the altar those who did not measure up to his idea of what an altar boy should be. Parallel to these ventures, he met the women of the parish. In matter of time, he met them first.

A group of twenty women came to the rectory on the evening of his first Sunday in the parish. He had heard his first full evening of confessions the night before and had said two Masses in the morning, preaching his first sermon on the theme: "By the grace of God, I am what I am; without it, I am nothing." The parishioners had found him interesting—"an earnest speaker, not a brilliant one." The women who called on him were spontaneously organized, not part of any regularly functioning parish group. They sat in the rectory parlor and chatted. The priest from Ireland was not at his ease.

"What county are you from, Father?" one of them asked.

"Cork."

"Musha Mary," the woman said. "What a pity it is that he isn't from Mayo!"

He laughed with the others who laughed and the ice was broken. He discovered then that most of the Irish in Holy Rosary were from Mayo or Tipperary. There were some Germans in the parish and some Negroes. Most of the Germans went to a German church.

When the ladies left Ned Galvin knew what he wanted to do. He waited a few weeks before facing the pastor with his idea. "I'd like to take a census of the parish," he said.

Monsignor McEnroe said, "Why?"

"There are some people who don't come to church and we don't know too many of those who do. I'd like to know all these people."

"You would, would you? Well, in regard to it, Father Galvin, if you start a job like that you'll be expected to finish it."

"I'll finish it."

46

"Start it, then, and bother me no more with it."

Father Galvin was surprised at the quick and easy approval, because he still walked in awe of his pastor and he had felt the fury of the McEnroe fire a few times, particularly when he was late for Masses, meals, events; a decided fault of his and one which Monsignor McEnroe did not abide in anyone. He did not know that the chancery office was more surprised than he at the sudden lull in hostilities in Holy Rosary rectory. For years it had been quite the normal thing to have a visit from Monsignor McEnroe on Monday morning, demanding the removal of one of his assistants, and a visit from the assistant in the afternoon seeking a transfer. The advent of peace was unbelievable and a topic for talk.

"How is your new assistant?" one of the older priests asked Monsignor McEnroe at a clerical dinner.

"In regard to him, he's all right," the pastor said, "as long as you don't disturb him at his prayers or say a hard word about Ireland."

No one could remember such a favorable opinion on any assistant from Monsignor James McEnroe.

So there was amity of a sort, and Father Galvin faced his census taking and other new activites while his pastor moved comfortably in the smoothly oiled grooves of habit. The monsignor practiced the art of walking as exercise and as a means of reaching objectives. He wore a tall silk hat and clerical clothing of a cut that had been out of fashion for twenty years. He carried a cane and he seldom greeted anyone. When the mood dictated he walked to one of the trolley lines, boarded a trolley car and rode to the end of the line. Most of the trolley conductors knew him and none dared speak to him. He belonged to the country club although he never entertained, did not associate with the membership and played no golf.

"In regard to it," he said, "it's the only place I found where I could take a shower."

Father Ned Galvin learned to work for, with, and around Monsignor James McEnroe. He looked forward to the return of Father Connolly, the other assistant, who had been on vacation when he arrived at the parish. Father Connolly, when he did arrive, made no difference. He was a pleasant, good-natured priest who did exactly what he had to do, astonished that anyone should seek to do more. For companionship and for conversation on the problems of priesthood, Father Galvin went outside the parish.

The other priests from Cork notably Father Ulick Buckley and John Delea were settled into parishes; Father Delea in rather far-off Queens County and Father Buckley in the Bedford Park area within strong walking distance or comfortable streetcar distance from Holy Rosary. Father Bob Barrett, having served him amiably in the first two weeks of Father Galvin's Brooklyn residence, did not maintain even a thread of further interest in the man from Cork. He wasn't missed. New York, in that fall of 1909, provided more excitement than any man could handle in his spare time. The Hudson-Fulton celebration was staged in September and Ned Galvin went with Father John Delea to Riverside Drive in Manhattan to see battleships of the United States and of foreign nations at anchor in the Hudson River, kite-like aeroplanes flying overhead and replicas of Commander Henry Hudson's *Half Moon* and Robert Fulton's *Clermont* moving under their own power. There were bands and parades and uniforms, history alive and moving on the river and above it and beside it. The visit of Halley's Comet provided an additional thrill and there were many people convinced that the end of the world was imminent.

Father Ned Galvin had been aware for some time of an unused parish asset. There was no existent outlet for the great energy of the young women of Holy Rosary who were devoted to the Church and its priests. Such womens' societies as existed were designed for and monopolized by older women. Father Galvin casually asked three or four of the young men if they would aid in keeping his census records and he was astonished that so many girls when they heard about his need, came to volunteer; a far larger force of girls than he could use.

Two of his first helpers were sisters, Ava and Vera McHale. Ava was eighteen, a Sunday school teacher.

"I talked so much about the new priest," Ava said, "that my father went over to the rectory one night to meet him. This was most unusual because my father was a quiet man who was more apt to avoid people than to seek them out."

Frank McHale was an editor on the staff of the book

48

publishing firm of McGraw-Hill and he had been drama critic on a New York newspaper. He liked Father Galvin in that first meeting and became one of the great friends of the priest's life. They had a strong bond initially in their love of music and the theatre and it was a bond that they developed.

"My father really loved him," Ava said. "I always felt that he took the place of the son that my father lost."

John McCormack, in the dawn of his great career, came to New York in October, 1909. He was billed as "The Irish Caruso" and he opened the Manhattan Opera House season as Germont in *La Traviata.* He sang a series of Sunday concerts in addition to his operatic roles, and Frank McHale obtained two tickets for the first of the Sundays. He had tickets, too, for Chauncey Olcott, an Irish romantic singer, who opened on January 24, 1910, in a musical titled *Ragged Robin.* It was the beginning of a long series of performances which the two men shared, including all of the Gilbert and Sullivan operettas which came to the Academy of Music on Lafayette Avenue, Brooklyn.

The taking of a parish census was a new activity in Holy Rosary. The old-line faithful Catholics were accustomed to a weekly call from Owen Brady, the sexton, who collected ten cents from each Catholic family as parish dues that were over and above anything contributed on Sunday. Father Galvin, walking up one block and down the next, carried no list with him; he rang every doorbell, not caring whether a Catholic, Jew or Protestant answered the door.

There were people in the parish who had not entered a church in years, although they were baptized Catholics; Ned Galvin was patient with them, even when they were hostile or abusive. Some of these people, he discovered, were living in marriages that the Church could not recognize. Often there were the complications of children, economic dependence and love for the other partner. When he could not remedy an invalid marriage nor demand its abandonment, he was depressed; but he kept the depression within himself.

"Do not lose faith in God," he would say. "God has never abandoned anyone. Come to the church if you can't

49

come to the sacraments. Come to Mass every Sunday. Ask God to help you."

Some cases of straying were simpler; none of them were easy. He listened patiently to all the reasons that men and women find for turning their backs on religion, for walking away from the Church, for denying the existence of God. He found mean little sins of the spirit which had warped the natures of people and he found the sins of the flesh.

In one of the poorer neighborhoods, he found an Irish girl who was afraid of him. It did not take him long to discover why. She was living with a German who drove a brewery truck and she was six months pregnant. The man would not marry her and she suspected that he had a wife somewhere.

"Do you love him?' the priest asked bluntly.

"Ah, no. I thought that I did. Fair out of my mind I was. But he has been so mean to me because I got pregnant. . . ."

She stopped suddenly as the door opened. The man who stood framed in it was a big man, powerful, in his late thirties perhaps. Father Galvin spoke to the girl.

"You're coming out of here," he said. "You'll not have your baby while living in sin with this man and you'll not go back to him. You've got a long life ahead of you yet."

"I've no place to go."

"I'll find a place for you. Pack your things." The priest turned then to the man in the doorway. "You heard me," he said. "I'm taking this girl out of here. It's no place for her."

The man did not speak. He watched the young woman as she packed her clothes in a small bag. She did not look at him until she was ready to leave, then she straightened her shoulders, looked at him once and walked past him. Father Galvin took her to an order of nuns which specialized in the care of unfortunate girls.

"And she made out all right, too," he said. "She made something of her life."

Monsignor Joseph Kelly to whom he related the incident, naming no names, long years after the event, said: "It took more than a bit of nerve on your part. Weren't you afraid of that big truck driver?"

Ned Galvin laughed. "Oh, no. I was able to handle myself in those days."

The young priest's ability to "handle himself" won the boys to him. When the weather warmed in the spring, he took the altar boys and the stars of the Sunday school classes to the beaches on picnics and he played games with any group of boys in a vacant lot when he found a spare hour.

"He was the fastest runner I have ever seen," Jim Hall, one of his altar boys, said.

The speed was not only in his legs; he had incredibly fast hands. He learned without any apparent difficulty to field a baseball and throw it, although he had known nothing of baseball until he came to the United States. He was interested in the boys' discussions of the game and the universal enthusiasm for the Superbas, who kindled great loyalty even when they did not succeed in achieving a high standing in the National League.

"Who are they, these Superbas?" he said.

It was a day of heroes and the boys recited their litany. There were Manager Dahlen and Zach Wheat, Hummel and Barger and Miller and Nap Rucker.

"A lot of Germans!" Father Galvin said.

He went, out of curiosity, to see "the Germans" play. The ball park was in South Brooklyn. Ebbets Field had not yet been built and the word "Dodger," applied to a Brooklyn ballplayer, was a word of the future. Ned Galvin liked baseball and occasional attendance at games. The reading of scores in the daily paper became a part of his life.

He had another paper that he read. His mother subscribed to the *Cork Examiner* in his name as soon as she had an address in America. The *Examiner's* big news had long ago been told by the time it reached him, but the small personal items about the people and the places he knew were fresh; bits of knowledge or information obtainable nowhere else. Sometimes, after reading the paper, he was homesick. His best remedy for that was his violin. In the semi-seclusion of his own room, he played the old tunes that he loved and almost invariably ended up singing them.

He was singing one night when his door opened abruptly and Monsignor McEnroe was standing in the doorway. He had three or four songbooks under his arm. "With regard to it, Father Galvin," he said, "I think I'll pass around the hat. Do you know 'The Rising of the Moon'?"

"I do."

Father Galvin played a few bars, then laid aside the fiddle as the pastor started to sing. The old man's voice was high and thin and had small regard for key, but he was faultless on the lyrics. Ned Galvin sang along with him, accepting a minor role, singing obbligato. They did "Killarney's Lakes and Dells," "Who Fears to Speak of Ninety-Eight," "Come Back, Paddy Reilly," and several others. When he had had enough, Monsignor McEnroe rose and left as abruptly as he had entered, without a goodnight.

The evening was, however, a thawing of ice. The pastor encouraged no initiative toward himself from assistants, but he made occasional friendly gestures of his own to Father Galvin. Occasionally, and not predictably, he would relax at the table and reminisce about his career as pastor of St. Patrick's parish, Glen Cove, when Long Island was mission territory. He would talk, too, about Ireland.

"Ireland never lets you go," he would say. "Wherever you may be, it never lets you go."

Seano, Father Galvin's brother and the companion of his growing, was now in the United States. He was working in Jersey City and much of his work was at night, so the brothers rarely saw each other. People in Ireland could not understand that nor comprehend American distances. A woman in Macroom wrote many letters to Father Galvin asking him to call on her son and find out why he did not write to her. Her son lived in Boston.

Father Connolly was transferred from Holy Rosary parish and an earnest young priest named John R. Mc-Coy came into replace him. The new priest was a balance for many shocks and disappointments. Father McCoy was six years older than Father Galvin, born in Ireland but brought to the United States as an infant.

He and Ned Galvin were friends from their first meeting. They shared books and bits of parish news and the problems that came to them. Their friendship was good for both of them and it was good for the parish. They divided the work that had to be done and, as a two-man team, sought more work rather than the evasion of that which was obviously theirs to do. Father McCoy's sister

52

smuggled dinners to him and he accepted them through an open window on the ground floor. Ned Galvin was amused at this but did not accept invitations to share a repast admittedly superior to rectory fare.

"One meal is as good as another to me," he would say. "Let us not waste the thoughtfulness of your sister on such as I."

In time, Father McCoy created a whole series of stories about Father Galvin's careless eating habits and careless-ness of dress; humorous stories told without malice or ex-pectation of belief to priests with whom he felt at home. Usually Father Galvin was present during the telling and Father McCoy, who did not know him during his first year in America, would pretend that he, Father McCoy, was the first one to see him.

"I ordered him a plate of ice cream," he said, "and when he tasted it, he told me to send it back for warm-ing."

It was a time of simplicity, of needing nothing beyond the easily obtainable, of comradeship, of humor that was anything but profound. It was a time, too, of dedicated work, of serving God without ostentation, of walking hum-bly. In the course of his census taking, Father Galvin found many good Catholics who had never been con-firmed, many fallen-away Catholics who, seemingly, had never known the Church or what it taught. He organized classes of instruction from these two groups and em-ployed the young women who had volunteered their ser-vices to him. In the course of time he had an Adult Education Center of a sort in operation, and there were few nights in a week that found the church basement dark.

Daisy Hall, a tall, thin girl in her early twenties, became an indispensable aide in all of the projects, and the Hall family, like the McHales, became close personal friends of his.

Monsignor McEnroe did not acknowledge any of the parish activity as existent. He let Father Galvin go his way without interference, which was in itself remarkable. Fa-ther McCoy, who had never succeeded in awakening even the slightest interest in himself from the pastor, was not as fortunate. When Monsignor McEnroe went on a short vacation, Father McCoy had all of the old-fashioned pull-bells replaced by electricity-operated bells, paying for the change with his own money. On his first day home, without a word of comment, Monsignor McEnroe called a contractor and had the bells changed back to the old system.

Father Galvin took the bad with the good as Monsignor McEnroe dispensed his moods and his tempers. He had been nearly two years in the parish before he dared to extend an invitation to anything; he extended one then with his fingers crossed.

"Monsignor McEnroe," he said, "John McCormack is singing tomorrow night across the river. Will you go and hear him with me?"

There was a moment of suspense, of silence that seemed to grow and expand in the room before the breaking of it.

"I will," the pastor said.

They went out together for the first time in their association; the pastor in his tall silk hat and old-fashioned clerical garb, the curate in a shabby suit that fitted him badly, a collar too large. They listened to one of the great voices of the age as it drew the magic from Handel, and a few minutes later caressed the lyrics of a ballad or an Irish lament. For one of his encores, the Irish tenor sang "Cockles and Mussels." The two men walked out into a crisp fall night with more stars above them than two men could count. Monsignor McEnroe was silent until their feet made echoes from the street in his own parish.

"Cockles and Mussels," he said. "Did you hear him sing it? A tune like that! I don't know, in regard to it, when I heard it last."

He started to hum and then his old, cracked voice, carrying the melody badly, rose in song; Father Ned Galvin sang under him, offering him accompaniment. They had not been drinking but the night was big with a clear sky and Brooklyn was asleep, and the memory of their evening had been banked deeply within them.

> *In Dublin's fair city, where the girls are so pretty*
> *I first set my eyes on sweet Molly Malone*
> *As she wheeled her wheelbarrow*
> *Through streets broad and narrow*
> *Crying, Cockles and Mussels! Alive, alive, oh!*

They sang to the night and no neighbor awakened from sleep to upbraid them, and no policeman appeared to distract them. They entered their own house and Monsignor McEnroe did not say thank you. Father Galvin knew that he would never say thank you, never refer to the evening again. That was the old man's way. He did not have to say anything; the evening had been a sharing and sufficient of itself.

The young priest lay awake for a long time that night and he experienced a vast content with the place in which he found himself. The music of the evening and a magnificent voice had brought Ireland very close to him But Ireland had never seemed so far away.

5 : : THE END OF A LIFE

The idea that he had been born to be a missionary persisted in the mind of Ned Galvin. He was able, over relatively long periods of time, to rationalize his mission, to tell himself that he did all in Brooklyn that a missionary priest could do in mysterious China; serve the faithful as their priest, seek out the drifters and the fallen-away, convert those from outside the fold. Inevitably, restlessness returned to him and the conviction that there was, over some horizon of his priesthood, work to be done which he was qualified to do and which he had not yet found. The restlessness could be triggered by a phrase, a photograph, a story or an advertisement.

He was reading an article in a magazine one evening about the territory of Arizona, which was seeking statehood. One paragraph in the story mentioned the church problem of supplying missionary priests to cover a vast territory of mountain and desert in which the Indians lived. Arizona was not China or India or Africa; it was a territory of the United States. Father Galvin nevertheless set the magazine aside and wrote a letter to the Bishop of Tucson, offering him his services.

It was nearly three weeks later that a reply came to

55

him from The Most Reverend Henry Granton. The bishop complimented him on his zeal and thanked him for his offer. "I have a poor diocese," the bishop wrote, "and more priests than I can support. For that reason I am unable to accept your offer. There is, however, a way in which you can be of considerable help. I shall be very grateful for any Mass stipends you can spare for me and my clergy."

The letter was cold water to a young priest who had been thinking in terms of offering his life. He received the bishop's letter in the afternoon and that night his bed broke down. Father Galvin reported the damage to Monsignor McEnroe in the morning and the pastor called in Owen Brady, the sacristan.

"In regard to it," he said, "get a stout box, Owen, or two if the size isn't sufficient. A stout box, mind you, and get those springs up off the floor so Father Galvin can sleep comfortably."

Owen Brady produced the boxes which he installed under the bed of Father Galvin in support of the springs. Father McCoy insisted on trying the "repaired" bed and he was awed by it. He remembered, however, his own attempt to change the bell system of the rectory.

"I suppose that if you spent your own money for a decent spring, the old man would throw it out and reinstall the apple boxes," he said. "But you'll need a hide of callous to live with it."

The comforts of living seemed to mean as little to Father Galvin as did the food he ate or the clothes he wore. He lived in the work he was doing, the work that he saw ahead of him. He was in great demand for sick calls. People who were gravely ill, or who had seriously ill relatives, sought him out, asking for him even when Father McCoy was on sick-call duty. It was, in part, the gentleness and sympathy which the Irish priest brought to human trouble of any kind, but it was more than that. Father Galvin brought a calm confidence to a sickroom. He seemed to know immediately the degree of gravity which confronted him. His faith was strong, certain, without doubt, and the sense of certainty was communicable.

There was a sick call one day to a young mother who had two desperately ill children. The doctor said that neither could live; that one had spinal meningitis and the other had water on the brain. The mother was running from one to the other, half-hysterical, not knowing what to do for them but convinced that something could be done and that she should do it. Father Galvin told her to sit down. He looked gravely at each of the two infants, then turned to the mother, indicating the child with meningitis.

"Give that one to God," he said. "If you do, we will ask Him for the life of the other."

He turned away from her then and built a fire in her cold stove. There was kindling and coal in two boxes but no one had thought of the necessity for heat. In a few minutes he heard the young woman crying as she knelt beside the child with meningitis. She rose slowly and turned to him.

"I did it," she said. "I gave my baby to God. I asked Him to take her."

"Good. Now, let us ask Him if we may have the other one."

He knelt with her and he prayed. While he was praying, the woman's sister came in with another woman. Father Galvin asked the aunt to wrap the ill child warmly and put her in the baby carriage. He told the other woman to make the mother lie down and rest. He walked with the child and the child's aunt to the milk station which had recently been opened by a group of doctors.

"We'll do this every day," he said, "and the child will have fresh air and milk."

The baby that was given to God died on the next morning. The other child lived, to be the subject of an article in a medical journal and to become ultimately a nun, Sister Frances Theresa, O.P.

With the warming weather of 1911, spring racing into summer, the mission fever returned to Ned Galvin. An Irish missionary, who was making a round of calls on pastors and, if permitted, giving talks to parishioners, came to Holy Rosary. He was granted permission to speak to the people of Holy Rosary and to take up a collection for the African missions. He was in the rectory for a week before the collection Sunday and Father Galvin introduced him to his friends in the parish and spent every minute that he could spare with him. The collection totaled five hundred dollars, two hundred dollars more than any priest had ever received from an appeal at Holy Rosary. As he

57

helped to count the money, Father Galvin expressed for the first time his own intense desire to be a missionary. The missionary did not raise his eyes from the task of counting.

"Forget it," he said. "You have a fine parish here and a fine pastor. Take my advice and stay where you are."

There was a cold finality in his tone which left no gateway open to a renewal of discussion. Father Galvin felt that all the signs a man could read were pointing the way back to Ireland, if not to Brooklyn. There had been the letter from the bishop of Arizona and there had been, too, a dinner on October 7, 1910, which the New York Maynooth Alumni gave for Father Daniel Walsh, spiritual director of Maynooth, who was on an American tour. Father Walsh had made prophecies about his hosts and when he came to Father Galvin, he said:

"Ah, Galvin out of all of you is the one who will return to Ireland. Yes, Galvin will return to Cork."

In 1911 there were many news items out of Ireland. King George and Queen Mary visited Ireland and, with the Prince of Wales and Princess Mary, visited Maynooth. Archbishop William D. Alexander of Armagh, Protestant Primate of all Ireland, died. The Galvin family moved to Clodagh. In other parts of the world, the Italians were at war with the Turks; China, through the agonies of civil war, became a republic.

Father Galvin was intensely interested in the Chinese news. He was a persistent patron of the Brooklyn Public Library and drew every book that they had on China, new or old. He had to read late at night after he finished his letter writing; the long letters home and to friends in Ireland and America. His parish activity gave him little time for himself and he was acutely aware of how swiftly time was passing. He was in his last full year at Holy Rosary. Cork would reclaim him from loan in May, 1912.

That summer he won the regional baseball junior championship with his team of Sunday school youngsters who did not have a school behind them and who were the only team in competition without uniforms.

Father Galvin was a glamorous figure now, still carelessly dressed but possessed of many skills, at a physical peak and magnetically attractive. One of the girls described him in a still existent letter as "tall and thin, with a

58

great big stride in his walk, like a sprinter." Another stated that he had "beautiful hands" and there was universal agreement about his voice: "a gentle, soft voice, with a lovely flavoring from Ireland."

It was an innocent era in America and a time of slow maturing for the young, but the girls of Holy Rosary parish were very much aware of the big priest who was the dynamo of every parish activity. They romanticized him and literally fought for preference on his work lists. He must have been aware of them and have known the commotion he created, but no hint of such knowledge ever crept into any of his letters, nor any comment that could be construed as personal. They were nice girls, his parishioners, some of them more helpful than others; only one girl received greater recognition than that. Irene Delap was the subject of a letter to his mother and her photograph, enclosed with the letter, was carefully preserved in his mother's home.

Irene Delap was twenty-two years old, a frail girl who played the piano beautifully. Her health would not support regular employment, but she taught in the Sunday school and took care of the altar at Holy Rosary. She seemed to have a sixth sense where the priest was concerned, to anticipate his thinking, to know what he wanted before he wanted it. Father Galvin obviously relied upon her for many things, and valued her devotion. One day when she was checking his list of poor families for the Christmas baskets, which he had made a feature of Holy Rosary activity, she laid her pencil down suddenly.

"Father Galvin," she said. "Can I be your sister?"

He was probably startled. "I will be very happy to have you as my sister, Irene," he said. "If you will kneel, I will give you a brother's blessing."

Irene Delap knelt and he blessed her, setting a wall between them forever. He wrote that night to his mother, telling her about the girl and about his acceptance of her petition to be his sister. "She is a sweet and lovely girl," he wrote, "but she is not well. She spends what strength she has for God." His mother did not misunderstand him. She referred to Irene Delap always with respect and sometimes as "my daughter in Brooklyn."

The coming of the new year had significance for Ned

59

Galvin. Time was running out. He was aware of the fact that his pastor considered him a feature of the parish and he knew that Father McCoy took it for granted that he would remain in Brooklyn. They had discussed the matter.

"Ireland doesn't need you," McCoy said. "Ireland ordains all the priests it needs. Brooklyn is a growing diocese. You have grown here, found your work and your friends here. No one remembers that you came on a three-year loan. You belong here. You are a Brooklynite."

Father Galvin laughed softly. "There are people who remember that I came for three years," he said.

The letters from Ireland, particularly from his mother, had had a new urgency in them of late, an anticipation, a sense of days being counted. That urgency communicated itself to him. He was more aware each day of passing time and he agreed inwardly with Father Dan Walsh; much as he loved Brooklyn, when the choosing time came, he would choose Ireland. The other alternative had eluded him but he had to settle it firmly in his own soul before he could be content; either he was born to be a missionary or he was not.

On a bright, cold morning in January, 1912, he went to his room after breakfast to pick up some letters which he had written the night before. He had a clear day and he was going over the river to Manhattan to the office of The Society for the Propagation of the Faith on Madison Avenue. Father Galvin believed that his answer must lie in that office. There were experienced men there whose careers were devoted to missionary work. They should be able to tell him if there was a place for him or, as others had done, tell him to forget the idea and work where he was, in the field that God had given him. He knew one of the men slightly, Father John J. Dunn, and would see him first, if possible.

He was walking downstairs when he met Mary Stritch, the housekeeper, on her way up. "Father," she said, "there's a sick call—one of the Dolan boys. His mother is very ill, he says."

"Father McCoy will take care of it. He has sick calls this week."

"That I know. But the woman is insisting on you, so her boy says."

"All right. I'll see her."

He went out on the sick call. He never liked to refuse when anyone wanted him to come personally. There was usually a reason which had importance to at least the person making the request. The call cost him an hour, although Mrs. Dolan was not as gravely ill as she believed. When he came back to the rectory there was another call awaiting him, again from a parishioner who asked for him specifically. Two such calls in a row were unusual and Father Galvin had a strange feeling that he was being blocked again on a path to the missions. His mother's instinct for signs, omens and physical symbols of the will of God was strong in him. This second sick call distressed him but he accepted it, resigning his Manhattan trip to another day.

There was a strange priest at the table for the mid-day dinner when Father Galvin returned; a thin, gaunt man with a narrow face, prominent nose and cold eyes. Monsignor McEnroe introduced him.

"Father Fraser," he said. "John Mary Fraser, who came knocking at the door. In regard to him, he is looking for people to go to China. This is my Irish assistant, Father Fraser. In regard to him, he's by the name of Galvin, Edward Galvin, and he's from Cork." The old voice donned the heavy robes of sarcasm. "He'll go to China for you, no doubt."

"Not likely," the strange priest said. "They esteem their comfort too much, all of them."

Father Fraser did not acknowledge the introduction by so much as a personal word to Father Galvin. He addressed himself to Monsignor McEnroe and he picked up a narrative which the entrance of the younger priest had obviously interrupted.

"You can't, and you won't, imagine China," he said. "Two priests may have to cover a district as big as the state of New York. You can't imagine that. You have priests, all you need of them, and nuns and brothers, and splendid churches, schools, hospitals. . . ."

His voice was unpleasant, lacking emphasis or inflection, harsh yet monotonous in its level quality. He discussed the food on his plate and stated that the total food on the table for one meal would feed a Chinese family for a month. Father McCoy raised his eyes from his plate, ob-

61

viously incredulous. Monsignor McEnroe snorted. At meal's end, Father Fraser reached his question.

"May I tell your people of China on Sunday and ask for donations to the missions?"

"You may not," Monsignor McEnroe said.

That settled the matter beyond debate. There was no cordiality in the parting. Father McCoy simply disappeared and Monsignor McEnroe, who always invited any priest-caller to his table and who never turned anyone away from his door empty-handed, did not even extend a limp handshake. Father Fraser looked as he had looked when he described the sorrows of China. Father Galvin stopped him at the door as he was about to leave the rectory.

"Can you come to my room for a few minutes?" he said. "I'd like to talk to you about going to China."

"You're young and Irish and emotional," Father Fraser said flatly. "You'll talk about China today with tears in your eyes and forget all about it tomorrow. But I'll talk to you."

He talked and there was a strange power in him that had not been manifest at the table which Monsignor Mc-Enroe dominated. His voice was still a harsh, dreary monotone, but he had a compelling quality. He did not hold out one gleam of glory, one hope of happiness, one single recompense. He pictured a people in need of nearly every human necessity and he was eloquent in the description of human misery, of dirt, of squalor. He conjured up hordes of men and women and children without God and he described the French Lazarists, the order with which he worked, as overwhelmed and outnumbered, needing reinforcements, pitting their strength against paganism while well-fed, overindulged Catholics in a country like the United States pursued their pleasures, oblivious of the struggle.

"You could turn your back on it before today," he said bleakly, "and your conscience would never trouble you. Now you know the need and you turn your back on Christ if you ignore China, which starves in all ways and particularly in its need for priests."

"I won't turn my back. I want to be a missionary. I've always wanted to be one. I'm a priest; Cork didn't need me. I was loaned to Brooklyn; Brooklyn doesn't need me. I'm slated for return to Cork. You say that China needs

62

me." Ned Galvin drew a deep breath. "I may live to regret the day I met you, but I'll go to China with you. Now, tell me how."

Father Fraser did not light up with enthusiasm over the fact that he had, apparently, gained a recruit. In cold, uninflected, carefully-measured terms he stated the procedure for joining the Lazarist Mission in China. A priest's bishop would have to release him for mission duty and the priest would have to send his release and his letter of application to Bishop Faveau in Hangchow. Father Fraser planned to leave the United States on March first and anyone planning to accompany him would have to be ready by that date.

That night Father Galvin wrote a letter to his bishop in Cork. He walked out with the letter and mailed it, then knocked at the door of Father McCoy's room when he returned. His fellow curate had been reading. He laid his book swiftly aside when he saw Ned Galvin's face.

"What happened?" he said.

"I'm going to China."

Ned Galvin made the simple statement; then, as if it appalled him, he covered it with swift speech. He told about his early desire for the missions, the long, suppressed years when he had not, seemingly, even a remote mathematical chance of breaking from the solid Maynooth ranks that marched out to the parishes of Ireland. He told of the incredible incident of the curate's cat which caused him to drop back into the class which was destined to be the first which could not be placed in Cork, the first in all the long history of Maynooth.

"I came to the United States. I was out of the pattern. It wasn't what I wanted; it was, I could believe, what God wanted. I am at the end of that. I have been asking Him to show me, in some way that I could understand, what next He wants of me. Today that priest came. If my plans hadn't been interrupted, I would have missed him. I didn't miss him."

"A pity, that!" Father McCoy joined his two hands, fingers touching, under his chin. "A less attractive priest I never met. And glib with statistics! Did it ever occur to you that God may want you here in Brooklyn, that He has showered you with reasons for staying?"

"It has. I've weighed the reasons for staying. Brooklyn,

63

for me, seems a preparation for something rather than the something itself. I feel this. I feel something inside of me. There has always been something in my way but I know what I want to do."

Father McCoy watched him gravely as he spoke. "Ned, I wouldn't go to China myself," he said, "but I won't say a word against your going if you think it over and decide that you are right."

Father Galvin wrote his account of that day of decision in his life and he said of Father John H. McCoy: "We had been very happy together, he and I."

His interview with Monsignor McEnroe was a stormy affair. The pastor paced angrily back and forth in the room, blasting China and enumerating a long list of reasons for staying in Holy Rosary. He ended with a flourish, announcing that he would never grant permission for a curate of his to go to the missions.

"In regard to it, Father Galvin, there's special men train in a special way for the likes of China. Leave China to them!"

The Most Reverend C. E. McDonnell presented a problem, too. Father Galvin wrote an account of that interview which is a masterpiece of narrative simplicity:

Bishop McDonnell received me with his usual kindness and, as we sat down in the reception room, he said with a smile: "I suppose you have come to make a complaint against the old man." I said I had no complaint whatever to make against Mgr. McEnroe, that he had always been very kind to me, but that I had come to inform the Bishop of my decision to go to China. He opposed it strenuously, spoke of the difficulties McEnroe had with former assistants, which were likely to recur, and ended by saying he would not give me permission to go. After a short silence on both sides, I reminded him as politely as I could that I was a subject of the Bishop of Cork and in Brooklyn only on loan.

Up to that point he had felt, I think, that my intention of going to China was a passing whim, but now he saw that I was in deadly earnest, so he rose up, came towards me and said: "Father Galvin, stay in Brooklyn and become a priest of this diocese." I thanked him for his kind offer, but replied that I had made up my mind to go. "You do not know the difficulties that lie ahead of you in that strange country and you will not get my approval." He accom-

64

panied me to the front door, opened it and bowed me out. When I was going down the steps to the street, he called me back. "I see you are determined on going to China," he said. "You will not be happy there and I want you to remember that there will be a place for you in Brooklyn as long as I live. Kneel down." He gave me his blessing; I said goodbye to him and went out.

"Walking out" to Father Galvin was a walk into the unreal. His life hung in the balance while he awaited a letter from the Bishop of Cork. If the letter was favorable, as no opinion yet had been favorable, he would be leaving for China in a few weeks, incredible though that appeared; if the letter proved unfavorable, he would face the choice between Brooklyn and Ireland, returning in all probability to Ireland. Life went on about him, involving him, while he waited; Masses every morning, confessions on Saturday night, sick calls at any hour, parish activities, visits from and to his friends and parishioners. In February, 1912, he baptized two babies, bringing his total, since August of 1909, to 249.

Priscilla Dowd, one of his younger group among the girls who taught and kept records and decorated the altars with flowers, reported on him at this time when no one save a few intimates knew that he was contemplating a mission career in China. "Father Galvin was a warm, wonderful person and so approachable. As a young person I could always talk to him. He used to come to our house and I remember that we would have *The Tablet* or some other Catholic magazine or paper on top of the other papers and magazines. He would always laugh and lift the religious papers off and bring the others to the top. That was a standing joke with us."

So there were even little things to do; dropping in at homes where one was expected, repeating family jokes, shifting papers on a tabletop, while a man's life held its breath and waited.

In Ned Galvin's mind there was another shadow, the shadow of a letter he must write, a letter which would be almost impossible to write. His mother was expecting him home soon and had reached the point now of counting the days till May when she expected him to leave. He had to tell her that he was not coming home, that he was going to China. He postponed the writing, telling himself that it

65

would be premature, that he didn't know, that the Bishop of Cork might frown upon his project, that worrying his mother unnecessarily would be a poor service. He did not feel easy or comfortable about the evasions in his mind, but the letter remained unwritten as the days between him and a final decision vanished one by one.

The letter from Cork, when it came, was brief; but it said all that was necessary:

> Farranferris,
> Cork.
> 15–2–12.

Rev. E. J. Galvin,
Holy Rosary Rectory
141 Chauncey St.
Brooklyn, N.Y.

Rev. E. J. Galvin has my permission to accept an invitation for the Chinese Missions.
The reports I have had of him are the very best.

> T. A. O'Callaghan O.P.
> Bishop of Cork.

Time which seemed agonizingly slow in its march during the period of waiting was suddenly at full gallop. There were so many things to be done in less than a week. Among other things there was a production of Gilbert and Sullivan's *Pinafore* which Father Galvin was directing with the assistance of Joe Finnegan. A fund-raising project, it had been Father Galvin's idea in a quiet time before his career at Holy Rosary had a time limit. The cast had been rehearsing for weeks in the basement of the church. The public performance would run three nights at Arcadia Hall, Halsey Street and Broadway. Three days later, Father Galvin would be gone.

He did not slight his *Pinafore* company in the time that he had and he did not release the news that he was leaving. He did, however, do impulsive things born of his own knowledge that he had friends whom he loved and that he would be leaving them.

He appeared at the McHale house one morning and asked Vera to go downtown with him. Vera was only twelve or thirteen but she was one of his pets. "We went down to Fulton Street," Vera said. "That was our shop-

66

ping center. He took me into a pet store and he bought a bird there. He also bought me an ice cream. It was the first time in my life that I ever had ice cream in the morning. We proudly carried the bird home. It was a present from him for us; for the McHales."

Pinafore was a resounding success, with the house sold out for the three nights. On the last night the word circulated Father Galvin was going away. He was appalled when he learned that the secret was out. He wasn't ready to meet people on that night in the role of a China missionary and he did not want to interject a note of parting on the triumphant paean of *Pinafore*. He left the hall before the performance was over. The company had to take its final bow without him. The following day, however, the rectory was virtually in a state of siege. The parishioners of Holy Rosary, with no shopping time, gave Father Edward J. Galvin a testimonial of human affection unequalled in the history of Catholic Brooklyn.

Writing about it, Father Galvin said:

> They gave me a Chalice and a purse of 500 dollars, but all the other little gifts would take up too much space if I were to tell you all. . . .
>
> On Monday and Tuesday before I left, there was a constant stream of people coming in all day to say goodbye and, of course, to cry like babies. I don't know how I stood it, now when I look back at it all. From 6 p.m. until 10 p.m., that parlour was so crowded . . . I never could get a chance of escaping to my room to take a rest unless when Mary [the housekeeper] called me just for an excuse to get me away from them. . . . Many of the little children came to say goodbye. . . . The Altar Boys wanted to know if I would need boys to serve Mass in China and if I did, they were willing to go with me and mama had given them permission.
>
> At 10 o'clock on Tuesday, I had to go to Mr. McHale's house to take one last cup of tea. . . . Mr. McHale never cried one time, but his face was actually black. If I was his son he couldn't feel my leaving more.
>
> At 12 o'clock I had promised another family that I would go and say goodbye, and though I felt tired I went, because it was the last night and I knew that they would be waiting for me. When I got there I found a crowd waiting, all friends, the best I have ever had or ever will have. . . .
>
> I left Holy Rosary at 7 o'clock Wednesday morning

67

February 25th. A crowd came to the station along with me and there I cried, as I had cried once before. Everything seemed to come before my mind like a flash. I was leaving all. God alone knew what was before me. The train had gone several miles before I realized fully where I was, and then I remembered the crowd of friends in the station, waving green flags, and saw one of the flags beside me on the seat, one that a lady had thrust into my hand as I stepped on the train.

Daisy Hall wrote her own account of that parting and it supplements Father Galvin's narrative: "Those who were at Grand Central to say goodbye hadn't traveled from Holy Rosary in one party as an organized group. Their going was a spontaneous action. . . . Father McCoy was there. He and Father Galvin threw their arms around each other. . . ."

On the train, Ned Galvin struggled with his letter to his mother. All of his emotional upset went into it, his doubts and fears, his concern for her and his sense of guilt at not having written sooner. It was not a good letter and he knew that it was not.

Mary Lordan Galvin received her son's letter on a clear morning after a night of rain. Her daughter Kate brought in the mail. A letter from her son was long overdue and Mrs. Galvin tore open the envelope eagerly. She read the letter and fell back in her chair, her eyes turned to the ceiling. Kate, who had not yet read the letter, says that her mother half whispered: "The Blessed Mother is above me, consoling me." Later the two women walked out into the orchard together and Mary Lordan Galvin was still in a daze. She stopped on the orchard path and stamped her foot.

"I will not curse my God and China, too!" she said.

Her body was trembling, her fists clenching and unclenching. Kate led her back into the house and she sat again in her chair. She did not weep but she buried her face in her hands.

"The tigers will eat him," she said brokenly. "The tigers will eat him."

6 : : LETTERS FROM CHINA

In 1912 Hangchow, capital of Chekiang Province, which Marco Polo called "the noblest city in the world," had a population of 750,000 people. It stood on the banks of the Ch'ien Tang, the most beautiful river in China, and commanded a view of the picturesque West Lake. Like other Chinese cities, it harbored much dirt and many odors but it housed, too, such beauty as that in the Lin-Vin, Temple of the Soul's Rest, allegedly the loveliest of all temples. Old in the Buddhist tradition of the country, Hangchow was a place of Buddhist pilgrimage, but its Catholic ties, too, were ancient. Friar Odoric, a Franciscan, who visited China in 1324-1327, wrote of it:

"Departing thence I came into the city of Cansay [Hangchow], a name which signifieth the City of Heaven and 'tis the greatest city in the whole world. . . . It is a good hundred miles in compass and there is not in it a span of ground that is not well-peopled. . . ."

Hangchow was Father Edward J. Galvin's goal in China but the route was a long and circuitous one.

The train which pulled out of Grand Central Station, New York, on February 25, carried the young priest to Toronto by way of Buffalo. Father Fraser's family lived in Toronto. "We left Father Fraser's home for China one night after supper," Father Galvin wrote. "His parents were old and not likely to see him again in this world but, at parting, not a tear was shed on either side."

Father Fraser was a trial as a traveling companion, particularly when he insisted on his right as senior priest to act as his junior's pastor. Father Galvin had his own money, but he was held to what he considered "semi-starvation fare." Besides limiting meals, Fraser absolutely forbade tipping and the long train ride across Canada became a nightmare of embarrassment to the generous, freehanded Father Galvin as the crew's dislike of the two priests mounted. The older priest read or slept or looked out of

69

the window. He sharply ordered his assistant not to speak to strangers and he indulged in little conversation himself. Occasionally, he would tell some grim tale of starvation or suffering in China or, looking at a man smoking a cigar, state statistically how many Chinese children could be fed for how long for the price of that tobacco. He put such estimates on everything he saw and, as Father McCoy suspected immediately and as Father Galvin did eventually, Father Fraser pulled his statistics out of the air with no basis on which he could rest them. Oddly enough, though it annoyed him, Father Galvin acquired the same habit and had a difficult time breaking it.

It was not until the two men were at sea that Father Fraser told Galvin about the Catholic Foreign Mission Society of America, founded by Fathers James A. Walsh and Thomas P. Price, with China as their projected mission field. This was the group that would ultimately be known as The Maryknoll Fathers. Father Galvin, for all of his reading, had never heard of them.

"Why didn't you tell me about this society sooner?" he said.

Father Fraser shrugged. "You didn't ask."

Ned Galvin was to discuss often that discovery of the existence of American missionaries in China. "If I had gone to Manhattan that day of Father Fraser's visit to Holy Rosary rectory," he said, "I would have missed the China path I eventually took and Father Dunn would have undoubtedly sent me to the Maryknolls."

It did little good to speculate on the Americans and what they planned to do when a man was already beyond the sight of land and pointed toward Asia.

In those days there was not a single American flag in the Pacific [Father Galvin wrote]. We traveled on the Empress of India, a steamer of 6000 tons belonging to the Canadian Pacific R.R. There were only about 30 passengers on board, mostly British officials and military men bound for Hongkong. After a fairly rough voyage, as is usual in the northern route, we arrived in Yokohama and went up to Tokyo, I was much impressed by the quiet efficiency of the people and by the order and the cleanliness of the country. Since then I have had opportunities of seeing the Japanese at closer range. Despite many glaring faults, they are a great people and, with the blessing

70

of God, I think they hold the key to the conversion of Asia.

We reached Shanghai about the middle of April. It was a small town then, but full of life. There was not a single auto in the street. The city was, for the most part, a vegetable garden. Our baggage was piled on a Chinese wheelbarrow and we followed it to the Lazarist Procuration in the Rue Chapsal just in time for lunch, traveling the next day by the Shanghai-Hangchow Railway to Kiashing where we expected to meet Bishop Faveau. He was not there so we went on to Tsefupong, in a small boat on a dreary wet afternoon. The Bishop gave me a very cordial welcome. It was Friday and, as is usual with the Lazarists in China, the supper consisted of a bowl of Chinese macaroni—with chopsticks.

After recreation and night prayers I was shown to a room by Father Asinelli in which a Trappist would feel perfectly at home. I slept, or rather lay awake all night, on a plank bed. We left the following morning for Hangchow where we arrived the same afternoon. Fraser departed the next day for the Vicariate of Ningpo and I felt as much alone as a small boy in a new school.

This was China but the immediate reality was the fact that the priests spoke French. Ned Galvin had studied French at Maynooth, but he had had the years in Brooklyn since and the academic tongue was not the same as the intimate exchange of Frenchmen who know each other well. His basic French was sound but he had to feel his way into the spoken language of his new contemporaries. Father Fraser had neither advised him nor prepared him for the China of the Lazarist Fathers and, having delivered him here, Fraser was gone. The Lazarists joked mildly about this man who seemed to have no talents as a missioner, no will to work for any time in the missions and who was their best raiser of funds.

Ned Galvin went to Hangchow immediately and was enrolled in the Chinese Language School. Chinese was a language of forty thousand characters and a reading knowledge of the language would carry one through China and Japan since the same characters were in use throughout. Speaking the language was another matter. There were dialects and inflections. The language of Hupeh, which had much in common with Mandarin, had four tones; some other areas had nine. There were colloquialisms and there was slang as in other languages, and the study of Chinese was not easy.

Ned Galvin received more than a hundred letters, most of them from Brooklyn, in his first week at Hangchow. Among his letters were two from his mother; the first was written on March 25, two days after receipt of his letter, and it was not reassuring; but the second was written on April 14, the day that the White Star liner *Titanic* crashed into an iceberg, and it commanded an immediate reply from the young priest in Kublai Khan's old city:

"My dear Mother," he wrote, "I received your letter today and I am very glad to know you are feeling so well about my coming here. As I told you in my last letter, I did everything for the best and there was no one who felt so badly about leaving you, and to leave the other friends, but I thought it was my duty to come, that perhaps I could do something when there was so much to be done. I always pray for you and those at home; almost every week I say a Mass for you and I never say Mass without remembering you all."

At Clodagh, in Cork, a woman had made the difficult journey from desperation and fierce resentment to acceptance and resignation; in China, a man tried to learn the language that he had to know and to write letters to the incredible number of people who wrote him. Many of the letters contained money and the assurance of prayers; more than a few promised to raise money for him if he ever decided that he wanted to come "home."

"The climate so far is good," he wrote in a June 8 letter to his mother. "Of course, the Summer is warm but not a bit warmer than New York. Just now a Chinaman brought in the *Cork Examiner* and a letter from Mary, the housekeeper at Holy Rosary. What strange hands a letter passes through! By the way, I would like to send you a little package of China tea. It grows here, of course. I suppose you never drank any. No sugar or milk. It doesn't taste well with either."

The *Cork Examiner* was his mother's personal gift, a gift that she could make out of her personal funds and one that had "sharing" in it. The *Examiner* was the paper which she read herself. It had followed her son to Brooklyn through all of his time there and his subscription was

72

re-routed to Hangchow, China, as soon as she had the address.

On August 12 Ned Galvin wrote another difficult letter to his mother. "The best and kindest friend I had has just died; poor Miss Irene Delap who wrote to you. . . . When I heard she was dead, I cried. She was a real sister. I will never forget her. Just before she died she asked for me, the poor little thing."

Ned Galvin's flow of letters slowed after that one. He was working hard on the study of Chinese and making phenomenal headway with it. He had his sure ear for music to help him and an actor's gift for learning and remembering lines; more importantly, he was a natural mimic. He had always been able to imitate voices and vocal mannerisms, to handle in speech any dialect or accent he had ever heard. He brought his gifts to the Chinese language and it capitulated to him.

On October 12, 1912, Father Galvin heard his first confessions in Chinese; a week later, he preached his first sermon in the language and was complimented by the Chinese and by his fellow priests. It was time to think of the active work ahead of him, and he tried to describe that work to his mother.

You must understand that every priest has a central station where his letters are sent. He leaves that station and travels on till he meets the first town, which may be 12 or 13 miles away from the Central Station. He calls the few Catholics around him, instructs them, hears their confessions, gives Holy Communion, says Mass, baptises the children, makes any converts he can and, after spending a few days there, travels on to the next town which may be another 14 or 15 miles. He goes through the same course there as he did in the last town and as he will in the next, and the next after. You must encourage them as best you can and tell them that you may soon come again, although God knows when you will return. After you are out two or three months you return to the Central Station, rest a week, read and answer any letters there are and then set off again in some other direction for two or three months more.

You will see poverty and misery such as you never saw, but no matter how poor the Catholics are, they will always give you the best they have, treat you kindly and ask you to come back soon. All these towns have a population of

10,000, 20,000, 30,000, 100,000, etc. You very seldom visit a town of less than 10,000 inhabitants. It is too small and you haven't time. There are 10 European priests and ten Chinese priests in this diocese and the population of the diocese is 20 million. There are about 15,000 Catholics in the whole diocese. If there were more priests, things would go on better but they can't be got.

Father Galvin had proved such a good student in the Chinese language that the order sent him to Shanghai to perfect himself in it. He studied there under a noted Vincentian teacher, Father Luke Ting, and acted as secretary at the Shanghai house of the Lazarists. His duties called for him to communicate in three languages, French, English and Chinese. He learned the problems of a large missionary order, the political, economical and mission map of China and he met a great many individuals. He maintained his astonishing personal correspondence, and added the schools and seminaries of Ireland which trained young men for the priesthood, telling them of China's need for priests and describing life in the missions. He did not return to the actual mission work until late in 1913.

"You can get no idea of the Chinese people from books," said the man who had read all of the books on China in Brooklyn's Public Library. "They are written to catch the eye and the money of Europe, but their greatest fault is their lack of truth. If one wants to do anything among the Chinese, one must get rid of that air of superiority which Europeans are fond of assuming. The Chinese are quick to detect anything in that way. You cannot imagine how they love a European priest who treats them as equals. I must say that I have found them a very lovable people, and very different from anything that I had expected."

7 : : JOSUE 1. 9.

The outbreak of the World War in 1914 brought grave problems to the French Catholic missions in China. Fi-
74

nancial support from France, never better than barely adequate and often much less than that, was severely curtailed. The heavier blow, however, was the recall of priests. The clergy in France were subject to the draft and missioners were not exempt from that call. As man after man went home, the demands increased upon those who remained. Ned Galvin was one of the veterans now. He had a large parish to cover and a pony to take him over the trails. He no longer ignored the smaller places entirely, although the larger places had a priority.

One day when approaching one of his cities, he was strongly attracted to a small village. Acting on impulse, he sent his boy ahead with the horse, gear and sacred articles. He went into the village with only his breviary and his small stock of standard medicines. People stared at him because he was a foreigner, but they were suspicious rather than friendly. No one spoke. Father Galvin's impulse was losing its initial momentum. There was no logical starting place for him when he was unknown in the community and apt to find enemies before he found friends. Suddenly he knew what to do. He squatted in the dust beside the main street and took his medicine bottles out of the bag. He stood the bottles, one by one, like soldiers before him, frowned at them and, very slowly, one by one, put them back in the bag. A few people paused to watch him; a few more, having passed, turned back to pass again. He ignored them. The bottles stood in line again and once more he disapproved them and put them away. By the time he completed his third line-up he had a small crowd gathered, watching him silently. An old woman pushed forward. She was frightened and she spoke nervously, obviously certain that the foreigner would be unable to understand her.

"My son is ill," she said. "You have medicine. Can you cure him?"

Ned Galvin raised his eyes. "I will go with you and see him," he said.

He returned his bottles without haste, careful, in fact, to be as deliberate as before. He rose then and went with the woman, aware that a number of curious followers were in his train. The small house to which he was led had refinements which identified it as belonging to one of the more comfortable families. The woman's son was young and he had a high fever. Father Galvin's prescience in the face of illness, often manifest in Brooklyn, did not fail him in China. He was certain after a cursory examination that the young man would recover, and he said so. He prepared doses from two of his bottles and administered them. He went into the other room then and talked Christianity to people who had never heard of it.

Late that night the young man's fever broke and there was no doubt in anyone's mind that he would recover. "That was a beginning," Father Galvin said. "I made many trips to that village and ultimately it became solidly Catholic, one of the strongholds of the Faith."

Conversion by the village, experience taught him, was the only worthwhile conversion. Individual converts were too much alone and, under Chinese conditions, unable to maintain either belief or practice in the Catholic faith. A village was usually inhabited by a single family, including all the uncles and the cousins and the aunts; once converted, a village prided itself on its faith and members helped other members in the observance of it. To hold the village or the group together in the absence of the priest, a catechist was necessary. A catechist was, preferably, a man better grounded in knowledge of the religion than the average Chinese convert and capable of instructing the backward Catholic or the pagan who showed interest. Catechists led the rosary at regular intervals, baptized infants and led the prayers for the ill and for the dead. A great demand was made upon a catechist's time and it was essential that he be provided with means of support. The drying-up of French mission funds made Father Galvin responsible for his own catechists and he mailed letters to Ireland asking for money, in addition to those soliciting priests for the missions.

At this time, Father Galvin inaugurated a custom to which he adhered all of his life; when he asked for funds, he added the alternative plea that the recipient of his letter give him prayers if money could not be spared. He wrote a letter of thanks for every contribution he received, no matter how small, and he wrote letters of equal length and equal warmth to those who wrote to say that they were praying for him.

In June, 1914, when the terrible heat came down and insects seemed to materialize out of vapor, Father Galvin

76

and other priests came in, under orders, to Hangchow. He was working in his room one morning when he received a summons to the provincial's office and was introduced to a firm-chinned man in his late thirties who was identified as the Reverend Francis Farmer, a Methodist minister.

"He would like to learn about the operation of our missions," the provincial said. "Help him in any way that you can."

The visitor was apologetic when he went out with the young priest. "I am certain that there are other tasks you would prefer to that of answering questions for a Protestant clergyman," he said.

Father Galvin laughed. "Not if you remember that my name is Galvin and not Calvin."

They were on a cordial basis after that first exchange and the Methodist minister was a good companion. To Father Galvin's surprise he seemed less interested in the operation of the Catholic missions than in the Church itself. He had read a number of Cardinal Newman's books and so had Father Galvin. They found mutual ground there and a subject for a long discussion on Transubstantiation which seemed to interest the visitor greatly and on which the priest's conviction was, of course, uncompromising. They spent most of the day together and, at parting, Father Galvin, with an inbred Catholic-Irish distrust of Protestants, was baffled.

"I didn't know what he wanted," he said.

He was not sufficiently impressed by the meeting to include an account of it in any of his letters that have survived; the detailed account was written by his guest. On May 6, 1915, Farmer wrote to Father Galvin informing him that he had entered the Roman Catholic Church. He became, ultimately a Jesuit priest and returned to China as the Reverend F. X. Farmer, S.J.

Father Galvin did not anticipate such an ending to the story on the day of their meeting. He returned calmly to the letter writing which the provincial's call had interrupted.

"This country is fertile but over-populated," he wrote. "China, in many respects, reminds me of conditions in Ireland. There are practically no industries. The whole population lives on the land and every available acre is under cultivation. . . ."

In many of his letters, Father Galvin stressed the affinity that an Irishman must feel for the Chinese. China had produced some of the world's most renowned scholars, poets and holy men, yet the majority of its people suffered from a lack of education and lived on the terms of its conquerors. The Chinese loved poetry and storytelling and their land was populated with invisible beings about which stories were told. They were a religious people by nature, devout when converted, willing to make sacrifices in support of their belief and loyal to an astonishing degree. They had an odd, off-average sense of humor and laughed easily when they felt at ease. None of this to a man from the green isle was at all strange in a people that he met far from home. The differences he encountered merely served to awaken his sympathy.

"Famine conditions drove our people to America," he wrote in one letter. "Those who went to America helped those at home and Ireland struggled on. But poor China has nowhere to go. She is despised and refused admission everywhere in the world."

In most of his letters Father Galvin was cheerful, even rollicking, and he told stories which excited young priests and seminary students in Ireland. His letters were anticipated, enjoyed, copied and widely circulated. Some of them were published in Irish and American newspapers. Ned Galvin had imagination, but he drew his stories out of personal observation and experience. He was a prodigious walker and he liked people. He was not repelled by the Chinese commonplaces. The sheds of human and animal excrement were a part of the country in which he found himself and, as a man of farm background, he understood the deep renewal need of overworked soil. He understood, too, why a Chinese brought his animals into the house in which he lived. When a man owned little, he watched and guarded what he had and kept it close to him. He was interested in China and in the Chinese, not critical. The warm tone of his letters, written during rainy weather or in the late hours of the night, explains the popularity of all that he wrote in the hundreds of places to which he addressed messages.

It is really a pity that one cannot give these people the attention they require and deserve. They are good, simple,

78

grateful people. During the priest's few days' stay, all the Catholics in the surrounding district come to the chapel. They remain all day. They come to tell you their troubles; they want to know what progress the Church is making in other places in the district; they like to hear of the war. In the evenings, when the day's work is over, I tell them stories of Ireland and America.

They cannot get enough of these stories and would sit all night listening. The women sit together in little groups; they are deeply interested in everything but they never ask a question, except some of the older ladies. The men ask all sorts of questions about Europe and America. Where are they? How large are they? How many Catholics? When I tell them there are 3,000,000 Catholics in Ireland, they are simply delighted. "And no pagans, Father?" I tell them, "No pagans!" I tell them about the persecutions and how we had to fight for our faith. Oh, they love to listen to these stories. Stories of school days, told with a good swing, bring roars of laughter. If you have ever experienced the pleasure of listening to your own Irish people telling stories around the fire on a winter's night, you will have some idea of what our talks are like. Nor are ghost stories wanting. I have a pretty good number of hair-raising ones and you can imagine the impression created. These stories open up the way of good work. They bring the priest and people together and if there is any shyness, it always disappears after an evening's storytelling.

In mid-year, to his delight, Father Galvin received word that two of his correspondents had committed their lives to China and were coming out to join him: Patrick O'Reilly, a Cavan man of Meath diocese, and Joseph O'Leary of Cork.

There was paper work and detail and many clearances to be mailed back and forth, so the two men would not arrive in China for months; but the knowledge that they were coming meant much to the lonely Irishman in Hangchow. He went back to his parish while the summer was still high, because the river was over its banks at Chuchow and there were ten thousand families homeless in the area which he considered his parish. He worked on relief, helping to obtain food and medical supplies for the flood victims, tried to take care of his Catholics spiritually and wrote word after wary word at night. Writing from Chuchow in August, 1915, he said:

"I am writing begging letters all of the time. During this month I have written more than 250 letters."

He was not politically-minded and he tried to avoid political commitments or entanglements at all times, but he was living and serving with the French whose country had been invaded and he was, inevitably, drawn into their concern, their love of country, their worry about the welfare of the families at home. He was surrounded, too, by the politics of China, the maneuvering for power, and his mind and emotions were involved with the ordinary Chinese who could do little about those who struggled for control of his destiny.

On September 16, 1915, Father Galvin discussed the situation, as he saw it, in a letter:

> There is a big discussion going on at present in China. As you know, China is a Republic like America. The President is Yuan Shih-Kai. There is a movement on foot to make him Emperor. It has divided the country and is causing great disturbance. The mass of the people care little whether they have a President or an Emperor as long as the weather is favorable and they have good crops. I think they are sensible. Yuan Shih-Kai swears by all the gods that he doesn't want to be Emperor, but he says, "the people are forcing me and what can I do?"

In the fall of 1915 Father Galvin fought his own war with typhoid fever and came close to death. He was ill for six weeks and he regained his health slowly. The flood, which had been responsible for his illness, subsided, and the people returned to the land.

Winter moved down the valleys and Ned Galvin watched the calendar. On October 16 Fathers O'Leary and O'Reilly sailed from Liverpool. They made stops in New York, Chicago and San Francisco; then they were on the high seas. Father Galvin went in from Chuchow to meet them in Shanghai on December 12.

The long trip had been a heady adventure for two young men whose previous travels, even within Ireland, had been limited. Father Joseph O'Leary wrote to a friend of their arrival in Shanghai:

"Father O'Reilly and myself stood there on the Pier, unknown and unnoticed. We could not understand or be understood. We found no trace of Father Galvin, not even

80

one face of a single European. We were in a new civilization. . . .

"Anyway, we decided to move on although where to go or what to do we knew not. The trunks and bags went ahead of us on two wheelbarrows while one followed on two Rickshaws, which are men-drawn wheelbarrows. . . . As we came along we saw a rather tall Monsieur L'Abbe bearing down on us. . . ."

There are three accounts of the meeting which followed, all in agreement on the main event, each adding supplementary data.

Father Galvin had been searching frantically for his lost reinforcements. He received his first clue from a policeman who had directed them; then he saw them, scared, bewildered, moving aimlessly. One of the men was much older than the other, of medium height and build, and that had to be Patrick O'Reilly. The taller, younger man with humor in his face would be O'Leary. Father Galvin was wearing the French flat hat and the dark soutane. He had a full black beard. He addressed the two men in French.

He saw relief break across the two faces. Father O'Reilly braced himself and with obvious effort launched into a description of the difficulties. Father Galvin listened patiently, nodded his head and replied in English.

"As fine a brand of Maynooth French as ever I heard," he said. "I'm Galvin, you Arabs. What do you mean by wandering all over Shanghai for me?"

The joy in his voice was a welcome. "Are ye long landed?" he said.

"Are we long stranded, would be more like it," Father O'Leary said.

The three men went to the procure which was staffed by Vincentians. Father O'Reilly needed dentistry, so it was decided that they would all remain in Shanghai for Christmas. Father Galvin schooled both men as he himself had not been schooled on what to expect in the mission. Father O'Leary was obviously reflecting the Galvin teaching in letters he wrote, and the following paragraph is significant:

"I wonder will Irish secular priests ever have an Irish Vicariate here. There is plenty of room for one in China. I believe if they could get one, they would be the most suc-

81

cessful missionaries that ever came here. The French are splendid, of course, but they are very conservative. They are gentlemen to their finger tips but they will almost legislate on the number of buttons on a man's soutane or the number of hairs in his beard. They are gone mad on rubrics."

The difficulty which Irish missionaries encountered in working under French priests emerges from the letter written by a man who had not yet worked under them, a man who was able to say, in all honesty, out of later knowledge: "I am absolutely delighted with China and with the French priests I have met." There could be a mutual liking and respect, yet no meeting of minds in the fields of method and procedure.

"We spent a very pleasant week in Shanghai," Father Galvin wrote, "during which they gave me the latest news from Ireland and between Joe's yarns and roars of laughter, we had many serious talks about the possibility of an Irish Mission to China. Father Joe strongly insisted that Ireland was ready for such a mission and that Maynooth was deeply interested. He gave me the names of priests and students who could probably be relied upon to support the project. I need not tell you how welcome that news was to me, and how surprising."

Even when confronted with the fact that Ireland, though beset by troubles within and living on the edge of the great war in Europe, had awakened from a long antagonism to an enthusiasm for missions, Father Galvin failed to see his own contribution to the change of attitude. In his letters, he had not merely called for more Irish priests, for any money that could be spared; he had made China a living reality to countless people. He had described the food, the great banquets in the city and the humble fare of a country home, the housing, the transportation. He had discussed the crops of China and the animals. He had painted pictures in words of great deserted temples, of pagan gods and goddesses. He had told anyone who would listen about floods and the courage of people and the great hardship which followed when the water overran the land. He loved China and had projected his love until others shared it. He did not, however, know what he had done. The two priests from Ireland knew,

82

however, because they were themselves the visible, tangible, living proof; they were the called, the first fruits.

"You have started a great movement," Father O'Leary said. "There can be an Irish mission society, but you are the key. You must go home and put before the bishops and priests of Ireland the necessity and feasibility of such a mission."

Father Galvin was startled and shocked. "Impossible," he said. "You are talking nonsense. I couldn't go, and if I could, I'd fail. I lack the ability and I'm nobody. It would take an outstanding priest to make a success of such a movement."

"An outstanding man who did not know China," Father O'Reilly said, "would not command the attention of the bishops."

Father Galvin looked from one priest to the other. He saw that they were in agreement and his jaw hardened. "Positively, no!" he said. "I am a missionary and I will stay in the mission."

The matter was dropped there without further argument.

The assignments came through and the priests separated. Father O'Leary was appointed to Kiashing. Father O'Reilly received orders to accompany Father Galvin to Chuchow on the borders of Kiangsi. The war-caused shortage of priests had changed the language-study program. New priests now had to study in the field where, even while learning, they could be of some service.

Father O'Leary wrote scores of letters. As Father Galvin himself did, O'Leary returned again and again to his objective, approaching it from every angle. He was convinced that the man who had made Ireland aware of China should return to Ireland and finish what he had started, settling for nothing less than an Irish mission to seek souls under Irish leadership in the pagan hinterlands of the Flowery Kingdom. He was not only persistent, he was eloquent. Father O'Reilly, in his quiet fashion, sustained his arguments.

"I candidly confess that the immensity of the task, and the necessity of having to appear before a body of Irish bishops frightened me," Father Galvin wrote. "I was afraid to go."

The year rolled up. Rookie priests became veterans.

Other rookies were ready in Ireland, demanding to know what they should do to become missionaries in China. The Galvin letters had been reinforced by the pungent, witty, compelling letters of Father Joe O'Leary and there was a harvest ready for reaping. Father Galvin was indecisive. The French missions had been seriously hurt by the war and they were deteriorating in terms of support from home. The good men on the working line in China would not last forever and their replacements were not in sight. It might easily be possible now to recruit replacements from Ireland, but still Father Galvin hesitated.

A few weeks before Easter, 1916, Galvin wrote to Father O'Leary. He mentioned that Father O'Reilly had suggested that the three of them start a novena, a nine-day prayer, for special guidance and grace in reaching a decision on the question of Irish participation in the Chinese mission. He said that he considered this an excellent idea and that he was so informing O'Reilly. He asked Father O'Leary to join in the novena. Almost as an afterthought, he mentioned that he was having trouble with a sore on the back of his neck which would not heal.

Father O'Leary wrote immediately, promising to join in the novena and also advising him to come to the parish house at Kiashing where there was an excellent nurse on duty, an Austrian Sister of Charity of St. Vincent de Paul. Father Galvin accepted the invitation and was seriously ill when he arrived. He had an infected abcess on his neck, one and a half inches in diameter. The nun lanced it and found that the infection went deep, bordering on the vital spinal area.

When the operation was over and after the patient had had an opportunity to rest, the nun spoke to him with firm authority. He had had an insect bite on his neck, she told him, and if he had been in normal good health, the insect attack would have been unimportant, a mere annoyance. "But you are run-down, overworked and without the proper resistance to disease," she added. "The next 'mere annoyance' may kill you."

She told him that he should leave the country and take a long rest, that it would be foolish and, from the viewpoint of his value as a missionary, very unfair to jeopardize his health by trying to work in his physical condition.

Father O'Leary was present during the lecture and when the nurse left, he said quietly:

"You asked God for an answer. You've had it."

"You may be right," Father Galvin said.

At Father O'Leary's urging, he wrote to Bishop Faveau, setting forth the details of his infection and asking for a leave of absence with permission to leave the country. The bishop replied without hesitation, expressing regret at his illness and advising him to take a trip home to renew himself. Father Galvin was feeling better when the letter came and when he was well, he was stubborn.

"I'm not certain that this is the right decision," he said. "I'd like to talk to Pat."

"We'll have him meet us in Shanghai."

The three priests had to live on their own funds while working in the French vicariate; donations, gifts and Mass offerings from friends and relatives. The trip to Shanghai was an expense out of their own pockets but all three men made it. They met in a room of the Lazarist procure in Rue Chapsal on Easter Monday, April 24, 1916, and the news in the papers was disturbing although unsatisfactorily brief.

There was a rising in Dublin, seemingly an armed revolt and fighting in the streets between the Irish rebels and English troops. The dispatch, hurriedly written, lacked detail but there was one long-winded sentence in it which caused the usually quiet Patrick O'Reilly to snort. The sentence read: "In our appraisal we are rather forced to assume that the situation here has perhaps passed the dimensions of a mere riot."

"An Irish riot," said Father O'Reilly, "is never mere."

It was difficult for a time to talk of anything but the trouble in Ireland, but such conversation had little upon which to feed. The three men could reach the point of agreeing that it would be bad for their families and their friends if the fighting spread out across the country from Dublin, but when they reached that point they stopped. Speculation was folly. They could be far wide of the mark in anything that they imagined.

Father Galvin had had another change of heart about leaving China. He did not believe that he could gain support by himself in Ireland or that he had any talent as an

85

organizer. He seized upon the revolt news in the paper as a sound reason for not going.

"I couldn't make myself heard above the sound of the shooting."

There had been some correspondence between Fathers Galvin and O'Reilly in which O'Reilly had stated an old belief in his family that cutting the Bible after saying a novena would provide the answer to any problem. He now reminded Father Galvin of their correspondence.

"We'll cut it, Ned," he said.

In the account that Father O'Leary wrote of this evening, he held the Bible and Father Galvin cut it. The understanding was that the verse at the top right hand corner, as one looked at the book, would contain the Divine Message for which they asked. It turned out to be Verse 9 of the First Chapter of the Book of Josue:

Ecce praecipio tibi, confortare, et esto robustus. Noli metuere, et noli timere; quoniam tecum est Dominus Deus tuus in omnibus ad quaecunque perrexeris. ("Behold I command thee, take courage and be strong. Fear not and be not dismayed; for the Lord thy God is with thee in all things whatsoever thou shalt go to.")

Father Galvin, still kneeling, read the verse aloud. Neither of the other men spoke. Father Galvin rose and walked around the room. He rubbed the heels of his hands together and returned to the Bible. He reread the verse aloud and took a deep breath.

"I will go, Pat," he said. "I have my orders."

He was a man who liked signs and he believed devoutly now that he had a task to perform and that some way it was his responsibility to accomplish that task. He was thirty-three years old and he had the United States and Ireland before him.

"Ah, sure," Father O'Leary said, "cutting the book, or not, he'd have gone. He knew what he had to do and that no one else could do it."

8 : : IRELAND—1916

The United States in 1916 was the most powerful of the neutral nations, a source of supply to nations at war and a self-proclaimed champion of peace. It was prosperous and confident, its citizens buying motorcars and luxuries at a record rate, its places of entertainment crowded, its cities aglow at night with bright advertising signs. Father Galvin was slightly bewildered by it. It had been a quieter, slower, sleepier nation in 1912 when he left for China.

He had sailed from Shanghai on June 16, and landed at Vancouver, taking the train to Seattle and then San Francisco. He stayed at the rectory of Dr. Peter Yorke, pastor of St. Peter's church, who was a friend of Father Joe O'Leary. Father Galvin had heard Dr. Yorke speak as a visiting lecturer to Maynooth while he was a student there. He was impressed and, as he was inclined to be with people of rank or reputation, more than a little awed by the tall, rosy-faced man who listened attentively to his declaration of purpose in returning to Ireland.

"Your timing is lamentable," Dr. Yorke said. "Ireland is engaging in war against England now on her own soil. Her sons, many of them, are wearing British uniforms and engaged in that terrible conflict against the Central Powers. It is no time to talk to Irishmen, as you will know if you reflect on it, about China and about going out to convert pagans. If I were you, I would settle into the diocese of Brooklyn or the diocese of Cork."

Father Galvin was emphatic in his refusal to consider Brooklyn or Cork as the end of his mission trail, so Dr. Yorke introduced him to Monsignor Cantwell, administrator of the Archdiocese of San Francisco and destined to be Archbishop of Los Angeles. Monsignor Cantwell was sympathetic, but he agreed with Dr. Yorke that it was an impossible time in which to talk about the formation of a new missionary society in Ireland, the United States or anywhere else.

"A priest who speaks Chinese would be a valuable man in the archdiocese," he said. "I can offer you a fine church and a house, and the Chinese of San Francisco as your parish."

It was, Father Galvin admitted, a generous offer and a most interesting prospect, but he was committed beyond any choice of considering it. He was discouraged when he left San Francisco and traveled east to Omaha on the Union Pacific. He arrived in the dark hours of the morning before dawn and checked into a hotel near the station. His only name in Omaha was his classmate from Farranferris, Father Con Collins, and he discovered when he called that Father Collins had been transferred.

> But I met Father Patrick J. Judge, a Maynooth man from the Archdiocese of Tuam who gave me a hearty welcome and practically compelled me to rest there with him for a day or two. . . . He showed the keenest interest in what I told him of China and eventually I took him into my confidence, told him what I hoped to accomplish in Ireland and asked his advice. He became intensely interested in the project and said that it was bound to succeed. His was the first word of encouragement I had received in the U.S.A. We became fast friends.

The feeling of fast friendship sustained Ned Galvin on his trip out of Omaha but his natural shyness when confronted by the hierarchy slowed him when he approached the residence of The Most Reverend George Mundelein, Archbishop of Chicago. He walked around the block before his courage was equal to making the approach. But Archbishop Mundelein had been auxiliary bishop of Brooklyn when Father Galvin left for China and he remembered him. "His eminence gave me a great welcome," Father Galvin wrote, "and when I told him that the object of my visit was to ask his advice regarding an Irish Mission to China, he became interested immediately."

Father Galvin, talking and thinking about China, forgot himself and was no longer shy. The archbishop was fascinated and cancelled two appointments in order to hear him out. "I pray God you will succeed," he said at length. "You will meet with difficulties but do not be discouraged. Don't waste time in the United States. Go straight to Ireland. If you get the approval of the Irish bishops, come

88

back to me and I will give you the freedom of the Archdiocese of Chicago."

Father Galvin had badly needed someone in authority who would take the mission idea seriously, discuss it with him and encourage it. "I left that great man, who was so much in advance of his times, with a heart full of gratitude and went down the street literally walking on air," he wrote. "He had given me encouragement such as I had never hoped for; he had told me that if the idea was from God, it would bear fruit and if the idea was *not* from God I would not wish it to bear fruit. That clinched and clarified everything. My part was to go on to Ireland, do my best and leave the outcome in the hands of God."

Ned Galvin was eager for Brooklyn when he left Chicago. There were his many friends of the priesthood; Fathers Flood and Buckley, Delea and McCoy. There were the people of the rectory; Mary Stritch the housekeeper, Mary Carroll the cook, and Owen Brady the sacristan. There were the families who had opened their homes to him and the people who had made a long trip to a chilly station on a gray morning to see him off. There were his ballplayers and his altar boys and a very special group of 120 young ladies who called themselves the Galvinians. Their dues were twenty-five cents a month, which they mailed to him in China. They promoted activities in his behalf, and had sent him one check for $2500. He had to see all of them. He had to see the grand old man of Holy Rosary, Monsignor James McEnroe.

Despite his eagerness he stopped one night at Garrison, New York, to visit the famous Father Paul of Graymoor. Father Paul Francis had been the Abbot of the Society of Atonement, an Angelican order. He and his friars and his nuns had come over in a body to the Roman Catholic faith and they were still in their old monastery. Their publication was *The Lamp*, and Father Galvin's first published articles in the United States had appeared in it. He wanted to meet Father Paul and his flock, to say thank you and to ask their prayers for his mission project. He had to walk five miles from the station to the top of the hill on which Graymoor stood. "A mere stroll in China," he said.

He met Father Paul, who had grown old but whose mind came swiftly to grips with ideas. Father Paul liked the idea of an Irish mission society but he talked at length on his own hopes and plans for Graymoor. The following morning, Mother Laura, whose convent of the Atonement Sisters was located down the road a short distance from the main building, sent a message to Father Galvin, asking him to call. She was a woman of quiet dignity who did not evade the fact that she had an object to serve and she did not indulge in any circumlocution.

"There are a number of students and there are lay brothers in Graymoor, Father Galvin. Father Paul Francis is the only priest. He had an operation a short time ago. If he had died, as it was feared that he would, the society would have ceased to exist. We still move under that fear. Father Paul needs an assistant, a priest who can help him and who can carry on his work. Will you be that priest, Father?"

Father Galvin had to say No, although he expressed his thanks. Father Paul himself had opened the door to him last night if he had wanted a career at Graymoor. There were many attractive features in the prospect. He walked down the road to the station and, as he wrote later: "I felt my own unworthiness. God had offered me so many alternatives, so many places in which I could serve Him happily. I felt humble before the many men who had only one apparent choice."

New York, too, had quickened. There seemed to be more people where Father Galvin had always believed that there were already too many. Brooklyn had changed more noticeably. The new bridges, finished in Ned Galvin's time, had invited the people of crowded Manhattan to cross the river. New houses had been built, and apartments, and commercial buildings. There had been other changes; familiar stores vanished from their well-remembered locations, strange stores standing in their places. Some of the old families had moved away and a great many strangers had moved in.

Monsignor McEnroe was the initial disappointment. He had not spoken to Father Galvin since their angry exchange when he had forbidden his assistant to go to China. He had not given him a handshake or a word of good-bye and he did not offer a handshake now nor a word of welcome. He acted as though he were meeting a stranger and he terminated the visit abruptly.

Father John McCoy was the contrast and the leaven.

90

He threw his arms around his former partner and slapped him on the back. "God, I'm happy to see you!" he said.

Father Galvin spent that night at the Murray Hill Hotel in Manhattan and the next ten days in the Hall home in Brooklyn; swift, breathless days of seeing people who thrust money into his pockets, who wanted to entertain him; who listened, rapt, to anything he wanted to tell them.

"The greatest friends of my life," he said, "the most wonderful people. They were all my family."

Those friends found him older, less boyish in his laughter and in his reaction to news of individuals and events, but little changed in the essentials; in his broad sympathy, his interest in the problems of people, his love of children. He still wore collars that were too big for him and his suit needed pressing; incongruously, as they had always been in company with his general shabbiness, his shoes were neatly shined, gleaming from the brush. He was thin but hidden sources of energy moved him. He walked briskly and he did not seem to tire no matter how many demands he was called upon to meet. He still liked to sing and he had some new ballads to old tunes, funny ones which he solemnly said were Chinese. He had too little time for singing or for lighter evenings of pure relaxation; there were too many people and too few hours.

He did not again see Monsignor McEnroe. This saddened him and he made a special effort when with other priests to speak favorably of his old pastor. Usually he climaxed any discussion of the pastor with some variant of the simple statement which he wrote many years later:

"Monsignor McEnroe was one of the most charitable men I have ever met. He never turned a poor person empty-handed from his door and I never heard him say a hard word about anyone. The farthest he ever went was: 'He knows enough, with regard to him.' I have always thanked God that I was sent to the Holy Rosary and to the old man and that I was associated there with two such splendid priests as Father Tom Connolly and then Father John McCoy."

On the 15th of August, he sailed for Ireland on a darkened ship with the threat of submarines haunting the journey. Halfway across the ocean the passengers heard the news that the bottled-up German fleet had come out, but they did not hear that the fleet had returned again to port until they landed in Liverpool.

England, with only a glimpse of it, was subdued and gray, with uniforms everywhere and an atmosphere of weariness hanging like fog over the people and all that they did.

Dublin had little meaning for Father Galvin in terms of memory or association and he spent only a few hours there before taking the train for Cork. Seven years had rolled over him since he had seen his mother and his family, but he had a prior responsibility before he could participate in the long-postponed reunion. He had to see the Bishop of Cork.

Bishop Thomas O'Callaghan was dead and his place had been taken by Bishop Daniel Cohalan, who had been Galvin's professor of Theology at Maynooth. He approached the bishop with a full knowledge of how much depended upon the interview. If Bishop Cohalan rejected his idea, he could go no further. No other bishop in Ireland would listen to him without the approval of his own bishop.

There was no cold and awesome dignity about Doctor Cohalan. He was warm in his reception of the young priest from China and he mentioned that he had had an interesting letter from Father Joseph O'Leary. He was prepared to listen and that was all that Father Galvin needed. Never better than an average preacher in the field of sermons, he took fire from causes and had a magnetic, almost hypnotic quality when facing one man or several hundred in behalf of an idea or a conviction. He was probably never more eloquent and persuasive than when facing the Bishop of Cork. Dr. Cohalan was caught up in the idea of an Irish mission for China and asked dozens of questions; then some phrase in one of Father Galvin's replies made him aware of the fact that the young priest had been in Ireland only a matter of hours.

"You haven't seen your mother yet?" he asked incredulously.

"No, Your Lordship. I came to you directly."

"Then go to her immediately. Leave everything else to me. Be back in two, at the most three, days. We will have another chat. I want you to see Cardinal Logue, a very cautious man but the one you must see. I'll have letters of introduction for you. No doubt your mother will be anxious to see you. Go along, now!"

Reporting this key interview to Father O'Leary, Ned Galvin concluded: "Joe, I could hardly keep back the tears."

He went down to Clodagh then and the place enfolded him, as his family did. Here was love and peace and family pride, his mother's fussing over him and cooking for him, his sisters looking at him wide-eyed, his brothers trying to impress him with the manhood which they had acquired in his seven years' absence. He was, only in a sense, a part of the life that they were trying to share with him.

He did not stay in his mother's home for as long as the Bishop of Cork had suggested. There were too many details to tie up, too many people to see. He had called on one of Father Joe O'Leary's correspondents during the few hours he had had in Dublin. Father Tom Ronayne had the missionary mind and attitude. He would have come to China to join Fathers Galvin, O'Leary and O'Reilly, if Father Joe hadn't asked him to wait. He wanted to be one of the first men in any Irish missionary society for China. He had ideas, friends, influence in odd places. Ned Galvin liked him immediately and regretted that his time was so limited. Father Ronayne was a man on whom one could build.

There was another man in Cork City, Father Edward J. McCarthy, a classmate of Joe O'Leary's. Ned McCarthy was a Cork man, too. Father Galvin remembered him as one of the young pack in the audience when he produced *Rosaleen Dhu*. McCarthy was committed to the mission if he could find a way to serve. Father Galvin drove in to see him.

"Within a few days of his arrival in Cork," Father McCarthy wrote, "he came to see me. . . . I remember how he jumped off the old jaunting car which stopped near the church gate. He came over to where I was waiting for him with that characteristic long, slouching stride of his; a tall, slim, dark-haired man with a very pale face."

Father Galvin, who remembered only a small boy, saw a tall, heavily-built, round-faced young priest who wore glasses with perfectly round lenses. The two men shook hands and walked to the Parnell Bridge. By the time they reached it, they were friends. They continued to Flana-

93

gan's Hotel where they talked through the day and most of the night.

"We could not hope to get very far by ourselves," Father McCarthy wrote. "We needed a leader who would command the confidence of the bishops. Father Galvin decided that he wanted a Maynooth professor. . . . He had a few men in mind, but while they were interested in his scheme they were not prepared to resign their Chairs and that was a first condition in Father Galvin's mind. In that he drew a blank."

It was not quite a blank. Ned Galvin was trying to feel his way back to Ireland, and Maynooth stirred more memories than any other place. He had a long talk with Dr. James McCaffrey, the vice-president of Maynooth, to whom Father O'Leary had written, and he carried some good suggestions away from the conversation.

Father Galvin, after that visit, was receptive to the suggestion which Bishop Cohalan of Cork offered when he handed him his promised letters of introduction.

"I have given much thought to your project," the bishop said. "Call it the Maynooth Mission to China. If Maynooth is with you, you won't fail."

Father Galvin went north to Armagh to see Michael Cardinal Logue. He then swung around the northern cities to see other bishops and some priests of influence. While he was gone, Father Thomas Ronayne wrote to Father John Blowick. Father Blowick, at twenty-seven, was professor of Theology at Maynooth and acknowledged as one of the most brilliant students who had ever worked within the ancient walls. He was a classmate of Father Ronayne's and more interested in missions than in his assured academic career.

In his letter, Father Ronayne told Blowick of Ned Galvin's hope that Blowick would join with them "to head the organization—as a Kitchener of the new army, so to speak," and invited him to discuss the matter. He received a reply by wire from Father Blowick setting up an appointment for September 4.

Father Galvin had allowed himself little rest. It was important to him that he enlist aid for his cause, but he was seeking, too, an understanding of Ireland, which had changed subtly during his time away. He knew how to listen and he had a sensitivity to the unspoken message

94

behind whatever an Irishman might say aloud. There was smoldering emotionalism everywhere, strong feeling which had no outlet. Support for the Irish Republic and its armed force had been small before the famous "rising" of Easter Morning, and there had been no great rallying of forces behind them such as the Republicans counted on when the revolt began. There were people in Ireland who had always agreed with the Republican principle that "England's difficulty is Ireland's opportunity," but there were a great many who felt that disaster for England in the war against Germany would be disaster for Ireland. There were a great many families with sons who were wearing the British uniform and fighting in the war.

It was the British, not the Irish Republicans, who had stirred up the country. They had executed the leaders, who would never have become martyrs if they had merely been imprisoned, and they had stretched out the executions, two or three a day, building suspense and dramatizing the roles of the condemned. The antagonism to England now was a pulsing thing, particularly among the young. Young men and young women talked of sacrificing, of tossing in their lives as the men in Dublin had done. There was a military twist to words and expressions in the language of the people and there was a fervor behind the singing of such sentimental songs as that of Thomas Ashe:

> Let me carry your Cross for Ireland, Lord!
> Let me suffer the pain and shame
> I bow my head to their rage and hate
> And I take on myself the blame.

Observers differed in their opinions as to whether this extra-emotionalism in the atmosphere of an emotional country would help the cause of a priest preaching China missions, or hinder it. Father Galvin did not doubt at all. He was certain that the mood of the country was in his favor.

"I went on to Dublin," he wrote, "and I learned from Father Ronayne that Father Blowick would see me the following evening at Tommy's house in Monkstown. I felt that interview would be an important one for me and for the Mission, so I tried to put my ideas in order and I said a few prayers, too."

95

9 : : A MAN NAMED BLOWICK

On the evening of September 4, 1916, some invisible church tower bells saluted eight o'clock as two priests entered Langford Terrace, Monkstown, Dublin, from the opposite ends, walking toward each other. They reached their objective, Number 16, with the taller priest a few steps ahead. Each priest must have suspected the identity of the other. Father Galvin's report read as follows:

"Having rung the bell I turned round and saw a young priest walking up the street. He . . . came up the steps to where I was standing. Evidently he wished to see Father Ronayne and I volunteered the information that I had already rung the bell. We stood there in silence. Tommy himself came down to open the door, burst out laughing and said: 'Do ye not know each other?' He then introduced me to John Blowick."

The meeting was historic, of far greater significance then either of the men could imagine. Father Ronayne, the priest in the middle, later described the two men as he saw them: "Father Blowick, the shorter of the two men was frail, refined, nervous, neatly dressed; he wore glasses. Father Galvin, in contrast, was rather untidy in dress—a rough, tough man who had been in hard action on the other side of the world and looked it, a man whom you felt could hold his own with anyone. He seemed, however, a bit in awe of Blowick."

In the first exchange, as the three men sought a relaxed mood of chatting, Ned Galvin discovered that Fathers Blowick and Ronayne owed their interest in China and Chinese missions to a visit of Father Fraser's to Maynooth where he lectured to the students in June, 1911.

"A cold, unpleasant man and one you would class as a miserable speaker," Father Ronayne said, "but he held us rapt and I've never forgotten him."

"Nor I," Father Blowick said. "I do not suppose that I was aware before I heard him that there was any nation so completely pagan as China. It was to me, as I listened to him, and it is yet, a biblical concept; the multitudes of people, minds to be instructed, souls to be saved. The Apostles faced a similar challenge. A modern priest does not expect it."

"No, he doesn't," Ned Galvin said slowly. "The strange thing is that Father Fraser couldn't stay on a mission himself. He spent all of his time traveling, recruiting, raising funds, organizing, almost anything but living the mission; yet we are all here tonight, talking about an Irish Mission to China, because we met him."

Father Galvin later wrote:

I put before Father Blowick the idea of an Irish Mission which had come to me in China. . . . I told him of Cardinal Mundelein and the help we might hope for in the United States, the deep interest which the Bishop of Cork and Dr. McCaffrey had taken in the proposal, and the priests who were ready to join the Mission if the Irish Bishops gave it their approval: Fathers Joe O'Leary, Pat O'Reilly, Tommy Ranayne, Ned McCarthy, Jim O'Connell and myself.

"But, if we are to hope for the approval of the Irish bishops, we must have a leader in whom they will have confidence," I told him, "and I am nobody. You, whatever you may think of yourself, are a professor in Maynooth, you have a standing with the Bishops, and your name is known to almost every priest in the country. When they ask who is in charge of the Mission, if one can reply, Father Blowick, a Maynooth Professor, then its success is beyond doubt, for the priests from Ireland have a love for Maynooth, and they will be proud to hear that a Maynooth Professor resigned his chair in order to lead the Maynooth Mission to China."

Father Blowick shook his head. The bishops, he was certain, would require more than Father Galvin was anticipating. This idea of a mission was not one of a guerrilla campaign against the pagans of China; it had to be an enduring thing or it was nothing. Money would have to be raised to build a college, because the existing seminaries could not be pillaged of their graduates indefinitely. A mission society would have to train its own men, equip them and send them forth, at additional expense for travel and maintenance, and maintain them again after they arrived

97

in China. Churches and chapels would have to be built, and houses for priests; schools, ultimately, and probably hospitals. A great amount of money would be required and it would have to continue to come in.

"Ireland will contribute enough to get us started," Father Galvin said. "The United States will help mightily when we can go over there and ask for what we want. Australia, too, will help."

"What happens if the United States enters the war?" Father Ronayne said.

Father Galvin was silent. That, of course, was a great imponderable. He had crossed the United States during the campaign for the Presidency which was still going on. Woodrow Wilson was campaigning for re-election on the slogan: "He kept us out of war." Charles Evans Hughes was challenging him and certainly not advocating American participation in the war. All that one heard, of course, was along the surface. One of the most influential Catholics with whom Father Galvin had spoken, mentioned the possibility of war and summed up tersely: "If Hughes wins, it is probable; if Wilson wins, it is certain."

"We don't know," Father Galvin said now. "We have to go ahead, war or no war."

Going ahead meant that they were to establish a society, finance it, build it a college and staff that college with faculty, design the platform of studies for a Chinese mission seminary and, so very important, gain backing from the bishops of Ireland and approval from Rome. The Rome approval would have to include an allotment of acceptable territory in China.

"Dr. McCaffrey suggested that we have a strong committee submit our idea to the bishops," Father Galvin said.

"He is right," Father Blowick said.

The three men talked seriously about individuals to be asked to serve on the committee. Father Galvin was out of touch with affairs in Ireland, but the other two men were sharply aware of the currents and crosscurrents in the ecclesiastical life of the nation. They rejected certain names because the men named were opportunists, certain to take over the movement if it seemed popular, certain to drop it immediately if it went out of favor. Other men were rejected as chronic joiners who never

98

worked, as dissidents who always gained attention by opposing measures, as hairsplitters who never saw the mass of detail they accumulated. In the end, the men who had survived scrutiny made up a long and solid list. Each man on it would have to be seen personally and convinced that he should serve.

The meeting broke up at dawn. Father Galvin stretched his long arms. "It looks as though it will take us a long time to reach China," he said. "I don't know what to tell Joe or Paddy."

"You'd better bring them to Ireland," Father Ronayne said.

Father Blowick said nothing. He, more than the others, had an idea of how long the launching of this project would actually take. He knew, too, that the infinite detail, the dealing with hierarchy and the preparation of documents, would be his. If he came into the proposed mission, he would be surrounded by work and buried under responsibility. He had no fear of work, but he was a man who could never take lightly the making of decisions which affected other lives.

"I am going to talk to my confessor," he said, "and I am going to pray. I'll make a retreat and I'll let you know after that whether I can take this on or not."

The next morning Ned Galvin went down on the train to Cork. He had to visit people who had written to him, he had to talk to prospective members of the committee. He and Father Ronayne divided a sizeable list of names and reserved another list for Father Blowick if he decided to join them. They were moving fast.

Father Blowick came out of his retreat and notified them that he had decided to resign his chair at Maynooth. He had duties at Maynooth but he arranged to use, on his day off and on weekends, a room in Father Ronayne's mother's house which she offered as the first office of the Chinese Mission. He, too, was caught up in the necessity for fast action. The three men had little time or opportunity to compare notes and, acting as individuals rather than as a group, they inevitably left loose ends which embarrassed them later.

Father Galvin, leaping all hurdles mentally, was optimistically seeking for a house in Dublin which would serve as headquarters for an Irish missionary college. An old friend and classfellow of his, Father John Henaghan of Tuam, had come to Dublin, too. He was immediately enlisted in the house hunt. The two men found a house in Terenure, in the Dublin area, which delighted them. They had no money with which to buy it; but it was there and it was suitable and they were pleased with themselves that they had discovered it.

The organization of a small but representative committee was smoothly accomplished by Father John Blowick. The Most Reverend Dr. Cohalan, Bishop of Cork, accepted the position of chairman. The other members were: John F. Hogan, D.D., president of St. Patrick's College, Maynooth; James McCaffrey, D.Ph., vice-president of Maynooth; P. Canon Lyons, P.P., V.G., Armagh; Michael Murphy, P.P., V.G., Kildare and Leighlin; T. Canon Langan, D.D., P.P., Ardagh; Daniel McCashin, P.P., V.G., Down and Connor; John Blowick, professor, St. Patrick's College, Maynooth; Edward Galvin, apostolic missionary of Chekiang, China. Father Blowick drafted a memorial to the bishops and invited the members of the committee to their first meeting on Monday, October 2, at the Gresham Hotel, Dublin.

There wasn't a cloud in the sky, no whisper of opposition to the dreams of the young men.

Then Father Blowick had a rude shock. He had written confidently to his archbishop, The Most Reverend Dr. John Healy, as soon as he had decided to resign his chair at Maynooth, informing him of the decision and requesting permission to sever his connection with the Archdiocese of Tuam. He received a reply on September 30, 1916, two days before the scheduled committee meeting:

"I am heart and soul with you in the noble work in which you are engaged, but I still do not like to lose such a man as you from the National College and the Archdiocese. Do everything you can for the Chinese Mission. It is a Godlike work. Get as many as you can to do the work but you yourself must stay at home."

John Blowick was upset. "I'll have to see him personally," he said to Father Galvin. "I can make him see what I have to do and why. I'll go immediately after the meeting adjourns, if you will take the committee resolution to the printer with the names of those in attendance who approve it."

100

Father Galvin agreed cheerfully. He foresaw nothing difficult in a task like that.

The meeting was held on schedule. Points were raised by various members and sentences reworded for clarity or emphasis or to correct any possible misinterpretation. The committee strongly approved the idea of the China Mission and of the men who wanted to establish it with its base in Ireland. They recommended it to the consideration of the bishops who were to hold their meeting within less than a week.

Father Blowick then went to Tuam and Father Galvin prepared the memorial for the printer.

"I visited Archbishop Healy on October 4th," Father Blowick wrote, "and, having discussed the matter with him, he gave me his consent verbally. . . ."

That difficulty seemed safely surmounted and John Blowick returned to Dublin. The bishops met on October 6 in Maynooth. Fathers Galvin and Blowick went to Maynooth and held themselves available, although the China Mission would not come up for consideration until Monday, October 9. It was tense, suspenseful waiting.

Fathers Blowick and Galvin were not admitted to the meeting of the bishops, so they could only sit within summoning distance and speculate. Just before noon, alarming news reached them that one of the bishops had opened a heavy attack on the China Mission idea as soon as it was offered for consideration. He objected to the memorial submitted as badly drawn. Names were signed with titles *prefixed* to them and "the promoters of the new mission scheme had stated that they would like to enter the Archdiocese of Dublin," but they had not asked the permission of the archbishop.

In his preparation of the memorial for the printer, which Father Blowick would have handled smoothly, effortlessly, correctly, Father Galvin had been out of his field and the result displayed his ignorance of the niceties of ecclesiastical etiquette.

The bishops adjourned for lunch and, as various versions of what was happening reached the two young priests, their appetites vanished.

The Bishops again assembled about two o'clock and they were on the point of rejecting the whole scheme [Father

Blowick wrote]. There are, I think, two things which prevented their taking this action. . . .

Father James Ryan of Cabragh Castle near Thurles was in Maynooth at the time of the Bishop's meeting. He was told of the difficulty we were in. He went to Dr. Harty, his own Archbishop, and said that he had a house and a large area of land which he would be prepared to offer to us for our new foundation. Now this fact had, we always believed, a very great influence in turning away the Bishops from a decision which, in view of the after history of our mission, would have been lamentable. It will be easy to realize our astonishment at what we always were to regard as the intervention of Providence in sending Father Ryan with his offer at this time.

The second point. . . . was this: the Bishop of Raphoe, Dr. Patrick O'Donnell, suggested to them that, before they would take any action one way or another, they would send for me and ask me to give them personally an explanation of the whole situation. At any rate, I was sent for by the bishops . . . and I explained as well as I was able the nature of our request. . . . First, we wanted leave to appeal throughout the country in order to raise money and, secondly, that we wanted their authority to found a college for the Chinese Mission. . . .

In the course of his remarks to me, Cardinal Logue said that it would be necessary for us to get the approval of the Holy See before the Bishops could be expected to give us any satisfactory approval. . . .

That night a friend of the mission sent word to Father Blowick that, after he had left the meeting room, his proposals had been watered down and that there would be no weight and no authority in the mild approval of the bishops which would appear in the document. The Bishop of Raphoe, the information stated, was charged with the writing of the approval.

Dr. Patrick O'Donnell was one of the strongest friends of the China Mission. Father Blowick hurried to his room and found the bishop surrounded by notes and weary of all of them. The bishop sighed with relief when the young priest offered his help. Father Blowick wrote a draft of approval which proved satisfactory, so much so that it was unanimously accepted by the bishops and passed without change for publication. The closing paragraph read:

102

The Bishops, having given careful consideration to this important memorial, joyfully approve and bless the project and earnestly commend to the generous help and support of the faithful the establishment of this Mission House for the training of Irish missionaries for China, who, in a spirit worthy of our missionary race, offer their lives for the propagation of the Faith in a pagan country.

> Michael Cardinal Logue, Chairman
> Robert, Bishop of Clayne
> Denis, Bishop of Ross
> Secretaries

This was triumph. This was sweet victory. Father Galvin wrote to Joe O'Leary in China. "I wrote you a letter last night from Maynooth re the approval of the Bishops. The whole thing appeared in this morning's Press. Man! It was powerful."

Such exuberance was swiftly blunted. The Archbishop of Tuam, Dr. John Healy, collapsed suddenly before he could write his confirmation of the verbal release which he had granted Father John Blowick. He was to remain in what was considered "a dying condition" until March, 1918. The Archbishop of Dublin refused Father Thomas Ronayne's request for a release which would enable him to join the Maynooth Mission to China.

"The proposed new organization has, as yet, no ecclesiastical status," he wrote, "and until it has, I cannot exempt a priest ordained for work on the mission here to transfer himself for work of an indefinite character elsewhere."

Ultimately, because he was a missionary in his heart, in his mind and in his personality, Father Ronayne volunteered his services to the Holy Ghost Fathers for the missions of Africa. He received, immediately, the release and the approval of the Archbishop of Dublin.

Fathers Blowick, Galvin and McCarthy could not grieve long with Father Ronayne. Their mail was heavy after the notice of the bishops' approval in the papers and many people sent money. Bishops vied with one another to be the first to open a diocese to a campaign for funds. Father Galvin developed the basic sermon and wrote a number of other guide paragraphs which could be used for variety or to illustrate points which might occur to the individual speaker. Three men came into the mission group, bringing their working total to six.

Father John Henaghan had been counted on for some time. Father James Conway had been an Honors man, Exhibitioner in the Arts, highly distinguished in his studies at Maynooth. James O'Connell had the distinction of being the first student to volunteer for China. As a junior seminarian, he had offered himself to the China missions when Father Fraser lectured at Maynooth. He had never wavered in his vocation and, although he was frail, he was accepted without hesitation. He was ordained priest in June, 1917.

The society, then, in October 1916, numbered eight men, two of whom were in China. There were a number of volunteers who could not obtain releases from their bishops, because there were so many priests in the British Army as chaplains that some dioceses were undermanned. Many priests applying were promised releases as soon as the chaplains returned and were, therefore, on the future book as far as the society was concerned. The men available worked hard.

"We spend most of our time traveling," Father McCarthy wrote, "by train, sidecar, bicycle. . . . We take on as many churches as we can ourselves. Ned told me the other day that China is nothing to the work we are doing at present. You can guess what it is to go around and interview parish priests, preach three sermons on Sunday, lecture in schools and convents during the week, visit every priest in the diocese as we go along organizing lectures etc., not a moment to ourselves."

In a less tense mood, Father McCarthy, as did the others, found humor in some of the experiences of this trail through Ireland. "I remember one day, I was preaching in Carndonagh in the north of Donegal," he wrote. "The parish priest in introducing me said: 'The next time you will hear of Father McCarthy, he will be martyred in China! I got £60 there."

The emotional response of the people was the astonishing reality of the mission campaign. Ireland was small and it had always been poor, often to the point of mass hunger. It was still poor and one had only to read the worry in the faces of people awaiting the posting of casualty lists to realize that it, too, in part at least, was in the war. There were shortages and men away and a tight, grim army of revolutionists gathering force in the land, but

104

country people crowded their churches and dropped their small coins in the basket—twopence, sixpence, a shilling—to finance the conversion of the Chinese who were far, far away from them.

Father Galvin tapped the emotional reserve of the people more surely than any of his confreres; did it naturally, honestly, with no false theatricals, no formula. He was, of course, the star attraction, the man who had been to China, and he had had to speak in many places where he had not planned to speak because the demand for him was stronger than his own resistance. He never made the same talk twice. He sensed what any given audience wanted, what would appeal to them.

The Chinese, like themselves, he told them, was poor and he worked hard. He prized his family and he was a faithful husband. Father Galvin described the family, the man, the way he lived and worked. His religion, he told them, was dominated by demons and by gods who were little better than demons. The beauty of Christ's life was a story such as no Chinese had ever heard before, the story of a carpenter's son and his friends who were fishermen.

Father Galvin had magic and hypnotism in him when he used these simple elements to hold his audiences rapt and motionless in Ireland while he transported them mentally to China. Their faith, the faith they knew and loved so well, became a precious jewel just beyond the groping fingers of a man so very like themselves who, poor unfortunate, had been born in China where there were so pitifully few priests.

"They listen to him with tears rolling down their cheeks," Father Blowick said.

Father Galvin did not seem to see the tears. He did not indulge in theatrical effects or expose his audiences to the contagion of his own emotion; he spoke quietly, almost gently. He had stories to tell about people he liked and he told them. The talks demanded much of him and he gave what they demanded.

"The health of all is pretty good, although the strain is fierce," he wrote to Joe O'Leary in China on February 24, 1917.

No matter how tired he was, Ned Galvin wrote to Joe O'Leary nearly every night. He was worried and concerned that he was in Ireland and that O'Leary seemed hopelessly caught in China. He had tried every stratagem he knew to bring both of his former companions home but the Bishop of Cork, one of the friendliest of men to the mission and to Father Galvin, did not believe that the two men in China should come home until other men were ready to go out. He felt that their presence in China gave the Mission, at this early stage, a validity that it would not otherwise have.

Ned Galvin made light of weariness when he wrote to Joe O'Leary, but in a late March letter to Father Blowick he wrote, "You should receive a letter from Rev. Richard Ranaghan (Down and Connor), offering his services for the Maynooth Mission. All speak highly of him, especially Ned McCarthy. Try to get him to come along at once as we need men badly. I am in wretched form. Belfast nearly killed me. I had to talk six times."

None of the men engaged could see the miracle that was taking place under their hands. They were too close to it. In less than a year, talking to people in large towns and small, missing regretfully all of the great Archdiocese of Dublin which was closed to them, traveling by train, side-car and bicycle, sleeping where they could, eating whatever was available, that small group of men who pioneered the Maynooth Mission to China raised an impressive sum of money and established access to future contributions. They stirred the imaginations of young people and they were besieged by would-be recruits.

10 : : YEAR'S END

Fathers John Blowick and Edward Galvin went to Rome in July, 1917. They traveled by way of London where they were delayed for two days.

Ned Galvin was depressed. He wanted to turn back. "There is nothing for us in Rome," he said. "We're foolish to show our hand. If we are to get good territory in China, they will have to take it from Italians. Can you imagine Rome doing that?"

106

John Blowick could imagine that. He knew, of course, that much of Ned Galvin's resistance to Rome was a growing, building, expanding discomfort at the thought of meeting hierarchy *en masse*. One bishop in Ireland was too much for Father Galvin and a group of them was a nightmare. In Rome the atmosphere would be foreign, the rank higher and the protocol tighter.

They boarded the steamer at Dover with Father Galvin still in a glum mood. There were a store of reminders that this was to be a hazardous journey. Germany's submarines were ruthless in their campaign for control of the seas. Father Galvin ignored the warnings and the silent symbols, undisturbed and unaffected by any thoughts of submarines, still worrying about meetings with Italian cardinals.

"In this, as in so many things," Father Blowick said, "he had the courage of a lion and the timidity of a mouse."

They reached Rome without incident and the city was misted in a fine rain. The rain contributed to the sense of unreality, the improbability that one could pass on a busy street the work of Romans and their slaves planned and accomplished some two thousand years ago. The two men stood on the edge of the Piazza San Pietro staring at the great dome of St. Peter's, the Vatican slanting off to the right. It all seemed so much larger, so much more impressive than it ever had in photographs. Ned Galvin let his breath out in a sigh.

"Lord!" he said. "I never expected to see it."

The *monsignori* at the Congregation for the Propagation of the Faith, Propaganda Fide, were affable and friendly but there was no sense of speed or dispatch. There were forms, procedures, due process, a going out and a coming back. John Blowick was a canonist. He knew exactly how these people at Propaganda Fide would act and how they would conduct meetings and interviews; he could anticipate them as he could usually anticipate the bishops in Ireland. One moved within a set of unwritten rules, like the rules of good manners, which one knew instinctively or not at all.

Ned Galvin remained uncomfortably in the background or offside, leaving details and formalities to his partner, unless some question pertaining to China was raised. He came to alert attention then, and his shyness vanished. His knowledge of China astonished Father Blowick as it did the priests of the Propagation of the Faith, under whose watchful eyes the individual missions bloomed and prospered, or faded and died. Father Galvin knew every mission in China and seemingly every town. If a town were named, he named the religious order or society responsible for it. When a tentative offer of a territory in China was made, he waved it aside instantly.

"No," he said, "it is miserable, mountainous country; poor, unproductive, anti-foreign, overrun by bandits. None of the missionaries now in China would touch it."

"Isn't that what you want?" a young monsignor asked. "A new, untouched territory for a new society?"

"No. We want a populous but neglected territory that is now in the hands of people who cannot take care of it. We suggest Hankow."

"That would call for much study and discussion," the monsignor said. "You know that the Franciscans have Hankow."

"And not enough men."

Father Galvin worried later that perhaps he had said too much. The atmosphere made him suspicious and he had a broad streak of suspicion in him under normal circumstances in familiar surroundings; a Chinese habit of taking everyone at less than face value. Sometimes he imagined that the French Lazarists and the Italian Franciscans would make common cause against him and against the Irish Mission to China.

Fathers Blowick and Galvin were a week in Rome before they saw Cardinal Serafini, Prefect of the Congregation for the Propagation of the Faith, and two weeks before they had their audience with the Holy Father, Pope Benedict XV.

Although the two priests had been briefed at the Irish college on the appearance of the pope, they were startled when they met him. He was short, thin, stooped, and he walked with a noticeable limp. His left shoulder was higher than his right and his features seemed to follow the same tilt, downward to the right. When he spoke, however, one forgot his appearance. He spoke in Latin and there was warmth in him. He was not a man extending a routine courtesy or engaging in an empty ceremony; he wanted to know about his guests. He asked questions about

108

Ireland, about the missionary society, and Father Blowick answered him. The Holy Father turned suddenly to Father Galvin and addressed him in French.

The world, he said in effect, was beset by calamities and monstrous evil. What did Father Galvin, who had served in the missions, consider the greatest evil confronting them?

Ned Galvin did not hesitate. "The holding of many sections by orders with few priests. There are not priests enough, Your Holiness, and the territories were assigned long ago. It is necessary to redivide and to provide an opportunity for new societies and young priests."

Benedict XV smiled, a quick creasing of his lips and a lighting of his eyes. He did not follow up his own question, but he blessed the men and their missionary society before they left him.

The following day, Fathers Blowick and Galvin received a letter addressed to His Eminence Cardinal Logue, a letter which crowned their trip to Rome. It bore the date of July 18, 1917.

Rev. John Blowick, who, with the approval of Your Eminence and the other Irish Bishops, has become the promoter of a College to be founded in Ireland for Foreign Missions, on a recent visit to Rome furnished important information to the Sacred Congregation of Propaganda concerning the above-mentioned project and the development promised by this undertaking.

In a letter of June 13th, I already intimated to Your Eminence that the Holy Father, from information given by me, had blessed and encouraged the seasonable project of erecting in Ireland the said College where young men prudently selected could be prepared for the great work of the apostolate in pagan countries.

As a consequence there is nothing to hinder a beginning being made now in putting the project into execution, commencing with the erection of the College under the guardianship of the Bishops and especially the Ordinary of the place where the College will be established. Care will be taken to draw up a provisionary scheme of rules and to give the institution at its inception suitable organization and solid discipline, informing this S. Congregation of everything by opportune means.

D. Card. Serafini
Prefect
C. Laurenti
Secretary

Father Blowick delivered Cardinal Serafini's letter to Cardinal Logue and, with the cardinal's permission, sent copies of the letter to each of the bishops. He came back, then, to Dublin, where the toilers in the field were gathering to hear the details about Rome. Spirits were high and everyone had stories to tell about experiences with collections, some of them funny but most of them touched with pathos.

Father Ned McCarthy's biggest thrill was preaching the annual pilgrimage sermon to twenty thousand pilgrims on Croaghpatrick. "After I'd finished," he said, "a quiet, well-spoken priest came up to me and asked me a number of questions about China and the mission society. He was a gray-haired man, somewhere in his forties, a parish priest at Ballyshannon. I enjoyed chatting with him but thought no more about him till a letter reached me a week later. It was from this same priest, Cornelius Tierney his name is, and he enclosed a check for one hundred pounds. All his note said was that this was the savings of a lifetime and his expression of faith in us."

Another priest had a letter from someone named Anne Cunnin in Enniskillen. "On last Sunday I gave you 2/6 in church," she wrote, " and I am discontent since. Enclosed five shilling order to you and may God enable you to get on with the work you have in hand."

The meeting was suddenly quiet. These men were feeling their responsibility to the people who parted with the savings of a lifetime or with their two shilling six, or their five shillings. Father Blowick did not want this meeting to grow solemn, to lose its edge.

"My favorite experience occurred at St. Matthew's parish in Ballymacarret, Belfast," he said. "Father Crolly, the parish priest, would not let me appeal in his parish because I lacked the requisite age in his opinion, so he asked for Father Galvin. When Father Galvin arrived, Father Crolly walked around him several times with an air of puzzlement and asked him if he had actually been a missionary in China. On Father Galvin's replying that he had, the old priest said: 'Well, the ways of God are not our ways'—and he allowed him to preach."

The meeting ended with everyone in a cheerful mood. Father Blowick was charged with the drawing up of a constitution and by-laws for the society and the tentative outlining of courses for the college. Ned Galvin decided to take some time for relaxation at Clodagh.

"I've given my mother precious little of my time," he said, "and her place down there renews me. I leave all my problems at the gate."

That might not have been literally so, but he obviously felt a vast content when he turned off the road and approached the house between the lines of laurels. Clodagh was part of his boyhood and he had fought out alone at Clodagh the decision which his parents had forced upon him by insisting that he go to Maynooth if his vocation to the priesthood was real. He went back now for a very short time, and he talked with his mother and his sisters and brothers and the neighbors in the evening, pretending to himself that nothing had changed, that all was as it had been. He worked around the place, doing anything that needed doing. "He sang while he worked," his sister said.

John Blowick was having a more worrisome time. Father James J. Ryan, who had so opportunely offered his home and land to the society as a college during the bishops' meeting, had been adding conditions and clauses to the offer ever since. He had a lawyer now, who had thought of a few restrictions which had not occurred to Father Ryan. The whole situation had become impossible and Father Blowick so stated in a report to the committee of society advisors.

The society had a new member, Matthew Dolan, thirty-two, ordained at Maynooth in 1910 and serving since ordination on the faculty of the minor seminary, Kilmore, Cavan. There was also a letter that Father Blowick read many times. It was from Father Cornelius Tierney, who had given his "savings of a lifetime" to Father McCarthy for the society. It was dated September 10, 1917. The letter stated that its writer had been haunted by the thought that he should volunteer for the Chinese Mission.

"I am now forty-five years of age," he wrote, "and I can understand . . . the difficulty of entering, at this time of life, on a completely new line of work and a strange climate. There is also the question of learning a new language when one's memory is not at all as retentive as it was twenty years ago. . . ."

Father Tierney had not yet talked to his bishop and would not until he heard from Father Blowick. He had had

111

a physical examination in Dublin and the doctor "pronounced me healthy all round so far as he could see." Father Blowick answered immediately but postponed any decision, keeping the door open to a man for whom he felt strong sympathy, a sense of involvement. He advised prayer and offered prayers.

The bishops' meeting claimed him then. He expected permission to build or buy a college in accordance with the wishes of Propaganda Fide and he hoped for strong support in seeking a decision on the vicariate in which the Irish missionaries would work; from those two propositions many minor hopes stemmed. Father Galvin came up to Dublin and decided to wait there. Father Blowick went to Maynooth and addressed the bishops.

> I told them that in interviews which we had with the Secretary of Propaganda, Monsignor Laurenti, he repeatedly emphasized the desire of the Holy See that we should lose no time in opening a college for students who wished to devote themselves to foreign missions. Secondly, he instructed us to form ourselves into a Society, bound together either by an oath or a promise, but that we were not to take any vows. Thirdly, he told us that the Bishops could approve of our Constitution and, finally, that the Bishops could deal with the foundations of the College.
>
> The Standing Committee of the Bishops received me with the greatest kindness and cordiality. . . . That evening, I called Father Galvin on the telephone. I told him that Bishops had promised to do everything we asked them. I remember, distinctly, his sigh of relief coming to me over the wire as I told him that news.

The next day, however, things turned out quite differently. One member of the committee of bishops pointed out that the Propaganda authorities had not mentioned China specifically in their approval and that the Irish missionaries could be sent to Japan. In that case, he said, it would be illegal to use the money that they had collected from the Irish people for a Chinese mission.

The bishops decided to approve the society's constitution and rules for one year only. They did not approve the buying of a building for a college, merely the renting of one. They agreed to write to Rome in behalf of the society and ask that Rome give it definite approval as a Chinese

112

mission. In the meantime, the funds which had been collected would be very largely tied up.

Fathers Blowick and Galvin held a despondent two-man meeting at the Wicklow Hotel. Propaganda ha it was true, approved them for mission activity without mentioning China. The Lazarists or Vincentians, to whom the Chinese missions had been entrusted after the suppression of the Jesuits, could not be expected to look kindly upon any effort of an Irish society to encroach on their special preserves. Moreover, the order which held the entire region dominated by Hankow was Franciscan—Italian Franciscans who, in Ned Galvin's opinion, would wield great influence in Rome.

"I'll have to be off to America," Father Galvin said. "We can use any money I get there."

"Let's see first what we can do about renting a college."

"You do that. I'll see what we can do in America."

Father Blowick took Ned McCarthy with him on the house-hunting tour. They found a number of old estates in midland counties, but all of them were for sale, none for rent. They heard of one they could rent near Shrule in County Mayo and they went there on a cold, wet day that was whipped by wind. Dalgan House was for rent at two hundred pounds a year, with the option of buying the property at the end of six months for six thousand pounds. It was owned by the Congested Districts Board of which the Bishop of Raphoe was chairman.

There was one obvious fault to this find; it was too far from anywhere, out of the mainstream of activity in Ireland, far removed from colleges, universities or libraries. Father McCarthy raised all these points and Father Blowick nodded.

"After all, we are planning to train missionaries," he said mildly.

They rented Dalgan. There was one more meeting then to vote on the society constitution as Father Blowick had drawn it. All of the men had been out on collecting missions in the dioceses which had not been covered before the tying up of their funds. They were finished now until after Christmas and Father Galvin was leaving for the United States, in spite of his mother's hope that he would spend the holiday at home and the fear of his family that he would become a victim of the German submarines.

113

The meeting endorsed the constitution, voted formally and unanimously for John Blowick as Superior and posed for a picture before adjourning.

"We don't know where we're going but we've made a fine start," one of the men said.

John Blowick, despite his new title, returned to the simple, unspectacular work that someone had to do. There had been a number of letters from Father Cornelius Tierney and now there was a decisive one:

"Though I have considered the matter carefully again and I have prayed earnestly for light, I can see no reason sufficient for delaying. So I have made up my mind to go now as soon as I can get arrangements made which will be about the middle of January. . . . I hope it is all for the glory of God. I feel anyhow that God is demanding this from me, and I hope I shall be able to serve a useful purpose in this good work."

The priest who wrote the letter was forty-five years old; the priest who read it was twenty-nine. Father Blowick answered the letter on the day that he received it—December 11, 1917. His letter was gentle, as his letters invariably were:

"I need not tell you how delighted we all are at your generous decision. The time you mention will suit admirably for coming. You hardly realize how much your presence will mean to us in the opening of the college. In fact it looks as if you were the one man needed. We shall have a great deal to do in the way of farming, etc. which your help will make very easy, while, without it, I do not see how we could go on. . . ."

The college at Dalgan was scheduled to open on January 29, 1918, with a formal opening on February 7. Father Joe O'Leary had finally been cleared and would sail for the United States in January. Father Ned Galvin was already in New York. The mission to China was in being.

PART TWO

The Shores of Yangtze

11 : : OMAHA

Father Edward J. Galvin, accompanied by Father Matthew Dolan, landed in New York on November 30, 1917. The United States was a nation at war. There were a great many flags, a great many uniforms, an air of high intensity and of great lofty purpose in speech and in printed word, but to two men who had seen wartime cities and who had crossed the Atlantic on a darkened liner, there was no reality in it. The United States was dedicated to a cause, sending its sons to fight for that cause, but far away from the shooting. The size, hustle, confusion and noise of New York, the great number of people, impressed Father Dolan.

"America is a big place," he said.

"It is that, powerful big," Ned Galvin said. "But it isn't any bigger than anyplace else, Matt, if you take it one small piece at a time."

It was the manner in which he had taught himself to think. He was facing an assignment which dwarfed him. He had no detailed plan of action, only the grand plan to which his mind had clung for years. He was going to visit bishops and ask them for permission to seek financial support in their dioceses. He was going to preach and plead for the money where he was given permission, and assign other men to the preaching and the pleading. He was going to establish a college and erect buildings. He was going to enroll young men with vocations and fit them as an invading army against the paganism of China. He did not know precisely how all of this was to be done but he had to do it; that was his only excuse for being in the United States.

On that chill November day, he had an army of one man and he was facing an America which, apart from a very small segment of Brooklyn, had never heard of him.

Father Galvin had called on many of the hierarchy on

117

his trip across the States in 1916 and the bishops had been kind; it did not occur to him now that none of the bishops and priests he had seen had ever expected to see him again, that they had expected his swift assimilation into the mass of Irish clergy and that they had felt sorry for him. He was back in America with his China Mission idea approved by Rome and with a letter of introduction in his pocket, "To whom it may concern," from Dr. Daniel Cohalan, Bishop of Cork.

The Bishop of Cork, speaking of the Irish Mission movement, said: "Was it sheer madness, or was it not, rather, the human foolishness which is the wisdom of God?"

Father Galvin, with Father Dolan trailing him mutely, called on John Cardinal Farley, Archbishop of New York. The cardinal had grown old with the war and he had many worries, but he received the two young Irish priests graciously and reminded them that he had been born in Armagh. He encouraged them to talk, and he listened. He was delighted with Father Galvin's account of the Irish campaign, the few against so many, and gave him a letter authorizing him to collect for the Irish Mission in New York. The following morning, Father Galvin found a check from Cardinal Farley in his mail.

Ned Galvin was jubilant on receipt of the check. He went to Boston to see another Irish Cardinal-Archbishop, and William Cardinal O'Connell not only gave him a fine welcome but sent him away with a thousand dollar check.

He came into Brooklyn for Christmas and stayed at St. Saviour's, with a great round of reunions with old friends. He had aid in seeking collections from Fathers McCoy, Buckley and Delea, who drove him around on calls to pastors. The mendicant aspect of the work disturbed him. He knew that he had to have money for missions and for missionary work and he did not mind, after working himself up to the effort, facing a group of people and asking for money; but calling on an individual pastor in his rectory was a different matter, a definitely embarrassing matter.

"I find myself going out to see the priests on my list, hoping that I won't find them at home," he said.

He received his share of rejections, despite Cardinal Farley's letter, but he scheduled appeals in a sufficient number of churches, to employ Father Dolan for many

118

weeks and to employ Father O'Leary when he came in from China. He saw Dr. McGlinchy, director of the Propagation of the Faith, and, at his suggestion, made a trip to Washington to meet Archbishop Giovanni Bonzano, Apostolic Delegate to the United States. Establishing the society in the United States was becoming as complicated as the Irish adventure had been and Ned Galvin did not want to face that; he did not have John Blowick with him. He needed a home for the society and he did not wish to infringe on Maryknoll in the east; he headed west.

Father Galvin left New York in a snowstorm and arrived in Chicago during the early hours of a blizzard which was reported as one of the worst in history. He called on George Cardinal Mundelein, Archbishop of Chicago, who remembered him from his previous visit and who was amazed that anyone should call on him in such a storm to talk about China. The cardinal had missionary societies headquartered in his archdiocese, notably the Divine Word Seminary at Techny, and did not believe that it would be prudent to accept another one. He could, however, permit Father Galvin's priests to collect in Chicago.

It was a pleasant interview but the society was still homeless.

As soon as the weather lifted, Father Galvin went to St. Louis. The Archbishop, John J. Glennon, said that he could not permit the society to locate in St. Louis and offered no reason. Later, the archbishop wondered about his own decision and stated publicly that he regretted it.

Ned Galvin had not changed a great deal since his last visit to America. He had gained in maturity but he looked young. His clothing fitted him badly and his collars were always too large; if he buttoned a jacket, the odds favored his mating the button with the wrong buttonhole. He appeared awkward but he had a strange grace. Wherever he went, he talked to people and he was a seeker of names: the mailing lists or membership lists of Catholic organizations, the names of individuals known for philanthropy or for their interest in China or in missions. He bought notebooks in dime stores and he copied names into them, working late at night on the copying wherever he roomed. He wrote an incredible number of letters.

He journeyed back to meet Joe O'Leary in New York

119

and it was one of the great reunions of Ned Galvin's life
He had had a long, difficult campaign to manage in obtaining Father O'Leary's release from China and there were
few people in the world with whom he felt as close. The
two men fell into each other's arms and pounded each
other's shoulders. They talked through most of the night.

Joe O'Leary had gone to China in response to Ned Galvin's letters and Joe O'Leary had endorsed, in China, the
idea of an Irish mission. Joe O'Leary was a pioneer, a
layer of first bricks, who had been deprived of his rightful
place in the establishment battles on the Irish front. He
was determined to carry his full share of the work in opening up America and he had called upon bishops all the
way across the country from the west coast. He had not
found one who was willing to welcome a new missionary
society into his diocese.

"They are afraid of us," Father O'Leary said, "afraid
that we'll bring small credit on them with our odd nation
and our strange way of doing things."

"And afraid we'll become public charges. Well, no matter. Matt Dolan is in Philadelphia covering a few parishes and I have an appointment at the chancery office.
Something good may come of that."

Father Galvin felt optimistic about Philadelphia. He took
Father O'Leary with him when he went down to keep his
appointment on February 26. They arrived in Philadelphia
just two hours before Archbishop Edmond F. Prendergast
died.

"It was beautiful but very sad," Joe O'Leary wrote, "to
hear the bells of the various churches toll out the seventy-
five years of the dead Archbishop."

Those bells were tolling, too, for Father Galvin's hopes
in the big Pennsylvania city. He and Father O'Leary attended the funeral and he left O'Leary to work with
Father Dolan when he returned to New York. The problem of a headquarters city was a serious one now. The
society needed a permanent United States address as a symbol of solidarity. Father Galvin had, of necessity, been
moving from one place to another with his address under
his hat. Psychologically, he needed a sense of home, a
place to which he returned periodically; but over and
above any need of his own he had to establish the Irish
Mission in an American city.

120

On March 17, St. Patrick's Day, Father Galvin arrived in Omaha, Nebraska. He had a long string of defeats and rejections behind him and he knew no one in Omaha except Father Patrick J. Judge, pastor of Sacred Heart Church.

"I'll introduce you to the archbishop when he comes back in town," Father Judge said. "A very fine man—Jeremiah J. Harty."

"I know. He was in the Philippines when I was in China. I remember hearing of him out there. He was rather famous as the first American archbishop to the Philippines."

Five days later, Father Galvin saw Archbishop Harty, a gentle man who listened to him with obvious interest and who asked intelligent questions. "I would like a little time to think about this idea of yours," the archbishop said, "and a little time to pray over it. Come back on Monday afternoon and we will talk again."

It seemed a long wait and when Father Galvin again presented himself at the episcopal residence, he was fearful. "I had learned to like Omaha," he said, "and I did not want to lose it."

Archbishop Harty prolonged the suspense with light conversation, then said gravely, "I have only one serious doubt about inviting your mission society to come here—I am afraid that Omaha is not big enough for your work."

Father Galvin had no doubts on that score. "I walked out on the streets," he wrote, "and I was happy. It didn't seem possible and I kept repeating the word over and over. *Omaha. Omaha.* I liked the sound of it. It was our home."

He had less than three hundred dollars and he did not know how, or when, he would have more. He went downtown, rented a singe room office in the Brandeis Building, and paid a sign painter to letter a legend on the door: The Irish Mission to China. That gave the office an identity. He bought an old typewriter, a secondhand desk, a chair and a beaten-up set of file drawers. He went down and met the owner of the Burkley Printing Company.

It was essential in Father Galvin's opinion that the society in America have a magazine without delay. A magazine could talk to people whom, perhaps, a missionary priest would never find, people able and willing to contribute money, small sums or large, to the support of mission activity. The society had a magazine in Ireland, *The Far East,* edited by Father Henaghan, but war restrictions limited the print order to ten thousand copies and none could be spared for the United States. Much later, the value of the magazine in Ireland was to be dramatically demonstrated when the printers went on strike in Dublin. Without a magazine, the society's revenue all but vanished. That, however, was in the future. All that Father Galvin had now was his own conviction.

The veterans of printer's ink at Burkley's were startled when the young priest walked in and calmly asked how much it would cost to print a magazine. He was, they discovered, the entire editorial staff. He would write the first issue and bring the copy to them. "I have some pictures of China," he said, "but I'm not an artist. I'll have to find someone to do a cover for me."

It was an expensive project to publish a magazine. The printing company would extend limited credit and Father Galvin had some money left. The combination of cash and credit would provide him with two thousand copies of the American *Far East.*

"You keep the type set up," he said. "I will order more copies as soon as I get some money."

He went back to the office and he told stories of China on the old typewriter. He wrote and illustrated an entire issue of a magazine and when the printers delivered his two thousand copies, he sat at the typewriter once more, addressing envelopes to the names in his notebooks. He borrowed money from Father McCoy in Brooklyn to buy stamps. He sent copies of the magazine to Fathers O'Leary and Dolan in the east, telling them to combine a drive for subscriptions with their solicitation of funds.

The solitary man in Omaha, who could afford only two thousand copies of the magazine he had created, was willing to guarantee future copies to all subscribers on sheer faith that the means would come to him.

The necessity for writing to a great many people was an inevitable result of obtaining a permanent address. After his Mass in the morning, Ned Galvin went to the office and hammered his typewriter all day. He went back after supper and hammered it until midnight. This, he felt,

122

was a waste, in the sense that he would probably be of more value to the society in speaking to audiences, with someone else doing the magazine and office work. However, he had no one capable of taking over from him, so he had to continue.

Ireland made many demands on him. Father Blowick, in his modesty and in his disinclination to thrust himself forward, had written a constitution which gave practically all decision power to the council and practically none to director. He had discovered in a very short time that his council, comprised of pioneers and comrades though it was, had a tendency to deadlock and that the members were prone to lay responsibility on him without granting him authority. He shared many of his difficult problems with Ned Galvin and, on his biggest problem, had to pass decision to the man in Omaha.

In April, Rome finally made a definite offer of a mission territory and it was in China. They offered the Irish missionaries the vicariate of Kweichow. Ned Galvin rejected it flatly. It was, he said, mountainous, thinly populated and without a single city of note, six weeks' travel distance from Shanghai, damp, malarial and unhealthy. The population, he stated, was aboriginal, scattered through an immense province, each tribe having its own peculiar dialect. "They were unprogressive, addicted to drink, and most of them in extreme poverty."

In a letter to Ned McCarthy, he said: "Mac, I have no doubt but that God will lead us where He wants us to work but, at the same time, we must use the reason He has given us and seek the place where we think we can do the most good and do it for the longest possible time."

In Ireland John Blowick stood firm on the principle that the society had two experts on China, Galvin and O'Leary, and that a vicariate that was unacceptable to Father Galvin would be unacceptable to the society.

The exchanges of many letters on the vicariate question ate heavily into the time of Fathers Galvin and Blowick and none of the other demands upon the men lessened because they were so engaged. In Ireland it had been great news for the society when Father Patrick Cleary, D.D., joined. He was one of the top men on the Maynooth theological faculty, although still a young one, ordained in 1911.

In Omaha Father Galvin, too, had made an addition to the ranks of the society. In 1915, when he was in China, he had corresponded with a young Irish priest who was then in Springfield, Illinois. The priest was Michael Mee, born in Monaghan County, and educated at St. John's College, Waterford, Ireland. Father Mee had wanted to come to China as a missionary but Father Galvin urged him to wait. His name was on the Galvin mailing list and he received a copy of *The Far East*. One bright day in early summer he visited the office of the society in the Brandeis Building.

Father Galvin saw a fairly tall man with a high forehead and florid complexion, a blond English look. There was twinkle of humor in the man's eyes even at this first moment of meeting and Father Galvin liked him instantly. Mee, he discovered, was now the pastor of a church in Illinois, but still eager to serve in the China mission.

Father Galvin signed him into the society conditionally, subject to the approval of Father Blowick and the council. He wrote a decidedly favorable report on the man for Father Blowick, expressing the belief that he would be valuable as a fund raiser in the United States and, ultimately, as a missionary priest in China. In conclusion he wrote:

"So much for Mee and mine; the rest is up to thee and thine."

Father Michael Mee was accepted and he was written into history as the first priest of the society admitted in the United States.

The first issue of *The Far East* was being printed in larger quantities within a month of the initial order. The Rome offer of Kweichow vicariate, although rejected by Father Blowick, had a salutary effect in Ireland. Cardinal Logue and the bishops lost their fear that Rome might send the Irish missionaries to Japan. Money was released that had been held fearfully against the possibility that it would be diverted from the object intended by the donors.

The American members of the society, holding every possible dollar above expenses against the society's possible requirements, felt the welcome release, too, of money to meet immediate needs. Father Galvin went to press with the second issue of *The Far East* while using the first issue as a giveaway. He hired a stenographer, Claire

124

McKenna, whom he had met when he was doing some work for Father Judge.

On June 21, 1918, John Blowick wrote: "Good news. We are now able to send you Ned McC with four others. They shall set off as soon as passports can be got."

There was always an odd diffidence between Fathers Galvin and Blowick. Ned Galvin had been impressed with John Blowick before he met him, certain that he was the man needed to give standing to the society in Ireland, but uncertain about how far Blowick could be expected to participate. In a remarkable letter, dated June 27, 1918, Blowick reveals his own feeling for Galvin as it seldom, if ever, came through in person or in letters; he puts behind him, too, what he most wanted personally within the society. Abridged, the letter follows:

> The big need now is for priests and, Ned, believe me, we are leaving nothing undone to get them. But I am very much of the opinion that no one who joins at this stage should be put up by us for Vicar. I am terribly strong on this—that no one will take the interest in China that the five of us have been taking for a good while. It has been our doing and we are, as I said to you that night in Tommy Ronayne's, "body and soul" in it. We may have differed, we may have vexed one another, but for all that, give me these five! I have settled for a long time past that the future Vicar, so far as *we* can arrange that, must go to China in the first batch and the reasons are just those that you have given me today. I'm getting courage and self-reliance when I find my views agreeing with yours. To my mind, also, there are two men for the job, you and Mac. I'll have no one else for my vote.
>
> For me to go to China as the prospective leader, No. Ned, understand me. You are the only man and only your death or your physical disability would release you in my eyes. I am ready to stake my life that God directly inspired this mission and that all will be well.

Before he received that letter, Father Galvin had written to Father McCarthy: "What I want done then is: Blowick for China, Cleary to take Blowick's place in Dalgan, Mac for *The Far East* here in Omaha, Leary and I to organize the work in the diocese here. Last, but most important of all, the name changed to the China Mission

Society and full powers from the council to erect it in Omaha under that name."

Ned Galvin knew, or should have known, that the only two Chinese-speaking men of the society could not be left to "organize the work in the diocese" but he may have meant what he wrote at the moment, or may have thought that he did. He was a complex character. The question, too, of who would lead the mission group which first went to China was being discussed within the society and there were many conflicting opinions. Not by any means was there unanimity concerning Father Galvin. Several of his contemporaries felt that he was too decidedly an individualist, that he lacked the qualities of leadership and that his carelessness in handling detail could be disastrous. There were reservations about Father Blowick, too; a feeling that he did not have the toughness to command in the field, that he was not strong enough physically for hard China service, that he was lacking in self-confidence.

On Friday, August 2, Father Galvin said Mass at Holy Angels Church and, as usual, walked back toward his home. Two powerful English Pitt bulldogs charged him, one of them gripping his leg, the other leaping to his shoulder. He went down under the attack and the dogs slashed him badly while he was on the ground. If several neighbors had not come to his rescue, beating the dogs off, he probably would have been killed. An ambulance took him to St. Joseph's Hospital where he remained on the critical list, very close to death, for several days. The dogs were, it developed, infected with rabies.

Later, when he was able to talk to visitors, Father Galvin tried to make light of the experience. "The dogs were English," he said, "so I can understand their attitude toward a solitary Irishman minding his own business. There's a bit of tradition behind it. Protestant they were, too, I am certain, from the way they went for the meat on a Friday."

He wrote a letter, too, to Ireland from his bed in the hospital. "Now here I am," he wrote, "getting treated for rabies and I am sure you'll say that I should have got it done long ago."

Down in the Brandeis Building, his secretary, Claire McKenna, was doing her best with the normally heavy incoming mail, telling the letter writers of Father Galvin's account. One of the letters she answered was from Mrs. Hall in Brooklyn, the mother of Daisy Hall. Mrs. Hall immediately sent three hundred dollars to pay hospital expenses. As word of their missionary's disaster circulated in Holy Rosary parish, other offerings, most of them small, poured into Omaha. To his old friends and parishioners, Father Edward J. Galvin was a citizen of Brooklyn, away on indefinite leave.

The last battle of the Somme was fought in France while Ned Galvin was in the hospital. Ferdinand Foch was made a marshal of France and Hsu Shih-ch'ang was elected president of China. He was recovering and on half duty when the American Army took the St. Mihiel salients and when his old benefactor, John Cardinal Farley, died in New York.

On September 19, 1918, Father Edward J. McCarthy left Liverpool for the United States, accompanied by Father James Galvin [a distant cousin of Ned's], Alphonsus Kerr, Michael J. McHugh, Richard Ranaghan and Alphonsus Ferguson. They had a rough passage in convoy, and did not reach New York until October 3.

> Father O'Leary, who was then collecting in Philadelphia, was at the pier to meet us. . . . [Father McCarthy wrote]. He told us that Father Galvin, who was no more than recovering from his rabies treatment, needed Father Kerr and myself *desperately*. I didn't believe the thing was that urgent, of course, and neither was it, but just the same he packed us off on the first available train heading west. . . . We arrived in Omaha on October 9.
> I took over the editorship of *The Far East* at once, and Father Kerr was business manager. We fitted rather snugly in that single room office. . . . Father Galvin was living in his small rented house at 2444 Templeton Street and we did not have room to spare there, either. He did not have a housekeeper so I had to do the cooking for a few weeks. We may not have thrived on it but we survived.

Ned Galvin had postponed house-hunting until he had aid and companionship in the search. He wanted a home where the society could be canonically established; the headquarters for the United States and the editorial office for the American edition of *The Far East*. They found what they wanted in mid-October.

The house was located at 5035 Bedford Avenue, a

127

frame house with four acres of orchard and garden. On November 11, 1918, Fathers Galvin, McCarthy and Kerr moved in. It was a day of whistle-blowing, of firecrackers, of wild celebration—Armistice Day. The war was over. The priests felt the relief of that as deeply as anyone. Their society had come into being during war and they had never had an opportunity to work for it in a world at peace. They had had no way of knowing in advance that the day for taking possession of their first American property would be the day of war's end, but they were delighted that it was so. It seemed an omen.

"When we got our few sticks of furniture together, we sat down to talk," Father McCarthy wrote. "Ned sat there with his legs straight out, a bemused expression on his face. 'Wouldn't it be fine now,' he said, 'if only we had a few students.' "

12 : : DALGAN PARK

While Father Galvin was setting up the American symbol of the Chinese Mission Society at Omaha, Father Blowick was establishing in Ireland, with staunch assistance, the great society symbol which was to be known in perpetuity as Dalgan.

Dalgan was a large, old, neglected Georgian house which had been abandoned for ten years. It was surrounded by nearly 250 acres of woodland and rather inferior pasture. The lovely house looked haunted; reputedly, it was. It was in surprisingly good condition inside. Beautiful rooms opened off the central hall, each with its carved marble fireplace, its frescoed ceilings, its artistically papered walls. The house, at the time of its building, had been the largest house in Connaught. It became, under the society, a place of classrooms and lecture halls, the headquarters of faculty. Homes were created for students on the grounds from war surplus barracks buildings of the British Army. The unit—main house and ground buildings —was identified as Dalgan Park.

128

There was no doubt from the beginning about Dalgan's dedication to the training of missionaries. The place was remote, isolated, in need of much work from many men. The actual opening of the college took place on January 27, 1918, and the formal opening, with the blessing of Bishop Thomas O'Dea of Galway, on February 7. There were eight priests and nineteen students.

For the students there was little time for homesickness or for brooding. Young men who were shy and diffident, or slow to make friends under normal conditions, found themselves in a fight for survival. They had to clean and repair, help with the establishment of sleeping quarters and dining quarters, haul and unpack and set up. It was to be a long, long process, the work on Dalgan, but the men who shared the work established firm ties of friendship. Songs were written and sung, jokes born, catch phrases coined. Dalgan became itself a society. In the early days, when the tradition was being formed, grumbling and complaints were drowned out by the cry: "Ah, sure, a missionary isn't supposed to be comfortable."

The faculty was given no more opportunity for comfort than were the students. Father Blowick was superior of the society, rector of the college, and professor of Theology, Canon Law and Rubrics. Father O'Connell, always plagued by ill health, assisted with correspondence and office work in addition to teaching English. Father Henaghan wrote editiorials for *The Far East* and held three posts as professor of Church History, Sacred Eloquence and dean of Discipline. Father Tierney was bursar, spiritual director and professor of Latin. Father Conway was professor of Scripture and English. Father McCarthy, until he went to America, was business manager and assistant editor of the Irish *Far East*, and professor of Philosophy.

The first young priests from Maynooth for the society were ordained on April 28, 1918, in the college chapel at Maynooth: Fathers Alphonsus Ferguson, Joseph Mullen, John O'Donovan, Alphonsus Kerr and William O'Flynn. Father Patrick Cleary also came to Dalgan. On June 29, 1918, the loosely organized movement of many names, commonly known as The Mission, was canonically erected as an ecclesiastical society in his diocese by the Most Reverend Thomas O'Dea, Bishop of Galway.

129

After the official ceremony the priests of Dalgan formed small conversational groups which grew silent and grew closer together as Bishop O'Dea strolled over with the obvious intention of speaking to them.

"I meant all I said to you up there," he said, "about the significance of you and all that. You haven't begun to realize yet what you are. You won't be any good at all, you know, until some of you are knocked on the head out there in China. You will want a martyr's room here in Dalgan."

It was a bright, shining June afternoon with a full quota of flowers in bloom and with the trees of Dalgan looking their best. Any thought of cruelty and violence and death was as far from the scene as China was. Father Blowick thought of that as he listened to the bishop. He was standing where he could see Fathers McCarthy, Henaghan, Tierney and Leonard in one group. He was always to remember that. At the moment his distance from China disturbed and troubled him. The society now had twenty-two priests—seventeen in Ireland, four in the United States and only one, Father Pat O'Reilly, in China.

As the year ran out, Father Blowick recalled Ned Galvin to Ireland. A letter from Rome indicated that another trip to the Holy City might be imminently necessary and he wanted Father Galvin with him when he discussed specific territory in China. There were restless, impatient spirits in Ireland who felt that any vicariate was preferable to an idle society and to the criticism of the people who had provided its financial blood.

On January 22, 1919, Ned Galvin sailed from New York on the White Star liner *Lapland*. He found Ireland different in mood and spirit than when he left. There was tension in the air. People were sullen, suspicious or fearful. There had been a number of policemen and soldiers shot from ambush, a number of ruthless reprisals.

"It's a bad matter and could tear us apart," John Blowick said. "We have forbidden discussion of all political matters at Dalgan and we do not permit the forming of groups, cliques or societies. Forbidding anything is useless, of course, if it means suppression. We have discussed together the necessity we face, faculty and students, and we are united on means and methods. There is no trouble on that score."

130

Father Galvin could see for himself that there was no rift between faculty and students. Father Blowick had introduced a system unique in Ireland, of fraternization between faculty and students; priests and students sharing the same tables, partaking of the same fare and indulging in conversation at meal times. However, Father Galvin could see, too, the weakness at the top, with a superior of exceptional ability hampered by too little authority. That, to him, was an evil, and he discussed with each priest individually the necessity for changing the constitution of the society.

"I have been here for almost two weeks," he wrote on February 15 to Father McCarthy in Omaha, "and I haven't been home yet."

He wanted very badly to go home, even if only briefly. His mother wanted to see him and there was a family event to celebrate. His sister, Kate, married to John O'Mahony, had given birth to twins on the second day after Christmas; a boy and a girl, christened Donal and Margaret.

In March the so-called "Asian flu," which had swept through many countries including the United States, fell heavily upon Ireland. Father Jim O'Connell was considered in critical condition as were three students. John Blowick, on a business trip to Dublin, was stricken there and taken to the hospital. Ned Galvin, on the second day of his long-delayed visit home, received word to hurry back to Dalgan since there were dispatches from Rome which only he could handle.

The dispatches were not as urgent as he had been led to believe, but once back at Dalgan he was trapped. All of Father Blowick's normal problems automatically became Galvin's. On March 24 John Blowick was operated on for appendicitis. He came through it spendidly but the date of his return to work was doubtful. Ned Galvin experienced the absolute frustration of dealing with a council which hampered and delayed, opposed and postponed.

"All the cranks in the Society seem to have found their way into the Council," he wrote on April 11. "They make me feel absolutely alone. I am just longing for Blowick to get back."

That afternoon he discovered that, by orders of the doctor, John Blowick would spend another month in Dublin recuperating. Father Galvin was desperate at the

131

thought of another month. Valuable time was slipping away from him. He could be spending that time profitably in the United States, or perhaps pushing the vicariate through Rome, or actually doing a missionary's task in China. He had no interest in teaching and no talent for it. The council opposition had taken personal form for him as it had for John Blowick. He wrote to Father Joe O'Leary in the States and told him that he would like to have him in Dalgan, that he could perform a valuable function there, "but not on the Council."

"The lads here, at least some of them," he wrote, "have a kind of suspicion that Corkmen are running the show."

There were bright spots of news. Father Pat O'Reilly had finally arranged his release from the French missionaries in China and was sailing for the United States. The Most Reverend Daniel Mannix, Archbishop of Melbourne, Australia, mailed a check for £100 to Father Blowick with a note, "I wish that I could make it ten times this sum." With the coming of spring, too, Father Galvin found charms in Dalgan that he did not see earlier. The student spirit was remarkable and there was a great sense of companionship in the ranks, a feeling that no one who failed to know Dalgan would ever belong in their select company. He discovered, too, such physical charms as Father Ned McCarthy had described:

"We had all fallen in love with Dalgan, with the quiet, peaceful woods and its lovely gardens bright with flowers, its sluggish black river winding its way through the grounds and reflecting in its deep dark pools, under dripping willows and tall ferns, the wealth of foliage and color along its banks."

Early in May, John Blowick returned to Dalgan. He was paler, thinner, but he had laid aside frustration and worry during his illness and there was an air of quiet competence about him. He had thought through what had to be done. There were changes necessary in the constitution and he had written those changes. The new superior would have more authority and the council less, but the function of the council was clearly defined. The society had been invited to open a headquarters for the securing of funds and men in Buenos Aires and he was in favor of it. He believed that Rome had taken time enough, that he and

Ned Galvin should go personally to Rome for a show-down.

Everyone, including Ned Galvin, was happy to have John Blowick back in command. The members of the council agreed with his plans and a slate was drawn of possible members of a new council, to be elected in early June with a superior-general. Matters which had caused dissent in the past were no longer important. A young society had moved with appalling speed, trying to accomplish in months the work of financing, building and educating which had taken years in the founding of other societies and orders. A period of rest, of slow-up, had been essential, and that period had been enforced upon men who had not realized their own need of it. Father Galvin, whose sensitivity was seldom apparent to casual acquaintances, summed up the meaning of the long months in a letter to Father Ned McCarthy:

> What you and I, or any man big or small, may do is of little matter; it is God who is, and has been, guiding the whole work. Now, more than ever, His hand is apparent. John's getting sick and Jim O'Connell's illness was the greatest thing that could have happened. . . . Mac, there is something very strange in this Mission. It seems to be God's very own and He is guiding it. He will enable it to complete the work He has destined it to do, independent of you or me or any other. Everything will come right. Have no doubt of that.

On May 28 Father John Blowick wrote to Father McCarthy: "The last letter [from Rome] which came yesterday states that we are going to Eastern Hupeh but that we must wait till Rome receives the schema practicum, etc. from the Vicar of the place. Caw and I have our passports for Italy and we await only the sign from Rome."

John Blowick's use of Ned Galvin's Chinese name was rare at this period. Father Galvin had been Caw Kung in China but he had not permitted use of the name on his return to Ireland lest it seem like a bit of swank in a group where he alone had China experience. Later he had barred its use even in letters from Joe O'Leary until the society had a territory in China. He did, however, like the name and so did his friends. Occasionally, it slipped out.

133

The "sign from Rome" was still delayed but the members of the society did not know that. They lived in a daily expectancy and life seemed to move at accelerated pace. The election on June 8 resulted in John Blowick's unanimous selection as Superior General, backed by a three-man council: Fathers Patrick Cleary, John Henaghan and Joseph P. O'Leary. Father Cleary was chosen also to be Vicar General and Rector of the seminary at Dalgan. Father Edward McCarthy's authority in the United States was extended and he was placed in charge of all the society's priests who were, or might be, stationed there.

Father Joe O'Leary was notified by cable of his election to the council but he could not leave immediately for Ireland. He entered a hospital in Philadelphia on June 9 for an operation which proved more serious than he anticipated, immobilizing him for a month.

With the elections behind him, Ned Galvin, accompanied by Father Henaghan, took off on a trip to London to, as he expressed it, "fish up a Chinese professor." They succeeded in obtaining a first-class teacher of Chinese for Dalgan—Mr. Ignatius Ying Ki, the son of a distinguished Peking Catholic, who was educated in Europe and who spoke English, German and French fluently.

A familiar spirit appeared at Dalgan during their absence, Father John M. Fraser. He had been trying to enter the Irish Mission Society when Father Galvin was bitten by dogs in Omaha, and had dropped all attempts when he was informed that Galvin was in the hospital. He was on his way to Rome now to get approval for a new missionary society he had established in Canada. Father Galvin, reporting in a letter on the Fraser visit to Dalgan, took him lightly:

"Father Fraser called here on his way to Rome," he wrote. "The lads here seem sorry for him. They think he is on a wild chase and that he has little sense."

Father Blowick, after a report from Ned McCarthy in Omaha that Fraser had stopped there and had repaid hospitality by trying to lure some of the men into his Canadian society, had less patience.

"I had to practically give Fraser the boot here," he wrote. "He tried to get one of the priests and even after I had definitely refused, he wired from Liverpool to him, to come and meet him there. So, I sent a wire that was meant to sting him off. I could not help it. Fraser tried to start a recruiting stunt here among our students but I stopped him in that, too."

Father John Fraser did not, however, suffer an utter defeat. He succeeded in recruiting one of Dalgan's most promising young students, Daniel Carey, who had come to the seminary from All Hallows.

On November 18, 1919, Father Blowick wrote to Ned McCarthy:

> Rome has written to me to say that Bishop Gennaro has consented to give us the City of Hanyang with a certain piece of country around it. Propaganda has ordered me to China to view the ground, to try to come to better terms with Gennaro and to then refer the matter to them again. I am going to Rome next week to see what we can do to hasten a settlement. Then I return here and Caw and I shall start for China as soon as possible in the new year. We shall go by America and you will have the "Pleasure" of seeing us both again.

Only between the lines did the jubilation at Dalgan come through. The young men who had brashly set about the founding of a mission society without taking into account the power of bishops in their sees, nor the necessity laid upon an ancient Church to move slowly on new things, had covered a long road, a much longer road than they had anticipated. They could see their goal now. They could see China and place a name upon their small part of it.

There was a bright surprise awaiting them, too, in Rome. While Fathers John Blowick and Ned Galvin were en route, the Holy Father, Pope Benedict XV, released his encyclical, *Maximum Illud,* the greatest papal dissertation so far on the role of the missions and of the missioner. The two Columbans, as the society's priests were now popularly known since their adoption of St. Columban as their patron, read it in the Holy City after their arrival. It was a long encyclical and rich in wisdom to a missioner's ears. Certain words, phrases, paragraphs spoke boldly to them and they remembered their audience with the pope. Echoes of what they had said rang through the encyclical and their own peculiar situation was reflected in it. Pope Benedict XV had undoubtedly thought his thoughts on the missions before they met him, but he had encouraged Father Galvin to speak.

The encyclical was perfectly timed. Fathers Blowick and Galvin were aware of it as a smoothing influence moving ahead of them, a great expression of the Holy Father's mind into which they fitted. It was not, however, insurance that they would be granted everything for which they asked. In their first day of argument they were definitely refused the great city of Hankow. The Italian Franciscans were firmly entrenched there with churches and other institutions. The city could not be taken from them and given to a new, untried society.

Ned Galvin's report to Father McCarthy in Omaha continues from that point:

> .... After some fierce thinking we determined to ask for Hanyang City (400,000 population), (half of Hanyang prefecture; Hankow City is the outer half) and the prefectures of Ngan Lu which lies directly north of Hanyang prefecture. Our Vic then lies north of the Yangtze and on either bank of the Han. I am quite satisfied with it. It is big enough and we will be able to take on that other prefecture in time. . . . Anyhow, it is all settled now. We got our Vic on December 9, 1919. That will be one of the big first days in Hanyang Vic.

John Blowick's letter to McCarthy was exuberant: "When in Rome, as Caw has told you, we had a most awful fight. It was downright thick and ignorant and our best card was the number of men that we could put in the field right away. The Vicariate is really a first class one and I am more than satisfied. . . ."

The two men returned in triumph to Ireland. They were again faced with time-consuming detail in preparing the first crew for China but they were no longer waiting; they were going, with an objective fixed. Fathers James Galvin and Edward Maguire were dispatched to Australia to open the first Columban house Down Under and John Blowick set happily to the writing of a welcome letter to a new member, Dr. Michael O'Dwyer, of the St. Patrick's College faculty, Thurles, who was not only a noted scholar but one of Ireland's great athletes. Father Blowick said in part: "I thank God that you have thought it well to

136

throw in your lot with us. If you could see the jubilation here!"

The other side of the joy and the cheering and the new surge of enthusiasm in the society was voiced by Ned Galvin in a letter to Father Blowick from Crookstown:

"I have been engaged here for some time past in fixing up family matters; problems again. I am leaving here for good. There is no use in coming back again. It would only mean more crying. I suppose every poor fellow on the team will have his own share to suffer in that way. Tomorrow I will be over mine and I hate to think of it. Hope you are your old self again and in good form for the trip."

On March 19, 1920, eleven missionaries left Dalgan as part of the first Columban team for China. They sailed on the *Carmania* from Liverpool on March 27. The bulk of them would spend some time in the United States on publicity and fund-raising activity, but three would go on to establish the vicariate in China: Fathers John Blowick, Edward J. Galvin and Owen MacPolin.

In Dalgan one man, Father Joseph O'Leary, sat alone, writing a letter. He was a real pioneer of the society but he had always found himself on the wrong continent during the march of great events. He had been in China during the stirring days when the society was learning its first simple steps. He had tried frantically to have a part in the effort, writing countless letters and contributing ideas; but he could not actually participate from such a distance and he sensed when he left China that he was not quite in step. He missed the last stretch drive for a vicariate because he was in an American hospital while Galvin, Blowick and company were in Ireland and in Rome. Now he was in Dalgan and his erstwhile comrades were headed for China.

We are doing our best to keep the cover on the pot at this side [he wrote]. But there is a mighty gap left unfulfilled in the absence of Father Blowick. You can guess what his presence would mean here. I must say I thought that I realized it fairly fully before he left but I did not. There is only one Father Blowick in this Mission. I feel now that I am somewhat of a stranded fish. Caw has left me, too, and, gee, I feel pretty rotten at times over it all. I do not think that I will ever be content here. I have tried as best

137

I could but I have got the taste of China and my heart is there. Although Caw was not here long, there was a great satisfaction in having him about. We slogged along together out there in China and I am just praying for the day when I will be out there again in a little bit of a parish where I can drop down to him once in a while.

The *Carmania* was scheduled to dock in New York on Good Friday.

13 : : CHINA 'CROST THE BAY

Fathers John Blowick and Edward J. Galvin were improbable traveling companions; men of different tastes and viewpoints, of diverse physical and emotional make-up, united in the serving of an objective but aware that the precise service required from each was yet to be defined. They had visited London and Paris together and Rome twice; they had half the world ahead of them in March, 1920.

It took the *Carmania* twelve and a half days from Liverpool to reach New York.

John Blowick was seasick a good part of the time. Ned Galvin was a more experienced sailor, sick occasionally on the rough voyage, but more often up and moving out on the deck. He had never been a typical tourist, never overly interested in a strange locale because of its history, scenery or political importance; his interest was sparked, invariably, by the relationship of a place to his own project, the work he was trying to do, the cause he was striving to serve. He did not keep a diary and he wrote few descriptions of places; but he wrote an amazing number of letters and the writing was tied to people and events with, surprisingly, the background coming through sharply without the need for emphasis.

He was walking the deck one sullen, gray afternoon with Father Owen MacPolin. It was a day for thought

138

rather than conversation, with the sea in a quiet, brooding mood and no wind worth the mentioning.

"Pole," he said suddenly, "I couldn't do the work in Ireland. Someone else has to do it. I couldn't do it in America. I know what I can do. It isn't in either place. I belong in China. I've always belonged in China. I never thought I'd be gone so long away from it."

Father Ned Galvin was not asking answers from anyone, nor expecting them from himself. The situation that would, somewhere and in some manner, have to be resolved was the ultimate place of John Blowick in the society. One could look back now and see how fantastic it would have been to attempt what had been attempted if John Blowick had not been one of the group. He was indispensable, and he had deserted a career of eminence and honor for one of hazard because he wanted to be a missioner. He had wanted to go to China and play a role in the conversion of pagans. He still wanted that and, for what he had contributed, he had a right to demand what he wanted.

There was a grave doubt that there would be room in China for the two top men of the society or that the best interests of the society would be served by having them there.

The *Carmania* clove steadily through the waters of the North Atlantic and men who were not immobilized aboard ship were making news. There were shootings in Ireland and a wave of incendiarism, aimed mainly at government revenue offices and police stations. Two motion picture stars, Douglas Fairbanks and Mary Pickford, were married in Los Angeles. An American novelist named F. Scott Fitzgerald married a girl named Zelda Sayre; Eamon De Valera, away from Ireland for a year, was still speaking and fund-raising in American cities. Irish prisoners of the British in Dublin were on a hunger strike and some of them were reported near death. Within the society, Fathers Luke Mullany and Romuald Hayes joined the ranks in Australia with permission from their bishop.

The three Columbans on the *Carmania* were, at least briefly, newsmakers when they landed in New York. The newsreel cameras photographed them and they were interviewed by reporters. They enjoyed the experience of watching themselves on the screen in a motion picture

139

theatre before they left the east. John McCormack gave a concert in New York and they attended it. To the delight of Ned Galvin, who had told the anecdote about Father McEnroe and himself at a McCormack concert, the great Irish tenor again sang "Cockles and Mussels" as one of his encores.

On April 18, 1920, Father Galvin wrote to Father Mc-Carthy: "John and I have been visiting Washington, Baltimore and Maryknoll. John will probably arrive in Omaha about the beginning of next week. Tonight we leave for Boston, probably on Wednesday night for Chicago. I am staying over here a little longer to see some people I absolutely must see."

This tour of the east served several purposes. Some of the lectures given by the two men were financially rewarding; others were good publicity or seed for future reaping in vocations or donations. The speaking was a small part of the journey. Ned Galvin wanted John Blowick to see and to be at least superficially familiar with the important American cities. He introduced him to the bishops and archbishops, the clergy and the editors on his own list and always as "my superior." Father John Blowick was superior general of the society and Father Edward Galvin was one of the troops. Even over John Blowick's protest, he was precise in his introductions and in encounters with the hierarchy, never shading the younger man's dignity by a line.

Those who heard John Blowick speak were always impressed with his poise, his sure grasp of a subject, his vocabulary, the sense he left with them that he was a man of exceptional background. Ned Galvin, on the other hand, had no platform graces. He was apt to look awkward and ill-at-ease, to gesture clumsily. He had trouble in giving face value to the letter *r*. However, after the first minute or two, the audience was no longer aware of details; it was caught up in a personality.

"Ned Galvin always leaves them in tears," Father Blowick wrote from Baltimore.

John Blowick went on to Omaha alone to a reunion with the exuberant Ned McCarthy, who had new offices in the Courtenay Building, two secretaries, a multigraph and other office machines, a circulation on *The Far East* of

140

approximately twenty thousand copies and a farm of 250 acres.

He was full of ideas, statistics, energy and jokes. There was no doubt in Father Blowick's mind, or in Father Galvin's, that Ned McCarthy was the ideal man to head the American branch. He believed in what he was doing, he had unlimited vitality, he literally pulled ideas out of the air, and people liked him.

The first detachment of Columban missionaries came into Omaha in late April. They had American assignments, speaking, collecting, recruiting, seeking subscriptions for *The Far East;* but as soon as there was a place in China ready to receive them, they would sail. The roll call of this first missionary group was Fathers Edward J. O'Doherty, Michael McHugh, Matthew Dolan, Cornelius Tierney, Richard Ranaghan, Timothy Leonard, Joseph Crossan, John O'Brien, Alphonsus Ferguson, Arthur Mc-Guinness and Thomas Quinlan. Fathers John Dawson and Michael Mee were delayed but were scheduled for the China trip.

The three leaders swung west on the last American lap of the journey and at Green River, Wyoming, they changed trains. Father Galvin moved blithely from one train to another without the topcoat he had been carrying. In the pockets of the topcoat, he had his funds and his passport. The train was speeding westward, away from his coat, before he discovered his loss.

"He was pale for an hour," Father Blowick said.

Through some deft action on the part of the Union Pacific Railroad, the coat caught up with Father Galvin on the west coast, money and passport intact.

On May 25, 1920, Father Galvin wrote to Joe O'Leary in Ireland: "We left Seattle this morning at 10:10 A.M. . . ."

The Pacific in June was gentler than the North Atlantic in March. The three men took this voyage in stride, without discomfort. Galvin, writing to Ned McCarthy on June 7, stated: "We are in sight of Japan. . . . We will probably reach Yokohama about noon tomorrow."

John Blowick's diary reports that they docked at Yokohama at 3 P.M. on June 8. He was excited about his first sight of the mysterious East; the shipping in the harbor, bales of merchandise and weird luggage in customs, the rickshaws and the necessity for walking when they reached

141

a hill too steep for the rickshaw men to climb with passengers. There was difficulty in locating a hotel but when they finally checked in at the Bluff Hotel, they had tea on the veranda; Ceylon tea, toast, marmalade, and loaf sugar. "As good as Dalgan," wrote John Blowick. "The best since we left Omaha."

After that initial difficulty in finding a hotel, it became Father MacPolin's responsibility to travel one day ahead of the others and locate a hotel whenever a stop was planned. He became quite adept at room-locating. "I did not learn to speak Japanese," he wrote, "but I did learn how to make Japanese motions."

Ned Galvin had only a mild interest in the cities of Japan. They had no place in his life or in the work that he had chosen to do. He remembered the bishop's prediction that they would be assigned to Japan, and not China, if they went out on missionary work. He looked at the Japanese with that erroneous prophecy in mind. "A harder type of pagan," he said, "a more rigid people than the Chinese." He did not know, of course; he was drawing on intuition as he often did.

John Blowick was thrilled with it all; the meeting of people, the saying of Masses in strange churches and chapels. He had no necessity for connecting anything that he saw to a personal purpose; it was enough that it was there, that it was strange or unlike anything he had seen before. He bought postcards and guidebooks in Yokohama at a shop with the delightful name of "Kelly and Walsh." Later he complained in his diary that nothing he saw was as beautiful as the postcard photographs. He found the road from Yokohama to Tokyo fascinating. "The road is one long street, about the width of a second-rate country road in Ireland. No sidewalks. The shops—and the houses are all shops—open full to the street." He moved in a mass of "pedestrians, rickshaws, motors, bicycles, motorcycles, carts drawn by men or beasts" and he felt sorry for the people who impressed him as "very poor and overworked."

Father Galvin did not write anything of Japan. He was impatient until they boarded the steamer which was to complete their journey to China. He relaxed then. When he reached China, his pen was eloquent, and he indulged

142

himself in a description of place and movement. He wrote of the arrival:

> I awoke on the morning of June 16 about 6:30 and went on deck to find that we were entering the mouth of the Wang Poo River. The Wang Poo and the Yangtze enter the China Sea at the same point. Over on our left the little village of Woo Sung marks the entrance of the river and 30 miles further up, also on the left bank of the Wang Poo, stands Shanghai, the commercial center of the East and one of the most cosmopolitan cities in the world. . . .
>
> About 11 oc. the Yawata Maru reached Shanghai. The river was filled with shipping; large ocean going steamers . . . lay at anchor a short distance down the river. They were surrounded by a flotilla of small native junks and were evidently taking on cargo. . . . Opposite the Chinese Bund lay a fleet of large merchant junks flying little red pennants from their mastheads. Here the confusion, hustle and noise was at its height. Along the river bank on either side are warehouses, go-downs and factories with tall chimneys which belch forth immense volumes of their black smoke.
>
> Along the English and French Bund, and facing the river, are a series of very beautiful and imposing buildings. Farther on is the Chinese Bund and lying immediately behind it is the Chinese City to which every tourist should pay a visit. It is a hive of industry with narrow, badly-kept streets and poor sanitary arrangements.
>
> As our boat drew into the dock we discovered several friends among the crowd. There stood Mr. Ying and his father, both of whom had traveled from Peking in order to meet us. Along with them was Mr. Tsu, a prominent Catholic who was a ship builder of Shanghai. Mr. Lo Jr. was there to represent his father, Mr. Lo Pa-Hong, one of the most prominent Catholics in China, director and part owner of the Chinese tramways. . . . There, too, stood Brother Faust of Dublin, waving his hat in welcome and smiling that cheery, encouraging smile which I knew so well. He is the sub-Director of the St. Francis Xavier School which has more than 800 pupils.
>
> From the pier we went in Mr. Lo's motor to St. Francis Xavier College where rooms had been prepared for us and where we remained as guests of the Marist Brothers during our stay in Shanghai.

This was China; less China, perhaps, than it was a great international city, but moving to a strange rhythm, creating

143

an odd music out of the heterogeneity of its traffic. A man felt it, aware in his nerves that no other place of his knowledge was like this. Tired though they were, and facing an early rising, the three priests were exhilarated, keyed up, and early sleep was impossible They sat talking with the brothers and ended up singing, sending the music of Ireland out into the night of China.

In the morning, Fathers Galvin and MacPolin said private Masses at St. Joseph's Hospital. Father Blowick sang a *Missa Cantata* which was served by Lo Pa-Hong and Mr. Nicholas Tsu, assisted by four little Chinese boys There was a choir of forty Chinese boys, all orphans. "About 400 people attended the Mass," Father Blowick wrote later, "and at intervals they chanted their prayers with that peculiar rising and falling inflection which one hears in all of the Catholic churches of China."

In the evening the three priests were dinner guests of Mr. Lo Pa-Hong. The dinner had twenty courses which included bird's nest soup, sharks' fins, bamboo shoots, chicken and ham, mandarin fish, a sweet made of beans and lemon flavoring; all the exotic dishes which they had heard about, or read about, without quite believing. They returned to the living room for tea, cigars and cigarettes. Father Galvin, by request, sang several Irish songs. The evening climaxed with a trip upstairs to a beautiful private oratory which was decorated with flowers. All in the party sang the *Ave Maris Stella* and the *Salve Regina* with one of the brothers playing the harmonium.

"What a beautiful evening!" Father Blowick said as they were on their way home. He turned to Father Galvin. "It wasn't new to you, of course."

Father Galvin laughed softly. "New enough," he said. "I rose high in my China station this night."

Shanghai, whether the high or the low of it, was only a way station. The objective was Hanyang in which the Columbans were to labor. Father Abraham Shackleton, who was not one of the first party of priests, located the city beautifully in a book that he wrote for the use of the society. The following are extracts:

The Diocese of Hanyang lies within the Province of Hupeh. Hupeh is the central province of China and part of the great Yangtze plain. It is drained by the Yangtze

144

and the Han. Unlike the Yellow River, which is aptly called China's Sorrow, the Yangtze is a producer of wealth in spite of the damage and the destruction of life which it often causes by flood. It contains within its watershed 180,000,000 people, or one-third of China's total population. The Han, which is the principal trubutary of the Yangtze, flows east through the middle of Hupeh and joins the Yangtze at Hankow. The greater part of the Hanyang Diocese lies within the plain between these two rivers.

At the junction of the Yangtze and the Han, lies Wuhan, the great metropolis formed by the three sister cities of Hankow, Wuchang and Hanyang. Of the three cities, Hankow is the commercial capital, handling the bulk of trade; Wuchang is the political capital and Hanyang, the oldest but now the most decadent. Hanyang was for a long time important for its Iron Works and Arsenal. The Hanyang Arsenal for Central China was of considerable importance and an objective for many warring generals of the past. The climate of the three-city area compares favorably with that of any other part of the world lying in the same latitude, e.g., Cairo in Egypt or New Orleans in the United States.

That was the target, the objective, the dream—present and future—of many missionaries.

The vessel bearing Fathers Blowick, Galvin and Mac-Polin from Shanghai docked at Hankow on June 26. The warm Chinese friendliness of Shanghai had followed them, or anticipated them. The nephew of Mr. Nicholas Tsu was at the dock to meet them and to put himself at their disposal. Father Covi, a Franciscan, was there to meet them, too. He was a quiet and friendly priest who explained that he was acting for the bishop, who was out of the city. He was a faithful host who offered them the hospitality of the Franciscan friary and who arranged for their Sunday Masses. On Monday he took them across the Han River on the ferry to the city of Hanyang.

"It is, sadly, a city of no Catholics," he said.

Father Galvin asked: "Why?"

"There are many reasons, as you will no doubt discover."

The exchange was brief, not followed up by either side. The Franciscan had been a surprise to the Columbans who had anticipated hostility. They had encountered open hostility from French and Italian priests in Shanghai, and a

Belgian had told them that the opinion in China was that they had gained a foothold in China dishonorably, behind the backs of the men who held the territory they wanted; that they had gone to Rome without consulting Bishop Gennaro and had worked against him in Rome.

"We are missionaries," Father Galvin said then. "We did not seek any territory where other missionaries were working and meeting the needs of the people. If Bishop Gennaro cannot staff the vicariates he seeks to hold, or afford to build the institutions they need, then he should welcome us in."

He would have replied as strongly to the Franciscans of Hankow, but they were not unfriendly. He was engaged, too, in a bewildering adventure at the moment. He was the society's expert on China. He had argued the geography and the economics and the population patterns of China for hours at a time in Rome, had lectured on these subjects in Ireland and in the United States, had answered questions and drawn diagrams; but, from the moment the vessel left Shanghai and started up the Yangtze, he had been as much a stranger as was John Blowick or Owen MacPolin. He had never seen Hankow for which he had campaigned valiantly, nor Hanyang which he had won. He saw Hanyang for the first time through a haze of heat.

The temperature was 103 degrees in the shade and there was no shade on the river although the motor launch from Hankow was equipped with a shielding canopy. The traffic of huge rice junks, lumber barges, houseboats and fishing boats was heavy and the sun blazed back from the surface of the water. The city came into view through a forest of masts. The three men and their guide disembarked and walked up into the town. Father Blowick was wilted. He looked at the poker-faced Franciscan and remembered that this man was Italian, the native of a sunny country.

"I suppose that you are accustomed to this heat," he said.

"One never becomes accustomed to it," said Father Covi.

They rode the Shing Mah Road, which was the main street of Hanyang, in rickshaws. The street was no more than eight feet wide and was choked with people around whom the rickshaw coolies cut their way miraculously

146

without collisions of any kind. Nearly every house was a store and the removable fronts had been removed for the better display of merchandise. Signs of all sizes, shapes and colors hung from the framework of the buildings, creating a touch of the picturesque to a scene which needed that touch. People were in motion everywhere and all of them were talking or shouting, demanding the right of way or indifferently blocking the right of way.

Ned Galvin watched it all and felt a vast content. This was not a city of China that he knew, but he was at home. The essentials were here, the people and the things that he remembered.

"Lord, how they talk!" he said. "They never stop."

They came to the great, black wall of the city, a huge mass of masonry twenty to twenty-five feet thick, pierced by an arch. The passengers descended from the rickshaws and walked through the chink in the wall. It was comparatively cool. Father Blowick touched the dark surface.

"This was standing here when Mary and Joseph went down to Bethlehem," he said, "when Jesus was born."

"Hanyang is older than Rome," said Father Covi.

Fathers Blowick and Galvin talked late that night. Their words were filled with pictures of the ancient city which was to be their capital, their headquarters, their responsibility. They had received various population estimates of Hanyang, from one hundred thousand to two hundred thousand people. There seemed to be no dependable source of figures, but they had carried away with them the visual impression of vast hordes, all pagan. There was no Catholic church in the city. Reputedly, there were about 120 Catholics somewhere in the suburbs. Father Covi said vaguely that they occasionally had sick calls from the Hanyang side of the river and, of course, answered them.

"The sooner we get ourselves established over there, the better," Father Galvin said. "We'll get the boys out here and put them to work. We've got the right place, John, the place where we are needed."

John Blowick agreed with him. Hanyang had thrilled him. It was a totally Chinese city, with none of the Europeanization of Hankow. It fulfilled his mental ideal of mission territory, of the kind of place he had dreamed about since he had heard Father Fraser one night in Maynooth. He and Ned Galvin were talking in a stifling hot

147

Franciscan friary of Hankow this night and MacPolin was somewhere in one of the other rooms—he had been present, too, when Fraser had talked of China. Probably none of them would be here, now or ever, if it had not been for Father John Fraser. Like the man or not, he had touched all of them. John Blowick voiced that thought.

"It would be easier to understand," he said, "if he had been a good speaker or an appealing man, if he'd made us see the best of China or made us see a little of what we saw today."

Father Galvin stared at the far wall. He held his lighted cigarette suspended halfway to his lips. "I know how he made me feel," he said slowly. *"God, it's terrible! I have to go there!"*

Fathers Galvin and Blowick were very close that night in Hankow, close in aspiration, in hope, in affection. They were not designed, seemingly, to be easy companions in the normal round of living, nor to share the same enthusiasms; but there was respect and appreciation for each other, perhaps a touch of honest envy on the part of each for gifts that the other possessed. "There was never any competition between Blowick and Galvin," one of their early companions wrote, "though the basis for it was there. I never saw a sign that either of them ever tried to outdo the other or that either of them ever deliberately sought an advantage over the other."

The day after the visit to Hanyang, Father Blowick had a visitor who identified himself as Dr. Francis Kung, a Chinese Catholic engaged in medical work among the employees of the Hanyang Steel and Iron Works. He had been told that Father Blowick was the superior of a society of priests which planned to locate in Hanyang, and he knew of some houses which were for rent. Fathers Blowick and Galvin returned to Hanyang with him. The houses, which were situated at Pai Yu T'ai, about a mile outside the west gate of the city, were the property of the Iron Works. They were built in European style and had once been occupied by Iron Works engineers and their families. The two Columbans looked at them, liked them, and rented them, all in the space of a few hours.

As soon as he reached Hankow, Father Blowick cabled Ned McCarthy in Omaha, telling him that a home had been secured; the young priests could come to Hanyang.

148

Those priests were scattered over a wide section of the United States, working in pairs and located in different cities, but Father McCarthy rounded them all up, secured reservations for them and, by July 24, had them headed for China—a remarkable piece of arranging which, when he had many times repeated the performance under differing conditions, was taken for granted.

The day after they had rented the buildings, Fathers Blowick and Galvin took the train to Peking. They wanted government permission for the opening of schools in connection with their mission, a complicated matter in China and one which, they were advised, must be negotiated personally in Peking.

There was one good express train a day from Hankow to Peking, leaving at 8 P.M. and arriving at 7 A.M. the second next morning, a 35-hour run. The Blowick diary classed the trip as "unpleasant" and the train as "stuffy, dusty, dilapidated and fearfully crowded."

Peking was a beautiful city and they saw it at the perfect time while its beauty was intact, but they did not succeed in getting the clear-cut authorizations they wanted. The structure of government was shaky and insecure, public servants were afraid to act or to take responsibility.

During the return journey, John Blowick made a tourist discovery in Tientsin which fascinated him.

"This city, too, has narrow streets," he wrote. "There are one or two wide and stately thoroughfares. If a street is narrow, it is called Ma Loo, that is, 'horse street,' or a street wide enough to permit the passage of a horse-drawn vehicle. If the street is more impressive, wider, it is called Ta Malu, meaning the 'great horse street.' Horsedrawn vehicles are rare in China."

The two travelers returned to Hankow on July 26. A letter from Ned Maguire in Australia stated that he had two Australian-born priests and five other volunteers awaiting only the permission of their bishop before joining the society. He had, in addition, what he called "a host of other volunteers," students and girls who wanted to be missionary sisters. He had netted about £7000 during the few months he had been working Down Under and he had just started an Australian *Far East*.

"We move fast, once we start," Ned Galvin said.

Father MacPolin had not been down to meet them and

149

they assumed that he was on the Hanyang side. "After we read our mail," John Blowick wrote, "we crossed over to Hanyang. The heat here is oppressive all of the time, day and night. We use Chinese mats for beds and we all have prickly heat."

MacPolin had been busy. He had hired Chinese labor, a few technicians, and he had the rented houses sound and shining. He had even made a beginning on landscaping. However, he was not happy about the cleaning job, which had been a bit haphazard when he was not on top of it. The three men located the ideal spot for a chapel, an upstairs room which had been two rooms until the dividing partition had been removed.

"We'll clean this room ourselves," Father Galvin said.

It was a resolution that he kept. He and Father MacPolin scrubbed and shined the room in their home which was reserved for God. Father Galvin wrote later to a student at Dalgan: "I strongly advise you the next time you go home to get your good mother to give you a few lessons in the gentle art of scrubbing, for I assure you it is more necessary here than theology or scripture."

In the meantime, having seen their houses, Fathers Blowick and Galvin went shopping for furniture. They knew that they would have to do most of their purchasing in Hankow where European styles, types and designs of everything were available, but they strolled through the shopping area of Hanyang which was uncompromisingly Chinese. Father Galvin saw a Buddhist altar in a shop and was enchanted with it. It was huge and solid and, apart from geometric design, plain. There were no images or obvious pagan symbols carved into it. One could not guess how the altar had come, divorced from all religious attachment or significance, to a corner of Hanyang, but here it was. The price was the equivalent of five American dollars.

"I want it," Father Galvin said. "It will be wonderful in that chapel. Impressive enough for a cathedral, it is."

Father Blowick was doubtful. "It looks as though it would weigh a couple of tons," he said.

"No matter, these people are great at handling weights. They'll get it up there."

Father Galvin bought the Buddhist altar. After the

150

chapel site and the altar itself had been cleaned, a small army of Chinese succeeded in installing it. The entire operation was of tremendous interest to people of every degree in Hanyang and, naturally, the doctors, engineers and executives of the Iron Works heard all about it. The three priests invited this group to see what they had done with their rented houses. They served refreshments and sat in a group on Hankow furniture. The engineers, although Chinese, had gone to college in England and, of course, spoke English. Poker-faced and Oriental in the carrying out of a joke, they discussed Chinese building, assuring their hosts that the appearance of a building in China was deceptive; that, for example, the Chinese did not build to resist a strong wind, which would be futile if the wind proved truly strong; that Chinese built to yield a little, to give way before strength. They told of some horrible examples of what had happened to various structures in the hands of Europeans who did not understand this.

In the midst of the discussion, Ned Galvin jumped up suddenly and hurried from the room. John Blowick, startled and a bit concerned, followed him, catching him at the foot of the stairs in the house next door.

"What in God's name is the matter with you, Caw," he said, "bounding out like that on your guests?"

"I want to take another look at that bloody altar," Father Galvin said.

The mail continued to come in for Father Blowick, wherever he was. The vicariate question was far from settled. He and Father Galvin had called on Bishop Gennaro who was upset and angry, claiming that they were trying to tear the heart out of all that he had built with his life in these missions.

"A lot of Latin exaggeration," Father Galvin said later. "He wasn't able to maintain what we are taking over and he knows it. Look at Hanyang, across the river from him. Not a single priest in the whole city."

He saw Bishop Gennaro again and the old man, while maintaining his position on territory and his determination to fight it out in Rome, was cooperative in other respects, so much so that Father Galvin could write in a cheerful tone about him in a letter to Father McCarthy:

Gennaro and all have been very kind. John has told you probably that Gennaro has put up a case against us on An Loo but I don't believe he'll succeed, and he said he'd do whatever Rome said. He gave me all the faculties right away and the boys will get them when they arrive. . . .

Everything considered, I'm well satisfied and rather glad that we are beginning at scratch in Hanyang. It is a kind of no man's land and so here we're perfectly undisturbed and can peg away as soon as we are ready. John and the rest of you have all the time ye want to put up a big fight in Rome if necessary, for we have all the room we require here for at least another year.

The vicariate question not only dominated letters, it crept into conversation at all hours, particularly when Fathers Galvin and Blowick were alone. John Blowick was going to Australia because it seemed obvious that, with the splendid beginning which Father Maguire had made, Australia would loom large in the future of the society. Father Blowick decided that he would return to Rome after Australia and stay until every point of Bishop Gennaro's was nailed down and the vicariate made secure for the Columbans against all appeals and all attempts to remove them; that the territory beyond Hanyang itself would be territory that the Columbans could work.

The role of Father John Blowick in the society was being written for him by the work that was being given to him to do. He and Father Galvin recognized that without discussing it. There was no one else who would carry the same weight with the Australians, and certainly no one who could handle the people in Rome as Father Blowick could. As for China, yearn for it though he might—and he still did, even looking at its negative side from close-up— Father Blowick knew that this was the area in which Ned Galvin moved with sure touch, the area in which no one could surpass him. The irony of the Blowick position was that he was too commandingly capable for second place anywhere in the society, and first place was firmly and honestly held in the one territory that mattered.

At this time, in various letters, Father Galvin was setting down his impressions of various people in China. It was a weakness of his that he was apt to be suspicious of people, that he anticipated hostility or opposition without sufficient justification for his anticipation; but it was a

152

strength of his that, discovering himself in error, he tried to correct the record. The Vicar Apostolic of Shanghai, Monsignor Paris, was a man whom, in advance of their meeting, he had regarded as an opponent and from whom he had expected no friendly gestures. On August 1 Father Galvin wrote to Father McCarthy:

"Monsignor Paris is a man of about sixty, with gray hair and a strong, intelligent face. He is, like most Vicars Apostolic, a simple, kindly man and, like all Jesuits, a gentleman."

In the same letter he comments on the heat. "It is frightfully hot, an inferno, here. For several days it has been 104, 106, 110; all of the time boiling with not the slightest breeze. No sleep is possible except in naps."

He had taught his companions to wear white Chinese garments instead of the priestly black, but Father Blowick wrote: "We must get a place in the hills for the priests."

Time was running out for Father Blowick in Hanyang. He and Father Galvin recognized the moment when all the words had been said, when the problems had received all the attention which they deserved, when the hopes no longer needed expression. They were parting and they did not know if they would ever meet again. That was not a thought that could be expressed. John Blowick reported their farewell in a brief paragraph:

"The night before I left Hanyang," he wrote, "Caw and I sat up half the night reading Burns to each other and the lines that tickled us most were those which you will apply to me the moment you read all that I've been saying; 'God knows I'm no the thing I should be—I'm even no the thing I could be.' "

There was one more day and a busy round of detail, then the night boat on the Yangtze out of Hankow. Father Blowick had six hundred miles of river to travel before he reached the sea, and thirteen thousand miles of sea before he touched again the soil of Ireland. He wrote of that evening to Father John Henaghan:

"Leaving Dalgan was about as bad as I ever experienced up to that moment, but then I saw a few of ye again and, anyway, I knew that I would have the company of the boys all the way out here. But that night on the steamer at Hankow, in the dark and the awful heat, saying goodbye and seeing Caw and MacPolin gliding off,

153

two white figures, into the night, with myself starting off alone around the world again, I was absolutely sick of it all."

14 : : MEN IN HANYANG

On August 17, 1920, eleven young Columban priests landed in Shanghai, the first mission band of the society in China if one excludes the team of Blowick, Galvin and MacPolin. They took the usual short tours of Shanghai and learned the feeling of assured veterans of the missions on their long trip up the Yangtze to Hanyang. Father Cornelius Tierney, the oldest priest in the group, the man who had given his life savings to the society before he gave himself, wrote a vivid description of the city which they had traveled so far to reach:

> We have just arrived in our new home and have got a look at a portion of Hanyang. . . . Words cannot describe it and, in my wildest imagining, I never dreamt of it being what the reality proves to be. The long winding street we passed through is so narrow that you could, by stretching out your hands, reach the houses on either side. The pathway is the antithesis of cleanliness, with here and there a little puddle of green glittering water; the smells varying from that of a suds tub after very dirty clothes have been washed to that of an open sewer in very hot weather. Our houses are very well located out of the town and fairly good. Each house has about 12 rooms besides a back portion for kitchen, servants, etc. There is an old lake overgrown with the lotus plant within a few feet of the house.

Father Galvin welcomed the first missionaries enthusiastically and started them immediately on the study of Chinese. Future mission groups would have at least the rudiments of Chinese before they came out, but this first band had to start their study of the language in China itself.

154

On the day after the new missioners reached Hanyang, Father Galvin's brother, Michael, was killed during a fight with a British contingent which he and other Irish Republican Army men had ambushed. The family decided against cabling the bad news and mail traveled slowly between Ireland and China, so it was many weeks before Ned Galvin heard the news.

The most interesting topic of correspondence, now that the vicariate question had temporarily quieted down, was the question of obtaining sisters to teach in schools and to provide the necessary contact with Chinese women which the priests could not hope to achieve. Father Galvin believed that it should be possible to recruit an order of sisters from the many girls who had volunteered in person or by mail in Ireland; to organize them, train them and ship them out. Father Blowick, bearing in mind the long struggle to organize and ship out priests, was doubtful that women could be made ready for mission service in less time. Father McCarthy did not believe that Irish women were the ideal choice for China service and he was advocating a serious effort to obtain nuns from some existing order in the United States. The resulting three-way correspondence was interesting even if, for the time being, non-productive.

Father Galvin was saddened by the news that Father Tom Ronayne was sailing for the African mission to Nigeria in September with fifteen other Holy Ghost Fathers. He walked back and forth across the room and punched his right fist into his left palm.

"Damn!" he said. "He was one of us. We should have had him."

The toils of the Chinese language had closed firmly around the Columban Mission crew and Father Tierney related eloquently the experiences of them all in a letter:

We have been working hard on the Chinese language for nearly three weeks. For the present we are not doing any characters. We are just learning to speak. We have a text book with a graduated set of exercises, each composed of a set of sentences; very simple in the beginning, increasing in difficulty. The teacher comes in and reads these out slowly, repeating each a few times. Then we take them down phonetically and repeat them for him to ensure that we have the correct, or nearly correct, sound. We are

155

getting a new set of sentences each day, with new words, and illustrating new idioms. In this way we have already got between 250 and 300 sentences and, of course, these will enable us to make up other sentences.

Father Galvin had no difficulty with the language as spoken in Hanyang, but there were local words and idioms, local inflections, which had to be learned. As he was looking forward to spending his life in or near this province, he studied as the new men did. To educated Chinese, however, he retained, all of his life, a Chekiang accent.

In October the College of St. Senan, an extension of Dalgan, opened in County Clare. It was a fine old mansion and estate located on the River Shannon at a place called Cahiracon, one of the beauty spots of Ireland. It was dedicated to the study of philosophy and students were assigned there before moving on to the four-year theology course at Dalgan. Dr. Michael O'Dwyer was appointed rector.

There was news from Australia, too, where Father Blowick was still visiting hierarchy and clergy. The first issue of the Australian edition of *The Far East* had made its appearance and was enthusiastically greeted. In three years it reached a circulation of thirty thousand.

On October 24, 1920, Father Galvin wrote on the flyleaf of his ritual, the book which he used for the administration of the sacraments, the following entry: "Mr. Patrick Joseph Wang was baptized by me today—our first baptism in China. Deo Gratias."

This Christian victory was overwhelmed by a pagan demonstration three days later. There was an eclipse of the moon over Hanyang and the event was signalized by a beating of cymbals and pipes and the hammering or rattling of anything which would create noise, preferably a loud noise. In Chinese mythology such an event signified that the Dog of Heaven was eating the moon and must be frightened away.

Father Richard (Dick) Ranaghan, unofficial photographer for the Columbans at Hanyang, took pictures of the eclipse and the Chinese noisemaking ceremonies. Ranaghan had come to China with cameras, including a movie camera, and a variety of paraphernalia associated with the

156

developing of film and the making of prints. He believed that eventually his cameras would be a tremendous Columban aid in the raising of funds and in the stirring of vocations.

Some time after this incident a letter came from Father Paul Waldron in Omaha: "I am writing to let you know that Doc Mee is now booked to sail for China on February 10 and arriving in Shanghai on February 26."

Father Galvin passed the letter to Owen MacPolin. "If I forget, Pole, or if I am not here," he said, "take care of him. He is one of the unusual people."

Father MacPolin made the note in his small book. "That fills the quota," he said. "We can't fit another unusual person into this place."

On November 14 Father Galvin finally received his long-delayed sad news from Ireland. He wrote to Father McCarthy in Omaha: "Please say a prayer for my brother who was shot by the police at Lissarda on August 22nd. He tried to do his duty as he saw it and, though I feel his death sorely, I have no regrets. May he rest in peace."

This letter was crossed by a letter and two immense packages from Father McCarthy; one of his inspirations. There were eighty thousand multigraphed letters enclosed signed with a plate made from a genuine signature of Father Galvin's. The letter, based on actual letters of his, described conditions in China and the problems facing missionaries, and frankly asked for funds. The envelopes were addressed to a first-rate Catholic mailing list. Enclosed in the accompanying letter was a check for eight thousand dollars to cover the cost of stamps. In Father McCarthy's opinion, these letters mailed from China would have an impact far beyond anything that American based letters could hope to have; in Hanyang the letters were appalling.

"Don't ever do anything like this again, Ned," Father Galvin wrote. "If this stunt becomes known in the United States as your stunt it would do an infinite amount of harm. When these 80,000 letters go through the mails in Hankow they will create a sensation in every Vic in the country. When O'Doherty went over the other day to Hanyang Postoffice and asked for $200.00 worth of stamps, merely a beginning, mind you, the whole office stood still with amazement."

157

The letters, of course, got mailed ultimately, and a great many contributions came in because of them. Once faced with the reality of this immense burden of letters, Father Galvin and his men had done a creditable job.

"We will have a good response from these letters," Galvin said. "The Catholic people, God bless them, always respond when they can. . . . Whatever it costs us in time or sleep, every letter must be answered. The man or woman who gives us prayers must be thanked, as is the person who sends us money. We have no right to ask for anything which we are too busy to acknowledge."

Ultimately, he gave that lecture or a variant of it to many groups and individuals who came to China, and no one lived up to it more steadfastly than he did. He would sit up, often by candlelight, in the country parishes after a hard day's work, to answer the letter of some old woman he had never met, a woman who wrote to tell him she was praying for him. It was a rule of life.

In December the Columbans moved. It was impractical to put long-range planning or extensive work into houses rented on a month-to-month basis. Mr. Kwok, sub-manager of the Iron Works, understood the problem. He was friendly with the priests and had been a partaker of their hospitality. He could do nothing to insure their possession of the houses but he did offer them an alternative.

About a half mile to the east of Pai Yu T'ai, between Tortoise Hill and the north wall of the city, there was a hospital that had been built by the American Baptist Mission in 1906. The difficulties of wartime operation had resulted in the abandonment of the mission in 1916. The entire plant had remained idle since. It was an attractive, quiet, secluded place on three and one-half acres of ground. The ground was low-lying, which was a disadvantage but, as far as Father Galvin could see, the only disadvantage. Through the cooperation of Mr. Kwok, he bought this property into which the Columbans moved.

The main building itself offered ample accommodation for the sixteen priests, and if the needs became greater it would be easy to enlarge it. It had four large wards and a number of smaller rooms. Adjoining this were a number of houses to be used as a kitchen and dwellings for the domestic staff. At a distance of sixty yards from the main building there was a house for the professional staff, eight

158

large rooms with adjoining accommodations for servants. Fifty yards further, there was a small church with two large rooms and three small rooms under one roof. In addition there was a small isolation hospital with nurses' apartments and a hall that would accommodate approximately two hundred people. The compound had a green lawn, shade trees and an encompassing wall.

The total cost of this property, payable in two installments, was twenty thousand dollars.

With money or without, living in one place or another, the life of the average Hanyang Columban was dominated by one central interest. Father Tierney stated it in a letter of December 3:

> We are still ding-dong in the language. It is the great business of our lives just now. Books, conversation with servants, all that can assist is called into requisition. We shall soon begin on Catechism, rather late in life for some of us to be learning the elements! But it must be memorized in order to meet the Catechumens. Well, all of this is a certain kind of drudgery but we don't feel it. In fact, we have got into the run of things to such an extent that we scarcely realize that we are in a strange country.

These student missioners had not been equipped to go out to the people, so no real attempt was made to spread the Faith during the first months in Hanyang. "The little oratory at Pai Yu T'ai had for long witnessed Sunday Mass without a lay congregation," Father Shackleton wrote. "Then, among the few Catholics of the district, their presence became known. Later came one old woman whom we welcomed like 'the first swallow of summer.' The 'first swallow' drew others in her train and so, slowly, a tiny congregation began to gather around the newcomers."

The tiny congregation was, of course, composed of former Catholics who had slipped away because they had no place in which to worship and no priest. Some of them had previously lived in Hankow or Wuchang or other places. The move to the property which had once been Baptist provided the Columbans with a church. The church, like the rest of the property, was in need of cleaning and rehabilitation after long vacancy. All of the staff and students contributed physical labor in the time be-

159

tween other demands and assignments. A letter of Father Tierney's reports the sequel:

> Well, we managed to get the little church opened for Christmas. We had a congregation of about 100 people—about 50 for Holy Communion. We had High Mass at midnight and Father Galvin gave them a short sermon in Chinese. This was a beginning which, of itself, was sufficient to make our Christmas a happy one. The poor people were very fervent. . . . During the night there were some of them knocking about the place. They never went home at all but were there until Masses commenced again at 6 A.M. . . .
> Later Christmas Day . . . we had our turkeys and plum pudding. Mr. Chang, our grocer, made us a present of these and some wine also. Some other people sent over fruit and some sent cigars and cigarettes. So, every taste was catered to fairly well. Then there was the usual singing of Irish and patriotic songs. We had quite an Irish Christmas in Hanyang.

Father Galvin was at his best during a holiday celebration like this. No one knew more songs and he had, on this Christmas, a warm feeling of sympathy for the young men around him. He had gone through what they were experiencing; the sharp ache that came with the awareness of Christmas in a land completely alien, a longing for loved ones, a memory of other Christmases. He whipped their spirits up and he led the singing and the songs were touched with humor or heavy sentiment. There was a bit of farewell about it all, too, although that was not stressed. The tight little community of men in Hanyang was breaking up. Apprenticeship under Franciscans in the parishes lay immediately ahead of each of them.

"The boys are going out next week," Father Galvin wrote to Father Waldron on December 30, "and I am going with them."

160

15 : : NGAN LOO

The first two priests to go out to the missions, the country regions of China, were Fathers Cornelius Tierney and William O'Flynn. Their post was Shinti, 130 miles from Hanyang, a city of fifty thousand of whom only 160 were Catholics. Theirs was the largest headquarter town and they came to it off a bleak river boat on a cold night with snow heavy on the ground.

Fathers Matthew Dolan and Arthur McGuinness went to Chang Tan Kow; Fathers Michael McHugh, Alphonsus Ferguson and Joseph Crossan went to Hwang Kia Shan; Fathers Thomas Quinlan and Timothy Leonard to Chi Wu Tai. They, too, traveled in cold and snow. Father Ned Galvin planned to allow them settling time and then follow, visiting each man in the field. He knew from his own experience the shocks in store for a young missionary in the rural regions of China.

The Chinese were curious people. They were drawn to anything new or strange or different. They wanted to know how mechanical things worked and what made them work. They wanted to know how foreigners differed from themselves, if foreigners did—in what manner, and to what degree. They watched, listened, observed, gathered in groups and stared, sometimes silently, sometimes with much conversation and laughter. There was no malice in this; they were people who lacked privacy, and who consequently did not value it.

One of the stern ordeals for a young priest in a small Chinese town was facing the problem of a bodily function, of waste elimination. There was, of course, no indoor plumbing and there were few privies. If privies were built, they were apt to be promptly torn down and carried away for the wood in them; but in the main town or towns of a parish, they could be secured fairly well. The accepted alternate was a trench with a pole supported on two uprights. A stranger, particularly a foreign stranger of another color, invariably drew a friendly, interested crowd of spectators if he sought bodily relief. Men, women and children shared the interest in him and he gained nothing if he tortured himself, as most new ones did, by waiting for nightfall. The night had as many eyes as the day, any hour of the night.

It was normal for a young missionary to develop physical ailments in his first few weeks while seeking to evade an interest which did not understand his attempts at evasion.

In the same general area of experience, even farm-raised young men from Ireland and the United States found it difficult to adjust to China's need for and intense interest in excrement, animal and human. The ancient soil needed it as a renewing agent and the acquiring of it was a quite matter-of-fact affair. In small towns or large, there was no subtlety to the odors.

All this a young missionary had to learn. He was committed to living in this area of earth, to abiding what he could not hope to change.

The small towns in a parish were many and a priest visited the main ones as often as he could, but there were towns which received no more than a single visit in a year. In the towns where there were a number of Christians, the priest tried to have a catechist who functioned in his absence, instructing, leading the Rosary or Stations of the Cross, holding the Christians together. The demands on a catechist, however, were many and it was almost impossible to find a qualified person who could give the time and still manage to support himself. If the priest could not afford the small wage the catechist had to have, a village was apt to grow careless in religious thought and practice. In a Christian town, the priest had a small structure reserved which served him as a church and as a dwelling place. If he had a good catechist, or devoted Catholics, the place was kept clean and habitable; but when carelessness set in, it was immediately noticeable in the deterioration of the church premises.

Young missionaries had to see the good villages and the bad and learn to live as they must, under the guidance of an older priest, before they could even attempt the facing of Chinese realities alone. Winter was the prime season in

162

which to go out. It wasn't comfortable but it was a time to learn.

Father Galvin was concerned about his first band of priests, as a group and as individuals; but he had other concerns. Fathers John Blowick and Ned McCarthy were in Rome, going through the patient, painful process of securing a satisfactory territory which would one day be erected into a vicariate for the society, insisting on the territory which stemmed logically from their assigned command post in Hanyang and rejecting courteously, with sound reason, the proffered alternates of the Franciscans who yielded good territory reluctantly. One of the alternates which appeared earlier had included working territory on two sides of the Yangtze. Father Galvin had replied to that:

> To show you what a terrible barrier the Yangtze is. About two weeks ago Gennaro invited us to Wuchang for the feast of St. Francis. It had rained all the day before and that morning up to 11 A.M. When we arrived at the Yangtze we found that no steamer could cross as it was considered too dangerous. Communications was cut off altogether. You can form some idea then of the difficulty of working a Vicariate, part of which is on either side of the river, when one day of rain makes the river impassable even for steamers.

Ned Galvin, however, was too far away from Rome. Mail was slow in traveling from one point to the other; a letter and a reply took prohibitive time. He had, then, to rely upon John Blowick to keep the record straight in Rome, to hold firm against all temptations to compromise.

On January 8, 1921, Father Blowick wrote from Rome to Father Galvin: "I had a great audience with the Holy Father. He took a deep interest in the whole thing. He asked me very deep questions and seemed quite touched by some of the facts and figures on poor China."

One of the Rome points which impressed both Fathers Blowick and McCarthy was the encouragement they received toward the organizing of an Irish order of missionary nuns dedicated to service in China. Before they left Ireland, there had been a movement tentatively organized under

163

the direction of Lady Frances Moloney, a Dublin social worker, but both priests had reservations about it.

There were more problems than that of the mission sisterhood in Ireland. The financial situation in Dalgan was so badly muddled, in Father McCarthy's estimation, that he wrote a letter of alarm to Father Galvin, who replied immediately:

"I had hoped that the fellows in Dalgan would give me some notion of the state of things; but they have not. I fear they made a terrible mess of things while John was away and if things are as bad as your letter leads me to believe, I pity the poor fellow when he returns to Dalgan. Our own small supply of money—it wasn't very much at the very best of times—has run very low and our expenses are increasing daily."

One of the extensions of the Hanyang Mission was medical service. Dr. Robert F. Francis, an American Catholic, volunteered his services and arrived in Hanyang in January. Within a month he had opened a dispensary. A few days later Father Galvin opened a small school and enrolled sixty boys on the first day.

It was the Lenten season and Father Galvin went out to visit the priests who were learning the front line principles of missionary life. He visited his oldest priest first, Father Cornelius Tierney, forty-nine, who was assisted by Father William O'Flynn at Shinti. They were well adjusted, and Father Tierney suggested a visit to the neighboring city of Fengkow. It was thirty miles distant. He and Father Galvin walked the distance along the banks of a small river and through an almost continuous chain of villages. The villagers, of course, were curious, stopping all work to watch them walk by. Most of the route was flat, marshy in spots, but for the last ten miles the land was fertile and intensely cultivated; wheat, oats, beans, and a great variety of vegetables. They arrived at Fengkow as it was growing dark. Father Tierney drew a deep breath.

"I wondered if you'd walk it now," he said softly.

"Did you have another way of reaching here?"

"Not a one."

"The more fool you to wonder then!"

The two men understood each other as only two men who have grown tired together can understand. They had shared a day, with much conversation and much silence,

164

solid walking and soggy walking. Fengkow was a city with a ten thousand population and a small Catholic church which waited in quiet isolation until a priest visited it. The two priests moved unobtrusively into the shabby church house and the word of their arrival spread rapidly through Catholic circles. The Catholics arrived in twos and threes and in entire families, tired no doubt from their own work of the day, but unwilling to show it lest the Shen Fu might want or need something from them. Father Tierney, who had been in Fengkow before and met its people, had a look of content. These were his people and they gave him great face with his visitor because of their concern for him. Father Galvin understood all of that—the Chinese Catholics and their priest—and how swiftly a good priest established a near-kinship with those under his care.

"A great people, Corney," Father Galvin said, when at last the two priests were alone. "They are like the Irish. When you've made Catholics out of them, you've made good Catholics."

The priests said Masses in the church in the morning and people came. There were people who wanted confessions heard and there were a few babies to be baptized. In mid-afternoon the priests walked seven miles to the village of Liao-Chia-Ho where there were seventy Catholics but no church. It was a chill, windy day with moisture in the air. They visited the Catholics and spent the night there, walking back to Fengkow the following morning. Another town, Shiao-Sa-Kow, was thirteen miles from Fengkow, a small place with eighty Catholics who proudly traced their Catholicity back for two centuries. Shiao-Sa-Kow did not have a church or a school but its Catholics met regularly, led by a catechist.

"They break your heart," Father Galvin said, "and there are others like them everywhere."

The thirteen miles back to Fengkow seemed shorter than the thirteen out. It was still cold but the wind had quieted. There was a wisp of warmth in the sunlight.

Father William O'Flynn was waiting for them in the city. The young priest had made an intensive trip with his Franciscan mentor, testing his knowledge of Chinese against the demands of a priest's work. His Chinese was primitive, limited and far from adequate, but he had

165

worked hard on the mastery of what he knew and, with a little ingenuity, could take care of the needs of the people, learning from them and with them. He was delighted to see Fathers Galvin and Tierney, proud that he was going to be pastor at Fengkow.

"Do you know what it means? Of course you do," he said. "Fengkow! In Chinese it means 'windy mouth'. And what will they say to that in Ireland? 'Willie O'Flynn is pastor of a place called "windy mouth." Imagine that now! A more apt place he'll never find.' "

The three priests celebrated Palm Sunday together in Fengkow and Father Galvin walked back with Father Tierney to Shinti. He returned then to Hanyang for Easter.

The final answer on the assignment of Ngan Loo, the Hsien county which Father Galvin particularly wanted in the Columban vicariate, was still suspended in Rome when word came to Hanyang that Bishop Gennaro was planning a trip to Rome. Obviously, if the bishop was going to carry to the Holy City his fight for the territory he held, there would be no decision until he had been heard. Father Galvin decided to explore Ngan Loo and see for himself if the Franciscans had any basis for a claim to it. He delayed his trip one week after he made his decision.

Every Columban who could get away came down to Hanyang when they heard that Romuald Hayes of Melbourne, the first volunteer priest from Australia, was coming up the Yangtze. Father Hayes, thirty, was a curate at Northcote, a suburb of Melbourne, when Father Edward Maguire of the Columbans went to Australia in 1920, seeking money and priests. He gave Father Maguire the equivalent of fifty dollars, which was all that he had, and he waved the thanks of the priest away.

"I will give you something more one of these days, please God," he said.

The "something more" was his life. He joined the Columbans and when Father Blowick went to Australia in 1920, he took Father Hayes back to America with him. He worked for a while in Omaha on *The Far East* and now he was on his way back, on assignment, to Australia.

Father Galvin left for Ngan Loo on May 4, after he had welcomed the priest from Australia. In a long, detailed report to John Blowick he related how, through all of the

166

country, the traces of a once widespread Catholicism, a successful missionary crusade, were evident; but it was equally evident that the effort had run out, that there was no longer a crusade. The Franciscans, who had once taken this country for Christ and who wanted to hold it, no longer had the priests nor the hope of obtaining them. The churches were crumbling into dust and decay, and the priests had vanished. The Franciscans had lost to paganism in fact what they sought to withhold on paper from the Irish society, which had the priests and the will to reclaim what had fallen away.

In places where there was a priest in residence, there was a difference in conditions described; but the mark of defeat and despondency was on the work of those who, by necessity, sent too few with too little against a great, teeming reality.

Never in my life have I been over any country where the possibilities of doing something big for God seem greater than here [Father Galvin wrote]. I have never met pagans like the pagans here. They are almost as friendly as the Catholics, and all are most friendly to one another. The pagans can tell you where every chapel in the surrounding country is, and, what is more, they can tell you how many Catholics are there. When you arrive at a Catholic house, the pagans come in, too, and they are very respectful, very polite, a very refined people although all of them are poor. It is not a studied politeness, it is the natural inborn politeness for which the Irish people are remarkable. Let us have priests and we will bring these people into the Church by thousands.

Father Galvin finished his tour on the evening of June 3. In his report he stated that he had covered 1,262 li in the province of Ngan Loo, 932 of which he walked. In a letter to Father Ned McCarthy, dated shortly after his return to Hanyang, Galvin, still under the spell of the country, wrote:

I have just got back from a month's trip through Ngan Loo and as I walked about 1000 li (330 miles) I am feeling a bit tired. Let me say that in all my wildest dreams I never thought Ngan Loo was so beautiful or so extensive. The country is very like the rich country around Maynooth, with this difference, that it is more beautifully

167

wooded, every inch under cultivation and teeming with life. The pagans are most friendly and consider it a privilege if you speak to them. The people are as simple as children. The atmosphere of Ngan Loo is almost as Catholic as Ireland. The people are living Catholic lives. I am convinced that all we need is priests to convert this Vic in our own lifetime. Gee, I couldn't help crying a few times.

16 : : VICARIATE

There was a happier spirit in letters from Ireland in the latter half of 1921, particularly in the all-important letters that priests received from parents, relatives and close friends. The British Government had shown an interest in achieving peace and was offering Ireland the long-sought Home Rule in the form of dominion status. A truce and cease-fire went into effect on July 11. On July 26 Father Blowick wrote to Father McCarthy:

"Things are looking brighter and everybody is hopeful of a good settlement of the political trouble. The Irish Sisters of Charity will undertake to train our novices for us and we should be in full swing in September or October."

Irish nuns for China was a project which had engaged much of Father Blowick's time at a period when he was in constant correspondence with Rome on the subject of the vicariate, in close touch with building and other developments in China and the United States, teaching classes at Dalgan as a member of the faculty. Other men in the young society were also doubling and tripling on jobs, but no one, not even Father Galvin, carried as much responsibility.

On June 5, two days after Father Galvin's return from his Ngan Loo trip, Father James O'Connell died in Arizona. Jim O'Connell had been the first to volunteer for the China Mission while he was a student at Maynooth, but his health, unfortunately, never matched his ardor. He went no farther than Omaha on his way to China, and he knew that his time was limited when he went to Arizona in an effort to recover from tuberculosis. He offered his life for the society and for the success of the mission work in which he had been unable to participate.

Father Galvin learned of his death with sadness. Jim O'Connell was the first of the society to go. There would be others, of course, and many of them would go, perhaps, under far less peaceful circumstances. He laid the cablegram on the desk and went down the hall to the chapel.

There were other problems, one of them heralded by a terse letter of inquiry from Father Blowick and a long, impassioned letter from Father McCarthy that was more an editorial than an inquiry. At a time when Great Britain and Ireland were balanced in an uneasy truce, someone had made the charge that Ireland's missionaries had been registered with the British in China and that Father Galvin had accepted British protection for them; that they had been so registered and so protected during the time of the fierce fighting in Ireland.

"I wish to say very clearly," Father Galvin replied, "that the Mission has not accepted British protection. . . . The priest members of the Society now in China are British subjects by birth. . . . Therefore, [they] are as much subject to English law as if they lived in Dalgan. One of the laws, most strictly enforced by all the Powers, is that their subjects have to call at the Consulate and register their names within a stated period after their arrival in China under penalty of arrest and imprisonment for failure to do so."

He developed that point in a long letter, stating when and in what relationship he had dealt with the British Government since his arrival in China. A careful writing on the subject was required of him to answer any possible misunderstandings inside or outside the society.

It was a fixed rule of Father Galvin's to keep policy problems and worries out of conversations with the men on the theory that they had problems of their own and needed reassurance often that they were moving forward in a band of brothers. It infuriated him, therefore, when one of his priests received a letter from Omaha on the British protection question and shared it gleefully with most of his confreres. In reporting the matter to Father McCarthy, Father Galvin wrote:

"I have no blame whatever to the man who sent this

thing, but I ask him as one brother asks another to think well before he writes such things in the future. Give us a chance at this end. God knows we have troubles enough."

The "troubles enough" included one physical threat which looked ominous to the dwellers in Hanyang. Father Galvin wrote of that in another letter to McCarthy on August 3:

"Fierce fighting has broken out on the Hupeh border. . . . Four hundred dead were brought to Wuchang yesterday. Say a prayer for all of us here. We may be in the fighting line before this letter reaches you and even if it does blow over now, Hupeh has become the key to the situation. Sooner or later we are in for serious trouble."

The Columbans tried to avoid political involvement in China as they tried to avoid it in Ireland, but the situation was as badly confused in the one country as in the other. It was not easy to understand the motives of contending forces and it was difficult to remain clear of the contention. Father MacPolin tried to explain the problem in a letter to Dalgan:

> The Chinese are revolving here all of the time. We have no fixed government in this province now at all. You will probably hear a lot about Chinese wrongs in connection with the Pacific Conference, but you needn't have much sympathy with them. There seems to be no hope for them except for the foreigner to step in and run the country. A great many Chinese merchants are actually in favor of that. If you were here and saw what they are suffering from the ruffians who are in power you could understand it very well. There is not a steamboat on these two rivers which has not been commandeered these days. A whole lot of Tienmen and Nganlu are under water, owing to the breaking of bad dykes, and nothing is being done. Worse still, the rulers are flooding miles more by way of military operations. Even the Japs would be better than the present crowd.

In another letter, this one to Father McCarthy, MacPolin touched one of the human notes in mission life during the shaky, experimental period of its establishment in China. A motion picture sequence which Father Richard Ranaghan sent to Omaha received favorable comment from Father McCarthy and the MacPolin letter offered a report:

"Dick Ranaghan is like a man who has swallowed a sunset since he got your letter. The poor fellow devoted a terrible amount of planning and work and worry to the production of his masterpiece. He is already planning another one. . . ."

On September 6 Father McCarthy and the Omaha Columbans were laying the foundation stone of their new seminary, which inspired comment from Father Galvin:

> From the very day when Archbishop Harty gave me permission to open in Omaha, I nursed the idea that some time in the future we would have a house in the East. . . . When I went to Washington for the first time from Omaha, I actually looked around for some spot in the neighborhood of the University with a view to future developments. Of course, you are laughing loudly by this time. Please don't mention this to anyone for I am not as thick-skinned as I look. A house in Washington would give us a grip on the East which is the stronghold of Catholicity in the states.

Men who worked close to Father Ned Galvin did not consider him "thick-skinned." There was a basic shyness in the man under his superb sense of showmanship, a sensitivity that was not always apparent when he assumed the responsibilities of command; a mystical sense of faith that demanded much of a man and a calm acceptance of God's presence in the affairs of human creatures. He relaxed the tensions of leadership with music, as listener or participant, and often in the writing of verse. He might spend hours on a verse—his brow furrowed in concentration, burning one cigarette after another—then, when it satisfied him, touch a match to it. He cherished no illusions that he was a poet and he did not write for others; the writing of verse took him out of the endless round of problems and puzzles, cleared his mind, satisfied something creative in him and sent him back to his responsibilities refreshed. One verse of his from the fall of 1921 escaped the flames, one of the very few that did escape them:

THE YANGTZE AT HANYANG

Below the Temple moves the flowing river,
With long voiced murmur washing past the shore,

171

A tide, like life, that passes down forever,
Beside the waving shade of Ching Chuan Ko,
Laving the ships and rippling on the prows,
Coming from nowhere, goes where, no one knows.

A moment come and then a moment here,
Another moment, we are passed away,
Each strives a while, his little skiff to steer,
Till tides of Fate have swept him clear away.
For every dawn and eve repeat the same,
"Man is a floating bubble and a name."

We are but down upon the Winds of Time,
But tiny atoms on the sea of space,
As fleeting as the early winter rime,
That melts before the morning's genial face,
Yet, fear not; every act of good or ill
Bears fruit eternal and is living still.

Behind the Temple sinks the gorgeous West,
Tinting with ruby fire, the purple haze,
Making his last farewell appear the best,
Of glories glowing on departed days,
Peaceful his day is come, is here, is past,
Time is, Time was—too beautiful to last.

He came back from such efforts to the realities of finance, with an annual report to be made to Father Blowick. The report was accompanied by a note asking to be told of "any place where we are falling down" and adding, "Don't bother putting it in nice language. . . . We have no time for saying nice things."

Another letter to Father McCarthy in the same week deals with a different anxiety: "Art McGuinness is ill. The doctor says he has sprue, a disease of the intestines common in China. I have cabled for permission from Blowick and am sending him to Omaha. He is very young and has a very soft kind of nature. Don't ask him to do any work for the present. Art is a fine fellow and I can't tell you how sorry I am that he is leaving."

On October 19 Father John Blowick left for his fourth journey to Rome, where he would spend his thirty-third birthday. He was accompanied by his friend, Father Patrick Cleary. Bishop Genaro was there ahead of them, so there seemed to be no doubt that this was destined to be the climactic meeting which would lead to a final settlement of the vicariate question.

In Hanyang the most exciting event, once everyone had become accustomed to the smoldering threats of open warfare on the doorstep, was the arrival of the Irish Christian Brothers who would direct the establishment of schools. Owen MacPolin's report of their arrival reads:

"The Brothers are on their way from Shanghai. . . . and are due to arrive here on Saturday morning, November 5, 1921. . . . The old houses in Bei Ya Tai, which I fixed up for the boys when we first came to China, I have retaken from the Iron Works and they are now ready for the Brothers. . . . The staff of servants is *au complet;* carry-water coolie, buy-things coolie, cook, teacher, waiter, etc., etc."

The matter of hiring coolies in China was governed by rules and precedents. A foreigner with a certain type of house, a certain social standing, had to have a certain number of coolies. The Chinese community knew exactly how many he needed and it did not take advantage of him by padding the number. To oppose custom would be foolish. Everything would grind to a halt; one would accomplish nothing. Salaries were absurdly small but the coolies, needing their jobs, were happy in employment. As a system it was rather feudal, but it could only be changed slowly, if at all.

The Christian Brothers included one Australian strong man in their midst. He brought a punching bag and boxing gloves to Hanyang. The priests were fascinated.

On November 16 the big news broke, the news so long awaited. Father John Blowick cabled from Rome that the vicariate question was settled and Propaganda was granting most of the society's hopes and wants. Father Galvin was almost inarticulate with delight. He slapped Father MacPolin's shoulder.

"Pole, it's wonderful," he said. "We'll open schools. We'll get nuns out here. We can do it, Pole. All we ever needed was the word to go ahead. All we ever needed! Pole, we're going to do it!"

He and MacPolin talked into the pale hours of morning. It was a long night in Hanyang. On the following day, however, Father Galvin worried about Ngan Loo. He couldn't wait for a letter and he cabled his question. The

173

cable missed Father Blowick in Rome and was not answered until November 25, two days after Father Edward J. Galvin's thirty-ninth birthday. Until that assurance on Ngan Loo reached him, Father Galvin made no vicariate announcement. Through Father MacPolin, he made it now. Pole wrote to all the priests of Hanyang:

"A cablegram arrived yesterday from Ireland telling us that the Vicariate question has been definitely settled in our favour. Wherein all the brethren do rejoice exceedingly."

In the meantime, Father Blowick had written to Ned McCarthy in Omaha a brief version of the complete report sent to Father Galvin. It read in part:

> Thank God, the Vic is settled. Hankow has been ruled out but we have the Ngan Loo part and it makes a fine Vicariate. We have Hanyang, Mienyang, Tienmen, Anlu, Chungshiang, Kingshan, and part of Hanchwan. When the Vicariate will be erected and a Vicar appointed will depend on our priests. As soon as they know the language and are able to stand on their own legs it will be done. I called to see Genny [Bishop Gennaro] after the settlement and he is nice enough. The Fras [Franciscans] put up a fight, the magnitude of which you can scarcely imagine but as Drehmans said to me "it is a little miracle". Then, last night the Cardinal [W. Cardinal Van Rossum] sent for me urgently and said that we must change the name of the Society. He could make no positive suggestion but he did not like the name of Chinese Mission Society. Let me have your counsel in the matter *quam primum*.

Father McCarthy replied: "As my personal choice I would suggest St. Columban's Foreign Mission Society if the Cardinal wants it with a wider significance than 'Chinese.' [This of course, subsequently did become the official name of the society.] That is what we are known by among the students and our priests are called St. Columban's priests."

For once, Father McCarthy had to yield the prize for pungent phrasing to another member of the society. Father MacPolin wrote from Hanyang: "It is now felt here that poor St. Francis has lost face, indeed. I do not think that this is to be wondered at, as anyone with the slightest acquaintance with the two saints would choose ours in a fight."

174

On December 25 Father Galvin wrote to Father Blowick and the letter is a dramatic contrast to the Christmas letter of only one year earlier:

We had a very happy Christmas here. The priests arrived a few days before the feast. [This was the second group of missionaries from Dalgan, given six weeks of promotion and fund-raising duty in the United States en route to China. There were seven of them, led by Father Patrick O'Reilly, who was Father Galvin's comrade on his first time out.]

We had Midnight Mass in our chapel in the city, an attendance of 400, with 90 communions. The chapel looks neat. On Christmas day we had high Mass in Hanyang and the chapel was packed. Most of these people are not yet baptized but we will baptize 50 in two weeks time. In Woo Sin Meao where Father Mee is in charge, the little chapel was also filled and Dick [Ranaghan] had a good congregation in Ying Woo Dzou which is about a mile outside the city on the Yangtze bank. The young priests said their masses in Bay Ya Tai and some of the Priests said masses here; so we had masses in five places, in Hanyang and the suburbs.

All the young priests are well although a few of them are rather homesick.

17 : : A MATTER OF NUNS

Nearly six years had passed since three priests sat in a room in Shanghai and cut to a page in the Bible seeking guidance. They had believed then that a missionary society could be formed, staffed with Irish-born and Irish-educated priests, financed by gifts from the Irish and the American people. They had not foreseen, nor even imagined, the many obstacles that would lie between them and the realization of their dream, nor the time that would be consumed. They were older now and the dream had become a reality. Their missionary society had come into being. It had seminaries in Ireland and the United States, with an impressive number of young men being educated for mission work; it had money contributed by the generous, the self-sacrificing, the people of great faith; it had a mission headquarters and a home on the foreign soil of Hanyang, China; it had a vast territory delivered to it by Rome, with responsibility for all the souls within it. The three men, whose dream it had all been, stood humbly in the accomplished reality. Father Joseph O'Leary was in Ireland as manager of *The Far East*. Father Patrick O'Reilly was in Hanyang, out to China again with the latest detachment of priests which arrived in December. Father Edward J. Galvin was actively on the firing line, responsible for whatever was done or left undone.

Father Galvin had felt a new, fresh surge of vitality, as all members of the society had, with the news that the vicariate had been granted. "I am giving the boys their places," he wrote, "and there is as much excitement here as in a hive that is going to swarm."

It was mid-winter, but he went back to the shabby little villages and their neglected churches. He wrote on January 23, 1922, to Father Ned McCarthy:

> I have just got back from the country and I am nearly frozen. I was out in Ngan Loo for more than two weeks and it was the coldest weather I have ever struck. Everything was frozen down and not a thing moving. However, after some difficulty, I succeeded in getting to nearly all the places the priests are going to and in making arrangements for them. The people are delighted that we are coming and the priests will have a big welcome. Dick [Ranaghan] was along with me to his place. Ko Chia Dzae, and he got a great reception. The Catholics came out to meet him with flags flying and there was a crowd of about 400 people assembled at the Mission. They are a great people and Dick will do fine there. In all the other places, the people told me they would turn out to receive the priests if they knew when they were coming, but now with the snow, I can't say just when they can get there.

He was full of plans for building and rebuilding, for training catechists and paying them, for opening schools. He wanted to swoop through this vicariate like a great wind, gathering in souls for Christ, and he had no doubt that the souls were ready. He had talked to Catholic Chinese who had been too long without a priest and who

176

were as excited as he was. He wanted to serve those people and the many neighbors who, almost certainly, would become Catholics if a priest came and a church were opened for worship.

Father MacPolin listened to the great plans, the big projects. He was a solid man, with a live and sparkling sense of humor. Tall and powerful, he was a former chaplain in the British Army who carried himself like a soldier and who had a nice sense of command. He was procurator at Hanyang, responsible for money if not in complete command of it, and he was also the superintendent of construction.

"Look, Caw," he said at length, "all of this is fine but it will cost money. We fixed our roof last year, Chinese tiles, and it cost $1800 Mex, about 900 Gold. We finished a 50x20 school and it cost $2000 Mex without furniture. If you're going to rebuild Ngan Loo it will take time."

"God will provide what we need," Father Galvin said. "He always has. He wouldn't have given us the vicariate if we'd impressed Him as cautious types who'd be afraid to work it."

There were warnings from Ireland, too, about finances, warnings to go slowly at a time when, in Father Galvin's belief, they should be moving full speed ahead. Father Galvin was inclined to discount Irish anxieties as mere "nerves," chargeable to the political situation.

On January 22 His Holiness Pope Benedict XV died. Missionaries all over the world mourned him as one of the great mission popes. No one knew much about his successor, Pius XI, and there was concern about inevitable changes in policy.

"I am glad that we had our vicariate settled before we had a change at the top," Father Galvin said.

He was concerned about nuns. His plan for education called for teaching sisters at the highest levels. He also believed that Christianizing the vicariate on the large scale he envisioned would be possible only through reaching the women. He needed women to reach women. In China, men could not do it.

Late in the previous year, Father McCarthy had grown impatient with him because he delayed the decision to seek American nuns.

You put me off [the fiery McCarthy wrote] saying that you had put the proposition up to the Irish Sisters of Charity. If those Irish Orders have not enough of the missionary spirit to jump at a thing like that, you ought to just let them sit there. All the damn nonsense we heard and wrote! About all the Irish Sisters who volunteered! Now, when it comes to a showdown, there's not a quorum to start a little house in China.

Mind you, I cannot definitely guarantee to get you an American Order. . . . but I would try very hard to get what I consider the best and most progressive Order in America and I feel fairly certain that we could succeed if we go about it in the proper way. It would be a very great privilege to get them for they are in demand all over the country. Every bishop and priest who wants to put up a decent academy and high school wants to get the Loretto Sisters.

In January, 1922, with all plans moving forward, Father Galvin was no longer hesitating on the matter of American nuns. He was not in an oratorical or scorn-heaping mood as Father McCarthy had been, because he remembered how long it had taken eager, willing priests to reach China. He believed that the Irish nuns would be working in the missions some day as young Irish men were; but he wanted American nuns, and he wanted the Sisters of Loretto at the Foot of the Cross as soon as they could possibly come to Hanyang. He made himself clear in a letter to Father McCarthy:

"Hanyang is not a thing of beauty. The streets are narrow and dirty, the houses low, badly built and dirty. In summer little boys go quite naked, the little girls wearing pants. Men wear cotton pants, naked from the waist up. Women fully clad. Better make this quite clear to Mother General. The people are simple and inoffensive. The Sisters will be as safe in the streets of Hanyang as they would be in any city of the U. S."

While letters went back and forth between Fathers Galvin and McCarthy, the Columban nuns were established on February 1, 1922. They had been in a dreamlike formative stage since 1916, but now there were twelve novices with three Sisters of Charity to train them and that small organization had substance if not size. They were in being.

All problems crept into letters despite the involvement

178

with new duties and new assignments. Father McCarthy wrote from Omaha to Father E. J. O'Doherty:

"We are delighted to hear all the good news coming from China these days. It is fine to have 'the Question' settled. I suppose the boys will be starting out for Anlu any day now. Doc Mee described Anlu as 'half old Christians and half devils' and added, 'those wanting martyrdom will go to the latter.' From the tone of the remark, I presume the Doc has no desire for martyrdom, at least not at his present stage in the illuminative way."

Father O'Doherty answered immediately: "Regarding Anlu, this talk of the Doc is all sheer nonsense. I suspect we have the pick of the pagans of China in our district. From my own experience they are a fine people. The question is now settled and I think we should settle down to wholehearted cooperation with the Franciscans."

With the competitive strain lifted, and free of their contention for the same mission territory by the decision of Rome, members of the society, universally, were feeling friendly to the Franciscans, finding virtues in them, a little ashamed of their former hostility. Father Galvin sounded the new note in a February letter to John Blowick:

> Ever since we came here our relations with the Franciscans have been, on the whole, the very best. Monsignor Gennaro always treated me very kindly and the V.G. has been exceptionally kind. On a few occasions recently I did get a few minor complaints from the Franciscan priests but they were due to misunderstandings which I cleared up. Both the Franciscans and ourselves understand the necessity of harmony and charity and I feel that with fair luck, we are likely to become very good friends.

In another vein, Father Galvin wrote that he was having some trouble with priests who drank, two in particular. He recommended the recall of one of them and announced that he was not permitting the serving of liquor in Hanyang and was setting a good example himself. He urged Father Blowick to insist upon students at Dalgan taking the pledge that they would not drink.

"Our priests will be very much alone," he wrote. "There

will be difficulties and days of depression. If a man has any taste for drink, he is lost."

One direct result of the troubled political situation in Ireland was the shrinking of donations. Father Blowick was alarmed, in the face of the cash decline, at the size of Father Galvin's building plans in China. He cabled Galvin to meet him in New York.

On his arrival in the States, Galvin went to Omaha and on May 1 said the first Mass in the Bellevue Seminary chapel there. It was a solemn moment for Father Mc-Carthy who had built the seminary in the face of many doubts and many difficulties.

On his way east to meet Father Blowick in New York, Father Galvin stopped at Nerinx, Kentucky, to see Mother M. Praxedes, Superior General of the Sisters of Loretto at the Foot of the Cross. He knew that he needed the Loretto Sisters in Hanyang, he knew why he needed them, and he was a most eloquent and convincing individual. Mother Praxedes was impressed by him.

On May 27 Father Blowick, accompanied by Father Henaghan, landed in New York and Father McCarthy arrived from Omaha. Father Galvin was already on the ground at the Murray Hill Hotel. It was the first time that the four men had been together since November, 1917.

Father Arthur McGuinness wrote from Omaha to Father MacPolin in Hanyang: "Caw escaped from Omaha as quickly as possible. He did nothing while he was here but talk about Hanyang and tell a lot of stories which were supported by yours truly. I had to go to confession recently, so you can draw your own conclusions."

Father MacPolin, in Hanyang, had his hands full with the money balance shrinking alarmingly, construction projects demanding his presence on inspection, and personnel generating problems as a routine matter. He was, nevertheless, caught up in the feeling of possession that had come to all the China hands of the society with the granting of the vicariate. China and the Chinese were close to him now. He wanted other people to know them, to understand them, at least a little. He wrote many letters, and one of the most eloquent is long:

Everywhere in China the country seems to be swarming with people, teeming millions! One must travel in China

180

to realize the meaning of those words; 'Every rood of ground maintains its man!' Hardly a square inch seems to be left untilled. The implements of cultivation are of the most primitive type; hoes and wooden ploughs drawn by a single bullock. Save for the railway, the means of communication between the towns and villages are anything but modern; narrow footpaths across the fields, wider tracks some three or four feet wide and sunken five or six feet below the surface of the surrounding country, either because of centuries of use or because they also serve as river beds during the rainy season, are the only roads to be seen. Over the ruts rumble those peculiar country carts with wooden axles and single piece wooden wheels, drawn by bullocks or a pony.

Along the footpaths the country man trots beneath the weight of his bamboo, balanced across his shoulders with two huge bundles suspended from either end; or, again, staggers from side to side in making frantic efforts to preserve the balance of his extraordinary barrow. What a clumsy invention that barrow is! It has but one large wheel placed somewhere near the center of gravity while the load is placed on either side. In order to lessen the effort required to preserve the balance, the handles are placed as far apart as a man can reach, the weight being borne by a rope passed from either handle across the back of the neck of the human beast of burden between. The China man struggling with his barrow typifies the struggle which he wages for existence with unremitting effort and infinite patience.

The Chinese—with his barrow, with his uncles and his cousins and his aunts—was waiting for Father Ned Galvin, and Father Galvin knew that he was waiting, with a need for churches, for schools, for priests. He had little time for America. He wanted to get back to China. He could see in his mind the neat, clean, future churches in those villages he had visited, newly created on the morrow and staffed with priests. He told Father Blowick how much it would cost at the very beginning and Father Blowick said, "Impossible!"

Father Galvin did not like the word, "impossible," and he had no sense of money. Everyone who ever worked close to him said that he had no idea what a steamer or railroad ticket cost, even on routes which he had traveled often. Unless someone thought to press it upon him, he would leave Hanyang for Hankow without a cent in his

181

pocket. If cigarettes were available, he was likely to chain-smoke; if he went out without money, as he so often did, he would do without cigarettes or food or anything else that an ordinary man considered essential to his health or his happiness. He was neither extravagant nor thrifty. He merely lacked the love and the understanding of money.

"He thought nothing of cabling me a request for ten thousand pounds," John Blowick said, "and he would want me to wire it to him."

Father Galvin saw only the need for money, the use to be made of it, not money. In the meeting at the Murray Hill Hotel in New York, he had force, persuasiveness, a touch of impatience, an occasional flash of temper and a great deal of calm, good-humored conversational argument. He was convinced that all logic was on his side, that he was nothing if not reasonable.

Blowick, in Galvin's eyes, made only the negative point that the society did not have money for the program which Galvin proposed for China. Galvin said that he could remember when the society had much less money than it had now and the Lord had provided it. Today's situation was very simple. They had contended a long time with Rome for the vicariate they now held. They had made and proved the point that the Franciscans did not have the men or the money to serve all the territory they controlled. "Are you trying to tell me now," he said, "that we should sit still and not do anything? Leave those villages as the Frans left them?"

The meeting did not settle any vital issue. Father John Blowick did not love or understand money, either, and had never lived intimately with it. He had not been attracted to the China Mission by any vision of the desk he held—the post of command and concern about finances. He was not at his best when called upon to say No to a forceful, aggressively sure man like Galvin. In the end he won only the concession that Father Galvin would space out the doing of necessary things and undertake no frills or luxuries for the time being.

Father Galvin headed back to China without waiting for the dedication of the new seminary in Omaha on June 29. Fathers Blowick and Henaghan attended.

The seminary, with twelve students, was a new building

182

on a bleak, bare hill, without a single tree or a shrub of any kind. Omaha was nine miles away. On that morning of the dedication John Blowick thought that this building, in its isolation, called for the same kind of faith that Father Galvin talked about when he planned to build without money and expand without money, and conquer China for Christ.

A cable dated July 20 to Reverend Edward J. Galvin arrived in Hanyang two days before he did. It was signed by Mother M. Praxedes and read: "Votes of the General Chapter were in favor of Chinese Mission. Letter follows."

The writing of the cable, and of the letter which followed, were the two final official acts of Mother M. Praxedes as superior general of the Sisters of Loretto at the Foot of the Cross. Her term of office ended at the General Chapter which voted 43 to 18 in favor of Loretto entering the China missions. Her successor, Mother Clarasine Walsh, worked out details with Father McCarthy. The Sisters of Loretto agreed to assume expenses for transportation, about $450 per sister, and to assume support of six sisters in China. Father Galvin budgeted one dollar per day for the support of each priest in China, and it was assumed that the nuns could be supported on the same basis.

Ned Galvin's mind always started building upon an accomplished fact as soon as the fact was accomplished. Now that the future aid of nuns was assured, he moved to a next step. Chinese girls could be taught to do embroidery; there were women who could teach them. He had seen Chinese embroidery in Hankow and Hanyang and it was beautiful. Once he had women to supervise them, he could gather and house a number of young girls who would learn the catechism and the art of embroidery. If he had them for two years in his school, they could go back to their villages—and he would obtain them from the villages, not the cities—to be a positive influence on others and possessed of a skill which would be respected, as any skill was respected in China. Some of those girls might develop aspirations, vocations, working with the sisters. His mind leaped ahead.

"Pole," he said, "some day we'll start an order of Chinese nuns here."

The Columban Sisters, attracting far less attention than

183

the Americans, quietly became an order when nine nuns received the habit on October 4. Their constitution had been drafted by Father John Blowick and their rule was the rule of the Sisters of Charity. The first superior of their convent was Mother Mary Camillus on leave from the Sisters of Charity.

In China, four new Irish Christian Brothers had reinforced the original three. They had 121 boys in their school, fifty-six of whom were boarders. The boys ranged in age from thirteen to twenty-one. On Christmas in Hanyang there were over four hundred Chinese at Midnight Mass and there was a policeman on duty before the church to unsnarl the traffic.

Father McCarthy, from Omaha, brought the year fittingly to a close with one of his pungent epistles, a reply to Father Blowick's letter which sought employment for a staunch lady supporter of the society:

"There is absolutely no place here that we could fit in a woman of her character and disposition unless she were a Sister. I will guarantee to keep this show running with Sisters around, no matter what kind they are, but you can't do a thing with lay women. As a Sister she would be a fine woman to work anywhere, but she has too much personality to fit into our work as a lay woman. Nix, John, on women with personalities."

18 : : DUNG HSI

The new Apostolic Delegate to China, The Most Reverend Celso Costantini, visited Hanyang. Father Galvin reported to Father Blowick that the delegate was "pleased and surprised with everything."

A less official report went out in a letter of Father MacPolin's: "We had an official visitation last week and, as Joe Crossan said, 'The Han was groaning under the weight of Ecclesiastical Dung-hsi.' I am sure that you have heard Art use that very expressive word often. It means 'things.' It is a word of such wide use that if Aristotle had

184

written in Chinese, it would have been one of the Categories."

In his report of March, 1923, Father Galvin listed thirty-one Columban Fathers, eleven schools, twenty-eight teachers and 362 people in the Hanyang vicariate and in Hanyang City, including the suburbs. He was hiring native teachers where he could find qualified people, and so were the priests whom he sent out to the smaller towns. The right individual in a small town or village could be teacher, catechist and a valued assistant to the priest.

Despite good resolutions and honest effort, expenses mounted. There were needs to be filled, opportunities to be seized. On March 22 Father Galvin sent a formal request to Father Blowick for £15,000 to build a college for three hundred boarders for the Irish Christian Brothers in Hanyang. Father McCarthy had expensive projects in mind for the American Columban establishment and was committing his money in the United States rather than sending it to China. In Ireland, Father Blowick faced the endless demands, the necessity for supporting a series of projects which had become living things, and his money was running out, the source of it no longer free and flowing.

Father Galvin found a letter in his stack when he came in from a mission swing. He read it, frowning. It was from Father Dan Carey who, as a student, had left Dalgan to go with Father Fraser. He was a priest now and in China, alone on a station to which Father Fraser had assigned him. He did not feel that he had anyone in back of him or that he was serving as he could serve. He wanted to be taken back into the Columban Society.

Father Galvin crumpled the letter in his fist. "Some people didn't know how damn well off they were," he said.

At approximately the same time, Father McCarthy wrote to Father O'Leary in Ireland that he had had a mid-April visit in Omaha from Father Fraser, who wanted to amalgamate his Canadian mission society with the Columbans. "He has two seminaries," Father McCarthy wrote, "one at Almonte . . . and one near Toronto. . . . His whole organization in Canada is worth between $60,000 and $70,-000. He has 22 students and 4 priests."

Father O'Leary said that he had no personal objection to absorbing these missionaries, but he did not believe that

185

Ned Galvin would touch them. He was eminently correct about that. Father Galvin wouldn't and didn't.

On May 23 Father Galvin wrote: "I wonder if I forgot to tell you that we have four Chinese priests, ordained on Pentecost Saturday. Two of them said their first Masses here in the City on Pentecost Sunday. They are nice lads, about 26 to 28 years old, and after a vacation of a few weeks, will go right into harness."

These young Chinese had received all their seminary training from the Franciscans, of course, and came to the Columbans with the vicariate.

The weather in June was warming up and the heat of the plains was terrific. Father Galvin effected an innovation which was later widely copied by other missionaries. He purchased, and fixed up simply, a mountain retreat for the priests during the two hot months. It was in the province of Kiangsi at a place called Kuling which, although a legitimate Chinese place name, sounded like a word devised by a punster. It was above three thousand feet and offered swimming, fishing and hunting. Half of the Columban priests went one month, the other half the following month. A man attended a one-week retreat, usually conducted by an outside priest, and spent the other three weeks in whatever manner appealed to him; outdoor sports, loafing, writing, reading books. It was a necessary relief from the terrific heat of Hanyang, from the demands of the Chinese language and the ruggedness of Chinese living.

Everyone in the society was shocked on July 3, 1923, when Father Charles Cullen, Father Richard Ranaghan's assistant at Ko-Chia-Dzae, died suddenly while Ranaghan was away. Father Cullen felt unwell after saying his morning Mass, returned to his room, and died there, quietly alone. He was twenty-seven years old and had been eighteen months in the mission field. He was the first Columban to die on the mission firing line. His death, initially a mystery, was later ascribed to sunstroke.

Two other Columbans escaped death on successive days in August. A bandit army swept down on Lungho and a houseboy, at the risk of his own life, warned the pastor, Father Daniel Ward, who fled and hid on the banks of the river. His church was unharmed.

Father Michael McHugh, pastor of Tsao Shih, had a

closer call. Some of his parishioners came running to tell him that bandits were coming. He consumed the Blessed Sacrament which he removed from the tabernacle, then ran toward the river. The bandits were fanning out through the village and McHugh plunged into the water. He used a floating log to conceal himself from riflemen on the shore, and when he reached the far bank he looked back to see his church in flames.

These attacks were the first experienced by the Columban priests, and Father Galvin went on a round of the mission stations to talk to the men and to set up methods of escape in case of future raids. Chinese armies had been engaged for a year or more in a series of incomprehensible wars which seemed to be based solely upon the personal ambitions of certain leaders. Some of the armies employed had fared badly and the former soldiers, in many cases led by their former officers, were still extracting a living from the country by violence.

The United States lost its President in August when Warren G. Harding died.

There were eight new Columban priests traveling as a group to China in October, 1923, and two more Columbans, Fathers Patrick McAuley and Francis Murray, traveling with the long-awaited Loretto nuns. The Lorettines numbered six. Father Galvin met them in Hankow, and one wrote of their reception:

> . . . . Father Galvin ushered us into a cemented courtyard where dozens of little girls and young women were gathered to greet us. . . . Father took us to the church where we offered fervent thanksgivings. We were then shown our new home. It is delightful; two two-story Chinese houses. Very quaint. We are situated inside the city walls while the present compound of the Fathers and Brothers is outside the walls. We have three rooms in one home and four in the other. A kitchen adjoins one of our houses and the church the other. Our entire place is surrounded by a high brick wall. . . .
>
> The side door of the church opens into our house. The buildings are completely furnished . . . and the thoughtful Procurator, Father MacPolin, thought even of writing tablets, pens and ink, and mirrors. Excepting chairs, the Fathers had all of the furniture made in their own carpenter shop. The Columban Fathers have prepared like brothers for us. . . .

187

We went to bed at the usual time but one of our number did not sleep well. During the night she caught something soft, about the size of a mouse. She held on to it, afraid to hold and afraid to let go. Her first impulse was to cry out, but the others were asleep and she did not wish to disturb their slumbers. . . . She finally decided to throw her undesirable captive out the window. Taking good aim, she threw—and, lo, her whole bedspread was going. She was holding a tassel of her spread!

Hanyang was a city where no church bells rang. The song of the city was the song of toil, blended of voices and turning wheels, the pound and snarl of machinery, the rhythmic thudding of running feet. The Sisters of Loretto heard the city before they saw it and when they saw it, as when later they saw Hankow, the overwhelming impression was of an enormous flood of people forever rolling by. Each new priest felt the force and the weight of those people, the sense that they were pagan and so many, and the messengers of Christ were so few. Father Galvin, already a veteran of China, had come to a stop on a street in Hankow when he first visited it with Fathers Blowick and MacPolin. He had looked at the people.

"They are so bloody numerous," he'd said.

The sisters were impressed by the children. In public streets that stank, that abounded with fetid puddles and piles of filth, the children were like bright flowers, garbed in red and green and purple and yellow. The boys had their heads shaved, with a small, rectangular patch of hair in front; the girls, with heads similarly shaved, had small circles of hair in back, from which tiny pigtails fell, the ends tied with bits of colored cord. They were loved and esteemed, these children, fondled by mothers and boosted high on the shoulders of fathers, although economic conditions compelled the parents to let them go too early, surrendering them to adult necessities before they were adults.

Father Galvin wrote his verdict on the new arrivals in an October letter to Father McCarthy: "The Sisters of Loretto arrived and they are a real dandy bunch. They are quite happy here and we are all swinging into work on Monday. If they don't do Big Work with a capital B, you may never again believe a word from Caw. That's that and I couldn't add another word to it."

Father Tom Quinlan also wrote to Father McCarthy, without any comment on the nuns:

> I'm afraid that the earliest news, and the latest, is bandits here and bandits there and bandits all along. Up to a short time ago a common question among the Chinese was "Have you had a meal?" I'm afraid that is quickly changing now into "Have you seen the bandits?" Honest to goodness, the country is swarming with them. They are divided into inter-provincial and local. The inter-pros sometimes have up to a thousand men in a band, and they do things on a big scale. They often clean up a whole town in a night and they sack, burn, kill as the notion takes them. It was an inter-pro crowd (Hanan-Hupeh) who kidnapped Father Melotto and hauled him around for three months with them. During that time he had to witness all their deeds of plunder, murder and rape. Finally, because the authorities would give no money for his release, the Chief shot and bayonetted him and left him to die. This was the climax of his twenty years experience in China.

The system of assigning newly-arrived priests in Hanyang had changed within the short time that any system had existed. Since all the priests now received their grounding in the Chinese language in Dalgan, Father Galvin believed that they should go out with little delay to the parishes as assistants to other Columbans, improving their use of the language in actual parish work and settling into the experience of the country and the people. Owen Mac-Polin wrote to Father McCarthy on November 15:

"The new arrivals have just left for up-country. We hope that the brigands do not get them."

November 23 was the feast day of St. Columban and the forty-first birthday of Father Edward J. Galvin, who sang the Solemn High Mass at the Loretto convent church. Bishop Gratien Gennaro came over from Hankow with a number of priests. The Sisters of Loretto made two cakes and some fudge. They played their victrola, one of the prizes they had brought from America.

The Loretto nuns were already beginning to feel like veteran China hands. Thirty boys and girls started school

189

in the Loretto compound a little over a month after the arrival of the nuns in Hanyang. By March, 1924, there would be eighty. It was an unplanned development. The children, cheerful and curious, made it a practice to gather and wait patiently for glimpses of these strangely garbed foreigners. When the sisters became aware of this attention, they went out several times a day to talk to the children. They were unable to speak Chinese, but they would draw pictures of commonplace objects on pads and speak the English names of these objects.

Thus casually a school started, staffed with Chinese women teachers in addition to the nuns. It was called "The Little School," and followed the regular Chinese primary school curriculum: reading, writing, arithmetic, physical education, politeness and respect to elders, plus a little religion and a little English.

The big school, of course, belonged to the brothers. One of the Lorettines wrote home in November: "The Irish Christian Brothers teach the boys. They have over 200 pupils in the High School. The Brothers have shown us great kindness, not the least of which was to bring us a watch dog which we have named 'Jeff' in memory of the good ship which brought us hither. They cautioned us, however, to keep a watch on our watcher lest the Chinese steal him and have him for supper some evening. Since he is fed with foreign food, he is doubly desirable."

The problem of changed diets, which bothered many of the priests had seemingly little effect on the Sisters of Loretto. Another letter said: "You would never believe the appetites we have developed. Sister Stella was in Hankow with me and everywhere we went the beggars followed her, pulling at her sleeves and shawl. They didn't bother me, so when we told one of the Fathers about it, he laughed and said: 'You know, the Chinese think that all fat people are rich!' "

There were such human things, so many warm and human things; but behind the scenes there were worries and tensions, some misunderstandings.

On December 3 the Holy See formally erected the Prefecture Apostolic of Hanyang and declared it to be the special field of the missionaries of St. Columban. On December 7 Bishop Gennaro sent his congratulations to Father Galvin. It was December 14 before John Blowick

190

sent a cable, notifying Galvin of the decision from Rome.

Father Galvin was incensed by this delay and could see no excuse for it. He did not reply to Father Blowick until December 26 and his letter was cold, with no trace of friendliness.

In the meantime, the Columban church at Hsien-tao-chen, a city of thirty thousand population, was blessed and formally opened on December 7. It was a handsome structure, the gift of William Cardinal O'Connell, Archbishop of Boston. Three flags—of China, the Irish Free State and the United States—flew in the compound on the day of the formal opening. The parishioners set off firecrackers. Father Edward J. O'Doherty, who had been ordained in 1903 and who had more inner stamina than men far younger, was installed as pastor.

Father John Blowick was ill and those close to him were concerned. He would not take the rest they recommended and he forbade anyone to write about the state of his health to either the United States or China. He had various controversial matters under discussion and he did not want to complicate the resolution of problems with what might seem a plea for sympathy. His nerves, however, were troubling him, and his digestion was bad. He did not sleep well. Most of his work had to be done by others.

On December 14 Father McCarthy reported to Father Blowick: "We have at last, purchased property in the Buffalo area. It is situated 2½ miles from a little town named Silver Creek, 30 miles south of Buffalo on the shores of Lake Erie. . . . Our property consists of two hundred and sixty acres of prime grape-growing and alfalfa land, one large frame house with eighteen rooms, fitted with electric light, hot water heating, gas, water. The cost. . . . was $70,000."

In Hanyang, on December 19, Bishop Gratien Gennaro died suddenly in the episcopal residence. All past controversies, disagreements and contentions were brushed aside and forgotten in the hour of his dying. Father Galvin spoke for himself and for the priests associated with him:

"I have always found him a gentleman and a real priest. He was loved by his own priests and people, and respected by all who knew him. May God rest his soul. Amen."

The year ran short of days.

The letter of a Sister of Loretto described the last holiday:

> In the early morning of Christmas Eve the coolies began decorating the church. We would go in and commend them heartily as they proudly showed us each new ornament. All of the decorations are paper. Great strands of purple wisteria are caught up with immense scarlet balls, green festoons all intertwined with butterflies. Flowers unknown to us are looped around conventional designs composed of all the unblending colors known to man. The church finished, the coolies turned their attention to the yard. This was crossed and recrossed with Chinese lanterns, then an acetylene lamp was suspended from our beautiful big tree and all was in order.
>
> Christmas was just what we expected it to be, a busy, happy Christmas. We had midnight Mass and our little Church was crowded. Every available nook was filled and even standing room was hard to find. From about 7 P.M. until midnight, the people kept reciting their prayers and singing hymns. Their patient, prayerful expectancy is wonderful. Confessions were heard from an early hour on Christmas Eve.
>
> The people came from the small parishes down the river and they came from the country. They carried with them their dishes and stoves and set up little cafeterias, all over both courtyards. All must needs pay their respects to the Sisters, so we had a busy day. We opened up the school room and let those who came from the country arrange their sleeping quarters. They spread little comforts on the floor and on the tables which serve as desks and they thought they were in Heaven.

Father Galvin ended his year by writing a letter to Ned McCarthy in Omaha: "Many moons ago you told us that we might expect a harmonium which, we had informed you, we deeply desired. We are still expecting it. May the Kings load thee with their gifts during 1924 and after, and may they bring us that harmonium."

19 : : DAMN NEAR A BISHOP

The General Chapter of the Columban Society was scheduled for May, 1924. Out of it would come new appointments, new definitions, a new approach to problems. The field men, particularly in Hanyang and Omaha, firmly believed that they could justify the demands which they planned to make and that they would have a freer hand after they had asserted themselves in conference with their contemporaries. They had definite demands to make and they were not in a mood to yield anything. Father Blowick, as he revealed in a letter to Father McCarthy on March 1, had no personal ends to serve, nothing for which he felt inclined to battle.

"I have been out of the Mission for the past four months," he wrote. "I have done no work. There was nothing seriously wrong but I was rundown and I really, truly could not work. I must try to make up for it in the few months that remain. The work will be done better, no matter who takes my place. I am about done up and, certainly, the Mission has got beyond me now."

Father McCarthy was distressed by the letter as other men close to John Blowick in Ireland were distressed by his personal attitude. There was a general agreemnt, which needed no written expression or the casting of votes, that the society would not be in existence if the hand and the mind of John Blowick were subtracted from its history; a general agreement that he was entitled to anything which he might ask of the society. The General Chapter would vote, among other things, on a superior general. If Father Blowick was not elected to succeed himself, the vote for another man might be interpreted as a repudiation of the man whom the society, in gratitude and in esteem, would not repudiate. Yet, what could men do if Father Blowick felt that he was unable to serve, if he genuinely felt as he expressed himself in a letter?

Father McCarthy decided that he would discuss the mat-

193

ter with Father Galvin when Caw came through the United States on the way to Ireland and that they would both be in a better position to assess the situation when they reached Dalgan and talked to Blowick himself.

Father Galvin, too, faced the problems of men—discouragement, homesickness, illness, fatigue. He expected such problems and accepted them without undue excitement. Usually a man could be brought back to normal by visits from other priests, a summons to headquarters on some matter labeled as important, an unscheduled rest or an opportunity for relaxation. With one priest, however, none of the regular remedies would hold. Father Matthew Dolan wrote a letter, stating flatly that he was going home and that he wanted to withdraw from the society "on the ground, that, owing to the incompatibility of the Chinese and myself, there is no use in my holding on here any longer."

No one could influence him to change his decision. He returned to Ireland and rejoined the Kilmore diocese, where he distinguished himself as a parish priest.

Father Galvin left Hanyang on March 1 and picked up Father McCarthy in Omaha. The two men sailed for Ireland on April 26.

There was an electric current of excitement in Dalgan as the chapter members assembled from the faraway stations. That evening there was a performance of *The Pirates of Penzance* by a cast recruited from the student body at Dalgan. This was, of course, a salute to Father Galvin whose long loyalty to Gilbert and Sullivan was certainly no secret; but it was also a salute to John Blowick who was no less a Savoyard. Several times in his life, Father Galvin stated that he had never met an enthusiast of Gilbert and Sullivan whom he had not instantly liked.

There was much fun and clowning and good fellowship. Father Dick Ranaghan, elected to represent China at the council, declared: "I stood on the street in Dublin and there were no British uniforms. I looked up at Dublin castle and there was *our* flag flying there. Nobody can tell me that our boys didn't make a good treaty."

The men who had been away for a long time were delighted at the absence of British flags, British officials, British soldiery, and the solid Irish look of the country, the feeling of independence in the people. There was no

194

prosperity yet, but everyone felt that it was coming; that it would take time but not too much time.

Father Blowick was thin and there were streaks of grey in his hair. He had spoken individually with the members of the council and they knew that he considered this meeting his last as an officer in the society. Most of the members had failed to agree with him that this would be so. They were shaken, however, when he spoke now at the formal meeting about finances.

The Irish division of the society was in debt, with overdrafts at the bank; the United States division was in the same situation, although the total debt was less. Current figures were not available for Australia. To men with little knowledge of bookkeeping, debt was a frightening liability. They did not take into account the fact that the society had acquired land and constructed buildings, erected seminaries and churches, hired teachers and catechists. There were assets balancing much of the liability, but the figures labeled "debt" were chilling. Father Blowick knew that the situation was not as desperate as the figures indicated, but he had failed to convince individuals and he had no hope of convincing the group. He faced the chapter with a feeling that he would not again be called upon to play an active role in the direction of the society.

The election was a solemn affair. Dr. Michael O'Dwyer was elected Superior General and Father Blowick, expecting nothing, was elected Vicar General and First Councillor. The new superior general had not been a member of the chapter, and his selection by the men assembled was a tribute to his strength, his gift of command, the confidence other men had in him. The chapter was not honoring him so much as entreating him. The society considered itself in deep trouble, and it needed a man who could hold it together and guide it back to solvency.

Dr. O'Dwyer's first directive was blunt and simple: "Land is not to be purchased by any Director of the Society without the express written permission of the Superior."

Directors were also notified that they would, hereafter, operate on budgets. They would be required to estimate their expenses in advance and have them approved, or disapproved, at Dalgan. They would not be permitted to ex-

195

ceed their budgets without special permission, which would be granted only in exceptional circumstances.

Ned Galvin had played his part in the deliberation of the chapter and in the election of a superior general. He was appointed Director of China by Dr. O'Dwyer who told him:

"You had better run home for a few weeks before you start back, Ned. No telling when you'll be in Ireland again."

Ned Galvin went home to Clodagh. It might be ten years, he thought, before he had another visit and many things could happen to a family in ten years.

He spent time with his youngest sister, Kate, and her husband Jack O'Mahony, who was, most of the time, an easier companion than his own brothers, saving and excepting Seano who was, in a sense, his other self. Kate's twins, Donal and Margaret (who was called "Winnie"), were between five and six now, an interesting age.

It did not occur to Father Galvin that the boy and the girl would remember his visit all their lives, because he did not give any thought to being a great man in his own family, nor to the fact that even small children are sensitive to greatness.

He took the two youngsters with him one afternoon to see Clodagh Castle. The castle was only a half mile away and they had seen it often, but not with a big man who told them stories about it and who laughed with them at the things which they considered funny. He walked with one of them on each side of him, holding their hands; then, suddenly, he stopped, freed one of his hands and reached down to touch the grass.

"Ah, now," he said, "it's too wet for small people to be walking. We'll have to turn back and see that castle another day."

There was genuine regret in his voice that a child could recognize. The "other day" never came, of course, because he was always running out of days wherever he was. He had created a memory, however, in the minds of two children and they continued to walk with him, each of them, long after he was gone, holding his hand until he freed it to pat the wet grass. He went away to other parts of Ireland and to England to buy things for his mission and then he went across the ocean to America. He crossed another ocean eventually and went back to China.

196

By order of the superior general, the mission force in Hanyang was reduced by four priests. Fathers Tierney, Ward, O'Reilly and McGoldrick were ordered to the United States to initiate a drive for funds and to solicit funds in friendly dioceses.

Dr. Robert F. Francis, who was operating the infirmary in connection with the Hanyang Mission, had a contract which provided him with his board, room, medical supplies and two hundred dollars a month. He was a good man and his contract was not unreasonable; but there were good European doctors available to the mission staff across the Han river in Hankow, and the Columban Mission could no longer afford to supply medical service. Dr. Francis was notified that his contract would expire at the year's end and would not be renewed.

The list of slashed services and plugged financial leaks grew long as Dr. O'Dwyer and Father MacPolin, whom he had taken away from Father Galvin, read the records and analyzed them. Cuts and changes and restrictions hit the United States as well as China. Father McCarthy wrote an anguished letter from Omaha to Father Joe O'Leary, who was delighted to be back in China.

"We never knew what we were letting ourselves in for at that last Chapter," he wrote. "I am glad that I made that fight for Silver. Creek last year. If it had been deferred until now there wouldn't be the ghost of a chance of getting it through for the next ten years."

A letter from the new superior general to Father McCarthy, dated August 29, said much between the lines on another topic: "Father Blowick is going to Lourdes on the pilgrimage. Ned, you won't forget to say a special prayer for him. Get the lads to pray for a very special intention, letting them know what it is. . . . I think he must have a good rest and I am trying to get him to take it. He is an exceptional soul. . . ."

Those who had served close to Father Blowick during the crucial year, 1923, when society finances got out of hand, were aware in intuition, if not in documentation, of what had happened to him. A scrupulous person by nature, he took responsibility seriously, searching his own conduct and his own decisions on matters affecting other persons. An intangible of 1923, difficult to measure, was the death of his father. It had happened when everything else

197

seemed to be going wrong. The Blowicks were a close family in loyalty, in affection, in faith. It was said that Ned Galvin's parents had opposed his going to the missions; John Blowick's parents had approved their son's going without reservation, even though it meant the surrender of a brilliant academic career at Maynooth. Ned Galvin had gone to China and John Blowick, with his headquarters in Ireland, had assumed the dull, difficult, necessary responsibility for the whole society which was, perhaps, the seed of his trouble.

"John Blowick is a beautiful character," his successor said. "I have never known a man of such good judgment in matters exterior to himself, of such hopeless judgment in matters pertaining to himself."

Father Galvin had made mistakes, too, some of them expensive. But he did not look back or relive decisions made, or torture himself with speculation on how a certain matter might have worked out if he had handled the affair differently. He faced problems honestly, did what he could with them and moved on to other problems. He was capable of intense concentration and he could become thoroughly conversant with the many sides of an involved situation in a short time. His decision on a situation often seemed like snap judgment rendered solely on intuition, and sometimes it was; usually, however, there had been more thought given to the dilemma than a bystander credited. He was a much simpler man than most people realized. He drew ideas from the world in which he moved; from people, from print, from personal observation.

Father Galvin arrived in the United States on his way back to China. Wherever he was, for an hour or a day, he was willing to call on bishops, speak to groups of ladies, write articles on the missions or give interviews to the press; anything and everything that would help to raise money, gain friends for the Columban Society or make people aware of the missionary effort. On that trip across the United States in 1924, however, there was a new element which he had never encountered before. The Ku Klux Klan, anti-Semitic, anti-Negro and anti-Catholic, claimed a membership of four and one-half million men. It wielded tremendous political power and he was told that in Colorado, where Catholics were the main target,

198

the KKK had elected a governor, a United States senator and a mayor of Denver.

"It's a sad kind of madness," he wrote, "and they tell me that some otherwise respectable people are afflicted with it. I am sorry for them."

He boarded the *S. S. President Lincoln* on October 14 and sailed for China.

The work had gone on in his absence. The priests had their parishes organized and there were fewer bandit raids. There were seventy-one girls in the Loretto school in Hanyang. At the end of a year in operation, the embroidery school was turning out forty-six sets of vestments which, thanks to arrangements made by Father Galvin in New York, were distributed by Benziger Brothers.

At Silver Creek, New York, Father McCarthy's pride and joy, St. Columban's Preparatory College, held its formal opening ceremony on October 7, 1924. In Ireland the Missionary Sisters of St. Columban had professed seven nuns. The society was growing and reaching out, increasing in numbers and influence, despite the storm cloud of debt which hovered over it.

On October 29, while he was still at sea, Father Edward J. Galvin was appointed Prefect Apostolic of Hanyang. He learned of the appointment when he landed at Shanghai.

"Great was the expectancy in our little world at Hanyang for the arrival of the Prefecture's new Prefect Apostolic, Monsignor Galvin," one of the Sisters of Loretto wrote. "The Fathers had a special launch prepared to bring him across the river from Hankow with a band of music. . . . Christian Brothers, Loretto nuns and their pupils went in procession to the Soo Wan [St. Columban's compound], the pupils lining up on either side of the avenue. Monsignor gave his blessing to all as he entered the gate and stopped to greet everyone along the way."

Outwardly, Father Galvin took the new rank, the congratulations and the adulation with dignity, with smiles for old friends, without any show of pride or ostentation; inwardly, he was shaken. The world of pomp and ceremony, of ecclesiastical rank, of forms and the rules of protocol, had never been his world. He had been uncomfortable with it in Ireland, all but demoralized by it in Rome. He was a working missionary, and that was the end and aim to which he had held since he first dreamed of priesthood while working on the land of Clodagh. He sat down and wrote to Dr. Michael O'Dwyer at Dalgan:

"The appointment came to me not as a blessing but as a burden and a cross. I tried to escape it and failed. All that remains for me to do now is to take the cross that God has sent, to take it up cheerfully and carry it until He tells me to put it down. There is no more to be said and I don't feel like saying more, for I cannot remember any time in my life when I felt more miserable than I do at the present moment."

Letters, cables and packages were flowing in to Hanyang. The little band of missionaries, the newest society in the Church, was scarcely secure yet in the working space assigned to it, and Rome had honored it with rank and honor for its leader in China. The choice of the man to be honored was popular, too. A great many people in America and Asia had met Ned Galvin and remembered him; he had friends who followed him with letters and with offerings wherever he went. The cables from Brooklyn were ecstatic.

In Hanyang, Father Joe O'Leary had drawn a difficult assignment.

I am just 'moidered' these days studying the ceremonies of a Pontifical High Mass [he wrote]. The Prefect is formally appearing in his full regalia and insignia of office at Midnight Mass, Christmas. A few hours ago, I finished reading a ceremony tract. As a result, I went to the Prefect and told him candidly, "As far as I can make out, you are damn near being a Bishop, judging by this book." Man, dear, he got awful rude, and I was pitched out of the door with the remark, "It's all bloody fine but it is damn fellows like you that put a poor devil in for all this stuff. Surely to God, there is somebody in the mission to do this bloody thing better than I can. Look at the crowd of Big Bloody Idiots over there in Dalgan! Surely one of them could be spared for this thing!" The language is wonderfully becoming to an ecclesiastic of high rank. At the same time, Caw is in wonderfully fine fettle and he'll take the whole thing as a matter of course.

In his last sentence, Father O'Leary was, of course, a prophet.

A Loretto Sister described that Mass, which called for

200

so much preparation. "Monsignor Galvin, who had been rather reluctant about stepping into his new dignity, participated for the first time as Prefect Apostolic of Hanyang at the Christmas Midnight Mass. Our little church looked very pretty, all decorated about the altar with real holly. The Chinese had their decorations in the body of the church but they left the sanctuary to us. If it only had electric lights, it would have been a dream."

There were other Masses that Christmas Eve all over the vicariate. The following letter, written by one young priest from a small Chinese town in Ngan Loo, can stand, symbolically, for them all:

> I was to celebrate the Midnight Mass. The pastor would be kept busy in the confessional. I will never forget how it looked; the chapel with its freshly white-washed walls, the solid mass of people, some of the men standing out in the cold because we had no room for them in the Inn. There was a low murmur of softly chanted rosaries and litanies. The little old confessional over near the wall, with its line of penitents waiting patiently to take their turn, the women wearing the black veil that is customary in China. Over it all, the light of two oil lamps placed in brackets on each side of the chapel. I turned to the altar and I thought: How very much at home Christ must feel in our chapel. How very much at home!

20 : : THE HUNGRY TIME

There was fighting in many areas of China, the massing of men under various leaders, a feeling of unrest and uncertainty in the cities. The Communists were gaining power in the south and, although they had in the past been dismissed as a minor annoyance, they were a menace now, a fanatical force that won converts where it did not impose its will with violence. There were incidents in the three cities, and brigandage in the country surrounding them, but Hankow, Wuchang and Hanyang were reasonably quiet.

201

Monsignor Galvin saw no immediate danger to the people under his charge, but he kept close tabs on the political news. He had, at the opening of another year, a more immediate concern than the possibility of war. He had keyed the concern, unwittingly, in the last line of his last letter in the old year: "Money is fearfully short here at present."

It was to continue so. Letters from Dr. Michael O'Dwyer emphatically barred "extensions in any direction" and stated that under present conditions no more men could be sent to the missions. "We have a bitter bit between our teeth and we must all bear it as best we can," the superior general wrote. "The most I can promise to do for you, Ned, is to send you a sum sufficient to support the men."

That wasn't enough, of course. One had to be a missionary in China to realize how many other things there were. Monsignor Galvin had promised schools to good Catholics who had waited long for them, and he had determined at least to clean and restore the neglected, verminous churches or priest houses which he had found on his survey trips. He had catechists, very necessary people in the mission effort, who would work for little but who needed the little. There were small needs, small demands, from priests called upon to live uncomfortably in their parishes which were days of travel away from Hanyang.

He laid down one of those requests one morning and picked up a letter from Brooklyn. It was a short letter, containing a clipping which carried word that the Very Reverend James McEnroe, ninety-two, for twenty-two years pastor of Holy Rosary parish, had died on January 12, 1925. Monsignor Galvin read the clipping twice, his forehead wrinkling, his fingers tight on the paper. He passed it across the desk to Father O'Leary.

"In regard to him," he said softly, "may he rest in peace."

There were problems developing in many regions of the expanded Columban Society. On January 29 Father McCarthy wrote to Father O'Dwyer that he had just received a letter from John Blowick, who wanted to resign from the society and go to the diocese of Los Angeles.

"It would not do," Father McCarthy wrote. "Father Blowick has been overworked since 1916. . . . . A transfer

202

to the United States might be in order, but not away from us. We should offer him a teaching job and relieve him of the kind of responsibility with which we have burdened him."

The Blowick crisis passed, partly as the result of letters which Father McCarthy wrote to him as well as to the superior. No change was made in his status. He remained director for Ireland with the same kind of budgetary restrictions that fell on Galvin. One of Monsignor Galvin's letters expresses well how those restrictions chafed:

"You will be surprised to know that when a designated gift reaches here, it is tied up and cannot be used by us until it is liberated by Dalgan. For instance, if someone sent $500 to build a chapel, I couldn't use that money, not even for the purpose designated, until I had first budgeted for it and had it passed by the Dalgan Council. You will understand that I am finding no fault with this, but I think it will make quite a change in things."

A letter of Father Joe O'Leary's to Dr. O'Dwyer reveals the grim point which Hanyang reached at times under the new conditions. "Your money wires came just in time," he wrote. "After all kinds of straining we were down to the last £50 and there was nothing left if aid had not come."

Father McCarthy in America was feeling the strain, too. In March he wrote to Monsignor Galvin: "It is very doubtful if, under the new conditions in the United States, we can keep going at all, much less send any considerable sums to China. . . ."

On April 21 Monsignor Galvin wrote to Father McCarthy: "The Budget allowed us nothing for schools and we are closing them down. It is a severe blow and much of our past work will be lost, but we have no complaint at all. It is simply God's will and, in the end, it will be for the best, I know, although it is very hard to see it now."

Dr. O'Dwyer was a sensitive man under a gruff, tough exterior. He knew how his economy measures handicapped men who were struggling against odds at best, and he knew that the measures he enforced were unpopular. He accepted the unpleasant facts stoically. "At present," he said, "it is not a question of efficiency but a question of existence."

The rank and file—priests and nuns and people—felt

the restricting weight of budgets and new rules, but they had work to do and lives to lead within their own environments, and they often floated trouble on the bright balloons of humor, making the trouble light.

Father William McGoldrick, who had come to the Columbans from Australia, explained in a letter how those streets of Hanyang became dirty:

> Rickshaws are doing their best to run over you, babies are crawling along on the highway for want of a doorstep to crawl on. At intervals you will have to make way for a couple of water buffaloes that have no intention of making way for you. Unclean-looking dogs are barking at every corner. Add, besides, the fowl and the ducks, a few domestic pigs, far more at home in their surroundings than you are; these are the ingredients of a Chinese street. The housewives throw their garbage out through the front door and it further adds to your 'amusement' when your progress is summarily held up by an unexpected shower of dirty water.

The priests, as their own poverty tightened its grip and made them feel very poor indeed, looked more closely at the poverty around them. A rather strange thing was happening, as the letters of the time reveal. These priests from another land became more understanding, more Chinese in thought, entering into the Chinese community rather than remaining even slightly apart.

"When I look at the Chinese," Father Patrick Laffen wrote, "I never notice that they are yellow. Their short flat noses seem, to me, quite natural; and their slit eyes and their stiff black hair. But they are dirty? Ah, yes. But they are poor. It is easy for me to forgive the dirt when I look at the poor little dresses and the broken shoes of the children, and when I think of the anxiety of the father lest they be hungry."

Monsignor Galvin, beset by the necessity of writing many serious letters, often wrote the letters of observation which distinguished his correspondence over the years. He seemed to feel, too, some need to identify with the Chinese, to describe them, to make them known.

> The Chinese farmer's plow is identically the same as the one his ancestors used ages ago [he wrote]. It was good

204

enough for them. He often carries on his back the water to irrigate his land or the manure to fertilize his farm. When harvest comes he can do nothing better than reap it by hand and trudge with it for miles to the nearest market. And yet he is not morose or despondent. Nothing of the kind. The hardships of his life do not seem to interfere in the least with his natural good humor and cheerfulness, a characteristic common to all his countrymen. He can laugh and sing and joke better than many who are in more prosperous circumstances.

The priests learned that a really poor place was called by the Chinese "a one-pig village," while one a little better was called "a two-pig village." The terms caught hold and were used in a number of ways to describe conditions within the society itself.

The Sisters of Loretto had their schools in good shape, due in part to the income derived from the embroidery school, and were not contemplating any close-down, although they felt the poverty pull as the priests did. They regarded their Chinese girls with affection but they were women and they did not overglamorize them. One of them wrote:

> Our Chinese girls are vivacious, naturally cheerful and happy, quick to enjoy a joke, hungry for stories. Gratitude is something they will have to learn a great deal about before they will be able to understand that as we do. Most of them are keenly intelligent and they are all ambitious to learn. Whatever may be their good or bad qualities, the longer we deal with them the more we like them. Whether it is a matter of getting used to them, or that we feel there is something deeply solid about this strange race which gives glorious promise of future spiritual conquests, is hard to say.
>
> Whilst women in China are looked down upon, I honestly believe that the men are afraid of them. In the home the mother-in-law is ruler and she wields her authority with no uncertain hand. This is true of the Christian as well as of the pagan mother. We would not exchange our poor girls for anything. They are the portion allotted to us by God. Prayers for them are badly needed, for paganism is deeply rooted in their hearts.

The Sisters of Loretto were greater realists than many of the priests. They resisted quite well any leaping to happy conclusions about the conversion of the Chinese and they did not exaggerate a little cheerful goodwill on the part of either men or women as a stampede toward Christianity. Some of the older priests were cautious, too, a bit disappointed at the small result of so much work and at the strength of Chinese resistance to Christianity, which was often friendly resistance, despite its strength, but not to be interpreted as anything else. Before he left China for the States, reluctantly and under orders, Father Cornelius Tierney, one of the wisest of the missionaries, had written:

"I have come to the conclusion that human nature in China is nothing above the average, possibly a little below. There is a terrible dead weight of paganism all around and if we are to win this place, we'll have to take off our coats and pitch into the business in no half-hearted fashion."

There was nothing halfhearted about the budget-hedged effort of the Columban missionaries, reduced in numbers, given no hope of reinforcements, as they dug into their task in the villages. They could not improve the churches or the houses in which they had to live except through ingenuity and manuel effort. They expended that effort, and morale was surprisingly good.

Monsignor Galvin visited each man and he wore no badge of rank. His costume was the Chinese *i-fu*, a long white garment, much like the soutane but buttoned down the side. He walked where walking was possible and he lived with the man he visited, accepting whatever space the man had, refusing emphatically the pastor's usual offer of his own accommodations. Often he slept on the floor, rolled in his padded quilt, and he had a remarkable capacity for accepting or ignoring rats.

"They are used to running over the Chinese. They've been doing it for centuries," he would tell young priests. "They are a fact of life. They do not expect you to try to do anything about them and if you aren't hostile to them, the chances are they won't be hostile to you."

Young priests had a difficult time adjusting to rats, which were everywhere. So did the nuns. In the fact of demands for economy, the Sisters of Loretto seriously considered extinguishing their kerosene lamps at night, but they couldn't do it. "It is a comfort to have a light," one of

206

the nuns wrote, "because the rats come in through holes in the mudbrick walls, armies of them, at nightfall. They race over the floor and onto the beds and pillows."

The hot weather brought other problems. "The mosquitoes have been busy in Hanyang this year," another letter stated. "They work chiefly at night, sunset to sunrise. Another little pest, not so familiar to people in America, the white ant, can do more havoc in the woodwork of a house in one summer than an up-to-date wrecking company. Their worse feature is that they always work on the inside and you can scarcely detect them until the wood begins to crumple."

A young priest in one of the village parishes described the insect problem with greater pungency: "Early summer brought flies and bugs in unusual numbers. . . . There were winged bathroom beetles, kitchen flies, pantry moths, bedroom buzzers. Our little sitting room became their auditorium. It had the greatest seating accommodation and it most probably came nearest to the laws governing public halls in Flydom. Every available object was commandeered by them, tables, chairs, books, floors, walls. It got so that the cat slept in the open."

Monsignor Galvin tried to get all of the nuns and half of the priests in July, the other half in August, up into the hills at Kuling in the season of mosquitoes and white ants, small snakes and blazing heat. He rarely stayed there himself, except for short periods; but when he did, he was one of the best entertainers. One of the priests from Australia brought a new version of "There's Whiskey in the Jar" that delighted men raised on an Irish set of lyrics, or raised in America without either version. The nuns had a limited number of victrola records of American popular songs. Father Galvin wrote Latin lyrics to some of them and they made a great hit with both priests and sisters. He was versatile as a poet, singer, raconteur or mimic, and he worked up material for each gathering of priests, material which seemed entirely spontaneous when he used it.

The quarters of the nuns at Kuling were described in a Loretto letter of July 8, 1925: "This is a dear little bungalow set in a dream of a flower garden. . . . very far away from the village, but we love it because we see so few people and marketing is done by the coolies anyway. We

207

are about twenty minutes walk, or rather climb, from the Fathers' place but we have been having three Masses every morning up to the present. Here in Kuling we can get almost anything foreign. Why, we got corn on the cob today for the first time since we came to China."

The cool weather brought the Sisters of Loretto back to Hanyang and a touch of tragedy. Jeff, their faithful little dog, disappeared and they had frightful visions of his being slaughtered to make a Chinese holiday. Father Quinlan hurriedly organized a group of young Catholics and told them to find the dog and return it. His own boy brought the dog in within a matter of hours. He had already been marked up in colors for dismembering.

Various realities of mission life became urgent again. One Columban wrote: "I made a trip to Hanyang today to worry supplies out of the kindly but impoverished Procurator. 'Just give me enough to run my school for one more month, Father,' I said. 'We are rushing the education. One more month.' Amazingly I got a few dollars. . . ."

The superior general, Dr. Michael O'Dwyer, made his trip of inspection late in the year. He visited Silver Creek and Omaha in the United States, and reached Hanyang just before Christmas. Monsignor Galvin's subsequent report to Father McCarthy is illuminative:

> The Superior is here and is leaving for the country this evening. He has been working at many things since his arrival and he looks tired and worn. I had some long talks with him. He is worried, even more than he admits, I think, about the financial condition of the Society and as I see it, he has good reason to be. He seems to take a very dark view of things and is afraid of the future. It is worrying him to death. I realize the burden that the Society is trying to carry but I have the utmost confidence that God will not see her down. Her mistakes in the financial line are entirely due to inexperience and to a false conception of the will of God and the providence of God. . . . I'd hold every single inch of ground we have gained but I wouldn't allow any man to advance an inch farther until we have paid what we owe and until we are in a position to advance with security.
>
> I entirely agree with the Superior on this point but then we disagree on another. He thinks we must throw a number of things overboard if we are to weather the storm, as he puts it. I say throw nothing overboard

208

—to do that would be a want of confidence in God's goodness—but don't add anything. If we continue to spend blindly and to add more obligations and burdens while we are unable to carry those we already have, my view is that we will be lost.

The society had come full circle and was facing, spelled out, the dilemma which Father John Blowick had faced. Father Joe O'Leary's comment on the tour of the superior general was terse: "The spiritual part of his visitation was a real pleasure but when it comes down to books, money, and all that—well, I fear we are in for a hungry time."

War clouds were heavier over China as the New Year came in and General Chiang Kai-shek, one of the younger leaders, announced a definite break with Communist and pro-Communist groups in China.

During 1925, despite the shortage of funds, the Columbans of Hanyang had sent an exhibit to the Vatican Exposition. The responsibility for the exhibit fell upon Father Dick Ranaghan, of camera fame, and Father Joe O'Leary who, among many other activities, had made a special study of the Ming period. In April, 1926, word reached Hanyang that the exhibit had won the Holy Father's diploma of merit and a medal, which reminded nearly everyone in the society of Father Ranaghan's oft-quoted remark. He had written a long report, justifying his promotional and publicity activity against the threat that all funds for them would be withdrawn, concluding with the line: "There is no use in a fellow being humble if he does not show it."

Ireland, supplying the greater number of priests, had been quiet for a year in the history of the Columbans; but Ireland, too, had its problems. Dalgan was crowded, despite the village of huts that had been erected on the grounds to house the students, and the classroom huts designed to take the pressure off the main building. The society had grown and it was no longer practicable for the superior general and his staff to carry on their work in the midst of ever-expanding seminary personnel. Room was needed and a central location which would make it possible for the society staff to see and to entertain visiting Catholic hierarchy and guests from America, who would never travel to Shrule. In view of the state of the finances, another

209

building was a mad dream; but the building was necessary.

Father John Blowick was acting superior general as well as superior for Ireland during the absence of Dr. Michael O'Dwyer in the United States and China. Blowick had recovered a great deal of his confidence, and his health had improved. He had, of course, few problems concerning money, since there was so little money. On a bright morning in March, 1926, a letter reached his desk which caused him to whistle sharply. A Mrs. Mary Morton, widow of Wilkinstown, County Meath, was offering her house and farm to the Columbans "as a site for a college or whatever your need may be." She said that she wanted no compensation, that she wanted to make a gift. Father Blowick took the letter to Father Owen MacPolin, Procurator of the Society.

"What do you think?" he said.

"If it is absolutely free we can afford it," MacPolin said.

The necessary first step, of course, was to seek the approval of the Bishop of Meath, in whose diocese this property lay. After obtaining an appointment, Father Blowick went up to Clonard House, Mullingar, with Father James A. Kennedy. The Most Reverend Laurence Gaughran—genial, friendly, warmly hospitable—was an old friend from the days when the society was fighting to establish itself. He looked at Mrs. Morton's letter and laughed.

"An estimable woman," he said, "a lovely old soul with the best intentions in the world. She is giving her house and farm to every order and every society of priests and nuns in Ireland. On top of that, she owns nothing, nothing at all. She has a life interest in that property and she cannot leave it to anyone."

When he saw the disappointment in the faces of the two priests, the bishop added softly, "You couldn't use her house anyway. I'll tell you what you need."

He went on to describe a beautiful property called Dowdstown. It was on the bank of the Boyne near Navan. He was lyrical about it, rising to his feet and walking up and down as he described it. It obviously did not occur to him that the Columban Society was entirely without funds, and Blowick knew that he had no right to tell him. Bishop Gaughran had already done his share for the Columbans.

210

The two priests thanked the bishop, said that they would look at Dowdstown, and left. Outside on the cold sidewalk they said, "Why not?"

Dowdstown proved to be a gentleman's residence, vacant now, three miles out of Navan on the road to Dublin. It was approached from two entrances, the main entrance comprised of a good gate lodge and ornamental iron gates. A long avenue led to the house from either gate. The house itself, about forty years old, was built of stone with freestone facing and cut limestone dressing. A long narrow wing of a simple stone construction ran off the main house for about one hundred feet. The main house had a tower which commanded a view of the grounds, projecting bay windows, a turret and a cut-stone open porch. There was a long narrow hall, an imposing staircase, a salon, two drawing rooms, a library, a dining room and a bewildering series of pantries, larders and servants' quarters. Upstairs, there were twenty-four rooms. The house was furnished, the plumbing better than adequate.

Fathers Blowick and Kennedy were quiet, not looking at each other, as they walked out again into the cool, crisp air. There were 116 acres of woods and 279 of land, nine acres with outhouses, stables, etc. They could stand on raised ground before the house and see clearly the Hill of Slane, the hill on which St. Patrick had lit his flame in defiance of the lords of Tara. Facing that hill, across the property, was the Hill of Tara where the famous "harp that once through Tara's halls" had played. There were the remnants of a stone road on the property over which, it was said, St. Patrick had walked as a prisoner from the Hill of Slane to the Hill of Tara.

The price of the entire property, land and buildings and furniture, was £12,110 (approximately $58,750).

The two priests went back to Dalgan in a daze. There could not be a more perfect property. It would house the superior general and his council, any guests and whatever staff would be needed in the society's future. They knew exactly where to place the chapel. There was much stained glass in the house, an ideal note. In the future, the unpredictable future, there would be land on which to build. The Hill of Slane and the Hill of Tara! The path o'er which St. Patrick had walked!

"We could say a novena," Father Kennedy said hesitantly.

"We *will* say a novena," Father Blowick said.

In the morning, Fathers Blowick and Kennedy described Dowdstown House to a politely interested Father Mac-Polin.

"You are both crazy, of course," he said at length, "to waste five minutes dreaming of such a place, with not a shilling in the bank."

Fathers Blowick and Kennedy said no more about Dowdstown, but they prayed. On the morning of April 14, 1926, nine days after they had started the novena, Father Blowick opened a letter addressed to himself:

Dear Rev. Sir:

By direction of Mr. Patrick Byrne of 19 Zion Road, Rathgar, Dublin, we send you a check for £2000 to be applied for the purposes of the Mission to China. Kindly acknowledge receipt.

Mr. Byrne does not wish any publicity given to this donation but trusts he will be remembered in the prayers of the Missioners and of this Congregation,

Yours Faithfully,
CARTER O'MEARA
CUSSI and KIBRAN
Solicitors, Dublin

Father Blowick walked into Father MacPolin's office and laid the check and the letter on his desk. "It's the last day of the novena, Pole," he said.

Father MacPolin read the letter, looked at the check, and made the Sign of the Cross. "God wants you to have it, John," he said.

He opened negotiations for the purchase of Dowdstown House and the bank was happy to hold mortgages for the balance above the £2000. No one in the Columban Society ever met the benefactor, Patrick Byrne, and many letters addressed to him were answered in non-committal fashion by his attorneys. He had never been on any society mailing list of record and no member of the society could recall having met him. He never made another contribution.

"We do not call such things miracles," Father Blowick said.

212

On the day that Mrs. Morton's letter had been received by Father Blowick in Dalgan, Monsignor Galvin appeared before the Boxer Indemnity Commission in Hankow. Much damage had been done during the Boxer trouble in China to Catholic Church property in the territory now vested in the Columbans. Restitution, if restitution were made, would be payable to Monsignor Galvin for the society.

It was not until July that the American section received its good news. A priest in Chicago, who had died several years back, left his inherited fortune to the American branch of the Columban Society. His rather remote surviving relatives sued to break the will, and possibilities of a favorable settlement had seemed remote. On July 16 Father McCarthy wrote to Monsignor Galvin:

"You will be glad to hear that, at long last, Father McGuire's will has been settled. The Supreme Court threw out the appeal and the executor has distributed the estate. The actual share which came to us is approximately $250,000 which has put us out of debt and left us a substantial margin. Of course there was an awful lot paid from the estate to lawyers and for taxes but we ought to be glad that we got so much."

The freeing of the American section from debt relieved tension from the whole society. There was a long way to go before restrictions could be relaxed and budgets liberalized, but the well-nigh impossible task was now scaled down so that men could hope.

That July the living space of China was divided among war lords, commanders of strong armies, each of whom aspired to take over the entire country: Chiang Kai-shek in the south; Wu Pei-fu in Central China; Sun Chuan-fang in the Lower Yangtze Valley; Chang Tso-Lin in Manchuria and Northeast Chihli. Feng Yu-hsiang, the so-called "Christian General," held Kansu, Shensi, and Inner Mongolia. There was a certain balance but the situation was potentially explosive.

By the end of August the Cantonese were on the march and they closed in on the walls of Wuchang, the capital of Hupeh, which lay across the river from Hanyang. Hanyang contained a powder factory, an arsenal and an ironworks. Tortoise Hill, which threw its shadow over the buildings of St. Columban's, was the strategic defense

213

area. A letter from a Sister of Loretto personalized the situation:

"Sister Justa and I had gone down to Hanyang from Kuling. . . . Monsignor Galvin came in on September 1, just before noon, and called us into the parlor. 'You two have to leave Hanyang before dark tonight,' he said. 'The soldiers are only 10 li away from Wuchang and there is going to be heavy fighting here. You can either go back to the country or to the concessions in Hankow.' We decided to return to Kuling."

On September 2, from the safety of Kuling, the nun wrote again:

> Brother Harty and Father Fallon are staying at our compound in Hanyang. They have moved all of our possessions over to the Mission House but there isn't much hope of saving anything. If Hanyang is taken, the place will probably be looted and what looting does not take, fire will, unless some miracle saves our city from the fate of other cities in the war path. We do not know how long we will have to remain up here. It is a bit cold already and probably we will have to stay for another five or six weeks until everything has settled down to normal again. We shall await Monsignor's orders. He has enough to worry about without having six women on his mind.

The attack on Hanyang was staged on the night of September 5, which was sooner than the natives had expected. Heavy firing from the Han River opened the attack and snipers fired at the guards on the hill. A battle raged around the Hanyang Mission until dawn and the priests had no way of identifying the combatants; artillery, machine guns and rifles contributed to the frightful all-night-long racket. Monsignor Galvin and Father Jeremiah Pigott ventured out to scan the situation and were forced by a burst of rifle fire to throw themselves on the ground. While they were hugging the earth, some little distance apart, a shell fell between them. They waited long, agonizing moments for it to explode, knowing that to rise would court rifle fire. The shell was a dud and never did explode.

The Sisters of Loretto continued to send our letters and, astonishingly, the mail went through despite the embattled condition of the country. A September 22 letter read:

We are taking turns in sending out war bulletins these days. This week's bulletin still finds us sitting on the hill. Conditions are very little changed in Hanyang and Monsignor will not permit us to come down. All around us, in the valley below Kuling, there is heavy fighting going on. Tomorrow, three years, we left for China and now that we were just beginning to find ourselves becoming useful, God has put us away up here, idle on a mountain top. We have not heard from the Fathers in Hanyang for over a week but a minister who came up the other day told us that our places are looking a bit battered up.

On October 10, Brother O'Donoghue, who was trapped in Wuchang by the siege, wrote:

This, the 40th day of the siege of Wuchang, peace negotiations have been concluded. The City has surrendered to the South, the Cantonese. We now realize that all the information at our disposal during the past weeks has been misleading. Hupeh and the neighboring provinces are already subject to the new regime. In this city many thousands have died of starvation. The sights witnessed daily are revolting and deplorable. The helpless and the hopeless, the women with faces wan and haggard, the younger people with hands pressed against their stomachs, shouting with hunger, all like walking corpses, moving about, heedless of bombs or bullets. Within the city there is no burial ground and the supply of coffins has long been exhausted. Along the street, corpses lie around any old place.

With the surrender of Wuchang, the southerners tightened their grip on the three cities and there was an uneasy peace. The Sisters of Loretto returned to their quarters in Hanyang and the priests returned to their parishes. There was rejoicing over the fact that His Holiness, Pope Pius XI, had raised six Chinese priests to the episcopate, the first Chinese bishops of modern times. He consecrated the six bishops himself in St. Peter's Basilica on October 28.

The Columban Sisters reached China in November. They had never been lucky. Beset by many problems similar to those which had delayed the priests, they were long in reaching mission territory. When their first mission band reached their objective, China was torn internally by civil war.

The Columban Sisters, six in all, reached Hanyang on November 15, 1926. They were given a royal Hanyang welcome and escorted to one of the houses at Pai Yu T'ai, their temporary home, which the Sisters of Loretto had helped to furnish and make comfortable.

The arrival of Irish nuns in China marked a great day in Monsignor Galvin's life and he was in Hanyang to welcome them. He went back almost immediately to the mission where he had spent most of his time since the inauguration of the poverty budget. Since the men had to live on little and manage with little, he shared their little rather than live apart from them in what they would consider comparative luxury. Father Michael McHugh's description of his place, made before he was transferred against his will to fund-raising in the United States, illustrates the conditions which many priests endured and which Monsignor Galvin, who could not improve the conditions, shared.

The house in Yen Ja Wan, where the priest stops on his rounds of the missions, and where most of the new Christians are baptized, is almost as wretched as the cave in which our Saviour was born. It consists of a large central room with a small room on each side. The room on the right is occupied by Yen-dso-fa, his wife and four children. The room on the left and the central room have been rented by the priest. It is a real Chinese house without windows or chimneys. An opening in the roof of the central room serves for air and light. The rain and snow also take advantage of this aperture. A few glass tiles in the roof over the altar let in light for the priest to say Mass. In these wretched quarters a boys' school was conducted and a night school for men.

In Tsao Shih, the best mission in the district and the one in which the pastor lives for the greater part of the year, the room is rented from Yen-Fu-Tin (Joseph), the second man in the village to receive baptism. It is 24 feet long by 7 feet wide with mud walls, mud floor and no windows. A few planks resting on forms and covered with a bunch of straw make a very good foundation for a bed. The priest supplements this with some bedding which is part of the missionary's outfit when going the round of the Missions. Over the priest's bed is a kind of loft where some farming implements and cooking utensils are stored. The center of the room serves as

216

dining room and sometimes as a confessional. The other end of the room serves as a kitchen. The furniture consists of one chair and a small table. The house is over 100 years old. Bad as this house is, I can truthfully say that by far the happiest days of my life were spent here. Monsignor Galvin has spent several nights in this room when on his rounds.

Those rounds continued and, while Monsignor Galvin was away, a Sister of Loretto described an adventure in Hanyang:

I didn't exactly go to a pagan wake, but let me tell you what I saw. A pagan woman died and one of the Christians at the Embroidery School—we call her Bridget —asked me if I wanted to see a pagan laid out and I said 'Yes.' So, Sister P. and I went over, accompanied by Bridget, and we went into the house. My, what a shock! I expected to see a woman *laid out* and, instead, I saw her sitting up at the table. She was good and dead, too. I can't, for the life of me, understand how a dead person could sit up so straight. They must have had her strapped to the chair.

At the table were three bowls; one with rice, one with vegetables, and the third with sweets. There were two red candles burning and a bowl of incense. The hands of the dead woman rested on the table around the bowl of rice. She had on a blue garment, with red shoes, and on her head was a red crown. My, but I was scared! That night I could not sleep. Did I shut my eyes, I saw the dead pagan sitting up. I hope they won't sit me up when I'm dead.

The snow came down in China and December turned white. Monsignor Galvin decided to spend Christmas with one of his lonelier priests. He stopped at Yo Kow and wrote from there:

We had a great Christmas here, with High Mass, a big crowd and many confessions. We had a crib, too, if you please, and you can judge what it was like when I tell you that Bob and his masons made the animals. That camel sure was a wonder. Then there were mirrors that threw double reflections, and lights and flowers and a star. Oh, yes. We had it all. And the Infant! We bought a little doll in Yokow, dressed it and laid it there on the straw

217

in a little cradle of our own construction. You never saw anything like it. Luckily we had a real little statue of Our Lady which added the finishing touch. We stood back and looked with complete satisfaction at the results of our labor but Bob couldn't keep from laughing, nor could we see anything except the camel. Next morning, when the Catholics saw the wonder that had been created overnight, no words can express their delighted astonishment. There lay the Infant and His mother, the animals kneeling in adoration, the wise men from the East, the star, the shepherds, the dogs. There, before their eyes, was Bethlehem.

21 : : MITRE, CROSIER AND CROSS

Early in 1927 a series of small, flickering Chinese wars blazed suddenly into a great civil war which swept over the entire country. A serious situation developed in Hankow as the Cantonese permitted rioters to overrun the city. British women and children were evacuated and British marines were withdrawn to warships in the river. The Chinese occupied the British concession.

Father John O'Leary, a younger priest and not related to the famous "Father Joe," wrote on January 3 from Hanyang to Father McGoldrick:

"Yesterday the new Government was formally installed in Wuchang. I suppose they will keep going until they get Peking. The Protestant missions are getting it rough. The Catholic missions have had trouble, too; most of it in Kiangsi Province, but some in Hankow and in the Wuchang missions. In the city of Sianfu, besieged for over a year, it is reported that some priests ate a horse. Well, maybe they did."

Bulletins from Foochow on January 16 carried the news that American and British men and women had been beaten, and foreign property plundered. Missionaries were fleeing the city. Yale-in-China, the only institution of higher learning with western standards in the province of

218

Hunan, was compelled to close because of an outbreak of bolshevism in the institution and in the province.

The Columbans were hit on January 29. Father Frank McDonald was visiting Father Patrick O'Connell, the pastor at Ko Kia Tsui Mission. There was a large and ugly mob on the roads and flowing through the town. Signs and banners identified them as the Nung Ming Huei (Farmers' Union). They bore other signs reading "Down with Imperialism," "Down with Christianity" and "Down with Capitalism." There were two thousand of them and the priests stayed indoors to avoid antagonizing them.

Early in the afternoon, a smaller, rougher group called the Ren Dou Hwei (The Hard Stomach Society) started a demolition program on the homes of those considered unfriendly or opposed to their aims. They hammered on the door of the priests' house and, when they were not answered immediately, broke it in. Father McDonald had just risen to his feet when a brawny, broad-faced Chinese smashed a fist into his face. Other men followed the leader into the room, beating and kicking the priests, who were hauled into the open for the mob to abuse. Bruised and bleeding, they were forced to stand helplessly and watch the mob wreck the church. They were then marched off to captivity as prisoners of a jeering mob.

Word of the attack and the capture reached Monsignor Galvin who was out in the missions, the news racing from one village to another until it caught up with him. He hurried down to Yo Kia Kow where Father Crossan was pastor and where Monsignor Galvin knew the magistrate personally. The magistrate was reluctant to interfere with Communists under whatever name they adopted, but he was confronted with a most persuasive man. He sent out a detachment of soldiers, who effected the release of the prisoners on February 7.

Fathers McDonald and O'Connell had been in the hands of the mob for over a week, had been punched and kicked and flogged, badly fed and assured that they would ultimately be beheaded; but they were back in their parishes a month later. Father O'Connell, with the aid of his Catholics, rebuilt his church.

In February, despite all the unrest in the immediate vicinity and violence elsewhere, the Sisters of Loretto moved to a new convent outside the walls of Hanyang and

219

surrendered their convent, inside the walls, to the Columban Sisters.

Father Ned Lane wrote to Father McCarthy on February 14: "There is a lull in the storm here at present. Many churches and residences have been sacked and looted and the priests from the northern part of the Vicariate have come into headquarters. At present there is no indication as to how things will be in the future. We hear daily promises of protection but promises are cheap."

At Shanghai it was announced that the general strike had been ended "after 100 beheadings." The Irish Christian Brothers had reached the conclusion that higher education in China was a lost cause. They closed their college, packed their personal belongings and went to Shanghai at the strike's end.

On March 28, 1927, Monsignor Galvin wrote a report letter to Dr. O'Dwyer in Ireland:

> The political situation is by no means clear. If the National Government can hold together it should not, I think, experience much difficulty in becoming master of the whole of China, but a split has occurred; if it widens, it will mean chaos. Chiang Kai-shek is the leader of the Moderate Party. He, and those with him, are too moderate for the Left Wing. It looks as though the Left has the support of Russia.
>
> In a word, we are following the lines of all revolutions. It is impossible to say when stable conditions will be restored and it looks as if the missionaries will have many anxieties to face for some time. When peace does come we will have to work under the new China and if the extremists win, our difficulties will be increased. It is difficult to do mission work now. Our aim is to stay in the parishes if we can and not to move around too much. In such times as these, a breeze blows up very quickly, but I am optimistic.

Despite the optimism, on April 5 the American Consul told Father Quinlan that he must send the American nuns out of Hanyang; otherwise, he would send marines in to get them. On April 6 both the Loretto and Columban Sisters were sent to Shanghai. There they became the guests of the Franciscan Missionaries of Mary at Yang Shu Poo.

Chiang Kai-shek was in the ascendant in China and he

220

adopted a ruthless anti-Communist policy. Thousands of Communists were executed where his forces took control in Shanghai, Nanking, and the smaller cities. On April 14 the executive committee of the Communist International issued a statement: "With the greatest indignation, and with utter hatred for the hangman, we declare Chiang Kai-shek a traitor and an ally of the imperalist bandits, an enemy of the revolutionary Kuomintang and an enemy of the working class and of the Communists International."

Father John O'Leary, writing on this date from Hanyang, stated:

> It is always easy to raise an anti-foreign cry in China. Mobs make no distinction. The Communist side of the movement is serious. Should the Communists rule China, I am sure they would find no place for us. The exodus of Protestant missionaries started last autumn. There are few of them left now. In these later days, and especially during the month of April, many priests, Brothers and Sisters have withdrawn to Shanghai. In Hanyang we have scares and rumors every day. It will be a terrible year for us.

Monsignor Galvin, who returned to Hanyang from the missions on Good Friday, April 15, had no doubt of the danger in his vicariate. He said, "This is our testing time," and asked all the priests to offer Masses that Columbans would have the grace to do the duty demanded of them. A few days later, he issued the most quoted letter of his career, with a copy addressed to each of the priests under his direction:

ST. COLUMBAN'S MISSION HOUSE,
HANYANG, HUPEH, CHINA,
April 20th, 1927.

My dear Father:

There is a grave danger of war between the Powers and China. There is also danger of a clash between the Communists and the anti-Communists.

It is the opinion of all of us here that no matter what comes, we cannot desert our people. We can do nothing for them, perhaps, but we can stay with the people that God gave us and we can die, if it is His will. Our example will give them courage, perhaps to face death or persecution or whatever it is God's will to send. But whatever

221

He sends, the priest must meet and face it first.

In a critical time like this when it is a question of a priest giving his life, I do not believe it is the proper thing for me, at present, to order him to remain with his people. If a man is being called upon to face death, I'd wish above all things that he himself would freely and willingly offer his life to the God who gave it to him. If he is willing to stay and make the supreme sacrifice, then I will give him orders what to do and I will accept full responsibility.

Therefore, I ask the following: I ask the Pastor, first, to stay with his people. If he is unwilling to volunteer— and remember, he is quite free—I ask the assistant who is the senior by ordination to stay. If he should be unwilling, I ask the second assistant. I want only one priest to stay in each parish. If the Pastor stays, I order, under obedience, the assistant or assistants to come to Hankow as quickly as possible. I ask them to bring as little baggage as possible—just their summer clothes and anything else they can pack into one grip. In a word, with the exception of one priest in each parish, I order the others to come at once to Hankow.

To the priest who remains in each parish I give the following instructions: Stay in your central residence as long as you think it safe. If it becomes unsafe, hide where you can within your parish. If your parish becomes very dangerous, you might leave it for a little while, but not for long. We cannot desert our posts. Of course, the priests who remain are quite free to visit one another at any time for any reason whatever, just as they did in the past.

May God be with you all.

Yours sincerely,
E. J. Galvin.

Every priest in the vicariate answered this letter by volunteering to remain.

In more peaceful areas of earth, men and women were excited that May because a daring young man named Charles A. Lindbergh had just flown the Atlantic, solo, in a small single-engine plane. In Hanyang, Father Thomas Quinlan wrote a letter:

"Poor Ulick Burke had an unpleasant time, too. The Workers Union was strong in his place and they moved in on Ulick. They lived with him about three days, holding him captive. The farmers of the region heard of it and

222

held a meeting. They laid on the Workers. About fifty men and four women are reported killed. Ulick saw one lad being killed in the compound, and seven lads who took refuge in the cellar. . . . were discovered by the farmers, taken out and killed."

Word was received in June that Father Edmund Lane was to be Procurator for Hanyang, a promotion which fitted him more firmly into the role that Father MacPolin had played before him. There was official notification, too, that the superior general and his staff would move in July from Dalgan Park to the Dowdstown House near Navan which would, hereafter, be the society's world headquarters.

The big news, however, came on July 14, 1927.

Dr. Michael O'Dwyer wired his congratulations to Monsignor Galvin on his being raised to the rank of bishop. The Hanyang Mission was raised to the rank of Vicariate and he became its first Vicar Apostolic. He was named Titular Bishop of Myrina, in accordance with the Roman Catholic custom of keeping even its most ancient long-vanished sees alive through the naming of bishops to them.

When Monsignor Galvin read the cablegram, he snapped his fingers and tears came into his eyes. Father John O'Leary who brought it to him was about to offer his congratulations, then changed his mind. Galvin rose from his desk and walked around the room, rubbing his hand over his head. He did not speak to anyone, except in monosyllables, for two days.

The mail rolled in. A letter from Father Ned McCarthy to Father John O'Leary read:

> The pectoral cross has already been donated. The priests of the United States will present him with a mitre and I know that I can get a number of other friends to donate the crozier. Both the pectoral cross and the crozier are being made by Egan's of Cork. They have submitted very beautiful designs of Celtic work which, to my mind at any rate, are very artistic and very beautiful. The good friend who presented the cross asked me not to spare expense and I certainly did not. The same is true of the crozier. The mitre is a rather beautiful one. It is technically known as the Mitre Pretiosa a la Guglialmo, similar to that which was presented to Leo XIII by the ex-Emperor of Germany. The Pectoral Cross, I might say, is pat-

223

terned after the Cross of Cong and the crozier after that of Cormac, King-Bishop of Cashel.

Chiang Kai-shek's victories were mounting and the Communists left Hankow. There was a measure of quiet except for marauding bands of bandits—ex-soldiers, as a rule—who were trying to live off the country after their commands had been beaten and scattered.

Father John O'Leary took advantage of the lull to go on a long-postponed holiday. On August 13 the shocking news reached Hanyang that he was dead.

> Yesterday morning I cabled you the news of Father John O'Leary's death [Monsignor Galvin wrote to Dr. O'Dwyer]. It was a terrible shock. I had a letter from him the evening before to say that he was having the time of his life—and the next morning a letter from Father Devlin saying that he was dead. John went to Sung Ho to take a holiday. From Sung Ho, Tom Devlin and John went to Wu Tai, a beautiful spot in the mountains 50 li west of Sung Ho. Tom's short letter says that about a week ago both of them got some terrible stomach trouble, that both of them came to Sung Ho and that John died there at midnight, Saturday morning, 13th of August about 1 A.M. John was a great man, a man who gave the last ounce that was in him to Almighty God and to the work. He was one grand priest, may God rest his soul.

A man was gone, and it was not expected that he would go; but the daily pressure of mission work remained and someone had to meet it. There was correspondence, much of it, on when and where the consecration of a bishop would take place. There were many people in the society who believed that the consecration should take place in Ireland, but Monsignor Galvin said: "For a number of reasons I'd prefer to remain in China."

The letters that arrived in Hanyang, the warm expressions from men who did not normally try to express anything which touched emotion, moved Ned Galvin. He often sat silent at his desk for a long period of time with a single letter in his hand. He groped for words himself when he wrote to Father Ned McCarthy in Omaha:

> I can only say 'thank you' with all my heart. I know that between all of us there are feelings for one another

224

which we seldom express and which it is not necessary that we should express. As you say, Mac, I suppose that these arms or crest or whatever they are called (the insignia of a Bishop) are a necessity and I notice, too, that you went to great trouble about them. For that trouble I want to thank you. To me it makes no difference in what the crest consists. I was never made for such things, but the one thing I am rather anxious about is the motto, and what I want is *Fiat Voluntas Tua* (Thy Will be done). I hope that that might constantly remind us here in China that we are here not to convert China but to do God's will, and we don't know 24 hours ahead what that is.

To tell you the truth, Mac, I feel perfectly miserable when I think of this consecration. The date is not yet fixed as the Bulls have not arrived.

A letter from Dr. Michael O'Dwyer to Monsignor Galvin was as ill-at-ease and yet as filled with feeling: "Ned, keep up your heart and give the priests courage. I would not that the joy of your consecration be darkened by any cloud. God be with you. I shall remember you every morning at the altar."

The priests needed heartening, as a Galvin letter to O'Dwyer on October 6 plainly indicated:

Seumas O'Rourke and Mick Fallon are in the hospital with dysentery. Father Patsy O'Connell has been having malaria for more than a month and though he has gone back to his mission he is none too strong. Jim Linehan was also in with dysentery but is over it now. He is not by any means a strong man. Fonsey Ferguson pulled up in Kuling wonderfully and looks remarkably well. He is gone to Yo Ba as pastor and is very fit at present. During the troubles all of the boys kept very well but when the strain eased, I think a kind of reaction set in. Tom Ryan was very weak when he came down but about five weeks in Kuling made a new man of him. Dermody has malaria but he has gone back. Frank McDonald is having constant malaria.

Balancing the problems of the society, which were constant, and the weaknesses or disabilities of its men, was the fact that the black clouds of debt had lifted. The strict budgets had all but eliminated waste, expenses had been low, and the plight of the missionaries—as revealed frankly in their magazine, *The Far East*—had inspired a flood of gifts and several surprising bequests. There was no surplus to be expended recklessly, but the missions could once again meet reasonable demands. There were rumors that Rome wanted the Columbans to establish another vicariate in China and that the final decision would be made after the consecration.

The new director for China was Father Cornelius Tierney who had been storming Dalgan to take him off money-raising in the States and to return him to his mission station. He would not be sailing until mid-November, but his appointment was posted and announced.

The sisters of Loretto had been campaigning, using wiles and arguments on U.S. officials and on the apostolic delegate, to get back to Hanyang for the consecration of "our own bishop." Monsignor Galvin was amused when details came to him from friends in Shanghai and he wrote to Dr. O'Dwyer: "We thought we had the Sisters of Loretto safe from all dangers in Shanghai, but they have been running in tears to the Apostolic Delegate in an effort to get back to the front. Tears, mind you! But please, Doc, don't say a word about the tears. It is a sore point with the Nuns. Be sure now."

The Sisters of Loretto made it. They arrived in Hanyang in time to help with vestments and to help turn Father Galvin's church into a cathedral. Like everyone else in China, they were accustomed to using the words "Shen Fu," the Chinese term for priest. Now they had to learn to say "Gao Ju Chao" (or "Kao Chu Chiao"), the phrase for a bishop. They practiced saying it as they moved around the church arranging flowers.

The poor Columban Sisters, probably because they did not cry at the right time or in the right places, did not arrive until several days after the excitement was all over.

The dignitaries came into Hanyang on November 5: The Most Reverend Celso Costantini, Archbishop of Theodosia and Papal Delegate; Bishops Eugene Massi of Hankow, Odoric Tchen of Puchi, Louis Fatiguet of Kiukiang. Only a very few of the Columban priests with parishes could leave them.

At 9:30 A.M. on November 6, 1927, the procession slowly entered the church. The solemn ceremony began with Archbishop Costantini presiding, assisted by Bishops Massi and Tchen. There was a hushed interval of time at the laying on of hands which brought Edward J. Galvin of Newcestown and Kilmurry, Cork, into a long procession of men leading back to the twelve Apostles of Christ. The voices lifted in a *Te Deum* and the new bishop blessed his own people in his own church. He mounted the throne of dark teak, hand-carved and decorated for the occasion and for his reign; then young voices rang out with the stirring mission hymn in Gaelic, the ancient Irish language. This was a tongue that the cosmopolitan group in the church, speakers of many languages, had never heard before. The man on the throne had heard it, had grown up with it. His eyes filled with tears but he stood straight for the singing—and then it was all over. He was, for all the years left to him, a bishop of the Roman Catholic Church.

There was a catered dinner and many speeches. For the most part, the evening was devoted to humor, the telling of experiences, the singing of songs. The star turn of the night came when Father Joe Hogan played the "Marseillaise" and Bishop Fatiguet sang it, his white-crowned head held high, his full white beard reflecting the light. A venerable old man, away from France in the Chinese missions for forty-two years, he sang with the fire of a young Zouave.

Bishop Galvin wrote to Dr. O'Dwyer:

> As for myself, I felt quite cool through the ceremony. I don't know how others feel on such occasions, but there were three places where I almost broke down; at the Consecration, at the memento for the dead—I had a kind of feeling that John O'Leary was there and I had to hold myself hard—and then toward the end of the ceremony when all the priests sang the hymn of the society. When I heard it, it was like an electric shock. There is something in that hymn which is positively uncanny.
>
> When the Delegate was leaving he said to me, "You ought to be proud to belong to the Society of St. Columban. Tell the superior that I am proud of it and that I will tell everything to the Holy Father." I felt that it was not mere words, but that the man meant everything he said. You could see it in his face. It is the feeling of every priest here, Doc. We don't want to say much about it, but our feeling is one of thankfulness to God.

227

The consecration was scarcely over when the fighting broke out again in Hankow. The Nanking troops pushed into the city and General T'ang Sheng-chih's men set fire to the native city before they evacuated it. Thousands of troops and civilians, and deserters from the defeated army, roamed through the city looting and assaulting citizens. Bishop Galvin wrote of the situation: "The rapidity with which governments come and go is amazing. China is farther from unity than ever. Bandits are swarming over our vicariate. They are the ruling power of the country districts. It is discouraging."

The fact that a man had crossed a certain line, had risen in eminence and was joined to the hierarchy of the Church, separated him from his fellows, made old established relationships difficult. Father Edward McCarthy faced the common dilemma with a forthright letter beginning, "Dear Ned."

"I know you will understand," his letter continued, "if I retain my old way of addressing you. I have always had the feeling that once a man has been made a Bishop, that somehow or another a kind of barrier grows up between him and his most intimate friends. I have noticed it again and again and bishops have told me that they feel it themselves. There will be enough people addressing you formally and I would prefer that we be just as we always were, if it is all the same to you."

Bishop Galvin's reply was fully as forthright and much less embarrassed: "Yes, sure, the idea is to stick to the old name, Caw. Nothing better than that. I feel that I am going to be an exception, maybe, for I can see no difference, nor can others, between the Caw that was and the Caw that is. The Pectoral Cross arrived. It is simply a delightful piece of work. A thousand thanks for it and thanks to the priests. . . ."

The gifts for the bishop were staggered, arriving at different times after the consecration. The first that arrived was the mitre, in November. "The mitre arrived from Rome this evening," the bishop wrote, "and it is a glorious piece of work. It is also a perfect fit. All the Sisters were here this afternoon, having photos taken, and they admired it very much. It is far too beautiful for us here but we will wear it only on special occasions and the Sisters will take care of it. . . ."

228

The crosier did not arrive until after Christmas. "It is a beauty, one of the finest I have ever seen. . . . but far too good for a rough and tumble place like Hanyang. At present things are not at all so good. In fact we have more trouble and worry now than we had during any part of last year. Bandits are the trouble and we can do no work at all. The priests are holding fine. They sure are wonderful men."

The holding on the part of the priests had been far from easy. Father John O'Carroll was pastor at Yuin Lung Ho and Father William Walsh was his assistant. The town was a large one of twenty thousand inhabitants, with a local militia; but the bandits attacked it, routed the militia and set the town on fire. The priests quickly gathered a few of their valuables when the firing started in the streets, locked the doors of their church and their residence, and joined the throng of fugitives pouring out of the town. Together, they crossed the river under heavy rifle fire.

"Had we delayed five minutes more," wrote Father O'Carroll, "we could not have got out. God help the poor people! The countryside was black with them; Catholic and pagan, men and women, old and young, all rushing. No one knew, or cared where, except to get away from the bandits. The lamentations of those poor fugitives are still ringing in my ears."

Father Luke Mullany was saying Mass at Ko-Chia-Dzae. He had a good crowd of worshippers. Armed bandits entered the church and halted the Mass. They were well-dressed bandits wearing well-made *i-fus*, the long garments, with satin jackets and foreign felt hats. One of them carried an attractively carved cane. They seemed more curious than dangerous, and after they left Father Mullany resumed his Mass.

The next morning, the bandits returned while Father Mullany was studying with his Chinese teacher. The cook came in and warned the priest, who went immediately to the church and consumed the Blessed Sacrament. The bandits stopped him on his return to the house and demanded five revolvers. They did not believe him when he said that he had no firearms. They tied him to a veranda post and searched the house, looting it of silver spoons, blankets, alarm clocks, anything of interest or value.

The bandits were about to shoot the cook and the teacher, but spared them at the entreaty of a Catholic crowd which had gathered. The bandit leader than issued an ultimatum to the priest. If he did not have three thousand dollars for them in two weeks, he and his servants would be shot.

Bishop Galvin had a report of the incident before the two weeks had elapsed and a military company, sent at his request, captured the bandits. "Those bandits, despite their elegance, were not very bright," the bishop said. "If they had been, that could have been a bad affair."

The cares of a bishop were already moving in on Ned Galvin. He wrote of them, briefly, to Father McCarthy. "I had a cable from the Superior asking me to negotiate with Monsignor Clerc-Renaud about the proposed new vicariate. Say a prayer that I may do the right thing. I don't like the job and I was hoping that Corney (Father Tierney) would deal with it but I will do my best."

22 : : THE MEANEST WORRY

A few of the priests were in from the missions and kicking around ideas in Hanyang [Bishop Galvin wrote]. Someone said that Columbans could be divided into two categories—the Pious Poor Fellows and The Slick Hounds. They started naming every Columban they could think of and putting him in one category or the other. When my name came up, someone said that they couldn't classify a bishop that way, but he was outvoted. The group decided that I was a Columban, just as was everyone else. And do you know where they put me? They put me at the head of the list in the category of Slick Hounds.

The man who was the bishop could laugh at such things, and sing with anyone who wanted to sing; could bake a better cake than anyone in the Columbans, or cook a meal. He could sleep on a dirt floor of a Chinese house, wrapped in his blanket with the rats running over him, and he could walk up to a tough bandit chief and talk him down. He had done all of those things and they had been

230

easier to do as a priest than as a bishop. People watched a bishop. Whether he wanted to be or not, he was a symbol, no matter how earnestly he tried, he was never quite a human being.

It was an odd situation. Men, and particularly Irishmen, it seemed, had a critical eye for a man who forged ahead, watching sharply for signs of conceit or superiority. They tested him to see if he responded to the old catchwords and nicknames and friendly gestures. He was under the constant necessity of proving his humanity, his adherence to old codes, his allegiance to old loyalties. Still, with all of that, the very least of the critics expected the man to live up to his role. If he was a bishop, then for God's sake, let him be a bishop! He was supposed to be, overnight, a political power. a man of wisdom, a breeder of right answers. He dared not be more than the least of those from whom he came when in an easy moment offstage, nor less than the most imposing Bishop of Elsewhere when on public display.

"I knew how it would be and, God knows, I never wanted it," Ned Galvin said.

He had gone to the apostolic delegate two years before it happened and introduced the subject carefully, stating that the growing importance of the vicariate would ultimately justify the appointment of a bishop and that he wanted to groom a man for that post, slipping out of the line himself. The delegate had looked at him coldly.

"Never, but never, decline an ecclesiastical honor before it is offered to you," he said.

Well, that was that, and a man's life changed when the ecclesiastical honor came to him.

He felt the change when he traveled, when he went among priests of another district than his own. He went down to Yaochow in the province of Kiangsi on January 14, 1928, with Father John McGrath attending him. He met Bishop Louis Jean Clerc-Renaud, the Vincentian bishop of Yukiang Vicariate, who, in accordance with the wishes of the Holy See, transferred to him that portion of the vicariate which was to be known to Columbans as Kienchang and later as Nancheng. The district had a population of less than a million people, six thousand of whom were Catholics. The transfer was a formal affair.

The finances of the society were improving steadily It

231

was going to be possible to staff this new vicariate and do a reasonable amount of building and renovating. The society had received a rather surprising number of gifts and bequests designated for the building and furnishing of schools and churches in China. Money so given, or so bequested, could not be diverted to any other uses, even if there were urgent and pressing needs. Bandit activity and shortage of personnel during the budget freeze had made church and school building impossible and some of the donors, not understanding, were becoming impatient. They would have their churches and schools now in this new vicariate. Bishop Galvin planned to send Father Tierney down as a director.

The United States, too, was building as the budget restrictions lightened. A letter from Father Ned McCarthy to the bishop stated: "We are starting to build our new preparatory seminary at Silver Creek, N.Y. this spring. . . ."

Rome wanted the Columban Society to open another mission territory in India. Many priests in the society were in favor of it, because it represented an alternative in case of severe trouble in China, another place in which to work. Dr. O'Dwyer was not enthusiastic about India and, on a trip to Rome in January, discussed the offer and declined it.

News of the society in China flowed steadily back to the States in letters. In February one written by Bishop Galvin slipped outside the bishop's role, as so many of his letters did: "Early this month it was intensely cold and then we had a week's snow. It was fun while it lasted. The young priests recently arrived from Ireland, staged battles. . . . with any of us who had the bad luck to walk into them. . . . Watching them, we felt young ourselves, in particular when we had to scurry for cover from them. Since then we have been having wonderful weather. Spring is all about us and everyone feels young and ready for the work that lies ahead."

Edward J. Galvin was forty-five. He never mentioned his age and seldom referred to members of the society as "young" or "old." He still moved fast, gestured emphatically, walked with that distinctive thrusting stride, smoked a great many cigarettes and outlasted ordinary men on any difficult task that he undertook.

232

"You better get a few days of solid rest," Father Jeremiah Pigott, the Vicar General, used to tell the nuns, "because the bishop is coming in on Friday."

It was accepted as a matter of course that everyone in Hanyang worked harder, faster and for longer hours when the bishop was in town than when he was away; not because he commanded it, but because he set a terrific pace and was always surprised when people did not keep up with him.

There were priests—a minority, but an honest minority —who did not like Bishop Galvin. They felt that he would sacrifice a man to an objective, that he often took advantage of the men under him by talking them out of deserved vacations or trips home, that he was a stuntster and that it was undignified and unnecessary for him to spend so much time in country parishes, so little at his Hanyang desk.

Bishop Galvin knew that he was criticized on many grounds but he seldom answered what he considered "griping" or "grumbling," because he considered a certain amount of complaining a necessity in an organization of men, and himself as the natural target. If, for some deeply-rooted reason he could not get along with a man, or the man could not get along with him, the man went home for reassignment. In the early days when he had had trouble with two priests who drank, he had banned drinking for a time. But older missionaries told him that white men in Asia usually needed a certain amount of alcohol for various good reasons. He relaxed the rule and had had no serious trouble since. Some of the men drank, some did not; none of them drank to excess or let it interfere with their work. He left the decision to the man and he took a drink himself when he felt like it.

Father Edmund Lane, his bursar in Hanyang and as close to him as anyone, was to say later that "Bishop Galvin was the most extraordinary man I have ever known." But Father Lane also said: "Ah sure, he was a bit of a crank. He was a Cork man."

Another close associate said of him, "No, Ned Galvin never wanted to be the boss. All he wanted was for the man who was the boss to do things his way."

Whatever he was or was judged to be by his contemporaries, Time and China put him to the test again and again. His first great test as bishop came in May, 1928

Father John Lalor, the pastor at Yo Kow, was walking down the road to another of his towns, Yuen Ho, when he was stopped by bandits. They held guns against his body and ordered him to write a letter to his superiors for twenty thousand dollars, the price of his ransom. Father Lalor refused to write, but aware that his Chinese boy was in danger, said that the boy could carry the message orally. The bandits cursed and punched the priest, but they let the boy go, emphasizing to him that the priest would be dead in three days if the money was not paid. The boy carried the message to the mission at Tai Lin Miao to Fathers Fallon and McDonald, who sent word to Bishop Galvin.

"I haven't got twenty thousand dollars," Bishop Galvin said. "They probably do not expect so much. It makes no difference. If I give them any amount, I've told them how much a priest is worth. Every priest we have will be kidnapped then."

He tried to enlist military aid as he had done in the past, but the situation at Hankow was chaotic again and there seemed to be no one in authority, no one with regular troops in the vicinity of Yo Kow. He sent word to Fathers Fallon and McDonald to keep the boy with them and not to send him back to the bandits with an unpopular message; if the bandits sent a messenger, Fallon and McDonald were to tell him that the Columban Society did not pay ransom for its priests.

It was the logical decision, the only possible decision; but it was difficult to make and to adhere to, when the captured priest had a name, John Lalor, and a personality; when one thought of the long-headed man with a twist to his mouth and a twist to the humor that emerged from it, when one could remember his singing.

The bandits had no feeling about Father John Lalor except anger that he had not written the note when they demanded it. They were stupid men, drafted while young into one army or another, and taught nothing but brutality. They had never known why they were fighting and had no conception of causes. They were unemployed now, since their armies had been defeated and since their paymaster had vanished. They wanted to live well, if possible

234

—very well, if possible. It infuriated them if anyone came between them and their wants.

For four days they kept Father Lalor locked up in a filthy house without food. On the fifty day they gave him a bun. For six days they gave him three buns a day. A small group of them invaded his quarters and tried to make him eat a bowl of filth. An officer interrupted this morbid idea of fun, abused Father Lalor because no ransom had been received, and ended up by ramming a capsule down his throat. The bandits then took him out and threw him on the village dung heap.

Father Lalor was semi-conscious, but unable to speak or to use his arms or legs. The villagers, afraid that they would be in trouble if he died in their village, carried him to a field a quarter of a mile away and tossed him on a heap of wet straw. For hours, Chinese came out to look at him, curious, pitiless, indifferent to him as a human being, but interested in him as a spectacle. They lost interest when night came down—all except an old woman, who walked around him, talking to herself and rubbing a knife on her apron. She was driven away by a man and two boys who lifted the priest and carried him to the man's house. He was fed hot tea and, very gradually, solid food. Traveling only by dark, it took the man and boys two nights to carry the priest to Fathers Fallon and Mc-Donald. The Good Samaritan, the priests discovered, was a fallen-away Catholic who had been converted years before by the Franciscans and who had retained his feeling of friendship for the Catholic Church and its priests.

In less than a month Father Lalor was working again in his parish at Yo Kow.

There were homely incidents while drama held the stage. A Loretto Sister wrote: "Let me tell you about the well that the Fathers are having dug for us in the compound. . . . At 80 feet we had not yet struck water. We had expected to find it at 40. Sister S. and myself, each unknown to the other, made special petitions to St. Joseph about the matter. As you would expect, this morning they struck water. We are rejoiced beyond words for it means a great boon to us to have water here instead of having it carried in buckets from the Yangtze."

There was a new vicariate to open, too. Fathers Cornelius Tierney and Peter Toal left Hanyang and set off for their new assignment in Kiangsi. They boarded a steamer at Hankow at 9 P.M. and arrived in Kiukiang the next day. They spent the day with Father Morel and took the 9 A.M. train on Friday for Nanchang. Early the next morning they sailed on a steamer for Jaochow which they reached on Pentecost Sunday, too late to celebrate Mass. On Monday they started in a small rowboat for Yukiang and did not get there until Thursday. The following day, with Father Toal riding a pony and Father Tierney on a mule, they traveled to Ting-Kia-Pu. On Saturday they reached Kin Ki in a heavy rain. On Sunday they achieved their destination at Tsitou at about 6 P.M.

The new mission was not exactly next door to Hanyang.

June was always a hot month, but Father Michael Fallon was trying to get his church built at Tai-Lin-Miao. The laborers quit and he rather scorned them for it. He was wearing a sun helmet and he defied the blazing sun as he sieved sand and laid brick. He was ill that night, and he was dead in less than a week.

One of the Sisters of Loretto wrote of him: "By this time you have heard of the death of our dear Father Michael Fallon, the result of a sun stroke. In him we have lost a brother for he was the most unselfish of men, scattering acts of kindness wherever he went, constantly doing for others and then forgetting about it. No words will express how we shall miss him."

Another Loretto Sister in the same week touched the reality of living. "Two more of our children were baptized yesterday," she wrote, "and they made their first Holy Communions today. One of them was espoused on Sunday last. She won't be married for a couple of years. The parents of the bridegroom, who is one of the boys over at the Mission, sent her a present of two dresses, two rings and a pair of earrings. Poor little Rosa! She thinks she has the world at her feet."

By mid-summer, the Nanking Government, uncompromisingly anti-Communist, was nominally master of China. Later, in his *History of Hanyang*, Father Abraham Shackleton, Columban, was to say of this development: "It is generally admitted in China that the Nanking Government under Chiang Kai-shek was the most competent government that China had known since the founding of the republic. Close economic relationships with foreigners were

236

established; the city of Nanking was remodeled and improved; new treaties, beneficial to China, were negotiated and signed. From every standpoint, a new day was dawning for China."

The bishop still had his problems. There were Communist pockets and bandits on the prowl. There were dilemmas in the mail, too. Ever since he first went to China, his mother had written to him about each of her problems, and she always had new ones. He did his best with them. In July, 1928, the difficulty was his brother Pat, who had never married and who did not seem to have any desire to settle down. Mrs. Galvin had been left a sum of money for each of the children by her husband. She was still holding Pat's share in the bank and he was demanding it. Bishop Galvin's reply was that he was too far away to make any kind of a fair appraisal of the situation or to offer any advice of value.

"It seems, however," he said, "that it is up to Pat to show that he can make some decent use of the money. That money was got pretty hard and I wouldn't want to see it wasted."

His mother was not the only one who appealed for Bishop Galvin's aid or advice through the mail. A nun in Cincinnati, who was a stranger to him, wrote about a program she had planned for doing penance and for growing in sanctity through self-denial. He replied to her:

Now, about your prayer. . . . I think it is far too strict. It shows a beautiful spirit but human nature is weak and we must not tax it beyond its strength. Nor should we ask it to do things or make promises which are beyond its strength, nor ask it to do things or make promises which may lead to scruples. Look, Sister, you are trying to become more spiritual, to become a Saint. Get the advice of an experienced Confessor and follow it. Remember that sanctity is a slow growth. Lay a safe foundation and build gradually.

He had little time to answer such letters. He was trying to work out a satisfactory method of marketing the embroidery shop's vestments in the United States, and he was resisting the urging of friends that he go to the Eucharistic Congress in Sydney, Australia. There were new priests coming out from Ireland and the United States, and he was assigning men to the new mission in Kiangsi, making a few changes in his parishes so that he could shift men around.

His Holiness Pope Pius XI issued a statement on August 1 expressing his satisfaction at the conclusion of the civil war in China and his desire that "the legitimate aspirations and rights" of the Chinese people should be fully recognized. He recalled that he had been the first to treat China not only on a footing of perfect equality, but with a true and very special sympathy, by consecrating in Rome the first Chinese bishops. This frank and cordial recognition of Chinese rights did much to win prestige for the new Chinese Government and to reassure the leaders of the new China that Catholic missions would cooperate with lawful rulers in maintaining order and achieving progress.

In the United States, The Most Reverend William Turner, Bishop of Buffalo, blessed the cornerstone of the new St. Columban's preparatory seminary at Silver Creek, New York. The stone, as a perfect Ned McCarthy touch, was of Irish granite, a fragment taken from the ruined walls of the old Abbey Church at Bangor, in County Down, where thirteen centuries ago St. Columban was ordained a priest.

In 1929 the Columban Society, on the invitation of Archbishop O'Doherty of Manila and with the approval of Rome, expanded one more step and entered the Philippines. The first mission was Malate, which had been in the charge of the Irish Redemptorists.

Dr. Michael O'Dwyer visited Hanyang coincident with the setting up of the two new territories which symbolized a future expansion that many men could feel as inevitable and which no man could see clearly in terms of years.

"This will be a big society some day, Ned," he said to Bishop Galvin. "It is bigger now than any of us could have imagined even five or six years ago."

"It is. It is already difficult to keep track of the new men, to know who they are."

"That is a worse problem from where I sit, but the money pinch is easing a bit, thank God for that. Money is the meanest of all worries."

The two men had grown closer since the loosening of the tight cords on the budget. From the Hanyang side, for

238

at least two years, there had been a touch of formal chill. Dr. O'Dwyer had anticipated that and understood it. It had been his responsibility to disrupt the work of many men and to wipe out their gains, in order that the society in which they labored might continue to exist. It was a responsibility which compelled a man to make brutal decisions, to smother his own sympathies. He had not expected to be loved, and he wasn't. It was still necessary that he maintain firm control, a hard grip on vital decisions, and that was not the way of popularity. Yet underneath the gruffness, the firmness, the hard masculine quality of making decisions and sticking to them, Dr. O'Dwyer had a broad, soft streak of sentiment and he never liked to see anyone or anything hurt. It took the society he commanded a long time to know him.

On February 7, 1929, the first Columban nuns in China took their final vows. It seemed to bystanders that it had taken them a long time to reach that point. There were complaints against the organization in Ireland because no more nuns had come out since the first six came to Hanyang in November, 1926. To a society which was training young men for the priesthood and training them in the specialized art of the missionary, ordaining groups of them each year and sending them into action, it seemed incredible that so many young women stayed perpetually in training with none of them emerging as working nuns. Writing on the situation to Bishop Galvin, Father McCarthy said:

"Mother Finbarr of the Columbans has been promising Nuns to Silver Creek for over a year. You have no idea, Ned, how much we need Sisters at Silver Creek. We have 40 boys this year and next year we will have 60 or 70, please God, with a big building to take care of. Young boys are continually getting sick with different kinds of boy complaints. . . . the priests have to carry their trays to them and nurse them."

Father W. S. McGoldrick, who had gone to Omaha as editor of *The Far East* after his first tour of duty in China, returned in July, 1929, as procurator general for the society in China. His office, in Shanghai, was officially opened on July 4.

Father McGoldrick was remembered for many things—as a fine mission pastor and a brilliant editor; but to many

239

of the Columbans he was the man who had caught and portrayed so accurately the quality of Chinese curiosity. That curiosity was, to the young priest, one of the most agonizing forces with which he contended, the source of embarrassment and humiliation, of irritation and, in some cases, panic. Father McGoldrick wrote:

The Chinaman assumes the right to know all he can about his neighbor's business, and the neighbor never dreams of resenting this curiosity for invariably he returns the compliment. The first question is not "How do you do" but "Where are you going?" "Where are you coming from?" "What have you got in that parcel?" "How much did you pay for it?" If you are as polite as he, you will answer them all promptly. Your dining room at meal time will always be a popular resort. In a spirit of most charming friendship, your visitor stations himself at your elbow and informs himself as to whether you really like this thing or that. He does not mind sticking an unwashed finger into the gravy or the vegetable dish to make sure you understand the object of his inquiry, and when you jump from the table and flee to the privacy of your bedroom, you find that your audience is equally ready to transfer themselves to this territory also and no Customs officer will ever be half so thorough in his examination of your household goods as they. If you bang the door in their astonished faces they crowd around your window with unabated interest. The window has no shade or curtains and if you still insist on privacy, the best thing to do is to dive under the bed. You must not look on this as unfriendly or hostile. It is all quite natural to them— far more natural, in fact, than it is for you to hide under the bed. And if you intend to stay in China, you may as well get used to it right away.

Bishop Galvin was one of the men who had learned early to accept curiosity as he accepted all else in China. He did not give curiosity any strange garments or symbols of rank to ponder on when he went back to the missions after he was raised to the episcopate. He dressed as he had always dressed, and he was a parish priest ministering to them.

The role of parish priest was not easy in 1929. The civil war had interrupted missionary activity and it had spread Communist propaganda. There was suspicion, if not hatred, of the foreigner in the country regions, an ac-

240

ceptance of the Communist claims that religion was one of the foreigner's tricks, a device used to enslave men to the foreign imperialistic system. Some men, too, expected the return of the Communists, and feared anything which might make the Communists their enemies.

There were many Catholics who had abandoned the Faith and there was a wall of resistance between the priest and the people he sought to convert. The missionary society was expanding and growing stronger as a society, while the people for whom it was created fell away from it.

Nor was the day of the bandit over!

Father Timothy P. Leonard was a tall, heavy built man, with a face of good-humored homeliness. An exceptionally devout man, he was described by Dr. O'Dwyer as the happiest man in China, serious about serious things but blessed with the gift of laughter. Known by the Gaelic version of his first name, "Tadhg," he was one of the first group of Columbans in China and became pastor of Chi Wu Tai. When the new district of Kienchang was assigned to the Columbans, he was a pioneer again and went down as pastor in Nanfeng.

The bandits moved in on Father Leonard in July.

The priest was saying Mass in his church when the armed horde poured through both doors. He tried to consume the Blessed Sacrament, but a bandit snatched the ciborium from his hands and scattered the sacred species over the floor. Other bandits trampled on the wafers and tore the vestments from the priest's body. Shocked by the sacrilege of the profaned hosts, Father Leonard upbraided his captors. A husky bandit smashed him in the mouth. Bleeding, he was dragged from the church and, according to the testimony of a Chinese businessman who was ransomed, he was put on trial before three Communist judges in their twenties.

Father Leonard was found guilty of representing a church hostile to the people of China and friendly to the Nationalist Government, of being the spy and agent of a foreign power, and of deceiving the people by encouraging them to practice religion. His captors took him out, threw him to the ground and hacked him to death.

Father Tierney, investigating all the details of the priest's death, discovered that the women of the parish,

241

after the attackers had left, slipped quietly into the Church, scraped the sacred wafer fragments from the floor and consumed them.

Father Timothy Leonard was the first Columban to die violently in the missions of China. His death profoundly shocked the society. A priest who had known him in Ireland remembered that one night in Dublin, a group of young priests were discussing the possibility of martyrdom for those who went out to convert pagans. Father Leonard said then: "Oh, what of that? What is it, after all, but a bad quarter of an hour? And think of the reward!"

The new Kiangsi Mission lost another priest on October 30 when Father William O'Flynn died of natural causes.

The society grew in maturity as it absorbed the awareness of casualties, as men dropped out forever from its parishes.

The nun population was on the increase. In October a Lorettine joined the other Sisters of Loretto at Hanyang, inspiring them to chant: "Now we are seven." Six more Sisters of St. Columban left for China on October 15, charged specifically with establishing catechumenates for women. They reached Hanyang in early December.

On October 23 and later on October 29, the New York Stock Exchange went through its most disastrous trading experience. Fortunes were wiped out, and the American chapter known as "The Depression" began. In China, of course, as in the rest of the world, it was a topic for discussion, but no one saw it in its true significance.

Bishop Galvin had worries and problems that were closer to him and hence more real. The Chinese had been poisoned by Communist doctrine and were still being poisoned. The government of Chiang Kai-shek was giving no quarter to Communists, but it would take time to establish sound government throughout the entire nation. The area in which the Columbans maintained their two missions had both bandits and Communists. The Communists at the moment were working mainly in propaganda, starting rumors, talking to small groups of people, stirring up suspicion and making men and women fearful. Where they walked and talked the soil was poor for missionaries, and Bishop Galvin knew that the Columban Society had not yet proved itself or justified itself in China, despite minor

242

triumphs. There were men working in parishes who knew that, too.

"Missionaries in general are quite discouraged," Bishop Galvin wrote in November. "Some of them are entirely fed up, but then there are men who would never give up and who keep on hoping. China is a dark place at present for Mission work. Personally, I am not discouraged. I feel that we must look at the whole business with the eyes of faith, try to see God working it out in His own way and keep right on. A simple creed, but it is hard to get some men to see it."

The year 1930 was greeted in China by the most severe cold in sixty years. Bishop Galvin was out in the missions, and had been for months. He wrote from Bao San Chao:

"Here I am trying to open up a new parish. It is fierce cold and so much snow has fallen that the branches of the trees are smashing under the weight of it. Father O'Carroll is in Yo Kow, on the run. Yuin Lung Ho is infested with bandits and there isn't a single mission station in the whole district to which we can go. Father McDonald is likewise on the run. Father Cowhig is hanging on at Gin San City but dares not put his foot outside the walls. Sung Ho and Fengkow are about as bad as can be, also Ko Ja Dzae."

Father Ulick Burke was desperately ill in Tsan-Dan-Kow at Christmas and did not succeed in communicating with any one until the 29th. Father Patrick Laffan went in after him and tried to get him to Hankow. He couldn't get through the heavy, howling snowstorm that broke, and doubled back on his route several times, afraid that Burke was going to die. They were in the storm for three days before Father Laffan stopped at Hwan Chia San with a delirious patient on his hands, and sent a boy to Father Quinlan in Hanyang for help. Father Quinlan could not find a doctor who would journey in the weather, but he sent medicine and, as soon as the weather softened, went up to Hwan Chia San with two Columban nuns, Mother Theophane and Sister Ignatius. "The journey was pretty bad," he said, "but they did not complain." The sisters nursed Father Burke for ten days and then took him to a Hankow hospital where he recovered.

A later letter from Bishop Galvin, written in March from Bao San Chao, is vividly descriptive of conditions:

243

"North of Yo Kow every mother's son seems to be a bandit. Not a soldier to be seen anywhere. They are all away somewhere, freeing the country. . . . I am trying to start a parish here. I have been here since November. It was a terrible winter. The Han was so frozen that the coolies carried their "dung she" over the ice for several weeks and my little bottle of ink was frozen solid for three weeks. . . . I have never experienced anything like it."

One of the old Chinese was quoted as saying: "Surely a new god of cold must have been born. The old one was not so severe."

The winter was harsh and cold, too, in Omaha. Father Edward J. McCarthy was not huddling in a Chinese shack but he had his own difficulties and worries. The stock market crash had not only reduced the value of the Columban reserve funds, it had also ruined, or badly hurt, many of the society's generous friends and contributors. In a humble mood, however, he ignored all personal concerns when he wrote in January to Bishop Galvin:

> It is surely true that it is easier for a missionary to become a Saint than it is to try to convert others without being a Saint. His success can only be in proportion as he realizes that ideal in his own life. I don't think it matters much whether a man is a monk or a scholar, externally. The successful missionary must always be a contemplative at heart. The names do not matter. Our lives can only be reduced to a few fundamental laws: humiliation, suffering, prayer. They are, as it were, pegs on which we hang our work and if it does not hang on some one of these three, we are only wasting our time. If it is mean and servile, it conforms with the law of humiliation; if it is hard and painful, it conforms to suffering; if it is done for God, to promote His work, then it is prayer. At least, Ned, that's how I look at the thing.

23 : : THE CAPTIVES

One of the most suspenseful and exciting of all Columban adventures began in April, 1930. The ending was long delayed. None of the people involved in it had an advance hint or a suspicion of danger.

On the morning of April 16 five Sisters of St. Columban arrived in Sientaochen. Father Patrick Laffan, the thirty-two-year-old pastor, had proudly escorted them from Hanyang. They represented a triumph in his young life. He and his assistant, Father James Linehan, thirty, had one of the best churches in the vicariate, donated by Cardinal O'Connell of Boston; a school, and catechumenates for men and women. Father Laffan had campaigned for nuns and he was fortunate. Bishop Galvin wanted to discover if nuns would work well in the smaller communities, and Sientaochen was considered a safe city.

Sientaochen had a population of thirty thousand and was located on the Han River, about 150 miles west of Hanyang. It had its own militia company and had never been disturbed by raiders. Catholics in the city and the immediate region numbered approximately two thousand, over a thousand of them descended from families which had been in the Faith for more than two hundred years.

Bishop Galvin rode in from Bao San Chao on Easter Monday to welcome the sisters and to give them his blessing. Father Gerry O'Collins came over from Chang Tan Kow. The bishop, the priests and the sisters spent most of the week outlining plans and procedures for the work that was to be done in Sientaochen with the increased staff. The men stayed up late on Thursday night talking, because Bishop Galvin planned to leave on Friday morning. It was a rainy night and they could hear the beat of the rain in any conversational lull.

The Sixth Communist Army marched through that rain. They marched all night and they had the city surrounded while it was still dark. There was no alarm.

Bishop Galvin said his Mass at dawn because he planned an early start on his journey. He was pronouncing the *Ite Missa Est* when the firing started. It was heavy firing and alarmingly close to the church. Father Laffan later wrote in a letter to the bishop:

"I remember your getting up before the dawn, but it was the shots that awakened me fully. The same shots aroused the Sisters. . . . It was clear to me from the very first moment that the Communists were upon us. At any cost, we must save the Blessed Sacrament. The three of us were dressed and out together. There was no gate leading from our part of the compound to the Sisters' buildings and the church. We scaled the wall."

The three priests met Mother Lelia at the church door. She was followed by Sisters Dolores and Patrick.

"Mother Lelia and I went into the church together," Father Laffan's letter to the bishop continued. ". . . oh, but was I glad to see you at the altar steps. You came out the sanctuary gates to meet us and you had your amice in your hand. Father Walsh was kneeling at his thanksgiving. Father Linehan was at the altar consuming the Blessed Sacrament. You had told him to do so. Everything is before me now as if this were Friday, April 25th, and I remember each actor and the part each played on that awful stage."

Bishop Galvin was the leading actor in that drama and he knew it. There was no discounting the menace of those guns outside. Obviously the attacking force was being opposed by the town militia but if the attackers were strong, that could not last long, since the Sientaochen militia was a small one. The bishop sent Fathers Linehan and Walsh to bury the sacred vessels in the sandpile behind the church. He then conferred with Fathers O'Collins and Laffan.

Women and children were fleeing now into the church compound. Father Laffan, who went out to see that they took refuge in the church, was confronted by a Communist officer and two men who had followed the refugees in. The officer had a revolver in his hand and he pointed it at Father Laffan.

At that moment, Bishop Galvin stalked down the aisle of the church. He was the symbol of authority; a powerful, impressive man who moved and spoke with apparent confidence. He ordered the Communist officer to post his men where they would behave themselves; then he invited him to have breakfast.

The officer seemed dazed in the face of direct command and he accepted the invitation meekly, assuring the bishop that this was a peaceable expedition, that all these men with guns meant no harm, that no damage would be done. Over a cup of coffee and a slice of bread, the bishop sized up the man whom he had taken over, and decided that he was too weak to be of value to him. He got rid of him quickly.

246

The priests and nuns were having a makeshift breakfast, picnic-style. There was still a great deal of firing in the town but there was less fury in its occasional lulls, which could only mean that resistance was lessening. More soldiers had come into the compound, standing against the walls with rifles in their hands. They were dangerous-looking men, recruited early in life from poor and ignorant backgrounds, trained to do only what they were doing now, bodies which had never learned to take direction from minds or souls.

The primary worry of the priests was the fate of the sisters.

Father O'Collins stayed with the nuns in the catechumenate. It was a difficult task, because it immobilized him at a time when action of any sort was a relief to strained, tense nerves. He was a good man for this task, an Australian who affected a goatee, who normally talked at great length, a maker of legends of whom some outrageous stories were told—stories of eccentricity, not of character weakness.

The Communist officer returned. He had a captain with him who was pompously self-important. The captain addressed himself to Bishop Galvin. He said that he had come with orders to arrest two religious. However, since there were many more religious, he would have to arrest them all. Bishop Galvin conceded no more to him than he had to the other man. He took exactly the same attitude: that a Roman Catholic bishop outranked any Communist officer.

No, he said, the Communists could not arrest any of his people.

There was a sound of hammering and banging while the conversation went on. Bishop Galvin looked through the window. The soldiers were wrecking his church, the finest one in his vicariate. He turned with fury on the officers.

"You keep me here talking," he said, "and you have no authority over your men."

He stalked out of the room, ignoring the guns which were pointed at him. From the veranda he could see the soldiers engaged in a wild orgy of destruction. They were tearing down the Stations of the Cross and slashing, smashing and destroying anything and everything. They had broken into the wardrobe and were using vestments to clean guns. A soldier smashed the butt of his rifle into the face of the Blessed Virgin statue and the head fell to the floor.

They were a mob and there was no controlling them. Bishop Galvin knew that he could not stop them. He had stung the Communist officers, however, with his charge that they had no authority over their men; they felt compelled to prove him wrong. They strode over to the church shouting orders, and Communist discipline had a heavy hand. The looters stopped, came to attention and marched out of the church at a sharp command.

The bishop, joined by Fathers Laffan and Linehan, stood before the empty tabernacle in the church surrounded by the wreckage of holy symbols. The Communist officers stood with them, and the arrogance of the captain had come back to him with the exercise of his authority.

"I will take only two men now," he said. "The name of one of those men is La. He is a religious and we have reports on him."

The captain was frowning. It was possible that he did not remember the other name. The moment was crowded with suspense. Bishop Galvin, with a gambler's sure sense, knew that authority had passed from him to the captain, at least temporarily. He could not risk his strength, because he had to be in authority again whenever they reached the issue of the sisters. Still, he would not betray any man of his into the hands of the Communists. Father Laffan sensed the situation as the bishop did.

"I am Father Laffan," he said. "I am known as La."

The officer was momentarily surprised, then he snapped an order and two soldiers stepped away from the wall. "You will go with them," he said to Father Laffan.

"He must first have his boots and a few personal things," Bishop Galvin said. He commanded Father Laffan to get his things, as the captain had commanded the soldiers. The soldiers would have stopped the priest but the captain waved his hand. Father Laffan went in to Father O'Collins, who was with the sisters. "I am off," he said. "Give me absolution, Gerry. Will I be a martyr if they kill me?"

Father O'Collins gave him absolution, but he did not answer the question. Father Laffan hurried back. A boy
248

had brought his boots. As he put them on, he whispered to the bishop, "Write home for me, please. And if I ask you for ransom, don't give it."

The bishop was pale. "Ransom is not out of the question," he said.

Father Laffan rose, stamped into his boots. He walked away with the two soldiers, then turned and waved. "God be with you, Monsignor," he said.

Bishop Galvin did not believe that there was much hope for any of them in the compound, but this was a horror to endure. "To my dying day," he wrote, "that awful picture will always be in my mind, the picture of that brave man going out to die and asking me to send a last message to his mother. For I did not think of anyone else in his home, or in the Society. I saw only his mother and she seemed to be before me there with a vividness and reality which I can neither describe nor analyse. The Communists were all around me but I didn't see them."

He didn't see the Communists and he ignored them. Turning his back on them, he stalked away to the room where the sisters were with Father O'Collins. He had planned to tell them of what had happened, but he couldn't speak. They already knew, of course. Mother Lelia said softly:

"Offer him up to God, Monsignor. God will take care of him."

Someone kicked at the door and it flew open. Communist soldiers entered. Bishop Galvin told Father O'Collins to take the sisters into a rear room and strolled forward to meet the looters. They looked at him with hostility, but he was not hostile. They started to pull out drawers and presses, examined what they contained, and took what appealed to them. The bishop did not interfere with them. He looted, too, taking what he could of those things which the sisters might particularly value. A tall soldier who looted beside him opened one of the presses and took out a bottle of vinegar. He turned to the bishop asked him, in utter simplicity, what the bottle contained.

"Rank poison," the bishop said.

"Oh, yo," said the soldier.

He put the bottle back. The bishop, acting on intuition or impulse as he often did, said: "Wait! Look here."

249

There was a little secret drawer in the bottom of the press where the priests had kept wine when they occupied the house. The bishop opened it; there was one small bottle left. He handed it to the soldier who laughed, recognizing the label. There was no word of thanks but the laugh was friendly, a laugh of companionship.

Bishop Galvin made a round of the compound. There were a surprising number of soldiers, most of them standing guard, only a few looting. Back again at the sisters' house he met Father Linehan.

"I remember how tenaciously Father Linehan clung to the hope that we might find some way out for the Sisters," the bishop wrote. "When I told him I had just made a round of the whole compound and that every exit was barred, he said nothing. There was nothing to be said."

The captain returned with one of his officers and a half dozen soldiers while the two men were talking. He now had, he said, the name of the other man who must be arrested. "His name is Lin," he said. "We want him to go."

Father Linehan drew a deep breath. "I am Lin," he said quietly.

"His voice was even and steady," the bishop wrote. "He was quite cool though his face was very pale. He showed no trace of nervousness and he went out, followed by those Communist soldiers. For a long time after he had gone, I stood there; just stood there."

The bishop had to let his men go, saving his strength and resources for the issue of the nuns. He didn't know, and no one else in the compound knew why the Communist officers were so confused and uncertain. They were commanded by a short-tempered tyrant of a general who had finished the long night march and the capture of the town in a state of profound weariness. The general retired to sleep and no one felt free to elaborate, enlarge or change commands that he had given. At the time he went to sleep the general did not know that there was a bishop or nuns or extra priests in the town. His orders had been that the two priests known as "La" and "Lin" be arrested. That had been done, but his subordinates would not risk the arrest of a bishop, or more priests or nuns, until the general awakened.

A great deal had happened in what seemed a short time. The attack on the town had begun shortly after dawn. It was 8:30 A.M. when the bishop returned to the convent and told the sisters that Father Linehan was gone. Then he went into the dining room where Father Walsh was seated at the table, writing a letter.

"What are you doing?" the bishop said.

"There is no hope," Father Walsh said. "I am writing a letter to Dr. O'Dwyer so our people will know something of what has happened here."

"I'll go next," the bishop said.

"No. It is your duty to remain. You can do more than anyone else. I'll go next, then Father O'Collins. You stay to the last man and try to save the sisters."

"We'll see," Bishop Galvin said. "Hear my confession, will you?"

Kneeling on the dining room floor, the bishop made his confession to Father Walsh.

Father Laffan's "boy," the trusted man of all work, was named Mah, a minor character in the drama whom everyone, including the priests, had overlooked. He procured from somewhere a straw hat identical to those worn by the boys and messengers of the Communist officers. He wore the hat at the correct Red angle and he moved around busily, so no one in the Communist camp paid any attention to him. He saw the leading merchants of the town brought in and he knew the ransom demands made on them, demands met almost immediately in many cases. He saw the officers of the town's militia shot. He was around headquarters when Father Laffan was brought in and, later, Father Linehan. He heard Father Linehan questioned about the other people in the compound, especially "The one who is the general and wears red." Father Linehan's answers were evasive and the Red general was still asleep, so nothing could be done. Mah heard that, too, and he took a grave risk by hurrying to Bishop Galvin.

When he had heard Mah's account, Bishop Galvin knew why they had been spared so long. Their temporary safety rested on a man's need for sleep and the man would not sleep indefinitely.

He was talking to Father Walsh about that when the second band of looters burst into the convent. These were a more violent and unruly gang than the earlier ones. Anything that they did not want, they tossed on the floor and trampled on. They insisted upon invading the room where

251

the sisters were and they were many, strong men with weapons. They took the sisters' clothes out of the presses and threw them around the room. They tried on the shoes of the sisters, laughing. Bishop Galvin and the two priests stood with the sisters and did not interfere with them. What these men did to "things," after all, was not important.

"If they had touched the Sisters," Father Walsh wrote, "I would have grabbed a rifle and the fight would have begun."

There was a sudden shrill whistle from somewhere in the town, outside the compound wall. The looters stiffened and two of them cursed. Bishop Galvin waited a few minutes, then followed them out. He hurried to the front gate of the compound. It was unguarded, but to escape through that gate, in full view of the sentry, was quite unthinkable. He looked along the outside of the wall. The groups of soldiers who had been stationed there all day had gone.

"My God," he thought. "What if the back gate, too, is unguarded!"

He strolled back with no show of haste but, once inside the catechumenate, he ran at top speed to the back gate of the compound. The gate was unguarded. "I decided to make a dash for it and trust in God," he wrote.

He went hurriedly back toward the house, then stopped. There was an appalling difficulty, a sentry at the door. He walked toward him and his heart speeded. It seemed like a fantastic coincidence, but it was true—the sentry was the tall Communist soldier with whom he had looted, for whom he had provided a bottle of wine. The lesser Communists, the boys with big straw hats like Mah's, were now gathered about the house where the sisters huddled, looking for looting opportunities which the soldiers might have overlooked. Bishop Galvin approached the sentry and noted the recognition in the young man's eyes.

"Your people will be frightening the women inside," he said. "I will bring them to a quiet place in back."

"The sentry hesitated," Bishop Galvin wrote, "but he and I had looted together and we had spoken to each other as men. There was a kind of friendship between us. I had played my last card. For a second we looked each other in the face, then, with a shrug of his shoulders, he said: 'Very well. You may do it.' "

252

Quietly and slowly, the bishop went up the stairs and along the veranda to the room where the sisters were. It was no time for explanations or long speeches. He stood in the doorway and said curtly, "Follow me."

He gathered a small procession behind him: the nuns, the two priests, the two "boys," Mah and Gow. He led them past the sentry and into the women's catechumenate. Only then did he reveal his intent.

"Sisters, you keep close to me," he said. He looked at Fathers Walsh and O'Collins. "You stand at the gate of the compound until the sisters have reached the embankment beyond. When I signal, follow. Mah and Gow, you scout ahead of us. Ready? We'll make a dash for it. Bunch up close to me."

The boys scouted the gate, signaled "all clear" and vanished. The bishop led the nuns outside and along the wall which hid them from those inside the compound. The embankment was seventy yards away. Mah reached it, signaled in a seemingly perfunctory manner and dropped out of sight.

To the bishop, leading the nuns, that seventy yards seemed miles in length. This was country that had fallen into the hands of the Communists and he was electing to travel it with five foreign women wearing habits, strange garb which was certain to attract the interest of any Chinese who glanced in their direction. He reached the embankment and signaled to the priests.

Before him lay open country, dotted with trees and groups of houses. The strange band of fugitives, three groups of them, hurried across the muddy fields from one clump of trees to another, from one village to the next, through pools and puddles of water which patterned the country after the heavy rain.

The country widened and opened up, and this was an area of great danger. They had to be too long a stretch without cover or protection, visible from a great distance in any direction. Mah, traveling well ahead of them, was a source of strength. He weighed and assessed the villages, satisfying the curiosity of the villagers and reassuring them. Usually it was enough for him to state that they were fleeing from the Communists; that statement made friends for his party. In one village the women suggested

253

that the nuns change their attire and wear the clothes of Chinese women.

They had been traveling in an arc to the right, hoping to reach the Han. If they could cross the river, they would be reasonably safe. Twice they sighted Red soldiers, but the parties were small and Bishop Galvin's groups, moving through wooded areas at the time, were able to hug the ground and avoid being seen.

"It was a terrible pace," the bishop wrote. "I was glad that the Sisters who followed me were young Irish girls to whom brisk walking presented little difficulty."

To reach the Han they had to travel along a high, exposed dyke which stretched for miles. It did not seem possible that they could travel the length of it without being sighted by enemies. But they did, and reached a small village on the river. They were badly spent, covered with mud. They had walked twelve miles since they had left the mission about noon, and it was now after five. There wasn't a Catholic in the village they had reached.

"Along our route we received nothing but kindness and encouragement from the pagan people," Father O'Collins wrote. "They gave us such valuable information as to the best paths to travel. They were willing to hide us in their own houses should the need arise. They knew that we were fugitives from the Communists and they did not know how long it might be until they were fugitives themselves."

"In the little town on the river where we stopped and ate a meal of eggs and bread, we received a real homey welcome," one of the Columban Sisters wrote. "The men suspended their buying and selling, the good wives ceased to haggle over the prices of eggs and cabbages, the little children called to one another to come and see us. We made our perilous descent down the muddy bank to the boats through lines of admiring and very friendly people. They seemed to delight in looking at us. . . ."

The bishop saw that the sisters were settled into the boat which would take them to Hanyang in care of the priests; but when they expected him to board also, he waved his hand.

"God bless you now," he said. "I have two men to look after."

He resumed his walk, then, accompanied by the faithful

254

Mah, and in a little more than four miles reached Dow Wan, a Catholic village. The people crowded around him. They knew the Communists were close and they had heard many versions of the day's events. Knowing that the village was in the possible line of the Red march, they would not let the bishop sleep at the church. He was, instead, invited into the best house in the village, fed and given hot water in which to bathe his feet. A man was dispatched to Chang Tan Kow with a note of warning from the bishop for Father Sands, who was alone there. All night long, out in the cornfields and the mulberry groves, men of the village stood guard.

Word came in the morning after Mass that the whole Communist army had marched out of Sientaochen before dawn. There was no word of the two captured priests, so the bishop and Mah walked to the city. It was a subdued, sad place where people were mourning their dead and the damage to their places. In the compound of the church, fifty or sixty Catholics were at work, cleaning up the frightful debris and repairing damage. No one knew what had happened to Fathers Laffan and Linehan, but a Catholic named E. Pin volunteered to follow the army and try to find out. Another Catholic named Dzao stepped forward.

"He will not go alone," he said. "I will go with him." He looked up at the bishop, then dropped to his knees. "We may never come back. If we do not, remember our names when you are saying your prayers."

The bishop blessed them and they set out together.

Rumors of all kinds drifted in, the most persistent being that Father Linehan had been shot. The detail made the rumor frighteningly convincing, but a later report that seemed authoritative stated that the Communist army was marching to their stronghold at Red Lake and that the two priests were marching with them.

The bishop visited every Catholic town in the region and said Masses, in which the people joined, for the safety of Fathers Laffan and Linehan. He opened lines of communication through the people in these towns, too. The people said that messengers could pass safely in the Red Lake district if they had legitimate business to conduct and that many non-Communists went there. But they had to be poor people, unimportant people; otherwise, they

255

were in danger. When he heard that, Mah volunteered to carry a message from the bishop to Father Laffan or to his captors. The bishop wrote the message and the intrepid Mah went off with it.

In the meantime, Fathers Walsh and O'Collins escorted the Columban Sisters to Hanyang and conferred with Father Tom Quinlan, who went to the commander of the Nationalist Army in Hankow. The commander was a worried man. One of the northern generals had defected from Chiang Kai-shek and the cream of the army was pinned down until that general was brought to terms. Meanwhile, Wuchang, Hankow and Hanyang were in danger. Even if times were normal, Red Lake was practically impregnable, a stronghold of the Communists for a long time.

The British Consul-General, Mr. Russell-Brown, used British prestige and called on officials, high and low, in an effort to get rescue action under way. "If Fathers Laffan and Linehan had been his own brothers, he could not have done more for them than he did," Father Quinlan said.

Bishop Galvin stayed in the country where he was joined by Father Jeremiah Pigott, rector of the seminary in Hwan Chia San. The two trailers, Pin and Dzao, had been captured by the Communists but released after being allowed to see the two priests. They quoted Father Laffan as saying, "Tell the bishop that we are well treated. They want us to supply them with guns as a ransom. That, the bishop knows, is impossible."

The situation was now fairly clear. The Reds wanted ransom for the priests—not money, but guns. How long they would hold the men if their demands were not met was a grave question. They might torture or they might kill. The obtaining of guns, of course, was impossible, but the Red mind might set itself on an impossibility.

There were now other bodies of Communist troops coming up through the country on the way to Red Lake. Bishop Galvin and Father Pigott were in danger, and a Catholic family sheltered them.

"Never once did that family show, by word or look, that we were other than welcome, though our presence there was a source of danger to them," Father Pigott wrote. "Morning after morning we celebrated the Holy Sacrifice on an improvised altar. It was but a door supported on two chairs but we felt that He, Who was satisfied with a

256

damp cave some two thousand years ago, would now, too, be graciously content with what we could provide in this miserable Chinese shack."

There was no virtue in remaining within reach of the Communists unless the missing priests were served by that remaining. Bishop Galvin sent the word along his line of couriers and messengers that he was returning to Hanyang. Messages, if there were any, would follow him there. He went by night along the route that the nuns had taken, and a letter from the missing priests was there before him. It was addressed to Rev. J. O'Rourke.

Dear James:
    We are prisoners of the Communists. We are well and have been treated respectfully. We are at present before the Communist Council and it has been decided that we will not be liberated unless you supply the army with guns or money. Father Linehan thinks exactly as I do.
                                Remember yours,
                                P. Laffan
                                J. Linehan.
Address your reply to Fengkow Postoffice.

It was a letter which required translating. By addressing it to Father O'Rourke, Laffan had suggested that O'Rourke be questioned. The "Remember yours" was significant. Father O'Rourke "remembered" that Father Laffan had once told him that he would write anything if captured by bandits, but that he did not want any attention paid to what he wrote and that he did not believe in paying ransom for any priest; that the paying of even one ransom put a price upon the head of every priest. The words "Father Linehan and I are of like sentiments" was an expression of solidarity.

There was nothing that Bishop Galvin could do about the request for guns but, after conferring with a number of priests, he decided that in this exceptional case a reasonable ransom could be paid. Obviously, Fathers Laffan and Linehan were not going to be released or rescued.

Another letter came from the two priests and Bishop Galvin, with great difficulty, obtained the name of the Communist leader in Hankow. He conferred with him, and

257

the man agreed to go to Red Lake as a negotiator and see what terms the Communists would make.

"Remember that we are poor men," Bishop Galvin told him.

Another letter came after the Hankow Communist left. It was addressed, as were the others, to "Father O'Rourke," and was dated July 14, 1930. The priests had been nearly three months in captivity. Their letter read:

> These people say they have not received a reply to either of the letters we sent you. They will not stand for that kind of thing any longer but now determine that, within two weeks from the date this is posted, you have a messenger at Pei Lo Chi with 10,000 dollars. They say that on no account can the two weeks be overstepped.
>
> The hot weather is severe and the Communists do not like to have sick men on their hands. It is decided that, if the business is not carried out this time, both of us will be killed. Father Linehan thinks exactly as I do.
>
> > Remember yours,
> > Patrick Laffan
> > J. Linehan.

It was obvious from this letter that the Communists, whatever they had been before, were now in a mood to torture or kill. Obviously, too, the two priests were ill but still conveying the message that they did not believe in paying ransom. Bishop Galvin walked up and down the room with their letter in his hand. He had to wait now until the Hankow man had a chance to negotiate at Red Lake. It was going to be difficult waiting.

The story of Fathers Laffan and Linehan was world-wide news carried by all the press services and kept alive by the continuing interest in their fate. There was, however, much else to worry about in China.

The Communist armies had grown in strength and the Nationalists had developed frightening weaknesses, caused in the main by dissensions and jealousies, the personal ambitions of some of the lesser leaders. Despite the heat of summer, the Red armies were moving.

Father Patrick O'Connell wrote on July 20, 1930:

> I was sitting at breakfast. The district had been tolerably peaceful for the few months preceding, thanks to the

258

vigilance of the local volunteers, armed with pikes, who kept watch night and day. Suddenly a messenger rushed in with the news that a force of bandits, a thousand strong, had just taken a town a few miles away. A second arrived, saying that they were less than a half mile away. There was just time to saddle my horse, take the chalice and make a dash for liberty. As I emerged from the mission compound, I could see that the countryside was black with people, refugees, fleeing from the bandits, carrying what they could. When I got out of immediate danger, I ventured to look behind. All around the church, flames reaching to the skies were visible. As I proceeded on my way to Father John O'Carroll, 12 miles away, I could see village after village set ablaze. Several thousand houses were burned in a few hours. More than 10,000 peace-loving, hard-working people were left homeless and unless we can have some semblance of peace, how can they rebuild?

By July 31 the Red armies were pressing toward Hankow, Wuchang and Hanyang from three directions. It was an extremely hot day. Bishop Galvin and Father O'Collins arrived at the Loretto convent in late afternoon.

"You must go to Hankow tonight," the bishop told the nuns. "Father O'Collins will escort you. The Communist forces are dangerously close."

He went then to the house of the Columban Sisters and assigned Father Edmund Lane to take care of them. He had already dispatched Father Joseph Crossan on the all-important task of obtaining junks for transport. The two groups of nuns and their escorts left at dusk and crossed the Han to Hankow, where they were sheltered at the Canossian Institute. The bishop stayed in Hanyang and that night it rained.

The rains ruined the crops of China. On August 12 Father Michael McHugh, who had returned with Father Francis Murray to their parish at Chi-Wu-Tai, reported that their people were terrified by the inevitability of famine.

"There had been a fair promise of a rice harvest," Father McHugh wrote, "but after a few weeks, when the grain was turning yellow, a plague of locusts came and ate all the rice and other crops. I have seen locusts in flight in the air, millions and millions of them, like a heavy cloud obscuring the sun. I have watched crowds of men, women and children frantically beating tins and gongs, ringing bells and waving flags to frighten the insects away. Others were using brooms or branches of trees to kill them, but their efforts were all in vain."

Other letters to Bishop Galvin told of the rising water which overran the land. Houses, livestock and people were swept away by turbulent water and the Communists offered no assistance. The burning, looting and conquering went on where the land was dry.

The Columbans were maintaining posts under great difficulty in an arc below Red Lake, in an endeavor to establish dependable contact with Fathers Laffan and Linehan or their captors. Their many efforts petered out in confusion and contradiction, leading to the conclusion that too many Communist leaders were trying to negotiate for ransom, apparently competing with one another.

Father Quinlan, Father O'Rourke and Mah went to Shinti, which had been one of the finest missions, and found it in ruins. Mah then went into the Red Lake region as a messenger. He came back with a demand for a hundred thousand dollars and guns. He had learned, too, that the priests had been beaten and that they were ill.

Father Quinlan sent Mah back with the message that missionaries did not have guns or large sums of money. He offered to pay the living expenses of the priests for the time they had been in captivity. The Communists sent back a demand for twenty thousand dollars.

Father Quinlan made them an offer of three thousand.

At another communication post, Liau-Chia-Ho, near Sientaochen, Fathers Pigott and Walsh suffered out the summer heat while they worked with messengers and scouts, seeking information or a reasonable, fair offer for the release of the priests from someone who had authority. Like Fathers Quinlan and O'Collins, they had a number of inflated demands, obviously made at random with no sense of reality.

They, too, had word of the priests' illness, more detailed than anyone else had received. Fathers Laffan and Linehan had malaria and dysentery, looked pale, drawn and sallow, and had, assuredly, been beaten.

Bishop Galvin had ninety-five girls, students of the sisters who, like the sisters themselves, had to be transported to Hankow from a Hanyang that grew steadily more dangerous. He had letters about locusts, letters about floods, letters about burned missions and priests on the run. It was one of the very few times in his life when he gave up in China.

He wrote on August 22 to Father McCarthy in Omaha:

> The Vicariate is in a frightful state. No priest can put his foot in the greater part of Mien Yang and the northern country is almost as bad. It is a frightful time and I do not know where I am standing. I think the Society ought to look for some other field in which to work. Flesh and blood can't stand the strain that we are under here. Our hospital bills for this year have been fearfully high. At one time there were as many as ten in the hospital together, and there is always someone there.

A week later, he wrote in a similar vein to Father Joe O'Leary: "Until conditions change in China, much cannot be done and men won't last long under this strain. Under the circumstances I think it better not to confine ourselves exclusively to China."

A letter reached him from Father McCarthy who reported: "I called to see your mother while I was in Ireland. She is in splendid health and looking forward to seeing you in 1932. It may be that she will see you before that because I feel sure the Superior General will write you to come to the Congress next year, and if he does, I hope you will come through America."

"Not 1932 or any other time the way things are!" Bishop Galvin said. "I'm needed where I am more than I am needed anywhere else."

The affairs of the society were moving ahead, despite Communists. bandits and the uncertainties of China. On September 12 the new seminary of the Columban Fathers at Silver Creek, New York, was dedicated. It opened with sixty-five students, bringing the total student body of St. Columban's in the United States from three students in 1921 to eighty-three in 1930. On October 3, the feast of the Little Flower, the Missionary Sisters of St. Columban opened a new dispensary in Hanyang.

Since five members of their order had distinguished themselves as heroines of the Laffan-Linehan affair, with publicity all over the world, the erstwhile backward Columban Sisters had taken on confidence, assurance, a sense of competence and mission. There was a remarkable new spirit in the organization. The Columban Sisters had met China at its worst, had conceded nothing to it and were ready for other tests.

Chiang Kai-shek, after several important victories for his troops, was confident of an early peace in China. His casualty statement for seven months of civil war listed 30,000 Nanking Government troops killed, 90,000 wounded; rebel casualties, Communist and other defectors from his own command, 150,000; civilian casualties, directly resulting from hostilities, 30,000. Shortly after issuing his statement, Chiang Kai-shek was baptized a Christian by Reverend Z. Kuang, pastor of the Young Allen Methodist Church in Shanghai.

Father Tierney, writing from Nancheng to Bishop Galvin reported: "Here, things seem as if they would improve a little. The Civil War is, I believe, ended for the present, but it is to be feared that nothing has been determined and there will be another later on. The big danger, it seems to me, is Communism. The Reds already have a footing in many places in this Province and it will not be easy to rout them out."

The electrifying news came in November. The Spanish Franciscans at Yochow had been trying, as Father Quinlan was, to reach some kind of understanding with the Communists. One of their priests, Father Fernandez, was also held at Red Lake. Now, suddenly, the Communists were demanding four thousand dollars, payable in silver dollars. It must be paid immediately. At the same time, Father Quinlan's scouts reported that the Communists were preparing to pull out of Red Lake if Chiang Kai-shek moved against them as they feared. They wanted to collect for all of their prisoners, or get rid of them, before they had to move.

The Spanish Franciscans had been looted several times recently and did not have the money. Father Quinlan suggested to their representative that they try to borrow the money from Captain Forde, of the British gunboat *Tern*, which was lying five miles below Yochow, and volunteered to go with them to the naval vessel.

"Captain Forde received us with great kindness," Father Quinlan wrote, "but he did not have the required sum on his ship. Like the gentleman he is, he volunteered to go

262

with us to an American gunboat farther down the river. There, too, we were unsuccessful. The American Commander, however, went with us to a Japanese gunboat which lay close by and, luckily, the Japanese Captain had the necessary sum on board which he gave to us without the least hesitation."

Shortly after the Franciscan left with the ransom money, Father Quinlan received a message from Red Lake setting a price on the two Columban priests. The Communists wanted fifteen thousand dollars. Word through the underground indicated that the Reds were actively planning an evacuation of their stronghold. If so, they would be in bad humor and it would not be good to be a prisoner in their hands. Father Quinlan conferred again with Captain Forde and sent a wireless message from the ship to the British Consul in Hankow:

"Please ask Hanyang Mission to send priest with 15,-000 dollars. We shall wait upon H.M.S. *Tern*. Military move imminent. Utmost speed vital. Quinlan."

The Consul received the message on Tuesday morning and immediately got in touch with Hanyang. Bishop Galvin and Father O'Collins went to Hankow for the money and discovered that there was no steamer going to Yochow until Thursday. The lives of the two long-imprisoned priests were in the balance and Thursday might be too late. To carry a sum like fifteen thousand dollars on a Chinese boat was unthinkable; Chinese boats were pirated constantly. Bishop Galvin went to the man who had been his friend through long months of concern over the missing priests, Mr. Russell-Brown, the British Consul-General.

He outlined his dilemma and the Consul suggested gravely that the British Navy should have an answer to it. The two men called on Admiral McLean who, without hesitation, put the gunboat *Mantis* at Bishop Galvin's disposal and instructed Captain Howden that the lives of the priests depended upon speed.

The *Mantis,* with the somewhat relieved Bishop Galvin aboard, steamed full speed up the river. When night approached, Captain Howden came down from the bridge to consult with the bishop.

"I am faced with a great difficulty," he said. "It is the first time I have been up this river; the water is low and if

263

we steam through the night, there is grave danger of running aground. What am I to do?"

"It is not my place to advise on the conduct of a naval operation," the bishop said, "but if I commanded this ship, I would take a chance on running aground."

Captain Howden looked at him sharply. "I believe you would." He rose with a shrug of his shoulders. "Well, never let it be said!"

He went back to the bridge and the gunboat raced through the night. Captain Howden stayed at the wheel until he pulled beside the *Tern* in the morning, after the fastest trip on record ever made on the Yangtze.

Father Quinlan arrived on board the *Mantis* and had with him the faithful Mah, who was prepared to handle the transfer of money.

"I believe that I should handle it," the bishop said.

The others immediately disagreed. The Communists would see in a bishop the source of possible great wealth; they were thinking now in ransom terms. Reluctantly, he agreed to Father Quinlan's plan. Mah, average in looks and far above average in courage and mental agility, would carry the money to Pei Lo Chi, the point to which the Communists had agreed to bring the two priests.

Once Mah left, the great period of suspense set in. So many things could go wrong.

They expected the return of Mah on Friday, then all day Saturday. He had a white flag to hoist if he came up the shore. On Saturday night a terrific storm arose; wind and high water beat at the two ships, which pitched and rolled.

By Monday the storm had blown itself out and Mah succeeded in hiring a junk. He bore down proudly on the *Mantis*, wavering his white flag. "We pulled alongside the *Mantis*," Father Laffan wrote, "and a Lieutenant ran along the deck to help us aboard and to welcome us. We were safe at last."

The bishop and Father Quinlan rushed up from the wardroom and this was the moment they had not dared to imagine. Fathers Laffan and Linehan, thin and brown and scarred and shaking, but basically sound and alive, were home again after seven harrowing months.

That night the captain gave a dinner for Bishop Edward J. Galvin and Father Thomas Quinlan. "There is a little

264

game that we play in the British Navy on great occasions like this and, although we do not often use port, the game is called 'Pass the Port,' " he said.

Captain Howden explained the rules. Each man had an ounce and a half of Scotch in a highball glass which was filled with soda. If a man broke a rule, enough whiskey was poured into his glass to fill it. He had to take a drink, even if only a sip, whenever anyone mentioned the name of a celebrity, of anyone present, of any respected institution, of the Church, the Navy, the flag or one of the recognized governments. A man's glass was filled every time he swore, mentioned royalty or the clergy, talked shop, spoke the word "Communism," or told a joke at which nobody laughed.

A great many wires and cables were filed on the release of Fathers Laffan and Linehan. The most prized one, in closely guarded circles, was dispatched in the early morning by Captain Howden of *H.M.S. Mantis* to Admiral McLean at Hankow:

"THE CHURCH DRANK THE NAVY UNDER THE TABLE."

24 : : THE BIG WATER

The winter was exceptionally severe in Tibet where no winter is ever easy. The snows piled high; higher, in the places where records were kept, than any snow of two generations. In China, few people knew about the snows in Tibet and no one cared. It seemed then, to those who heard of it, the difficulty of another people and of no concern to a Chinese. No one, not even among the wise, predicted that the snows of Tibet were the tragedy of China.

For the duration of the winter, the snow stayed in the high, cold country, frozen and immovable.

The Columbans were given no time to celebrate the release of Fathers Laffan and Linehan. Before the negotiations for their release were concluded, another group of

265

bandits struck the new mission of Kiangsi. The news was slow in reaching Hanyang.

On November 14, 1930, at 6 A.M., a Communist detachment in uniform marched into the town of Shang Tang Hsu about 50 li (17 miles) from the city of Kienchang. Father Cornelius Tierney had come to Shang Tang Hsu to oversee the building of a house for Father John Kerr, the pastor, and he had gone to the church to say his Mass when the troops entered. They seized him and took him outside the church, where the citizens of the town were huddled in tight groups surrounded by soldiers. The invaders stripped the priest in the icy weather, tied him to a post and flogged him brutally in the presence of his people.

Father Tierney was then fifty-nine years old, probably the oldest Columban priest. Many Columbans had believed, when he was assigned to open the new mission, that he ultimately would be the society's second bishop.

Father John Kerr was visiting his outlying missions when Father Tierney was captured and it was a matter of days before the news reached him. Bishop Galvin and Father Quinlan were far from Shang Tang Hsu in a British gunboat negotiating the freedom of Fathers Laffan and Linehan. There was no immediate contact between the Communists and the Columbans, and the idea of demanding ransom seems to have been slow in suggesting itself to the priest's captors. Their initial idea seems to have been to beat and humiliate him.

On November 23 Father Tierney was able to send a personal message to Father Kerr, obviously without his captors knowing that it was sent. He said that he had twenty unfulfilled Mass intentions on his books and commended the saying of them to Father Kerr. Under a stone near the church door, he had hidden five hundred dollars in church funds. He asked for prayers that he might bear well any suffering that came to him.

Father Kerr disguised himself as a coolie and, at great risk, suceeded in going behind Red lines. He heard news of the captured priest but did not see him. When the Communists ultimately demanded fifteen thousand dollars for the safe return of Father Tierney, there were insurmountable difficulties in negotiating because of the distance between Hanyang and Kienchang and the poor communications.

On December 18 Bishop Galvin wrote: "Life has been an agony here during all these terrible months and, at the present moment, it is as dark as it could be. . . . Father Tierney is still a captive. God knows how it will all end. We need faith and courage. Only fifty miles from here a young Chinese priest has been murdered by the Communists. They stripped him naked and beat him terribly. They blinded him with lime and then, tying a rope around his neck, they slowly strangled him to death."

Far from China and its strife, but connected to it in purpose, seven Columban Sisters from Ireland landed in New York on December 23 on their way to the seminary at Silver Creek.

On January 1, 1931, the Columbans had sixty priests overseas in three missionary areas: Hanyang, China; Kienchang, China; Manila, Philippine Islands. There were 210 students in the Columban seminaries.

There was a feeling of optimism in Chinese political circles, a feeling that the country was taking significant steps toward unity and peace. Bishop Galvin shook his head over such talk. "Not much is being done to clean up the Communists at Red Lake," he wrote on February 15. "I fear these people have come to stay."

Later that month, Father Ned McCarthy wrote to the bishop from Omaha: "You are an amazing man and I mean this in all sincerity. In the middle of all your worries with bandits and Father Tierney and embroidery schools . . . . you come along with a letter asking me if I seriously think the Society could ever have a foundation in Bobbio [the place in Italy where St. Columban settled with his monks]. I showed it to our mutual friend Father Joe [O'Leary] and his only remark was: 'Ah, sure, that does it. He's gone altogether now, poor man.' "

On February 28, 1931, Father Cornelius Tierney died in Communist captivity, but word did not reach any of the Columbans until March 12. Father Michael Moran, one of the priests who had been trying to negotiate for Father Tierney's release, arranged for the body to be exhumed and shipped down river to Kienchang where he was buried.

"God rest him out there in his lonely grave among the bandits," Father William McGoldrick wrote. "He won't

267

forget us or his poor mission at Kienchang. And he won't forget his captors, either. When his prayers bring some of those same captors into Heaven, I know he'll have a warm and cordial welcome for them."

The death of men who had been close to him and close to the society oppressed Bishop Galvin. He retired into himself when a man died, either going to work in some obscure mission if there was a need at the time, or secluding himself in Hanyang and reading accumulated books. He had good taste in reading and remembered what he read, even to the extent of memorizing long passages which he could quote months later. Father McCarthy's book on St. Columban had impressed him greatly and he mentioned it in many letters. A letter to Father McCarthy provides a glimpse into his mind: "There has been too much poetry woven around these Irish missionaries," he wrote. "I liked your book because of the great effort you made to present Columban, the man of flesh and blood, of success and failure. It is only in that way we can learn anything from a man's life."

He had definite ideas on music, too. He wrote to Father Paddy O'Connor, editor of *The Far East* in Omaha:

> That piece of music [the mission song] reminds me very much of two other pieces, both of which are set to sad themes. One is "Danny Boy," the other is a Spanish, or rather a Mexican, piece called "La Golondrina" ("The Swallow"). This latter piece I could listen to for hours and hours on end. I know you are an humble man and if I did not know that, the above would never have been written. I have some kind of a strange love for that piece of music. Some pieces of music let loose some darned kind of a wild thing that is inside of me somewhere and that piece is one of them. . . .

Father Patrick O'Connor was probably the finest writer of prose in a society noted for good writing and he had a versatile hand for verse. He had written the lyrics for the mission song on which Bishop Galvin commented and the imagery of his writing reflects the time of stress during which the society was born, the crusading spirit which marked its history, the sense that society members had of conflict, of "winning China for Christ." Two verses of the song follow:

268

A trumpet sounds in the far, far hills
'Twere shame to answer 'No,'
But show the world ye are unafraid,
As Louis was in the old Crusade,
To take the Cross and go!
Then let not the knightly slogan die,
Nor the knightly weapons fall—
Till every land is His Holy Land
Where His lamp is lit and His altars stand
And His Cross is over all.
So flash out your blades for the splendid cause
And pray that your hearts be true,
To live and to fight for the grandest thing
That man could dream or singer sing
Or ever soldier knew.

Bishop Galvin had much of that soldier spirit in himself and his leadership was often of the rough, front-line campaigning type, but he winced when anyone associated with him was tough or uncompromising toward another Columban. One individual who had no patience with pussyfooting, evasiveness, or the sidestepping of issues was Father Edmund Lane. A fine, loyal individual, with an underlying streak of sentimentality, Lane nevertheless was breathtakingly blunt when he felt that right was on his side. It made the bishop squirm to hear Lane speak at times, or to read something that his bursar had written in a letter. He felt impelled on one occasion to write a softening personal word to Father McCarthy as a follow-up to a straight-punch letter of Lane's.

"Lane is a real, decent man," he wrote. "But sometimes he hasn't a nice way of putting things. You understand, Mac, that he always means well, so I hope that, if any little thing slips into his letters, you will overlook it."

And friends still died. On May 9, 1931, Monsignor John H. McCoy, his friend and ally at Holy Rosary, died of a heart attack. The cable reached Hanyang on the 10th and the bishop didn't speak to anyone all day.

The congress, or chapter, of the society, to which Bishop Galvin had been invited, met at Navan in Ireland. In the calm, cool light of retrospect, the men assembled were agreed that Dr. Michael O'Dwyer, who had had the courage to invite dislike and opposition, had served the society with skill and devotion. In gratitude and appreciation they voted him to seven more years as Superior General. His council consisted of The Very Rev. John Blowick, vicar general; Rev. Patrick Laffan; Rev. Edward Maguire; Rev. James A. Kennedy, secretary. Bishop Galvin lost Father Edmund Lane, who became procurator for the society. He also lost Father Thomas Quinlan, who was transferred to Kiangsi.

In China, it started to rain.

The rain of June was tentative—days of heavy clouds; swift, furious storms; a quick clearing and another cloud accumulation that built slowly. In July there was no respite. The clouds were constant and the rain was torrential over all of the Yangtze valley. A letter from Father Patrick A. Maguire describes the situation as those who worked in the valley experienced it:

"Towards the end of June the crops gave hope for an excellent harvest and the Government seemed to be having some success in suppressing the Communists. Alas! The rain began to fall. It poured incessantly day after day until it seemed as if we were having a veritable replica of the Deluge. . . . How we longed. . . . for real summer weather, for the days of scorching sun and suffocating nights, those days when to go on a sick call is torture, those nights so sleepless that dawn is heralded with joy."

The rain continued to beat and hammer and gouge the valley of the Yangtze. It filled the Eight Cliffs Gorge and the Wind Box Gorge, the Witches Gorge, the Ox Liver Gorge, the Horse Lungs Gorge and the Ichang Gorge. It inflated and enlarged the Chin and the Lin, the Yuan and the Tsu. All the rivers of China rose and beat against the dykes, and crept, inch by inch or foot by foot, over banks and restraining walls. The irrigation and transport canals caught the water and overflowed. Still the rain came down, without any rest or faltering, through all the hours of the day and night.

The protective dyke at Hankow broke before the pressure put upon it and an incredibly swift tide swept through the city, carrying before it men and women and the structures they had erected, the goods they had amassed. The homes of the poor, built mainly of bamboo, were the first to go. There was no time for warning, no time for

270

escape. Five thousand people were drowned in Hankow on the day that the dyke cracked.

Hanyang was flooded less violently. There was no sudden rush, but the water came into the city, ran along its streets and climbed the walls of its houses. Refugees from small towns and flooded farms were crowding in from all directions. A dispatch from Wuchang carried the estimate that 104,000 Chinese had been rendered homeless by flood in the tri-city area.

The Columban Sisters, who had just completed and occupied their new convent, surrendered it to refugees, and 436 women and children, most of them ill from exposure, were crowded into the rooms and corridors. Sisters Patrick and Ignatius, who had been trained as nurses, took charge of the relief work. Bishop Galvin wrote of them: "The two Sisters faced that terrible situation with a quiet thoroughness and efficiency that are beyond words."

In August the heavy snow masses of Tibet, built up through the winter, were melting. Water rushed down through every channel into inundated China, adding new dimensions to the widespread flood area. Water rose rapidly and thousands of people drowned in the depths of it. There was nowhere to go. Two-thirds of the Hanyang vicariate was beneath this newly formed sea. In Hanyang itself, hordes of emaciated refugees dragged themselves up Tortoise Hill and Black Hill to cling precariously to any small patch of land. The thousands who had crept up earlier out of the cold, muddy water granted space to newcomers reluctantly.

All the resources of the Columbans were thrown into the struggle in behalf of the helpless. Refugees who were still fit were recruited to construct sheds and straw tents as temporary shelters to administer to the sick and dying. Columban and Loretto nuns spent their own strength to the danger point in giving anticholera inoculations and in helping to bury the dead. The dead were a danger to the living and had to be swiftly removed.

The sisters were housed on high ground but St. Columban's in Hanyang, where the priests dwelt, was filled to a depth of nearly fifteen feet by flood water. Priests and students of the seminary tried to rescue canned food and utensils by swimming under water into the house.

The roaring rivers out of Tibet still carried the melted

snow. The rains of August were less constant than the rains of July, but there was only an occasional brief respite. On August 20 Bishop Galvin wrote:

"God help us, we are in a fearful plight these past few weeks. . . . The Yangtze is 53 feet higher than its normal level and it is still rising. The distress on all sides is appalling; thousands of persons drowned, thousands dying from starvation, millions homeless. It is heart-breaking to go out, to witness harrowing sights, to feel that you are powerless to relieve the suffering. The refugees are rushing in on us so fast that we simply cannot deal with them."

As an added horror, there were bandits in boats—in many cases, large parties of bandits in big boats—who cruised over the vast flood sea, robbing the poor people who clung with a few rescued possessions to housetops or bits of high land. The callous brutality of these bandits was difficult to credit. They rescued no one, provided no help in an extreme situation, robbed indiscriminately and were utterly indifferent to the value of human life.

Nearly all the priests were in from parishes which were completely inundated, working in Hanyang on the hills where the unfortunate huddled. "We have 250 refugees in our little compound which normally houses 90," a Loretto Sister wrote. "We have spent every cent which the Embroidery School earned from the making of vestments and yet we have bought food and clothing for so few out of these many. We have been helping in the public kitchens and we have been giving instructions to those who will help clothe the needy. You could not believe the need that exists and I despair of describing it to you. . . ."

Father Hugh Sands, the pastor at Chi Wu Tai, was one of the few priests still on duty in the outlying territory. Most of his parish was hilly, and a number of the villages were above the flood. With a small boat and a boy, he spent eight days making the rounds of the parish. The water, although it possessed the dimension of a vast sea, was in fast motion. Rooftops, fences, entire houses went swirling by, as did gaily decorated bits of wall, pieces of furniture and bodies—the bodies of animals, and the bodies of men and women, turning over and over.

All of the surviving villages were crowded and jammed with refugees. Father Sands visited them one by one, helping where he could in cases of illness, hearing the con-

272

fessions of frightened Catholics who could see death all around them. On the return journey he heard at the Catholic village of Tsao Shih, 15 li from his home base, that bandits, identified frankly as "Reds" by the narrators, were raiding the stricken villages, moving in on them in big boats.

He arrived back in Chi Wu Tai on Sunday, August 16, and the town, high above the flood, was quiet. A number of his parishioners were assembled in the church with a catechist, saying the Stations of the Cross. Father Sands joined them. He visited with its people after the Stations, then, tired from his journey, decided to take a nap.

A half hour later he was awakened by his terrified boy who cried out to him: "Father, the Reds are here!" Before Father Sands could rise, a thin, nervous, wild-eyed man with a revolver was in the room. There were two more strangers beyond the door.

As he was led out, the priest could see a horde of armed men looting his church, spreading out through the town and rounding up its citizens. He was taken aboard a small, crowded boat into which citizens of another village had already been herded. He spent that night and the following two days as a captive on the boat, cruising over the wide water. There were, incredibly, forty or fifty boats in the fleet and armed men made landings wherever people had found temporary refuge above the flood, taking loot by violence from desperate, unfortunate people. On August 18 the fleet crossed the Han at May Ming Dzay and reached the Red camp on the hilltop.

Father Sands was ordered to write to Hanyang for fifty thousand Chinese dollars. He refused. He refused again when they reduced the demand to twenty thousand. Finally, under gun threat, he wrote their ransom demand for 5500 Chinese dollars.

As soon as the note reached Hanyang, Bishop Galvin sent for the faithful Mah, who had served so well in the Laffan-Linehan affair, and asked him to locate Father Sands and to see what could be done to free him. It was still folly, of course, to pay ransom on demand. If it were that easy, the Reds would immediately start collecting priests. Mah, always a devoted teacher and an all-round assistant to priests, had gained new dignity. He was now referred to by his full name. He was Mah Hsien Sen.

Bishop Galvin was filling many roles in the developing drama of the rivers and the Reds. He worked with the priests and the nuns on the hillsides of Hanyang, making no claim to rank, and he planned for the purchase and the distribution of necessities. He wrote letters. In one of August 21 he said:

All around the Mission is that helpless, starving multitude. In all my years in China, I have never seen such a terrible sight. From the hill at the rear of the mission the entire countryside, as far as the eye can reach, is one vast sea of water. In Hankow the water is several feet deep and the only way of communication is by boat. No pen could give an adequate picture of this frightful disaster. We can do little to alleviate the sufferings but we are doing our best. In the Embroidery School of the Loretto Convent we have over 200 women and children. In the Columban Sisters Catechumenate there are 170. In another house, which I bought some time ago, there are 90. But everywhere the water is deep and we must come into the house by boat. All the refugees are living upstairs. In all, we have given shelter, and are trying to feed, 800 starving people here in Hanyang but out there on the hillside there are still over 100 Catholics, and thousands of pagans. We have nowhere to put them.

Last night a Catholic woman gave birth to her child out there among the graves on the hillside. God help us, it is all terrible. A few days ago I met a little Catholic girl of 17 or 18. She had been in the Embroidery School for two years and then went home to be married. What a haggard, famished little thing she looked when I met her, with two healthy children pulling at her breasts as if they would pull the life out of her!

The people are fleeing in thousands from the stricken areas, from the double terror; inundation and Communism. Refugees living in the open air with nothing to shelter them from the burning sun around St. Columban's; among the graves, they are huddled in thousands. To hear the little babies crying in the night is dreadful. Almost every woman seems to have two or three helpless children. Kindly ask the people, the priests and the Sisters, especially the little children, to pray for us. Ask them to pray for our homeless people, for the priests and for me.

On August 30 the Grand Canal, which had held firm till then, broke. Fifteen sections gave way north of Yang-
274

chow, flooding hundreds of square miles. Between six million and seven million persons lost their homes as the water tumbled relentlessly down into areas already covered to incredible depths. A release of this date from Hankow reported that in the three cities of Hankow, Hanyang and Wuchang, 250,000 persons had been drowned or had died from exhaustion, disease or starvation.

Writing on this date, Bishop Galvin said:

> I have never encountered such desperate people as the people who are camped out here on the hillside. Hunger has made them desperate. I am honestly afraid to go out. Every time I do, I am caught by the clothes. They hold on for dear life until I promise them something. I cannot feed every one. We are feeding 900—a drop in the ocean. It is estimated that there are 30 million homeless in the Yangtze Valley and most of them have absolutely nothing. I never knew what *nothing* meant until I came to China. Poverty is hard, but hunger is terrible. And the Communists? My God, what demons they are! Robbing and killing, right and left, they have taken the boats from the people and what little they were able to save from the flood. No money anywhere. It is a hard country. Every single one of our missions has been attacked and looted. Not one has escaped. It is a record to be proud of.

The Columbans were proud, too, of the Sisters of St. Columban who had started slowly in their vocation, then had found themselves as an order of nuns and distinguished themselves under fire. They excelled in nursing and hospital work, and the great flood was their challenge. Sister M. Patrick wrote:

> . . . Two little boys carry our baskets of medicine and make lengthy explanations when necessary. We have to walk for about twenty minutes towards Wushimiao, and when we can walk no farther we get into a boat. After leaving the boat we have another walk of about ten minutes around the enclosure of the powder factory, then a similar lake has to be crossed. Then our "beat" commences. We have a hill, a long stretch of road and a longer stretch of the Han bank. Lately another hill has been added. On land the people have straw mats supported by bamboos and use them for homes. The Bei-Wu (padded quilt) is spread on the ground in most cases, and the sick person or persons usually lie on the remote side of

275

it. As the poong-dze, or shelter, is no wider and not much higher than the bei-wu, we often have to crawl across the latter to reach the sick person. Most of the cases are dysentery and malaria cases. Daily baptisms average nearly thirty, with fifty in one day as the highest so far.

The same Columban nun wrote a report on the Father Hugh Sands case, as nearly every one was doing, in the letter from China. "There is no news of Father Sands. . . . Father [James] Loughran went up to try to get in touch with him and had. . . . an almost miraculous escape. The Reds surrounded the village he was in, but he hid under a Chinese bed and his 'boy' got a brain wave. He had a boat near at hand and had Father wrapped in a Bei-Wu, his head bound up in Chinese fashion, and carried him away as a sick man who was going to the doctor. . . ."

Father Abraham Shackleton, in his *History of Hanyang*, quotes an unnamed priest through an extract from a letter of August, 1931:

Father Aedan (McGrath) and I separated for a moment. When I next came upon him he was treating the most pitiful case I have ever witnessed or hope to witness again. An old Chinese woman lay helpless in her mat shed in the burning heat of August. The place was literally black with flies of the worm-generating, blue-headed type. From head to foot she was covered with worms. Father Aedan was bending over her, brushing the worms away. At that moment a pagan came to tell me that his daughter was dying. He took me a long way but we arrived just in time. I baptized her immediately and in five minutes she was dead. When I returned, half an hour later, Father Aedan, now joined by Father Jim Fisher, was still at his task. . . .

The flood, with all of its attendant horrors, continued through most of September. The reports of Father Hugh Sands which came in through Mah Hsien Sen, and from other sources, were few. He was, apparently, at Red Lake and alive. Ten thousand Chinese dollars in ransom would probably procure his ransom but Bishop Galvin did not dare to set such a precedent and Dr. O'Dwyer decreed bluntly: "If a demanded ransom payment would endanger other priests, it should not be made."

In mid-September, Bishop Galvin wrote to Father McGoldrick:

I have organized the priests, virgins and teachers into bands of Red Cross workers. Each priest has his refugee camp and his own team. They are on the job every day. They dispense medicine and, in general, help the sick as best they can. The Columban Sisters are working day and night. They deal with over 150 cases in the dispensary each day and take care of the sick in our own houses. They sure are great women. Everyone of us is working like the dickens. From the beginning of the flood until now, our priests and Sisters have attended 102,846 sick people. During that time they have baptized 4,223 dying pagan babies and adults. At the moment this work goes on as intensely as ever and we expect it to continue for many months to come.

Colonel and Mrs. Charles A. Lindbergh flew over eight thousand square miles of the flooded area in the making of an aerial survey for the Nanking Government in September. The nuns, to their great disappointment, did not obtain a glimpse of them.

There was a slackening of new water flow from mid-September onward and on September 29 the water started to recede. Small patches of land appeared in the vast watery expanses.

Father Sands was living, obviously in unhappy, unhealthy prison quarters, but he had in some manner obtained a pad of paper and he wrote many notes, some of which reached the outside world, ultimately falling into the hands of priests. In one letter he said that he was crowded in with sixty-six other prisoners, all of whom were held for ransom, and that the place was squalid, filthy, infested with vermin and rats. "There are," he wrote, "two buckets in two corners of the room, with no screens, and they are the W.C."

In another note he said: "The Commies tried to wreck a pagan temple near here. The pagan priests warned them but they did not stop. All the men became ill and the Commander did not recover until he actually handed over to pagan priests the money necessary to repair the temple. The spiritual world, of course, lies close to the Chinese people. Nature has predisposed them to be credulous, perhaps to be too credulous."

Two other Sands notes which "came out" were widely quoted in Columban circles. He wrote: "Fighting men are

277

seldom gentle or humane. While they remain fighting men, they cannot be so. A Chinese proverb says: 'A humane man is not fit to command armies.' The first business of the Reds is fighting, at least for the present, and so they must have the courage of warriors. Those who have watched them, and those who know best, can affirm that they have exactly that."

In another mood, Father Sands wrote: "Up to the time I arrived here, I had a sort of feeling that Communism in China was not exactly opposed to the Church, as such, and this seems to be the impression it tries to create when it first begins propaganda in a Christian district. I was quickly disillusioned."

Again, he wrote: "Nothing dries more quickly than a tear."

The writing, in the estimation of his contemporaries, helped him to retain his sanity and by not writing specifically of his captors, and seldom of his surroundings, he avoided trouble for himself and his messengers. In each letter, in addition to the type of material quoted, he did provide clues to his own health and mental attitude. Bishop Galvin was concerned on this score and had told Mah Hsien Sen that if Father Sands were ill or seemed in danger, ransom negotiations should be started immediately.

The receding of the waters did not noticeably simplify the situation in Hanyang. As late as October 25, a report stated that the Columban nun who ran the pharmacy prepared twenty-five medicine baskets daily. "The Bishop and several of his priests go every day to Deai Tien," Sister M. Patrick wrote. "Bishop Galvin said the other day that he never realized how many babies were dying and that he wished he had more Sisters to assign to Baby work."

Columban news was being made around the world in November, 1931, but it was difficult for those in Hanyang to concentrate upon events beyond their own tragic region. Fathers Owen MacPolin, Jeremiah Pigott and Edmund Lane, sent to Rome by the superior general, were received in special audience by His Holiness Pope Pius XI. An exceptionally large contingent of Columban priests left for the East; among them was Father John Henaghan, one of the original five who had launched the work in 1916.

Lastly, and of great importance, Rev. Patrick Cleary

sailed to China as ecclesiastical superior of Kienchang. Doctor Cleary was one of the original Columbans who came into the society during its organization period. One of the most brilliant of Maynooth professors, he had been appointed professor and rector at Dalgan and the Columban priests who came after him were, with a few exceptions, men who had studied under him. He was a tall, handsome, poised young man described by an associate as having "more the look of a poet than of a fighter, but watch out!" He was a surprise replacement for the matyred Father Tierney, because Columbans thought of him as a scholar rather than as a priest of the line, but his appointment was a popular one.

As the water went slowly down in China, the immense post-flood task began. One does not pick up again where one left off at a flood's beginning. The water, when it receded, left mud and silt behind, and dead human beings and dead animals. A house that has been under water carries an evil smell even when there are no corpses in it. Many of the houses contained corpses. Furniture that had not been carried away had to be dried and, if possible, repaired. Buildings and broken bits of buildings that had settled down on the wrong land challenged a man's strength to remove them, and he could not farm again until his land was cleared. The dwellers in towns faced discouraging tasks of drying out, cleaning out, replacing. China, always a strain on sensitive nostrils, never smelled worse.

Contaminated water, and the well-nigh impossible task of maintaining any sanitary regulations in the crowded refugee camps, were contributors to epidemic, the great terror that followed flood. There were so many people with nowhere to go, people who had lost everything they had owned and whose houses had been washed away.

The priests and nuns faced the problems of after-flood as they had faced their emergencies, and with no more spare time on their hands. The Sisters of St. Columban did the major work of nursing, but the Sisters of Loretto found few rest periods. A letter from one them in November, 1931, reported: "All of us. . . . are feeling fine, but too busy to breathe. Think of it—a Catechumenate; a school; 250 girls, making all the mattresses, pillows, sheets and pajamas for the Red Cross emergency hospital, visiting the camp, having each day Adoration till nine in the morning, giving meals to three priests, training their new cook, nursing the sick, burying the dead, giving cholera injections and oodles of other activities. We have no time to be sick."

It was the Chinese custom to chant prayers. Every evening, as the shadows moved in, the voices of men, women and children rose and the words of The Lord's Prayer floated in the chill air. In the Hanyang dialect, it sounded like this:

"Zy tien wo den foo dzai, wo den yuen ur min jen sin, or quai lingueh, eur dz tien shen yu dee, yu wu tien yen Wo den wong ur, jin er yung wo, wo wu yung liang, wu mien wo dzy yu ngo yee mien fung wo dzy dzeh, yow boo wo shoo shen yu yow gan, ly jow wo yu shung wo Ya-mong."

They chanted the Hail Mary, too, and this is the way it sounded:

"Sin ur foo Ma lee ya, men bay sin tung dzey, ju yu wu sha yen, noo dzung ur way dzamai, ur thy dz Ye so, bing way dze mai; Tien-Ju Sin-Mung Ma lee-ya, way wo den dzaylen, Jinchee Tien-Ju Jee wo den su ho Ya mong."

Writing in November to Father McCarthy in Omaha, Bishop Galvin said: "God is testing us in strange ways. No young mission, it seems to me, has had to face what we have gone through these last years. We certainly ought to be proud of the priests whom God gave us."

At the same time he faced the fact that his money was running out. With his churches outside of Hanyang closed by water or Communists, he had been able to divert all of his operating budget to caring for the unfortunate. A great many of those who were helped had ceased to ask for aid as soon as they had a fighting chance of survival without it, but there were a great many still on the two hills, pagan and Catholic, who would die without help and the winter was closing in.

The bishop called a meeting of his priests. He had built a fund from donations and bequests which belonged solely to the vicariate of Hanyang, money that had come to him rather than to the society. He had built it against any unforeseen disaster that might threaten the continued existence of the missions. He had hoped, too, that

280

it would grow to a point where the income from it would support much that became necessary in the operation of missions. Now the money was in the bank and the people were out there on the hill. He faced his priests and asked them what he should do.

There was no unanimity of opinion. These men were anticipating a return to full mission operation shortly. They knew how grievously the physical shell of the vicariate had been damaged. It would take a great deal of money to restore the churches, the schools. Each priest knew that his people, returning to wrecked villages and ruined farms, would need help as badly as these refugees in Hanyang. There had to be money in the future and it would be as badly needed then as in the bleak present. The priests pointed out the need as they saw it and they could offer to the refugee problem of the present only the hope that, if the spending of Catholic funds tightened, the unfortunate might seek aid from other sources. They spoke, too, of the danger that lay in the spending of capital. Yet no one, despite the individual arguments which were conscientiously advanced, wanted to abandon the people on the hills.

Bishop Galvin heard them all. It was part of his technique in handling men to seek the opinions and advice of even the youngest men under him not always agreeing with the opinions or acting on the advice, but listening patiently. He ran his hand through his hair as he invariably did when he was struggling with a difficulty.

"It will probably cost us one hundred thousand dollars, Mex, to keep these people alive till they can get along without us," he said. "We can't expect to raise anything close to that sum with appeals, but we have very nearly that much money in the bank."

He paused and looked around the table. "God gave us that money," he said, "and God gave us these people on the hills. We are going to give the money back to Him."

There wasn't a dissenting voice.

On November 22, 1931, Father Hugh Sands, still in captivity, wrote: "When the Reds came to Sien-Tao-Chen, they destroyed most of my belongings, including my violin. When they came again in October, they destroyed whatever they had overlooked on their first visit. This time they took my *Music in Ireland* compiled by Captain

O'Neill, a wonderful book and now, alas, out of print. When I had nothing left, they came and took myself. But I must not complain. It is all in a day's work "

On the next day, a long siege of bargaining between Mah Hsien Sen and the Communists came to a climax when the Reds agreed to accept four thousand dollars Mexican ransom for Father Sands. Mah delivered the money and one of the Communist leaders walked into the small room where the Columban was confined with thirty-two other hapless individuals.

"Your ransom has been paid," he said curtly. "You may go."

Father Hugh Sands straightened slowly. He had been bent over a prone Franciscan, Father Lazzeri, who was old and ill, trying to persuade the priest to eat some of the repulsive food which was their only diet. He looked up at the Communist and rose slowly to his feet.

"What about him?" he said, gesturing toward Father Lazzeri.

"Nothing. Nobody has paid his ransom."

Father Sands stood unmoving. Today was the feast of St. Columban; he had been praying to the patron for release, and the society, certainly, had stretched a point in his favor by paying a ransom. He wanted to go, to leave this stinking, revolting prison, but he was young and strong and he could exist in it; the Franciscan priest was old and growing weaker. This was a terrible place in which to die.

"Let *him* go!" he told the Communist. "He can have my ransom."

An hour later Father Sands watched the Franciscan walk out. The man had never been a pleasant companion. He was querulous, complaining, pessimistic, depressing. In accepting his release he was neither gracious nor seemingly grateful. Father Sands did not expect gratitude, nor did he resign his own hope of release in surrendering his ransom to a man who had no other hope of rescue. He wrote a note two days later which revealed the hope that he held:

"A dark, wet November day, cold and as cheerless as the stones that mark the pagan graves around me. And yet it is a day of hope for me, of a certain hope that I will soon be free to say Mass again. I am alone now. Father Lazzeri is gone. He is now on his way to Hankow."

282

Father Hugh F. Sands, on that November day in 1931, could not foresee the fact that it would be May 9, 1932, before he walked out of his prison and that for all of his life, he would suffer from the effects of his imprisonment.

In Hanyang another effort to ransom Father Sands had been started as soon as the incredible news was received that he had given his own freedom to another man. The Reds, however, raised the ransom price, certain that they would get it, and the Columbans could not encourage such tactics. Another stalemate developed. Hanyang, with the flood behind it, was still a place of trouble.

Bishop Galvin wrote on December 1:

> In the Columban Sisters' Convent which we converted into a refuge shelter, Father Crossan and I slept on the floor of the bathroom. It was difficult to snatch any sleep. In that house the lamps were never extinguished. The peace and quiet of a hospital ward were entirely absent; women and children tramped up and down the stairs the whole night long. There was a continual babel of voices, intermingled with the moans of the dying. The pitiful wails of sick and fretful children were never for a moment stilled. The people were dying rapidly, at the rate of four or five per day. Cholera takes but 12 to 24 hours to do its deadly work and is so infectious that the body has to be removed and coffined immediately after the patient dies. The coffins were carried out for burial in the early hours of the morning and a wailing crowd of refugees followed them to the door of the compound. Every day for two months, five carpenters were busily engaged making coffins. I could never pass the little shed where they worked without a shudder.

In December Father Patrick Cleary, accompanied by Father Joseph Mullen, reached China. They had bade farewell to Father Heneghan at Manila. After a visit with Bishop Galvin, Father Cleary proceeded to his own mission field at Kienchang.

In the United States three Columban fathers were ordained by The Most Reverend Joseph Rummel, Bishop of Omaha. Father McCarthy, writing of the event, mentioned that the depression was deepening in the United States: "investments frozen, people out of work, money to the Church much less and Communism on the rise, even in the Colleges."

283

The year 1932 began on a low note as far as political situations were concerned, but there were seventy Columban priests on active duty in the missions and 248 students in Columban seminaries. The second Columban bishop, The Most Reverend Romuald Hayes, superior in Australia, was named Bishop of Rockhampton, Queensland, Australia, by the Holy See.

In August, 1932, Chiang Kai-shek returned to power after more than a year in eclipse. He immediately launched a drive on the Communist forces which had held China in a paralyzing grip since the great flood. On November 8, 1932, Bishop Galvin could write:

"Peace has come at last but the war is on, the real war for souls. Thousands are coming into the Church all over the Vicariate. In Hanyang City, twenty more families handed in their names yesterday. It is the same story all over—a landslide of conversions. The sufferings of last year and of the years that are past are now bearing fruit."

Bishop E. J. Galvin was fifty years old on November 23, 1932. The flood and the Communists had put lines on his face but there was still youth in his eyes and he stood straight. The superior general visited Hanyang and his report confirmed that made by Bishop Galvin. Writing from Hanyang to Father E. J. McCarthy in Omaha Dr. O'Dwyer said:

". . . without more priests, care cannot be taken of 10% of those who are seeking admission. The remarkable thing is the number of well-to-do people or gentry, who are anxious to enter the Church. Apart from the Grace of God, there is no explanation except the relief given by Sisters and priests during the flood and famine, the prayers of the people, and the heroic endurance and sufferings of the priests during the Red Terror. Every available priest is up to his eyes in work."

One of the young priests, Father T. Frank Powers, saying his first Christmas Mass in China at Chi Wu Tai, had a surprise and wrote of it in a letter home:

"There is a thunder of explosives at the Consecration, and one can easily believe that another war has broken out. Nothing of the sort. Our pious Chinese, with their beloved firecrackers, are merely welcoming the Saviour who has come down to earth."

284

25 : : TE DEUM

The priests were out in the parishes again and the Communists had lost even the stronghold of Red Lake. "In Sien Taochen parish about 10,000 pagans have handed in their names," Bishop Galvin wrote. "One hundred pagan familes in Hanyang are now under instruction. We have day schools for women and night schools for the men. It is the same all over the Vicariate."

It was a new sensation to have pagans peacefully hammering on the door of the Church. It meant hard work for months and years ahead, but there was real joy in the contemplation of it. Morale in the society's large and small spots in China had never been better than it was in the months after the water had subsided. Men and women could look back and richly enjoy the incidents and events which they had not had time to enjoy in the time of happening.

There had been one dark night after a horrible day on the hills of Hanyang. It was hot and the air stank and the sick women and children were crying out. Bishop Galvin, who had been working hard himself since early morning, stopped to talk to an obviously weary Sister M. Michael of the Columban Sisters.

"I'm distressed, sore distressed," he said, "when I think that I am responsible for bringing you out to all of this when you could be happy at home in holy Ireland."

Sister Mary Michael blinked at him. Her eyes were red. "Ah, sure," she said. "Nothing at all so interesting as this could ever happen to us in Ireland, Monsignor."

There was one expedient of the flood months that was destined to grow into a great and vital movement. Bishop Galvin was baffled by the difficulty of working among the Chinese women, even when their need was great. Custom denied to men, other than the individual husbands, any approach to women, whether the man be priest or doctor. There were not nuns enough to take care of even extreme cases and it was obvious that too many women were dying. Faced with this dilemma, Bishop Galvin thought of the Virgins, women who had devoted their lives to the service of the Church as catechists or teachers. The flood had driven these women into Hanyang as it had driven in the rest of the people. Bishop Galvin called in one whom he knew and greatly respected. Her name was Paula Wu.

"Paula," he said, "I need the Virgins. I need as many as you can find. I want you to go among the sick and dying and the frightened, as the nuns do. The nuns will instruct you."

"That was August 15th," Bishop Galvin said later, "which suggested the name for this group. We called them 'St. Mary's' and they called their own society when they assembled in community, 'Sen Mung Tang,' which means 'Blessed Mother's House.' Paula was the first of the Hanyang Virgins of Mary. She was a kind and gentle soul."

The girls and the women assembled by Paula Wu did remarkable work during the emergency and they formed, ultimately, a splendid order of native born Chinese nuns.

The flood left orphans, too, in Hanyang, and children without parents made a strong appeal to Bishop Galvin. Poor though he was after a long period of extraordinary expense, he started the building of a two-story brick orphanage for boys in a Hanyang suburb on October 10, 1933. It housed eighty youngsters eventually. They came in at the age of eight and stayed until they learned crafts; boat-making, beer-making, jewelers' work.

Outside of China the St. Columban Society continued to expand. On October 2 a new seminary, designed to relieve overcrowding at Silver Creek, was opened at Bristol, Rhode Island. In November, 1933, the society entered Korea. Father Owen MacPolin was installed as superior and provided with a staff of young priests from the class of 1932.

The Sisters of Loretto at the Foot of the Cross took on the responsibility of a school in Shanghai. The school was known as Ecole Sainte Famille and had been operated by the Helpers of the Holy Souls, an order of French nuns which had found its pupils among the children of the White Russians; as the Russian numbers diminished, the nuns seemingly did not know how to build student enrollment to replace them. Sisters Mary Jane and Maureen went down from Hanyang to take over the school and other Sisters of Loretto started for Shanghai from Kentucky. Only then, with a staff committed, did the Lorettines discover that the Helpers of the Holy Souls were transferring their school to them, but not the buildings. In August, with the fall school enrollment less than a month away, Sisters Mary Jane and Maureen had to find school buildings in crowded Shanghai, equip them and attract students. They did it, and their student enrollment for the first year totaled 167.

Father J. Charles (Charlie) O'Brien arrived in Hanyang and, within twenty-four hours, was appointed secretary to the bishop. He lived in the bishop's house, learned to sign the bishop's name to correspondence and was closer than anyone else to the bishop himself.

There were times during this period when Bishop Galvin remembered vividly the dream he had had for China while he was still in Ireland, when active service on the mission firing line was only a dream. He had seen armies of priests invading China, churches being built and vast multitudes of pagans coming up from the rivers and down from the hills to Mass. He saw hospitals for their ill and homes for their orphans and schools for their children. He had clenched his fists and prayed desperately when that vision came to him: "If I ask too much, O Lord, I'll be grateful for the part you give me."

He had it all. There were worries and vexations and he had too few priests and too little money. He had to move slowly when he wanted to leap and to run; but the pagans, thank God, were pouring down out of the hills and up from the rivers.

"They simply mobbed the various mission stations," Father William McGoldrick wrote, "clamouring for instruction and for entrance in this wonderful Church which they had seen for the first time at close quarters when they flocked to Hanyang from the all-covering waters. Not dozens or hundreds, but thousands, asked to be received into the Church. . . ."

The key figure, of course, where priests were few, was the catechist. Bishop Galvin once defined a catechist as "a layman, experienced and exemplary, who takes up residence in the village and devotes his days and nights to teaching Christian doctrine."

Father Francis J. Herlihy, a young Columban, wrote a more intimate definition:

> He is the missioner's mouthpiece, his representative, his messenger, his alter ego. He has access to places and persons that the missioner cannot reach. He has command of intricacies of language that a foreigner may never hope to equal. He must be gifted with more than ordinary intelligence for on his judgement, his prudence and his tact will depend the solution of many problems, perhaps the conversion or loss of a whole district. He must be zealous and unflagging in his efforts if the Faith is to gain ground and not to lose it. He must be obedient or his activities will hinder rather than aid the plans of the priest. He must be a hundred other things besides: humble, that his official position will not antagonize the flock; pious and well-instructed that he may competently instruct others; well-educated, and in some sense a man of culture, that he may command respect, both for himself and the Church. Above all, he must be, in his own life and character, a man above reproach.

It is astonishing that priests should expect to find such men in the country districts of China, and more astonishing that they actually found them. A catechist had a full-time job once a priest employed him and although his wage was little, he needed that little. A priest with many towns and villages in his parish was often hard-pressed to meet his payroll, the living expenses of people who were all but indispensable.

Father Timothy Leahy had a hundred villages in his parish of Chang Tan Kow. He was one of the many Columbans about whom a novel might easily have been written. He was thirty-one when he turned to the Columban Society, older than most applicants, but he was that rarity among priests, a born missionary. He was in Hanyang in 1930 and when the flood came, he was one of the laborers. He was installed as pastor in Chang Tan Kow in October, 1932.

"I went out with the expectation that conversions would be slow," he said. "The people came to me. They asked for catechists. I foolishly promised that if they passed their catechism exam to the teacher's satisfaction,

288

they could come down in the off-season, after the rice planting, to my mission and spend six weeks intensive study prior to being baptized. That was towards the end of the year and I thought no more about it."

After the Chinese New Year, February, 1933. Father Leahy was sitting before his home, well wrapped, enjoying the pale winter sun, when he raised his eyes and beheld the whole horizon in motion; there was every kind of conveyance, wheelbarrows predominating, with all sorts of cooking utensils piled into them and human beings behind and beside them.

"It took well nigh miraculous organizing to house and take care of the horde which had descended upon me," Father Leahy said. "We had to rent a number of neighboring houses. In my house, in the church, in the school —everywhere, there were boarders. And from morning to night the buzz of catechism questions and answers, prayers and everything else that goes toward making a thorough Catholic. The buzz never ceased. As the Chinese chant their prayers you can imagine what this up-country philharmonic sounded like."

The flood of seekers after faith in Father Tim Leahy's parish was duplicated in other parishes throughout the vicariate.

The idea of the Church as something kindly and helpful and charitable had been firmly established in the minds of the people. [Bishop Galvin wrote]. In any pagan country where the masses have no clear conception of God and only vague, uninspiring ideas of the next life, they must first be attracted to the true religion by something that they can see and feel. It is through some medium helpful to their bodies, that one must reach their souls. If you speak to a pagan about serving God and attaining eternal salvation, you leave him quite cold. He does not understand you. But he does understand charity and sympathy and friendship.

On June 20, 1934, Bishop E. J. Galvin observed his Silver Jubilee, his twenty-fifth year in the priesthood. One of the Sisters of Loretto wrote: "Today Bishop Galvin came to say Mass for us in our chapel, praying for our intentions. He is a real father to us all. For the Bishop's Jubilee the Fathers wanted to have a big celebration, but

289

His Excellency would not have it. He told them to have a little dinner for the home folk and no more. We wanted to give a dinner here in our place but he said that he wanted prayers and he knew that we were praying for him, and that was enough."

In August, 1934, Father Edward J. McCarthy, who had gone through a serious illness, resigned as superior of the Society of St. Columban in the United States. He was succeeded by Father Paul Waldron.

There was more to the story of Father Ned McCarthy than was apparent in an official announcement and Ned Galvin grieved for him. The man whom he called "Mac" had been one of the first group of raw, inexperienced young men who launched a society with little understanding of what they were doing. Big "Mac" was the man who had joined young Father Galvin in Omaha; tireless, inventive, full of ideas, never discouraged by huge piles of work ahead of him. Round-faced, the owner of a good smile and a sometimes preposterous idea of what was funny, Ned McCarthy got things done and, right or wrong, stuck stubbornly to any idea that enlisted his interest. He wrote thousands of letters, bore patiently with the gripes, difficulties and discouragements of Columbans all over the map, and answered their letters. He was the genius behind the establishment of the society in the United States, the builder of its seminaries.

He was out now, less in rank, and illness was only part of the story. His situation was very similar to that of Father John Blowick many years earlier. Ned Mac had never understood money, although he believed firmly that he understood it very well. The society had been hurt in the stock market crash, and that had been a fairly common experience. The brutal blow, however, was the heavy obligation with which the society was burdened through Father Ned McCarthy's annuity scheme. He had sold annuities to Catholics for years through *The Far East* and if the stock market had stayed happily prosperous, his scheme might have worked out. When it crashed around his ears, the society was stuck with a staggering long-term debt. The planner and designer of a scheme so disastrous could not remain as head of the society in the United States.

Nothing whatever could be done about it and Father

290

McCarthy's health broke under the strain and the worry and the sense of failure. There was irony in the fact that one of the pioneers, after a series of Herculean accomplishments, should pass from a position of influence at a time when the society was entering upon its period of greatest glory.

Father Troy, a secular priest and a cousin of Father Leahy's, said his Mass on Sunday, September 9, in Tsan-Dan-Kow and wrote a letter that afternoon: "There must have been a thousand people all told," he wrote. "This is the parish where, two years ago, 16,000 people applied to enter the Church. . . . Given sufficient men and money at that time, it is most likely that 8,000 of these people could have been instructed in the course of two years. As it was, though the Bishop helped to his last penny, the Tsan Dan Kow priests were forced to confine their activitities to some 3,000 of those would-be converts. . . ."

Men and money! Bishop Galvin struggled with those two problems, more than a little desperate at the knowledge that people who wanted to be Catholics were being lost to the Faith. "A family converted in this generation may mean a native Chinese priest or Sister in the next," he wrote. "A village of twelve families which becomes Catholic this year, by natural increase will become, perhaps, twenty-five Catholic families in twenty years. On the other hand, one possible conversion halted today may mean ten thwarted for the next year. It is heart-breaking for a missionary to be confronted, in a year of special opportunity, with an insufficiency of men and resources."

He decided to do something about that problem of men and resources. His sacrifice of money in behalf of the people during the flood months had been almost miraculously compensated. Readers of *The Far East*, learning of the suffering in Hanyang, had sent in an unprecedented number of offerings. The readers of *The Far East*, however, could not do it all. Through correspondence with Dr. O'Dwyer, Bishop Galvin made his own plan for meeting the increased need of the years ahead.

He was invited to the Eucharistic Congress in Australia in November. He would go from there to the United States and spend time in fund raising. He would then go to Rome and report to the Holy Father on the great

291

awakening of faith in China. He would go home to Ireland and talk in behalf of vocations. It would mean a long absence from Hanyang but the time for that absence was favorable. He was needed less, it seemed to him, than at any time since he first came out.

The National Eucharistic Congress at Melbourne, Australia, was held December 2-9, 1934. Bishop Galvin arrived a week early, looking forward to Australia and to the event. He had no forebodings, but the Australian visit was to be one of the notable failures of his life.

The congress was the creation of The Most Reverend Daniel Mannix, Archbishop of Melbourne. In attendance were ecclesiastical dignitaries from all parts of the world, including His Eminence Joseph Cardinal MacRory, Archbishop of Armagh and Primate of All Ireland.

Despite the spiritual splendor of the congress, the assembly depressed The Most Reverend Edward J. Galvin. The atmosphere generated in a gathering of highly rated prelates was too heavy for him. Despite all the dictates of reason, he withdrew from the social gatherings at which attendance was not compulsory and participated in small, intense, mission-operation discussions at which he was the only participant of top rank. One of his friendly contemporaries remonstrated with him on this:

"Look, you are missing the cream of this gathering," he was told. "These bishops do favors for one another. They borrow stories and anecdotes from one another and tell them at home. You are missing financial support and word-of-mouth advertising and a pleasant time. These meeting zealots can do nothing for you or anyone else. They are shooting off steam. Nobody will pay any attention to what is said or done at their debating sessions. Those meetings are arranged to keep them busy, to give them something to do."

"They make sense," Bishop Galvin said. "They are discussing mission problems."

He must have known that there was much truth in what the other man told him, but he did not establish the friendly relationships that he might have established among his highly ranked brethren, nor with the laymen who associated themselves with bishops.

"He did practically nothing in Australia to help further the standing of St. Columban's Society," a disappointed
292

commentator wrote. "He let slip a great opportunity to boost enthusiasm for the Chinese Mission."

As a climax to his Australian debacle, Bishop Galvin accepted an invitation to make an appeal for funds in Brisbane. In accepting the Brisbane offer, the bishop acted against the advice of Father Luke Mullany, Columban superior in Australia. Father Mullany had reason to believe that it would have been better to have waited in Melbourne and conducted his appeal for funds there, where the society was better known. Immediately after the congress, Bishop Galvin went alone to Brisbane, where he met with only moderate success.

The bishop did not delude himself that he had done well in Australia or that he had accomplished what he had hoped to accomplish.

"The best day I had," he wrote later, "was the day at the Sydney Zoo with Luke [Mullany]. They have a troupe of chimpanzees there that are an embarrassment to people."

The Columban missions in the Philippine Islands were a second stop on the bishop's tour and one to which he looked forward with keen anticipation. He was interested in the missions and their problems and he was eager to see again that original of the society, Father John Henaghan.

Time had done little to Father Henaghan save sprinkle gray in his hair. He was tall and erect, with deep-set eyes. Men in the society said that he was Ned Galvin's only rival as a storyteller. The two men sat and talked of the force that dominated their days; the mission and its people, the drama and the humor of it.

"You know, Ned," Father Henaghan said, "these Filipinos are strange beings. They are Catholics from away back, even when they've forgotten that, and you can become very encouraged about them. Then, somehow, they always let you down."

Bishop Galvin laughed. "On another day, in another mood, you'd say something else about them," he said.

They went out to visit the church and Father Henaghan said, "I find it hard, even after Ireland, to understand the concern of these people with saints. Everyone has his favorite and the first thing that any Filipino does when he enters a church is head for his saint's image. They ignore the main altar entirely."

The two priests entered the empty church. A Filipino couple, man and woman, entered the church a few minutes after them, marching solemnly down the center aisle to kneel devoutly before the main altar. Bishop Galvin chuckled. Father Henaghan spread his hands apart resignedly.

"As I told you, Ned," he said, "they always let you down."

While Bishop Galvin was on his journey, three more Columban Sisters sailed for Hanyang. More importantly, the first Columban Sisters sailed who were assigned to Monsignor Patrick Cleary's mission which had been erected into the prefecture of Kienchang in 1933. Their assigned work was a registered school, an orphanage, a catechumenate, a dispensary and a community of virgins. In the latter, young Chinese girls were to be trained in the religious life.

Monsignor Cleary's report on his town was without pretense: "We have no electric light but we have telephone wires enough for a county. We have no water supply, no plumbing, no hospital, no bakery, no beef, no mutton. But we import Palmolive soap and Parisian cosmetics; we get an occasional case of Korean apples and Sunkist oranges. . . we may even have our share in a case of beer or a box of Three Castles cigarettes. We cannot purchase a bolt or a screw or a nail . . . but we have wireless and machine guns and armored cars."

Bishop Galvin celebrated St. Patrick's Day, 1935, in San Francisco. He reached Denver on March 22 and one of his calls was on Monsignor William O'Ryan, whom he had met in Europe years before.

In a public address quoted by the *Denver Catholic Register*, Monsignor O'Ryan said: "I believe that Bishop Galvin has done more and greater work for the Church than any Irishman for centuries."

On March 25 Bishop Galvin wrote from Omaha to Dr. Michael O'Dwyer:

"I am feeling pretty well. I have heard from Ireland that my mother has lost her mind. Ned Mac went to see her and she didn't know him."

Worries about conditions in Ireland or in Hanyang might distress him, but Bishop Galvin was in the United States for a purpose and he did not let himself be diverted from that purpose. He saw bishops and Catholic leaders and he talked to groups. He had cities which he liked, and he had friends, but he was not influenced by liking or friendship; he went where he seemed to have the best chance of financial support. Occasionally, very occasionally, he could be himself, with no specific end to serve, no funds to raise.

On April 25 he went to Loretto, Kentucky, where he was requested to bestow the habit of the Sisters of Loretto on each of thirteen postulants. Among the thirteen were two young Chinese girls from his own vicariate. The occasion was the 123rd anniversary of the foundation of the Sisters of Loretto. Before he left Loretto, the bishop wrote to each of the Sisters of Loretto in Hanyang, enclosing in every letter a violet from the garden of Loretto's motherhouse.

Bishop Galvin had two devices that he used when he was granted an opportunity to speak before Catholic assemblies anywhere. He offered a parish an opportunity to adopt a parish in China by making a payment of one thousand dollars and promising to maintain interest. The adopting parish was given the name of the Chinese parish and of its pastor, who could write letters and send pictures, reporting progress made. In groups where no adoption plan was practicable, the bishop offered membership in the Mission Auxiliaries of St. Columban for one dollar and the promise of a prayer every Sunday; in addition, each member was guaranteed one personal letter from China each year. Both of these ideas were new and the bishop was highly successful with them. Because the need was constant and forever urgent, he cabled money to Hanyang regularly.

"I have met no mean priest except one Irishman, and he was a narrow one," he wrote from Chicago. "He gave me twenty-five dollars to get rid of me. Peace be to him."

Father Paul Waldron, in Omaha, worried about the bishop's health and his lack of care for himself. When the bishop went to Minnesota, Waldron urged him to take a few days for a Mayo Clinic checkup and did not even receive a reply to his suggestion. Several times he urged time out for dentistry and finally Galvin exploded, "Don't write to me any more about dentists!"

His correspondence was usually pleasant on the personal side, with few complaints or criticisms, but he went sharply on record May 24 with one of his favorite priests of the society, Father Paddy O'Connor, editor of *The Far East*. "I would be very grateful," he wrote, "if you would not refer to me as the founder of the Society. That is just not true."

There was another flood in China, and in parts of his vicariate; not as monstrously overpowering as the big flood, but bad enough. The bishop read the newspaper accounts and watched for mail. One of the Sisters at Loretto, Kentucky, sent him a copy of a July 11 letter written by a new nun in Hanyang:

"This morning we visited the Chinese Sisters at St. Mary's, Hanyang. . . . On the occasion of our visit, the water having risen during the night, we found the Sisters using a door for a raft and floating around on this improvised sampan through their rooms. . . ."

Not until July did the bishop reach his beloved Brooklyn. He had encountered vast changes everywhere he went; great highways, heavy automobile traffic, large cities grown larger. He had seen radio towers in great numbers and had listened to fine programs, remembering the crystal set to which he had listened with a headset when he first came to Omaha. He was not, however, prepared for one change in Brooklyn, because for once no one had written to him.

On January 31, 1934, two youngsters had deliberately and wantonly set fire to Holy Rosary Church. There was little that the fire department could do and the old structure was destroyed by flame. The new church on the old location, with its bright and shining rectory, had no associations for the man from China. At the invitation of Monsignor Joseph Kelly, pastor of Holy Rosary, he made his home in the rectory while in Brooklyn, but the neighborhood had changed, too, and the people. Most of his friends had moved elsewhere.

"The Bishop of Brooklyn [The Most. Rev. Thomas E. Molloy] was very fine," he wrote to Paddy O'Connor, "and he gave me the freedom of the diocese. 'It goes without saying,' he told me, 'that we couldn't refuse you anything.' "

There were other cities along the east coast to be

296

visited and then a return to Brooklyn. On October 27 the bishop wrote to Father Paul Waldron: "I am all in just at the moment." He had, on that date, started his day with ten Masses at which he preached. In the afternoon he talked to a mission circle, then carried the Blessed Sacrament in procession for two hours. He had dinner with a group of priests, made a speech and listened to several. He went home after 10 P.M. and wrote letters.

The bishop's nocturnal habits impressed his host in Brooklyn. "During the day we saw little of him," Monsignor Kelly wrote. "After breakfast he went off visiting priests. . . . After supper he retired to his room and typed letters until 11 P.M. [Then he] declared recreation. He visited the kitchen and fixed himself a meal of bread and butter and milk. . . . I joined him one night. . . . [and] never missed after that while he was in the house. We had a most interesting hour of conversation until midnight and sometimes for an hour after that."

Father John F. Cowhig in from China, joined Bishop Galvin in November and took over the speaking engagements. The bishop had his reservation to sail on the *Rex* for Rome on November 16—tourist class.

Monsignor Kelly and his two curates, Fathers Hugh Kenny and Bert Reardon, pleaded with him to let them buy him a first-class ticket so that he could travel in accordance with his status as a bishop. They brought the matter up at the dinner table where they had him neatly surrounded. The bishop listened, then pushed back the dishes from in front of him and, leaning on the table, said:

"Wouldn't I look well on the promenade deck? A missionary bishop who goes around begging? Wouldn't people be entitled to the thought that I was spending their money on myself and on my own comfort?"

Father Reardon went with the bishop to buy some traveling bags, replacements for the two he had: one without a handgrip and the other held closed by a length of rope. As representative of the rectory, Reardon was instructed to buy good bags, but the bags which the bishop selected, and insisted upon having, cost $2.98 and $1.98 respectively.

"I carried that $2.98 bag up the gangplank of the *Rex* for the bishop," Monsignor Kelly wrote. "It was heavy,

297

and knowing what it had cost, I said a short prayer that it wouldn't burst before I got it up."

"It was wonderful having him in the house, a little like knowing St. Paul personally," Father Reardon said.

In Rome, Bishop Galvin had mission affairs, detailed and tedious, to discuss with Propaganda. He had an audience with Pope Pius XI.

"He knew far more about China than I expected him to know," the bishop said.

Bishop Galvin was in Dalgan on December 15 and ordained twenty-six young priests on the 22nd. He reached home, at Clodagh, on Christmas Eve.

His mother was in bed. She had been confined to her bed for two months or more. He went up to see her, and his brothers and sisters were in the room. "Mother," Kate called out. "Look who's come to see you."

Bishop Galvin walked to the bedside and she looked up into his face.

"I don't know him," she said. "I never saw him before."

He tried to tell her who he was and she closed her eyes. "Whoever you are, God bless you," she said.

The bishop wrote to his cousin, Jim Murphy, in Dorchester, Massachusetts:

"Next morning as I came down to Mass, I dropped into my Mother's room. I had on my soutane. As I opened the door, she sat up and stared at me. 'Oh, Father Ned,' she said, 'you have come back, and they never told me. You were away a long time.' I went downstairs and said Mass for her. I brought Holy Communion to her. From that time on to the day she died, she knew me the best of all. . . ."

"It is what the bishop wanted to believe," one of his brothers said, "but she never knew him any more than the others. She never knew him at all."

Ireland was having a severe winter. On January 20 the temperature dropped to six degrees in many places and there was snow on the ground.

On that January 20 a bulletin was issued at London which stated: "The King's life is moving peacefully toward its close." At five minutes before midnight, King George V died.

Bishop Galvin visited old friends and said Mass in many homes.

298

I dropped in to see everyone [he wrote]. Julia Mickle almost got a fainting spell. She was baking a cake. She couldn't shake hands with me. She didn't know what to do and all that she could say was that she was shamed forever. . . . In North Cork I called to see the mother of a priest. She never knew where she was until I was in the kitchen. She was gasping for air. "A bishop in the kitchen," she said. "Oh, my God! Let me out in the yard until I faint." She had two daughters but they fled. I said that I wanted tea and some hot cake. The two girls came in, the tea was made and the hot cake was just great. They all got over their fright and we got on famously.

It was a relaxed time in the life of Bishop Galvin, a time for picking up old memories and turning them over in his hands. He stayed into the spring. "The whole country has improved wonderfully," he wrote. "New houses are to be seen on all sides, and flowers and trees, and white-washed houses all show signs of new life and prosperity. The people are well dressed and autos are everywhere on the roads, which are remarkably good."

A woman whom he described as "a bright lady" asked him if, in all his travels, he had ever seen any place as nice as Newcestown. He assured her solemnly that he had not.

"I was in Newcestown many times," he wrote to Jim Murphy in Dorchester. "It has not changed. It is the same place you know. I liked to ramble around there and to think of the people who are gone. . . . It was good to be home, even for a little while. Nothing changes in New-cestown except the children. The youngsters spring up like daisies. I didn't know one of them."

Such simplicities engaged the bishop's time and attention as earnestly as did the profundities which dominated much of his life. He wrote joyously about small incidents in Ireland, about a new chapel which he described as "a plain, decent building," about Clodagh and Kilmurry: "The people here, in fact through all of the country, are so friendly when they get over their first burst of shyness. They are a great people, full of faith and goodness. There is no rush. It is all so peaceful and so placid. It is a country in which the people enjoy life."

299

Bishop Galvin did many things and saw many people but he did not go too far from where his mother lay.

> She got weaker daily [he reported], and when all expected it was the end, she would rally again. She was a very strong woman. But on March 17th a decided change came and next day, about noon, she turned her head over on the pillow and died as quietly as if she were going to sleep.
> She was buried in Kilmurry with them all. There was an immense crowd of people and a large number of priests. I said the Mass and Bishop Cohalan said the prayers at the graveside. So, in God's strange way, I was with her to the end. I anointed her and gave her all the last sacraments. It was a strange feeling to be anointing one's own mother. God rest her soul, she was a good woman. . . .

One returned to the demands made upon one. "I am planning to leave here for China early in June," Bishop Galvin wrote to Paul Waldron in Omaha. "I am glad that I came home if it were only for all the talks we had at Navan with the Superior and, especially, with John Blowick."

A few days later he was with his favorite brother-in-law, Jack O'Mahony, Kate's husband. Jack O'Mahony's eldest son, Donal, was now seventeen and had already completed his studies at Farranferris. He was going to De La Salle Secondary School in Macroom for the fall term and was definitely committed to becoming a Columban. The bishop was proud of his nephew, the first member of the family close to him to seek a mission career, but he was still reserved with him on the subject of his vocation. The bishop did not glamorize a missionary's life and did not like others to glamorize it. He was worried about the boy's obvious hero-worship of himself. He did not believe that anything less than a clear call to the missions was enough to power and sustain a vocation and he had assumed a negative attitude toward the boy's aspirations from the start.

On June 19 he wrote to his sister Kate, Donal's mother, and the letter reveals the problem which he had in communicating with those whom he held close in affection.

> I sail tomorrow for New York. I was lonely leaving you all. I was glad we had those days out and I shall long

remember the two days that Jack and Winnie, Donal, Mary and I had together. Winnie said I was sarcastic but you can tell her that I might have cried any minute during those two days and a man has to cover that up somehow. . . . I didn't say goodbye that evening to the children. I couldn't. God be with you, Kate. It was hard to leave you all but I am going back to China with happiness in my heart. It was good, oh so good, to come back and see you all, to lay Mother in the grave, and now let us go on with what God wants us to do.

While the bishop was traveling on his return trip, great and little dramas were being enacted in China. Father Francis McDonald wrote: "At the end of June I had 92 baptisms in Tienmen City and bright prospects of many more to follow. At all of which no one is more surprised than myself. Tienmen City, notoriously barren, with a long-standing anti-foreign reputation! That this city should see 300 or 400 pagans attending Sunday Mass regularly is nothing short of miraculous. . . ."

At the same time, a different type of letter was being written by a Sister of Loretto at Hanyang: "One of our banana trees yielded a stock of bananas for the first time and we were all so pleased. But the Big Wind came and broke it so 'Yes, We have no bananas'. . . ."

On July 3 Bishop Galvin wrote to Paul Waldron from seminary at Silver Creek: "I arrived from Ireland on June 28, stayed a few days in Brooklyn and came on here. I will leave for Chicago July 5 and will probably spend a few days there; then Omaha. I am writing this just to say that your dentist friend still does not interest me."

One of the two days in Brooklyn had included a visit with his old friend, Frank McHale, eighty-four now, feeble, blind, but delighted that the bishop had called on him.

The United States did not hold Bishop Galvin long on this trip through; he was eager to reach "home" again. On August 30 a Sister of Loretto in Shanghai wrote a letter to Kentucky: "Another of our joys was the arrival of Bishop Galvin. It seems like a different country to know that he is back again."

The bishop returned to see a dream of long standing solidly achieved, thanks mainly to the architectural talent

301

and efficiency of Father Joe Crossan. Facing the convent and the buildings of the Sisters of St. Columban stood the newly completed Cathedral of Hanyang, mother church of the vicariate.

PART THREE

The
Long
Twilight

It snowed in Hanyang as 1937 opened. A Sister of Loretto wrote: "The heaviest snow since the Sisters came to China fell last week. Our compound looked like a fairyland. Those big feathery flakes had fallen for a day and a night. All of China's squalor and unsightliness were hidden under the pure blanket sent from heaven."

For Bishop Galvin the letters, reports, personal memos and official documents were piled up as the snow was piled. His secretary, Father Charlie O'Brien, with staunch assistance from many priests, had kept routine affairs rolling. Father Pigott had made decisions that had to be made. There was, however, no substitute for the bishop and many matters awaited him, or poured in when it was known that he was home. They demanded attention if not action.

The society was spreading out, finding its missionaries in demand in new territory. Late in 1936 eight Columban Fathers, under Father Patrick Usher, landed in Bhamo, Burma, to open a new mission assignment by Rome. This was the upper half of the huge Mandalay vicariate. Within six months, the territory of St. Columban's missions in Korea, with headquarters at Moppo, had been erected into the prefecture apostolic of Kwoszu. The Right Reverend Owen MacPolin was the first prefect apostolic.

The Sisters of St. Columban, in January 1937, established a high school in Shanghai for Russian girls, the children of exiles. In Hanyang, on January 31, the first branch of the Legion of Mary in China was established, with Father J. Joseph Hogan and Eugene Spencer in charge.

On January 11, Frank McHale died.

The news, the personal messages, the statistics of the society flowed across the bishop's desk. The society now had 132 priests in the mission fields of China, Korea, Burma, the Philippine Islands. In St. Columban seminaries

305

230 students were preparing to continue and to expand the missionary work in progress.

> In 1936 [Bishop Galvin wrote] we had a total number of 6,040 adult baptisms. . . . That total is almost three times larger than our adult baptisms of last year. It is only four years since our Vicariate was the home and the headquarters of Communism. Our priests and people suffered exceedingly. Those were dark days, days of danger. It was a testing time for priests and people. Thank God, they stood the test. The fury of Communism waned and passed. Peace came to Hanyang and, with it, the greatest wave of conversions that any Vicariate in China has ever known. In four years we have instructed and baptized 15,524 pagan adults. There are 17,000 others asking for instruction. The instruction of these converts is a laborious task. It requires kindness and patience. It has to be individual and thorough.

Father Jerry Pigott amplified the thought on instruction: "One must realize that in the midst of a dense pagan population it is imperative that the instruction of the converts be thorough. Badly instructed Christians will never be anything more than a burden to the Church and never far removed from apostasy. Our method here in Hanyang, as indeed the policy outlined by Bishop Galvin for the whole Vicariate, is to insist on the family, not the individual, as the unit."

Figures can become flat, statistics dull, and the solemn statements of serious purposes boring. Some of the priests assigned to missions knew that instinctively, and thought in terms of color. Father Patrick O'Connor, who had been editor of *The Far East*, had a feeling for the beauty, the drama, the reality behind a seemingly prosaic report. He wrote this:

> 1500 baptisms in Mo-Wang-Tsui since September, 800 in Tsan-Dan-Kow. Mo-Wang-Tsui! Tsan-Dan-Kow! To millions of eyes these can be only names, difficult Chinese names, to be stared at on a map or in a mission report. But I remember them as places, places where sunlight falls on the faded whitewash of mud-brick houses and on bright fields of young wheat, places where now the blossoms are pink on the peach trees and the new leaves are fresh on the willows, places where human beings like

306

you and me walk and talk, know joy and sorrow, live and labor and die. When you see these Chinese place names *that* way, you appreciate better the realities of 1500 baptisms in Mo-Wang-Tsui, 800 baptisms in Tsan-Dan-Kow.

The political situation in China was relatively calm. In December of 1936 Chiang Kai-shek had been kidnapped and briefly held captive by Communists. A Sister of Loretto expressed the general concern over that. "The Generalissimo's being taken prisoner cast gloom over all. Now there is great rejoicing all over China, and rightly so. A Mass of Thanksgiving was sung in the Hanyang Cathedral on December 28th for the General's release. Our Sisters and our girls attended."

By April 30, 1937, Carl Crow, an authority on China, wrote: "In the spring of 1937, China was enjoying the greatest measure of peace and prosperity it had known in a quarter of a century."

In February the thirty-third International Eucharistic Congress opened at Manila, Philippine Islands. Among the speakers on the program was Father Edward J. McCarthy, in partial eclipse since he moved from his post as director of the society in the United States to a missionary assignment in the Philippines.

At Omaha in January, a new bursar reported for duty —reported reluctantly and without confidence or enthusiasm. His name was Father Timothy Connolly. He had joined the Columban Society in June 1934 and everyone who joined, seminarian or mature priest, had to spend a year at Dalgan. Father Connolly went to Dalgan and in 1935 was sent to teach Latin and Greek at Silver Creek, New York. Late in 1936 his appointment as bursar for the American region reached him and he could not believe it.

"Wrong man," he said. "Somebody has slipped his rocker. I don't know a bloody thing about figures, money or bookkeeping."

When he was convinced of the validity of the appointment, he threatened to quit the society. Finally he yielded to obedience and discipline. He arrived in Omaha during a howling blizzard in January 1937, feeling forlorn and incompetent.

307

He enrolled almost immediately in a correspondence accountancy course. From that beginning he went on to become perhaps the greatest bursar the society had ever had in any region. The society in the United States was a million and a quarter dollars in debt when he took over. He paid off the debt, built a seminary at Milton costing six hundred thousand dollars and piled up an impressive surplus. He performed some financial magic for other regions, too, but he dismissed it all with a shrug.

"I was temperamentally unfitted for the job," he said. "Absolutely and positively unfitted for it in every way."

In Hanyang the sisterhood of the Virgins of Mary, Bishop Galvin's pride and joy, was under the direction and training of the Sisters of Loretto. The catechumenate and the dispensary represented their two great fields of activity. The catechumenate proved a blessing in Hanyang City. Women converts from the four city parishes were sent there for instruction. The dispensary catered to a large section of the city and the surrounding country. In one year it treated as many as 27,000 patients. A number of the Virgins received their nursing diplomas from the Chinese Government.

In every way the Columbans were entering into the lives of the people and the people were meeting them more than half way. The society throughout the world felt the great surge of energy that flowed into it from China. Bishop Galvin, having tended to all the paper work that he felt like touching, was out again in the missions, in the villages and the one-family towns and the country parishes.

The Sisters of Loretto, too, felt the call of the country. One morning in May, five of them caught the small steam launch from Hankow, bent on the adventure of exploring a country parish. They reached Father Patrick Maguire's parish of Tsai T'ien about 1:30 P.M. A boy from his school met them and they went to Hwan Chia San by chair. One of them wrote an eloquent report:

"The varieties of country green are surprising. Some of the wheat was already ripe for harvesting. More of it was still green. The Chinese beans were finished but the peculiar dark green plants remained. The rice is a vivid, vivid green. Mosquitoes! Oh my! There is a Chinese proverb which says that a thousand mosquitoes come to one

308

mosquito's funeral. We had a ten hour sampan trip home, which was not comfortable, but this was one of the pleasantest outings of our lives."

As Father Joe O'Leary once said: "It takes very little to amuse a missionary. If he insists on being amused, he had better accept that small truth early."

27 : : MARCO POLO BRIDGE INCIDENT

The year 1937 was the Chinese year 4635 and the Year of the Ox. The wise men said that it would be a good year for youth, health, the male sex and positive action. For the first half of the year, certainly, no one could have proved the wise men wrong. Conditions generally were exceptionally good for China, and the male sex seemed to be doing nicely. There were, of course, rumors.

It was said that, since the capture and release of Chiang Kai-shek, steps were being taken to insure friendly relations between Soviet Russia and China, with Russia agreeing to terminate its support of the Chinese Communist party and to offer economic aid to China. It was said that the Chinese Communists were urging Chiang Kai-shek to make war on Japan as a means of achieving a united front; that Chiang was insisting that a war with Japan would be suicidal while the Communist army remained in an independent position in the northwest. It was said that Japan planned to take over five northern provinces of China and place them under a puppet governor; that Soviet Russia could not, and would not, permit such a takeover.

Early in July the Japanese troops stationed in the Japanese concession of Peiping marched out for maneuvers. This was customary for the troops of all the powers with concessions in the ancient capital, a means of keeping soldiers in physical training and a device to maintain top discipline. The Japanese maneuver assignment was to center about a bridge which one Japanese force was to

309

attack, another to defend. The area in which the action was staged lay near Wanping, thirty miles from Peiping.

On the evening of July 7, 1937, a detachment of Chinese troops attacked Japanese soldiers at Lukuochiao, the Marco Polo Bridge. Shots were exchanged before the Chinese withdrew.

There were many conflicting reports of this engagement, each side blaming the other for making the first hostile move. Rumor said that this time the Japanese maneuvers were planned to create a provocative situation and a clash with the Chinese which would justify further military action. Rumor also said that Chinese Communists had planned and carried out the attack on the Japanese to force the united front to which Chiang Kai-shek was cool. One listened, and one believed what one wanted to believe.

The incident of the Marco Polo Bridge, however, has gone into the history books as the initial encounter, if not the cause, of the Sino-Japanese war.

The Japanese showed no interest in compromise and, in response to the Chinese demand that Japanese troops be withdrawn, ordered reinforcements moved in and mobilization in Japan. There were scattered skirmishes and an aerial attack on Tientsin.

The Columbans were solidly pro-Chinese. In fact, they considered themselves Chinese. They were aligned loyally in sympathy with their own people.

On August 6 Mother M. Linus, the vicaress general of the Sisters of Loretto, visiting China with Mother Ann Marita, secretary general, reached Shanghai from Hanyang. On August 9 two Japanese were killed by Chinese, and soldiers moved into positions all over Shanghai.

Rumor said that this was a shrewdly planned diversion to turn the developing conflict into a battle for Shanghai where the Japanese had not prepared to fight and where the Chinese were much stronger than they. Chiang Kai-shek, rightly or wrongly, was credited with a clever move.

On August 14 Chinese bombing planes, aiming at a Japanese warship and a concentration of Japanese ashore, missed badly and released their bombs in the middle of Shanghai. The dead were estimated at 582, the injured at 870. Three Americans were killed and two wounded.

Bishop Galvin in Hanyang received the news of the

Marco Polo Bridge, from Peiping and from Shanghai as successive shocks. His churches, all of them, were filled on Sundays. There were long waiting lists of pagans seeking instruction in the Faith, and the society was moving forward with schools, hospitals, dispensaries, orphanages. War, the ultimate disaster in any event, could swiftly wipe out all that he and other Columbans had built.

He wired the nuns in Shanghai to leave their convents and take refuge in the French concession which did not seem to be affected. Sister Mary Jane, the superior, sent out all the nuns except Sister Maureen, who remained with her to keep watch over their house.

On August 20 Mothers M. Linus and Ann Marita cut their inspection trip short and left for the United States. Mother Ann Marita was taken ill the day following her arrival in Los Angeles and died within a few hours.

On August 23 the embankment at Hanyang broke and released a minor flood upon the city. Most of the land between the convent and the boys' orphanage was under water. Bishop Galvin went out to survey the damage. Father Charlie O'Brien accompanied him.

"You know, Charlie," the bishop said, "poor old Hanyang is a black sheep of a mission, always in trouble with one thing or another."

Trouble was spreading the length and the width of China. The Japanese, with grim efficiency, were stepping up the war. Japanese bombing squadrons raided Nanking, Hangchow, distant Nanchang in Kiangsi province and many Chinese army bases in Kiangsu and Chekiang provinces. Japanese troops crossed the Great Wall and entered the province of Shensi. The Japanese Navy began a partial blockade of the east coast of China along eight hundred miles.

On the night of August 30 a rain-soaked coolie came to the bishop's house seeking a priest. His family had been driven up on the hill by the flood waters and his father was very ill. Father O'Brien talked with him and Bishop Galvin heard part of the conversation. He had been writing letters but he rose from the desk and came striding out, a tall, dignified man with tired eyes and untidy hair.

"What is it, Charlie," he said. "Who's ill?"

"I don't know. I never saw the man before. It's his father. He's waiting to guide me."

311

"What's the matter with the man?"

"I don't know that, either, but it sounds like cholera."

Cholera was in virtual epidemic at that time. Bishop Galvin's body stiffened. "Cholera! You stay here, Charlie. My Lord! You're a young man! I don't want you fooling with cholera cases. You stay right here. I'll go."

He meant it and his word was law when he gave orders. He went on the sick call and the case was cholera.

The year stormed on and the Chinese were inept in the face of the Japanese. The Japanese were better trained, better disciplined and better equipped. The Chinese was not military in his mind or his temperament. When, for one unavoidable reason or another, he found himself in an army, he became a courageous, enduring soldier and he did not lack the tiger qualities of cruelty, savagery, pitiless fury. But the Japanese, man for man, was a better fighter and the Chinese soldier knew it. There were few Chinese victories and there were many deplorable Chinese mistakes. Chinese aviation was notably bad, as evidenced by the accidental bombing of the *S. S. President Hoover,* a Dollar Line passenger steamer.

On September 24 the Japanese bombers came over the three cities of Hankow, Wuchang and Hanyang. The raid alert sounded in Hanyang a few minutes after 4:15 P.M. and the all-clear did not sound until 6:45. Nine hundred people were killed in the three cities. No bombs fell close to the Columban properties, although two hundred homes were destroyed in Hanyang. "One must see an air raid to realize its horror," one of the nuns wrote. "It is a fearful thing."

Heavy rain and great, gusty gales punished Hanyang from September 25 to the end of the month. As soon as the weather moderated, the Japanese bombers returned. Nightly plasterings with bombs became the expected thing, but the Japanese were wily. When they were expected, they swung to other targets, returning when their foes relaxed. One had to worry about them every night whether they came over or not.

In early October Bishop Galvin asked the Lorettines for volunteers to nurse wounded soldiers who were coming in too fast for the Red Cross to handle. All eight of the Lorettines volunteered immediately. The Sisters of St. Columban were already on nursing duty, working in the two

312

military hospitals which contained two thousand beds. Their catechumenate was used as a temporary hospital. The catechumenate's church was converted into a ward and the dispensary became an operating room. Funds for the necessary equipment and upkeep were made available through the directors of the Irish Sweepstakes who sent £2500 to the International Red Cross in China. The soldiers received in the catechumenate came from the northern battle front in drafts of from two hundred to three hundred. The mortality rate was high, for the men came with unattended wounds and many died of gas gangrene.

The Irish sisters were at their best when given emergency nursing duty of this kind. They rose to it magnificently and it was the story of the flood days all over again: the going to the aid of those in need, not asking what they believed or why.

The Japanese War Office officially numbered the Japanese casualties in the war with China at 9,640 slain as of October 24, 1937—5,173 on the Shanghai front. The campaign in North China had taken 4,467 lives. The War Office estimated that the Chinese deaths on all fronts had reached 425,000, with 250,000 dead around Shanghai.

That was the measure of the war.

On October 20 Father Dick Ranaghan was killed in an automobile accident in Iowa. Gifted with humor and words and an uncanny skill with cameras, his contribution to Columban publicity was incalculable. He had taken motion pictures in the missions and exhibited them in the United States. He met Bing Crosby and convinced him that he should make records of "Adeste Fideles" and "Silent Night." Bing agreed and said that the Columban Fathers could have the royalties from the sales. The record became the largest selling one in the world, but the Crosby organization forgot the Columbans. Royalties were divided among missionary organizations and others; the Columbans' share was small.

A short time before he died, Ranaghan wrote: "Heretofore, my picture taking has been an amateur sideline. I have had to build my scenario around what I had. Some day a man will receive an exclusive appointment from his superior, go out with a scenario already made up, and film the story with the preconceived plan. When that day

313

comes, you will see some missionary movies as exciting as anything the commercial screen can offer."

There was sufficient motion picture drama in and around Hanyang to satisfy most people. In Father Tim Leahy's parish of Tsan-Dan-Kow and in Father Jim Vallely's parish of Mo-Wang-Tsui there was drama of another sort, despite the war which marched across the country. In one area of a hundred square miles, every single family had turned in the names of its members to Father Leahy as wanting to become Catholics; all these in addition to the overwhelming number of converts he was already trying to instruct and enroll. To help in this extraordinary situation, Bishop Galvin sent four Sisters of St. Columban to take charge of the women catechumens. Father Leahy had Fathers Wang and McCormack assisting him, and five native Virgins of Mary.

In Hanyang the wounded continued to pour in. Sister M. Leonarda, Lorettine, wrote:

> Now here is how the Sisters of Loretto go into action. Armed with our religious garb, white apron, hemostat, probe, a pair of scissors and a few other similar instruments, we venture forth to fight infection. On November 15, 1937, Sister Justa, Sister Stella, two Chinese Virgins of Mary and I were introduced to war conditions. We were escorted throughout the entire camp by one of the staff doctors. In introducing us, the doctor told the men who we were and why we were there. They were told that we came free of charge, that we expected no reward whatsoever for our services. Most of these men had never before seen a Sister. In the afternoon . . . we dressed a few cases. The next morning we went six strong and worked from nine till twelve. At home, six busy Nuns and fifty Chinese pupils worked tirelessly, making shirts for the wounded. . . .

Toward the end of November the Sisters of St. Columban were asked to take care of an extra 250 wounded. They turned the old Cathedral of Hanyang into a hospital and accepted the responsibility which was not long in coming. On the 10th of December, 217 men landed in their emergency hospital. They came from the battlefields on stretchers, in rickshaws, some on the backs of coolies, some carried in saddles made by two men joining hands.

314

The sisters and the doctors worked most of the night taking care of the worst cases which had not been dressed in a week. The odor was frightful.

The Japanese established a new provisional government with headquarters at Peiping, which they renamed Peking. It was announced that the three guiding principles of the new regime would be: (1) vigorous opposition to the government formerely located in Nanking and to the Kuomintang (Nationalist Party); (2) the complete eradication of communism; (3) the heartiest cooperation between Japan and Manchukuo.

On December 13 the Japanese Air Force for a change was guilty of some careless bombing when three bombers hit and sank the U.S. gunboat *Panay* in the Yangtze.

Two natives of Hanyang, brilliant graduates of Bishop Galvin's minor seminary, whom he had sent to Rome for advanced studies, were accepted and enrolled in December at the Pontifical Union College de Propaganda Fide.

At Christmas Bishop Galvin, as was his custom, was out in the missions. When he could do so without making an issue or a display of it, he visited the man he rated as the loneliest priest. A Sister of Loretto reported on him in a letter of December 26:

"We got a note from the Bishop thanking us for a basket of eats we sent to him in the country. He is in one of the flooded districts and the church has been turned into living quarters for 100 women and their small children. The priests' dining room is serving as the room for confirming, baptizing or anything else. The Bishop examines each person for Confirmation and then the people know that he has a personal interest in them. It is wonderful to know the man, Bishop E. J. Galvin."

In Europe Hitler and Mussolini moved from one triumph to another and there seemed to be no coherent answer to the force they represented. In China they were distant and incomprehensible. The Spanish Civil War was distant, too, without any real significance for people who lived where the Japanese Army marched. The times were out of joint but each man looked to his own ache.

Rumor said that the Communists, having maneuvered Chiang Kai-shek into a war with Japan which he did not want, were holding back now, contributing little to the vaunted united front and planning future triumphs after

315

the Generalissimo was eliminated. Rumor on the other side snorted indignantly at this, asking how the Communists could possibly hope to profit from a victory by the Communist-hating Japanese. In Hankow, Agnes Smedley, an uncompromising Communist and a fluent conversationalist, was a powerful influence on a group of articulate and influential British and Americans; Sir Archibald Clark-Kerr, the British Ambassador; John Davies, U.S. Consul in Hankow; General Joseph Stilwell; Captain Evans Carlson of the U.S. Marine Corps; Edgar Snow and Freda Utley. With the exception of Freda Utley, all of this group leaned more Left than Right, and the argument that the Communists were actually dedicated to agrarian reform was readily accepted and transmitted to the United States where it colored public opinion.

The greatest friend the Columbans and other Catholic orders and societies had in China, Lo-Pa-Hong, often called "China's greatest Catholic," was assassinated on December 30, 1937. The assassins claimed that he was friendly to Japan and engaged in a plot to create a Japanese-controlled puppet government in China, an allegation which was never proved. Catholic China mourned him.

The Japanese continued to bomb the three cities. After the seventh air raid at Hanyang on January 6, 1938, Father Gerry O'Collins visited the Loretto nuns. "I'm here on a mission," he said. "I have to count you and make sure that nobody is missing."

From Bishop Galvin down to the youngest, newest member of the missionary team, good conduct demanded that air raids be accepted as a fact of life, as something inseparable from life in Hanyang. There was no attempt to take them lightly and certainly no one who lived through them could do that; but people who had work to do could not afford nerves, panic or hysteria. The bishop himself set a perfect example. He took the necessary precautions and stayed under cover during a raid, but he was out immediately after the all-clear sounded, doing what he could for those who had been unfortunate. He did not engage in, nor tolerate, fear talk or morbid discussion.

"We're in God's hands," he said. "If what we are doing is in accordance with His plans, He'll let us go on doing it."

316

On January 31, 1938, the Chinese New Year, 4636, came in, but without the usual celebration in Hanyang. It was the Year of the Tiger and the ordinary people were afraid that the Tiger, in this cycle, was Japanese.

On the day that Austria ceased to exist, consumed by an expanding Nazi Reich, Hanyang had three bombing raids, two by daylight and one in the dusk. "The spotlights played on the planes beautifully," one nun wrote. "To watch them is to experience great poetry, and there is sheer terror in the entire spectacle."

In April Father Edward J. McCarthy visited the Sisters of Loretto in Shanghai. "We had a couple of grand visits with him," a Sister of Loretto wrote. "He seems quite well and is very much wrapped up in his work in the Philippines."

The bounce and the zest and the easy humor were dulled in Ned Mac, but he had always been a missionary at heart and he adapted well to front line work. It pleased him that he was important to the Lorettines. They remembered that he had staged a one-man crusade to enlist Loretto at the Foot of the Cross for work in China with the Columbans and that he had laid the foundation for the service they were rendering, the experience that was theirs. They told him so and he smiled.

"Very few people remember," he said. "No reason why they should."

Another gay adventurer of the society's beginnings, in a very real sense one of the founders, lost his sense of laughter in 1938. Father Joseph P. O'Leary had been ill for more than a year and had had disappointments in his society work. Upon his discharge from the hospital, he requested the society to accept his resignation and then transferred to the disocese of San Diego in California.

On April 29 the nineteenth bombing of Hanyang inspired Sister M. Leonarda to write a particularly graphic letter: "The paper gives 400 as dead and does not know the number of wounded. All night they took bodies out of the debris, mangled bodies still breathing but with no chance of living. We simply waded in human blood for hours. Even the walls were spattered with blood. We got a wounded leper but had to send her home. Some of the Mission staff will attend her. I worked elbow to elbow

317

with Fathers McDonald and Spencer. My! They are men. God bless and keep St. Columban's priests."

A few days later she wrote: "I saw the first body louse in my life today. Horrors!"

The Japanese campaign had developed a beautiful military pattern by May 22. They had taken Suchow and Haichow and they controlled the Lung Hai railway. They had forty Chinese divisions, 250,000 men, trapped in a pear-shaped area four hundred miles in extent.

Another Columban missionary died in July, a Hanyang veteran, Father Peter Gabriel, who had gone home to Australia with tuberculosis in 1937 after seven years of active parish work.

The twenty-third bombing of Hanyang was described by Sister M. Justa, superior of the Sisters of Loretto: "On July 19 we had a most dreadful air raid over the Wu-Han cities. . . . There were so many blown to bits. Right after the all-clear signal had sounded, four of us went down to the place of horror. . . . Groups of people stood stunned; others were wailing over the ruins. Electric wires mixed up with the debris were smoldering. The burning sun was beating down pitilessly and the black hawks hovered over all."

Bishop Galvin wrote his own account of the same raid.

Jerry [Pigott] and I got to the spot as quickly as we could, followed by some priests and sisters. We found a panic-stricken people in the streets; relatives, men and women, tearing frantically at tons of wreckage in a vain endeavor to free the buried. Timbers, bricks, mutilated bodies lay around in one tangled mess. We could do nothing for the dead but, aided by the police, we got the wounded onto improvised stretchers and sent them on to the Columban hospital where the old Cathedral was being made ready to receive them. The old cathedral has seen some history but I doubt if it ever saw anything as pathetic as that motley crowd. Though some of the cases were bleeding to death, there was hardly a groan in the old church.

In another letter, Sister Justa picked up the narrative. "Next, cholera began to spread and the [St. Columban] Sisters took in the victims of that dreadful disease. If cared for in time, a cholera patient can get well and many have actually got over it. They cannot, however, be left alone. The St. Columban Sisters look after the hospital in the daytime and the Chinese Sisters of St. Mary and the Sisters of Loretto are on duty at night. One of the St. Columban Sisters had typhoid but, thanks be to God, she is getting better."

The Japanese Army, methodical and unhurried, was closing its trap, grinding the Chinese divisions to pieces, moving relentlessly toward the three cities.

Father Timothy Leahy came into Hanyang from the mission at Tsan-Dan-Kow for some needed supplies when the bombing was at its height. "To a greenhorn coming from the wide open spaces," he wrote, "it was edifying to see how casually the bishop, priests and sisters took those dreadful bombings in their stride. . . . On this particular day, the bishop announced that he had been reluctantly persuaded to attend a meeting [that] was to be held under the auspices of the British Chamber of Commerce in Hankow. He was more than willing to add his mite but like many men of his stature, he was shy and diffident among strangers and distrustful of self."

There was nothing about the meeting when the bishop reached it to alleviate the shyness or the diffidence. A large room was filled with business men, mostly British, American and French. There was a lot of self-importance, assertiveness, talk in broad generalities. No one paid any attention to Bishop Galvin, who sat quietly attentive, until one of the men turned suddenly and said:

"We haven't heard from Mr. Galvin. Maybe he has something to say."

Everyone looked at the bishop who rose slowly to his feet, a tall man with lines in his face that China had traced there and iron in his jaw that was mainly of his own casting.

"Since you ask me," he said, "everything that I have heard today is a lot of balderdash. No sense of reality in it. You have a fortnight, no more. Here is what you've got to do. . . ."

He told them how many people were trapped with the Chinese Army inside the Japanese pincers and he had a shrewd idea of how many would be capable of fleeing and the directions in which they would move. He knew how

319

many miles would be covered each day by a frightened, destitute swarm of human beings.

"At least 85,000 of them will reach here," he said. "They will reach us in three waves, a day apart, carrying at least a half dozen diseases with them, needing shelter and practically everything else that is a minimum need of a human being."

Edward J. Galvin was an eloquent speaker when a subject moved him. "He would have been a great rabble rouser if he had gone into politics," one of the priests said. A number of people stated that he had a mesmeric quality, that he hypnotized crowds. Certainly, he held the group at the British Chamber of Commerce in Hankow motionless. He was a man who had handled helpless multitudes in several large floods. He knew how much food a human being needed in a day to survive and how much that food would cost. He knew how many would need clothing and how shelter could be most efficiently and cheaply provided.

"You'll have to have enough rice on hand to feed 85,000 people for a month. You have to have it purchased and stored before they reach here," he said. "They will have no means of cooking anything. You will have to have cooking kitchens ready and staffed. Ultimately you may have hundreds of thousands of people on your hands. From the beginning you will need doctors, nurses, hospitals. Babies will be born in the mass of refugees."

The men at the Wuhan Refugee Zone Committee meeting, who had talked grandly in terms of vague, generalized dogoodism, had not looked at the realistic picture until the bishop flashed it before them. Listening to him, they knew that he spoke the truth, that this reality would be theirs to face "within a fortnight."

Before the meeting adjourned, Bishop Edward J. Galvin was appointed to take charge of the food committee for Hankow and Hanyang. "He soon came to exercise a profound influence over the executive committee for the whole zone," Father Leahy wrote. "To those who knew him, this was not surprising. . . . He was aware that no matter how grave the crisis should become, he had in the priests, Sisters and Brothers of Hanyang a solid, coordinated group ready to fall into action wherever needed. Most important of all, he knew the Chinese and their ways

320

much better than did the foreign community in semi-Western Hankow."

The bishop wasted no minutes going into action. On August 12 a Sister of Loretto wrote: "Have you heard what we are going to do next? We are going to Hankow and run kitchens for the war refugees. Bishop Galvin was appointed to conduct them. The Government is giving him a huge amount of rice. They are going to put up 100 kitchens and each kitchen is to feed 1,000 people. Each kitchen will have a Sister looking after it."

On August 16 Bishop Galvin moved to Hankow because it was obviously impossible to handle his big new assignment from Hanyang. Father Charlie O'Brien, his secretary, was to follow him within a week.

A few hours after the bishop left Hanyang, the Japanese bombers were overhead again, one hundred planes for the thirty-first bombing of the city. A Loretto nun wrote:

"Today was a dreadful day for Hanyang. . . . Fires all about, houses down, people killed, bombs falling like rain. . . ."

In addition to city raiding, the Japanese were alert to any Chinese activity on the ground. Another Sister of Loretto reported in a letter:

It is so hot. The sun is burning up everything. They are taking all the machinery from the iron works here and sending it up the river somewhere. They had many, many junks full of boilers, tanks, everything all lined up along the Hanyang waterfront, waiting to take them up. Someone must have given word where it all was, for the Japanese planes came yesterday and bombed the river front all the way to Yin-Wu-Chow. The big dyke between here and Yin-Wu-Chow was crowded with people. They always went there to lie down, thinking that, since they were away from the houses, they were safe. The dyke got the biggest bomb and all the people on it were blown to pieces. Just how many were killed, no one will ever know. Many boats filled with refugees went down and those on land could not be counted because they were completely dismembered. Sisters Simeon, Clementia and Isabel went over as soon as the all-clear sounded. The Chinese Sisters of Mary were there and some of the Fathers.

In Hankow Bishop Galvin was involved in a huge operation which involved talking to scores of people in government and out. He made a great many decisions and he gave a great many orders. He was still a bishop, however, with people of his own who had need of him or who commanded his thought for one reason or another.

On September 18 Sister M. Leonarda wrote one of her last letters from China. She had a spine ailment which made it imperative that she be sent home for treatment, and the trip to Shanghai was laced with peril. She was feeling badly at having to leave China and oppressed with a sense of failure that she could not continue her work when every pair of hands was needed. She wrote:

"Slow, steady rain all night and all day. Quite a drop in temperature. Bishop Galvin called in the afternoon and we had a long talk. He is the grandest man I ever dealt with, so big and yet humble enough to be interested in the likes of me. I am quite satisfied to go since it has been so decreed. Now that things are so dark here, it would be good to stay and help but there is no certainty that I would even be able to stay up."

There was a problem priest. Father X could not drink and handle the lonely, responsible job of a missionary. Invariably, even if he took only a social drink, he ended up by drinking too much. Bishop Galvin had warned him and worked with him, but had finally reached the point where he felt that there did not seem to be any answer but to pull the man off his parish and, when possible, ship him to the United States or Ireland. Something happened then which the bishop described in a letter of September 10:

> The town was heavily bombed. Father X escaped after just finishing Mass. His Catholics were out counting the planes when the bombs began to fall. He sheltered as many as he could in his house, hiding them under tables and under beds. Walls fell on top of them. They dug out, minus shoes, socks and hats. X remembered the Blessed Sacrament and returned to the wrecked church. The tabernacle was untouched in the ruin. He consumed the Host and escaped then to the river with some of his faithful Catholics. He had scarcely crossed the river when the second bombing raid leveled the town. It is something to dwell upon. The Lord spared him. Maybe the Lord wants him. Who am I to stand in the way? I will take care of him.

322

On September 16 Dr. V. K. Wellington Koo reported to the League of Nations that one million Chinese had been killed since the beginning of the conflict with Japan on July 7, 1937. He said that thirty million others had been wounded or made homeless. "Since January 1, 1935," he said, "there have been 2,204 Japanese air raids on civilian populations of China and more than one million Japanese soldiers are operating on Chinese soil."

The Japanese made no report. There had never been a declaration of war between China and Japan, and the Japanese never referred to war. All that happened in China was but an extension of the Incident of the Marco Polo Bridge.

On September 25, 1938, at Dowdstown, outside Navan in County Meath, Ireland, the cornerstone was laid for the partially erected missionary college of St. Columban. It was a dull, wet morning which cleared to a dry, pleasant afternoon. His Eminence Joseph Cardinal MacRory presided in the presence of the papal nuncio and fifteen other dignitaries of the Church, hundreds of priests and a large gathering of laymen. The *Drogheda Independent* reported: "The purple and scarlet robes of Hierarchy blended well with the snow white surplices of several hundred priests in procession. . . ."

Father John Blowick was one of the many priests contributing his share of contrast against the color of hierarchy. He was content. This was the land which had come to him miraculously; the land across which St. Patrick had walked long ago from the Hill of Slane to the Hill of Tara. The building, when completed, would be a thoroughly modern seminary but the name it would bear had meaning forever for Columbans. It had been pre-christened "Dalgan."

To Father Blowick fell the assignment of the day's last speech. He made that speech short and he gave to the laying of the cornerstone a memorable sentence: "The lamps which burn before the tabernacles in China, Korea and Burma and the Philippines have been lighted by the pennies of our people."

In Hankow refugees were pouring into the city. Bishop Galvin had been asked to assume the chairmanship of the Wuhan Refugee Zone executive committee and had been unable to refuse in the face of the emergency. It was obvious that the other members of the Committee, however willing they might be, did not know how to deal with the problem of a frantic, disorganized, hungry multitude descending upon a living city. He still retained his chairmanship of the food committee and the two jobs demanded most of a twenty-four hour day.

Ralph Mortensen, field secretary of the American Bible Society, served on the governing board of the International Red Cross for Central China with Bishop Galvin in 1938. He describes him thus:

> When I recall Bishop Galvin I can safely say that he was very vocal at every meeting. He always had something to contribute to the Board of Directors, some plan or policy that often became the plan or policy of the Board. His sense of humor never failed him. Even the occupation of the Japanese could not daunt him. His perspective and sense of balance were, on the whole, common sense that appealed to most of the Board members. To sum it up, he was a pillar of strength in the joint relief work done by the International Red Cross for Central China.

The Japanese were stepping up the bombing program as their troops moved closer to the three cities. Battered, shattered Hanyang was virtually deserted and Hankow was bulging with human life. Everyone, foreign or Chinese, dreaded the coming of the Japanese infantry. The intensity and callous brutality of the aerial bombardment seemed a fair indicator of what one could expect from the enemy's troops.

"Tuesday, October 25, was a day of horrors," Father Charlie O'Brien wrote. "Shortly after noon, the Chinese began to dynamite public buildings, Japanese property and the whole Japanese concession. There was a steady series of explosions until the whole sky was alight and the air filled with smoke. The most thorough job of demolition I have ever seen was carried out by the Chinese on the Japanese concession. Not a single building was left."

That should have insured rough treatment for Hankow if it were not already insured. A Sister of Loretto, in a letter to her motherhouse, tells what actually happened:

> There was no more bombing after Sunday, October 23.
> On Tuesday evening, October 25, the soldiers retreated

from Hankow. The unexpected happened. Hankow fell and not a shot was fired. The quiet of the occupation simply stunned everyone. On Wednesday afternoon, Bishop Galvin called in a car and took Sister Justa and myself to see the refugee kitchens in the German concession. We went by the Bund and behold! We saw Japanese ships sailing, or rather, steaming up the river. The evening was grey, the boats were grey, the smoke was grey. There was a weirdness about it all. I found it hard to realize that this was a conquering army. There was a strange stillness in the air. Was this the dreaded 'crisis'?

The following day press releases carried the story to the world. A typical dispatch read: "The occupation of Hankow by the Japanese was completed ten months and fourteen days after the capture of Nanking. Scarcely a shot was fired. Only a few hundred soldiers remained. Many of them had been wounded in defense of the city. The Japanese have also occupied nearby Wuchang and Hanyang. By evening the Yangtze River was filled with Japanese warships and transports."

The Japanese commander and his staff met with members of the various foreign-dominated committees and the few Chinese city officials who remained in Hankow. Bishop Galvin attended the meeting. It was a menace to health for so many refugees to be crowded into a big city, the Japanese officer said. It could not be permitted. There was an area beyond the city limits where they could be encamped. It was called Wu-Shen-Miao. They must be moved.

Bishop Galvin voiced the most eloquent protest. There had been over ninety thousand refugees at the last count, although the official figure still read 85,000. That many people could not be moved in a body. They had to be moved, if moved they must be, in sections, with facilities set up for them before they were uprooted.

The Japanese commander said that he understood that, but the moving must start immediately; moving people, moving facilities.

Bishop Galvin made the point that there were forty-four kitchens set up and staffed, each kitchen feeding 2500 persons twice a day. It was a staggering job to think of moving both people and kitchens. "We have given

325

them food sufficient to keep them alive," he said, "not to power them on long marches."

The Japanese, commander and staff, were unimpressed. They had another item. The streets of Hankow in the native district were a disgrace. There were piles of human excrement and many other unsanitary conditions. The commander wanted those streets cleaned immediately.

The native streets in Hankow, or any other Chinese city, were more often a disgrace than not. They were, however, kept under reasonable control in ordinary times. Under the constant Japanese bombing all public work had ceased. It was hopeless to think of depending upon volunteers for the onerous job of cleaning Hankow's streets. The committee decided to hire men for the job. Moving the 85,000 refugees was a more difficult problem and that problem was Bishop Galvin's.

> The burden of fulfilling this military order [Father Leahy wrote] fell on the shoulders of Bishop Galvin. He it was who organized the movement and trudged along on foot with those thousands of destitute refugees from the 'safety zone' of Hankow to a safer area.
>
> An incident occurred during this sorrowful exodus. It is only one of hundreds of similar incidents witnessed by his priests through the years but I choose it because it helps to explain the magnetic quality of Bishop Galvin the man, and helps, too, to explain the extraordinary affection he inspired in the hearts of those who were close to him. Among those thousands who were expelled from Hankow was a poor crippled Chinese boy; terror and fright stared from his eyes as, unowned and unattended, he painfully hobbled along. The bishop lifted him on his broad shoulders and carried him safely along that sorrowful trail and down through the densely crowded streets of Hankow.

Bishop Galvin's affection and concern for children showed in act and utterance all of his life. At this period of the capture of Hankow he wrote a statement in a letter to a benefactor about Chinese children:

> A little Chinese girl, given a fair opportunity, [he wrote] becomes a real Catholic in one year. She is the most loyal person you can possibly want and full of the will to do everything right. That is one of the surprising things about

China, her wonderful Chinese women. If she is ever to be lifted up, they will do it. They all really belong in the Church; it fits them like a glove. What a pity that so few of them are in it! They just do not know it, not yet, and we are too few to bring it to all of them.

Men, women and children—good and bad, promising and unpromising—the Chinese went to the camp outside the city where the Japanese wanted them to be. Ultimately, most of them would have to return somewhere, to find something on which to build again. They would do it because, on the record, they always did it. Flood and famine and epidemic and war drove them from their homes, made them temporarily dependent; as soon as they had even partially recovered, they went back. They were not a people who would live indefinitely on charity or on another man's rice. Bishop Galvin knew that, as did the other members of the committee. In the meantime, the air was growing cold.

A meeting was held to consider the purchase of firewood [Father Leahy reports]. It had been decided to purchase a certain quantity and at a certain price. Bishop Galvin ventured the opinion that he could secure the same quantity on far more favourable terms. Naturally the business men present were a little skeptical but it was agreed that he should be allowed to make the attempt. Bishop Galvin returned to Hanyang, in which only a few people continued to live, set his wheels in motion and purchased the wood. There was amazement all around when the bill was presented and much good-natured banter at the Bishop's expense. Mr. Marker, head of the Hankow Chamber of Commerce, told him that if he ever thought of retiring from Hanyang there would be a place for him in his firm. To which Mr. Dupree replied, "You keep out of this. I saw him first."

Purchasing wood and other supplies, attending meetings, making decisions on scores of questions involving the Japanese occupation could occupy only a part of Bishop Galvin's time. He was a priest, with priestly duties, and he had a deep human concern for the people at Wu-Shen-Miao.

"In the center of the area marked out as the new zone stands the Methodist Mission," Father O'Brien wrote. "The

327

Superintendent, Mr. Gedye, thoughtfully offered Bishop Galvin one of the dwelling houses. . . . The Bishop accepted the kind offer. On November 2, he took up residence. . . . Father Pete Leddy and I joined him the next day. The Zone Committee met and immediately appointed Bishop Galvin director of all departments. From now on, food supply, housing, sanitation, public order; everything was on his shoulders."

A Sister of St. Columban wrote:

> During this winter an epidemic of cholera broke out among the refugees and Bishop Galvin called for nursing Sisters. Three of us got our marching orders at noon on November 6, Feast of all the Saints of Ireland, and by 3 P.M. we were seated on top of our baggage on board a truck and en route for the field of action. Bishop Galvin and Father Paul Hughes accompanied us and Brother Colman was at the wheel. The building chosen for the isolation hospital was the old disused police station to which we had taken refugees a week earlier and we now set about fitting it up. Ventilation was not lacking as there was not a door or a window in the place. It made a good ward and next day we received the first patients, 16 cholera victims. They were almost belond help. Five of them died the following morning.

There were other sisters who had marching orders. Father O'Brien wrote: "The management committee strongly urged the Bishop to send for our Sisters and, upon the offer of another house in the Methodist Hospital grounds for their residence, [he] consented. The first band—St. Columban Sisters, Lorettines and Chinese Sisters of St. Mary—came on Nov. 6. Their number increased as time passed until, at the peak, seventeen Sisters were living in one small crowded house and doing a tremendous amount of work."

The Japanese had their own peculiar problem; they were combat troops, not an army of occupation. They had their own ideas on how matters should be handled; they were officious but preferred to work through the Chinese or through foreigners, provided anti-Japanese activity did not complicate the relationship. They were ruthless where opposed by hostile elements.

Sister M. Patricia, Lorettine, wrote: "Sister Justa asked

Sister Stella and me to go live with the Chinese Sisters, that we might be a kind of protection to them. . . . There were about 45 Sisters in the Chinese community. The Japanese officers called almost every day. The Sisters went to the chapel when they came. We had to meet these officers on all occasions. Some of them could speak English and some Chinese. We always took them upstairs to the chapel. They removed their hats and bowed toward the altar."

Living under Japanese supervision, facing the winter and taking care of refugees—all of this constituted a way of life. A Columban nun graphically presents the scene:

> Bishop Galvin has 41,000 refugees on his rice list tonight and, day after day, more people are flocking in. We have three camps and a long stretch of river bank to look after. The Sisters give out rice from 9 to 12 each forenoon and from 2 to 2:30 in the afternoon. One of the Sisters specializes in caring for the old men and women.
>
> The Methodists have been very friendly to us and on every occasion they have shown appreciation of the work we are trying to do. In hospital and in camp, in the streets and the byways the Catholic Sisters are hailed in all quarters as ministers to the ills and the wants of a suffering people. We are very happy in our work.

28 : : THE LIVING AND THE DEAD

The Japanese were driving hard against the Chinese Army in other areas of China and bombarding resistant cities as they had bombarded Hankow, Hanyang and Wuchang. They commanded and controlled the three cities with a fairly loose rein as long as there was no resistance. Refugees, despite the winter weather, were drifting away, responding to the instinct which called them to their homes, though many did not know if the homes still existed. By early December, affairs were so sufficiently quiet in Hankow that Bishop Galvin went out to the missions for a tour of confirmations.

There had been news in other parts of the Columban world during the heavy bombardment and during the frantic days of resettling refugees, a period when news from the outside registered dimly. "Peace in our time" at Munich had been a news item without seeming depth. There had been little time in which to note General Franco's victory in Spain.

In November Fathers Thomas Quinlan and Patrick Brennan had arrived at Syunsen in Korea to develop the new mission of Kang-Won-Do. It was the second Columban mission in Korea and extended for some two hundred miles along the sea of Japan, supporting a million and a half people in a ten thousand square mile area. There were eleven good churches, staffed by twelve Korean priests.

On December 13 the prefecture of Kienchang was raised to the status of a vicariate and formally renamed Nancheng, the name which had been in common usage for some time. Monsignor Patrick Cleary was named Vicar Apostolic. This was extremely good news from Hanyang's Columban neighbor in China, but the distance and the unsettled conditions made it impossible for anyone from Hanyang to pay a personal call.

On February 6, 1939, Bishop Galvin resigned his position as manager of the Zone, but he appointed Father Jack O'Carroll to represent him on the management committee. In the late spring, the executive committee turned over the remaining cash assets to the Hankow International Red Cross Society and dissolved the Wuhan Refugee Zone Committee.

That adventure was over.

On February 10, 1939, a great warrior, a sturdy and uncompromising realist, Pope Pius XI died. He was succeeded on March 2 by Eugenio Cardinal Pacelli who assumed the name of Pius XII.

On March 18, with the approval of Rome, two Sisters of Loretto undertook the task of shaping elected members of the Virgins of St. Mary into a community of Chinese nuns. Sister M. Justa was given the responsibility of forming the new Chinese sisterhood. Sister Justa had adapted well to the ways of the Chinese. She spoke the language perfectly, Mandarin and several dialects. Her years in

330

China had bronzed her olive skin and with her high cheekbones she resembled the Chinese.

On March 23, 1939, King Victor Emmanuel of Italy stated that the Rome-Berlin Axis of October, 1936, had been extended to include Tokyo, Budapest and Manchukuo.

On April 8, an echo from old, worrisome days was sounded in Hanyang when bandits invaded Chang Tan Kow and brutally beat Fathers Timothy Leahy and Martin Croffy, who were both hospitalized.

On April 16, 1939, Monsignor Patrick Cleary was consecrated bishop in his grey brick church in Nancheng. It was, consistent with the history of Bishop Cleary, a missionary consecration, out of reach of many friends, inaccessible even to many of his colleagues in China and practically within earshot of the war. He was consecrated by Bishop John O'Shea of Kanchow. Owing to war difficulties, two priests were authorized to assist in place of the two co-consecrating bishops required by canon law.

In Hanyang there was an air of excitement, a feeling that happy history was repeating itself. As the unselfish labor of priests and sisters during the flood had turned thousands of pagans inquiringly toward the Church, so had the labor of those same priests and nuns under the stresses of war awakened the interest of new thousands. A Sister of St. Columban wrote on April 29:

"There are over 200 families under instruction. We are teaching the women and girls and. . . . the men-folk go to the Cathedral compound. Bishop Galvin himself instructs them. His school opens at 7:30 and he remains with them for three hours. Another 100 families will start next week. . . ."

A few days later, a Sister of Loretto wrote:

The Japanese are courteous and all that we have to pay now, going to Hankow and returning, is a bow and a registering of our name. Our mail is now delivered by carrier. We don't even know where the post office is. It is taking letters a long time to come, but they do arrive. . . . On Easter Sunday, April 9, we were greeted with the Christmas number of the Denver Catholic Register, a big picture of Santa Claus on the front page.

Hanyang is so peaceful and things have so gone back to normal that you'd never think there had been any war. Towel factories are clicking away and vendors crying out

331

their wares and the big crowds elbowing one another just as in the days of yore. Trucks and autos run on the main streets now and the shops are full of soap, matches and cigarettes. Our old blacksmith is back across the street and it is good to hear his clang-clang.

The first Columban Sisters in the Philippines arrived in Manila on Thursday, May 25. There were five of them, and they were hailed by Father Henaghan as makers of history. "Believe it or not," he said, "I knew the society when it did not have any sisters, in the Philippines or in any place else."

On June 10 a Loretto Sister sent a catching-up-on-the-news letter to Kentucky which adds color to the atmosphere of peace and confidence which had built up in Hanyang:

"One yard is an immense bouquet of white and pink oleanders and our tomato plants are in bloom. The cabbage plants are all eaten up by some kind of bug. . . . The weather till now has been delightfully cool and our yard is all smiles."

"In July," another of the sisters wrote, "Brother Colman brought us a new dog, Rex, and a king he is, just about ten months old now. . . ."

Such trifles dominated the mail out of Hanyang. There seemed to be a grateful grasping at the reality of a world in which trifles could once more be sufficiently important to be noted. There was still violence in China but it was far away. The Japanese in Hankow were a nuisance, officious and arrogant, inclined to set up regulations that seemingly had no purpose save to satisfy the urge to regulate. They did not, however, interfere with religion or the exercise of it and, until the heat of summer brought all activity to a halt, the Chinese Catholics were intense in the practice of their religion, their pagan neighbors interested and inquiring.

Bishop Galvin, as he always had in the past, created a cheerful atmosphere for the priests who took a one-month vacation in July or August. He was in high good humor, ready for a songfest at a moment's notice, prepared to buy beer but wrapped in the pretense that he was imposed upon, a victim of sharp traders. He had stories to tell that he had amassed on his long journey to America and to Ireland.

He liked to tell stories about priests of the vicariate in their presence, and he was not above inventing, exaggerating or distorting an incident. He based his stories on common experiences, on the things his listeners knew from their own lives. He had one about an escape from the Reds. It built up with a mass of exciting detail.

"Then here we were, Tom O'Rourke and myself, running out across the field to the rear and half the Red army shooting at us. All I was thinking about was running fast enough, God help me, to keep my tail out of the way of a bullet. Tom was running in great leaps, and as he bounced along with the bullets behind him, he was wheezing out a message. 'Goddam it,' he was saying, 'I've got to go back and get my pipe.' "

The bishop was always entertaining in conversation. One trick that he had was the dropping of a simple, semi-startling statement into a moment of silence, such as: "It was a big surprise to me the day I learned that Omaha macaroni is sold in Italy." The less such a statement had to do with whatever had been under discussion, the more effective it was, and he always dead-panned such material.

Inevitably, even at vacation gatherings, serious topics crept into the conversation and flashes of the deeply spiritual. One day a tired priest who had only recently come from a lonely parish launched into an account of his troubles with parishioners; bickering, gossiping, getting into family feuds and creating insoluble problems which they expected a priest to solve. From such a takeoff, the other priests began talking of similar problems and annoyances with their parishioners. The topic was negative and the bishop did not believe in negative discussions; but he did not believe, either, in pulling rank or in saying anything that would imply a criticism of the majority's choice of a conversational topic. He puffed quietly on his cigarette and when a lull in the conversation occurred, he leaned forward.

"I spent one Christmas week in Bao San Chao," he said. "It isn't much of a place when it's at its best and that Christmas the snow was deep there and the wind was blowing day and night. My boy became involved with a

333

village couple, no excuse for him or for them, and I no sooner got that settled than another couple came over to tell me their troubles, with an old woman after them who was part of their troubles herself. I was so cold that I didn't believe I'd ever warm up and I wasn't very well fed. Then, suddenly, I thought: These people are just like the people who were around Christ, full of jealousy and quarrels and greed and trickery. How boring He must have found them! Yet, how patient He was with them. Who am I to be impatient with them on Christmas Day?"

He hadn't opposed the discussion of faults in the congregation; he had joined the discussion. The complaining stopped.

One of the veterans of Hanyang said later: "When we go out on the missions . . . we always make some provision for the stay, a certain amount of useful eatables and other amenities of civilized life. Not so the bishop. There is the usual packing of the Mass outfit and such necessities; but, for himself, the proverbial razor and toothbrush, and he just walks out as he is."

It was a good summer in 1939, filled with hope despite the presence of the Japanese and the sound of sabre rattling around the world. Bishop Galvin was at his best and the priests of Hanyang felt that they were entering upon a new era in the conversion of China.

On Friday, September 1, 1939, Germany launched an attack on Poland. This brought declarations of war upon Germany by England and France, and brought the Russian army into an attack upon the Polish rear. The European War was in process and Asia thought of it in just such terms—"a European War."

A journalist assigned to China wrote of this period: "Early September arrived and suddenly the world was at war. . . . [But] not until the German offensive in the spring of 1940 did the war lend itself to Shanghai's small talk. China was still the supreme topic of the day. Europe's war seemed remote and unnatural. For many months it scarcely ruffled the surface of the Far East."

The Columbans had bad news of their own. Rev. John McGrath, Hanyang veteran, had died at Silver Creek on August 5. On October 2, in Chicago, Bishop Galvin's supporter and friend, George Cardinal Mundelein died.

The day following, Hankow was shocked and shaken

when attacked by Chinese bombing planes; it was the first time that had happened.

On October 6, 1939, a great event occurred in the history of St. Columban's in China. Thirteen Chinese Virgins stood before the altar in St. Mary's Chapel, Hanyang, to receive the habit of the Sisters of the Blessed Virgin Mary. For eight years and six months they had prepared and prayed for this day. Six months postulancy preceded their reception, but the preparation had begun eight years earlier when they had taken charge of refugee women during the great flood of 1931-1932. They lived a community life, following a simple rule drawn up by Bishop Galvin; they studied assiduously, taught the women converts of Hanyang, took a practical course in medicine and were ultimately sent to three parishes in the country where they took charge of dispensaries and instructed hundreds of women.

On October 10 Sister M. Clementia, Sister of Loretto and superior of the native Chinese sisters in Hanyang, wrote: "The other night the statue [of] Our Blessed Mother seemed to beam, and the glow worms were enhancing the beauty of the night. In the stillness we could hear the men in the front part of the compound with their Seng gu fu, Malia [Hail Mary]. They believe that the louder they chant the more apt she will be to hear, I suppose. Anyway it is one of the most beautiful of sounds in all the world. When I am dying I want to hear—off at a little distance—Seng gu fu, Malia."

Several days later Bishop Galvin wrote to Omaha:

Our thanks are due to Almighty God who, in His merciful providence, preserved us from harm during the past year and who has permitted us, even in the midst of war, to reap the greatest harvest of souls in the history of Hanyang. It has been a difficult and dangerous time for priests and people, a year of suffering and of great poverty, a year of hard work under very trying circumstances; but the harvest has been great and, on our knees, we give thanks to the good God. Our adult baptisms in this year of war reached the astounding total of 9,056. The new converts have been carefully instructed and are good Catholics. We baptized 972 children of Catholic parents and 5,625 pagans in danger of death, a grand total of 15,653 baptisms. The Catholic population of Hanyang

335

Vicariate now stands at 51,554, our Catechumens number 37,000. It is God's time in Hanyang.

29 : : THE YEARS OF SILENCE

The Japanese attacked Pearl Harbor, Hawaii, on December 7, 1941, in the twelfth moon of the Chinese year 4639, the Year of the Serpent. With the declaration of war by the United States and Great Britain against Japan, and the Chinese Nationalist Government against Japan, Germany and Italy, all American and English priests and nuns immediately became enemies of Japan. They were confined in internment camps while the Irish, citizens of a neutral and presumably friendly nation, were permitted to follow their normal living pattern in China.

The might of Japan was released in a series of sledge-hammer blows which had the United States fleet in the Pacific reeling. Japanese troops landed in the Philippines and by Christmas Hong Kong had fallen. There was news of Japanese successes in Midway and Wake before the Japanese in Wuhan confiscated all radios.

"A matter of security," they explained politely.

There was no longer access to news. The available Chinese newspapers were purveyors of propaganda, controlled by the Japanese and making no attempt at balanced or objective reporting. Mail no longer came through and it was an act of faith to mail a letter and expect it to reach any destination outside the Japanese zone. One of the last pieces of mail to get through was a release of the Sisters of St. Columban.

There were now, the release said, 110 Sisters of St. Columban. They had houses in Dalgan Park, Navan; Silver Creek, N.Y.; a motherhouse in County Clare, Ireland; three houses in the Philippines with 13 nuns, and three houses in China with 21 nuns.

Bishop Galvin had received letters containing personal news before the lid came sharply down on all communication. His niece, Winnie, was married, and her twin brother,

336

Donal, was in Dalgan, within two years of ordination as a priest of St. Columban. The bishop answered before the attack on Pearl Harbor but, even then, he included the line: "I am sending this to Ballymichael and I hope that it will pass censors and submarines."

Father John Blowick, according to the last mail through, was still on indefinite sick leave. He was home in Mayo and details of his condition were few.

The mail stopped and there were no more answers to anything. The small Catholic world of the Hanyang vicariate had to settle into the silence of non-communication, arrange for its own survival and learn new rules of operation.

The Japanese were not hostile to the missions, or to the missionaries, but they obviously considered them a problem. They were perpetually suspicious and they came to the various Catholic buildings at odd hours, obviously hoping to surprise some rascality in process. They were patiently thorough in their examination of premises, possessions and equipment of any kind. Bishop Galvin wrote in his log book of one search:

> An amusing incident occurred in a certain convent where I was leading the search party. We entered one of the Sister's cells upstairs, and there in the middle of the floor was a pair of shoes almost large enough to fit me. The Jap pounced on them and said: "There is a man hiding in this convent." We protested that the shoes belonged to one of the Sisters, but he would not believe it, so there was nothing to be done but to produce the Sister in question. She came forward and held up her foot for inspection. The Japs grunted their astonishment—and the referee gave the round to Hanyang.

The morale of priests in the outlying parishes was a problem from the beginning of the world war. The parishes were sufficiently lonely under normal circumstances, but with rich, balancing compensation when there were occasional trips to Hanyang to anticipate, or visits from other priests. The work of the missions was itself a compensation for loneliness; the devotion of the people, the ardor of new converts coming into the Church. The widening of the war changed all the conditions. A priest was pinned down now. Under the regulations laid down

337

by the Japanese, a pastor was permitted to function only in the parish where he was known, in the area to which he had been assigned before December, 1941; he could not be transferred or replaced. Bishop Galvin could recall a priest to Hanyang City but he could not send a priest out if he came in even briefly. There could be no gathering of priests, no vacations at Kuling or anywhere else, no drive for conversions which would bring groups of Chinese together.

The bishop was himself severely restricted, although the Japanese obviously respected his rank and permitted that rank latitude in which to express itself. He could make visits to priests in the parishes, but only under narrowly defined conditions. He had to fall back upon his typewriter and his pen, with no assurance that the letters he wrote would reach the men to whom he addressed them. Often the best way to send letters was in care of Catholic river men.

He wrote on April 20, 1942, to Father Abraham Shackleton, who was alone in the parish of Tou Wan:

> We here and you there are sitting under a cloud. To lie very low is the only method and hope for the best. Our color is against us. That is the great trouble. I don't know what the next few months will bring. 190 of our two nationalities [American and British] are being moved out of here within a few weeks. Do we go next? Wednesday is the Feast of St. Joseph, who takes care of the whole Church. I am going to suggest to the priests around here that we say some special prayers for guidance and protection to St. Joseph and St. Columban, two great saints, and that we continue it for the duration. You might do the same.

There were many letters because there were many problems and the bishop did not want any priest to feel alone. By one device or another he kept his American Lorettines out of the detention camp until June of 1942. But Sister Stella and Sister Clementia finished their teaching assignments for the year on June 4 and the bishop could not protect them after that. He kept the Dutch Lorrettine, Sister Nicholas, in Hanyang for another six months, then she had to go. He had, then, of his Loret-
338

tines, Sister Patricia, who was Irish; Sister Justa, who was Czechoslovakian, and Sister Isabel, who was Chinese. The sisters who went away were allowed to take only what they could carry and their destination was unknown.

According to the news which reached the Columban group, the war was going strongly in favor of Japan and there was no reason to doubt it. The Japanese were too airily confident, some of them condescending, and it was easy to deduce even without propaganda-laden news that they were winning. The Columbans tried to carry off the assumption of indifference, although they obviously were not as convincing as the Columbans of Korea.

At a little after bedtime on February 18, 1942, two Japanese guards burst jubilantly into a dormitory in Korea where seven captive Columbans slept. One of the guards shouted hoarsely, "Ho! Ho! Singaporru has fallen!"

One Columban rolled over sleepily and said, "Is that so?"

A priest from one of the parishes reported on the efforts that were being made to save face in his village, even though everyone was aware that China was under the control of Japan, that food was scarce, prices high and many necessities almost impossible to obtain.

> One of my good friends is a pagan [the priest wrote]. I do not know his name. I always call him Lao Ban, which means "proprietor." He has a tea shop and attends personally to the pouring of the boiling water on the green tea leaves for his guests. He is very old and has no one belonging to him, so far as I know, except a little grandniece. Whenever I pass his place he comes forward with a dignified, smiling bow of salutation. On points of etiquette we have much to learn from the Chinese. Even in remote corners they all seem possessed of a wealth of native charm and refinement. They hate rushing.
>
> "Is the Venerable Proprietor well?" I inquire.
>
> "Father he is extremely well."
>
> "That is good. Has Fortune favored the important business of the illustrious proprietor?"
>
> We go on like that for several minutes and there are those who will say that I waste my time. I will admit that, in terms of words, it all seems meaningless; but the day is brighter and more pleasant when I have seen Lao Ban and have spoken to him and have resumed my way.

339

The Columban Society in Hanyang was hard pressed for money and none, of course, was coming in. It was necessary to conserve in every possible way. The schools were closed down. There were no frills whatever to living. Of course, even if there were money, there would not be sufficient food to eat; it wasn't available. Bishop Galvin worried about those under him and tried not to think of those beyond his reach. He taught classes every day in the convent of the Sisters of Mary, the native nuns who were the delight of his soul.

Sister Clementia, one of the Sisters of Loretto who went to the detention camp, wrote of Bishop Galvin at this time:

> I think that many people misunderstood Bishop Galvin. He was a man of very strong ideas. We used to say that he was "hatching bugs." That meant that he had one idea and that all his strength and energy went into the accomplishing of that idea, whatever it was. He was liable then to forget himself, his friends, everything except the object, or objective, on which he was centered. Until that one thing was accomplished he could think of nothing else. If people met him for the first time, or if they came on any other business that would distract him from that one idea, they would have thought that he was a terrible man, or they would have regarded him as a man who didn't have any sympathy or feeling for other people, a self-centered man. It wasn't that at all; he was merely hatching bugs.

There was much bug hatching in the bishop's life during those war years. He felt that his time was being wasted, that there were people who needed him and that he could do nothing for, or about, any other human being. He tried to find answers for individual problems which came to his attention and he was aware that all of the others pinned down in Hanyang were also feeling wasted, just as he was. He visited the various groups regularly and he promoted evenings of relaxation.

Irish songs were always sure-fire with the Sisters of St. Columban, and the more familiar they were the better. But he sensed that the Irish repertoire had grown a bit flat to the Lorettines who responded politely but whose enthusiasm was a bit forced. He devised an answer to that problem by writing Chinese lyrics to the old, familiar

340

Irish airs. The result was startling and his rendition of the songs was cheered. The Columban colony of Hanyang set about the task of learning the lyrics and the bishop wrote more, including sets to two American musical comedy numbers.

The nuns liked to tell about the stern side of Bishop Galvin which was such a rich balance to his gentleness. He liked no one in China better than he did the young girls who came in from the country with the hope that they would be accepted as candidates for the Sisterhood of Mary. The girls, however, were rough and crude and they had much to learn. With one of the early groups, the bishop noticed that some girls, after a meal, brushed off the tables with their hands, scattering crumbs and fragments onto the floor. He lectured them, saying that they must never do that again; but on another visit, he saw one of the girls repeat the offense. He singled her out immediately and told her that she had just done that which, under obedience, she was not to do.

"Now," the bishop said, "we must offer up a prayer of reparation."

He made her kneel down with him and they offered the prayer. That incident became part of the tradition of the Sisters of Mary, something to be related to each new class or group which came in.

"There are many sins of omission and commission while these raw country girls are being shaped," a Sister of Loretto said, "but nobody ever, under any circumstance, brushes anything off the table onto the floor."

These stories came out because trapped people sought for them in their memories as a leaven to the monotony of days without events. Father Gerry O'Collins was oft-quoted. He was a man who had left phrases in many memories. He once said, "When I am away from China, I have a nostalgia for its yells, its bells and its smells."

Without rhyme or reason or logical explanation, an occasional letter came in from the world outside. In September, 1943, Bishop Galvin received a letter from home which had been mailed in November, 1941.

Even without authoritative news, the Columban community knew when the tide of war turned against the Japanese. The officers with whom they had contact became more arbitrary, nervous, unreasonable. For some

341

reason known only to the Japanese themselves, Bishop Galvin and his priests were moved out of their own headquarters in Hanyang to the outskirts of Hankow, with no official arrangements for their housing or food. A number of Protestant missionaries were in the same plight. The Baptists, who had an immense compound which enclosed a number of residences, offered hospitality which was gratefully received.

Bishop Galvin, as was only to be expected, became a general favorite with everyone [Father William McGoldrick wrote]. He was given one of the mission residences where he lived with a number of the Hanyang priests. And there, their Catholic life proceeded as undisturbed as at home. One remark of the Rector of the mission is worth recording. A number of the missionaries had come to spend the evening at the 'Bishop's House' and they were seated on the verandah. "I can just hazard a guess," said the Rector, "as to what our people at home would say if they even suspected that there was a Catholic Bishop and his priests living in our mission here, and that one of the rooms in his residence had been converted into a Catholic chapel where Mass was being celebrated every morning."

Father McGoldrick, after relating this incident, adds his comment. "The good people at home will have no reason to regret this incredible action of their China representatives. May God reward and bless the good Rector and his helpers."

As abruptly and as unpredictably as the move out, the bishop and his companions were moved back again to their own headquarters at Hanyang. The war was definitely going against the Japanese now and huge fleets of American bombers swept across the skies above the Yangtze. The Columbans came back in time to bear the full weight of the American bombing.

Our food was very poor [the bishop wrote]. Indeed it is no exaggeration to say that one lived in a kind of semi-starvation during the whole war. Poor food and other things had sapped our strength, so that we were ill-prepared to stand the nerve-wracking air raids which became a daily, and nightly, feature of these cities during the last year of the war. We had no protection and no money to construct an air raid shelter. When the urgent alarm sounded, we left our compounds and sought safety in the fields around Hanyang. Later, when fighters engaged one another in the air, it was considered safer to remain indoors, so we took refuge in the church together with a terrified mob of pagans and Catholics. That was the procedure every day for a whole year, and almost every night.

Frequently the planes returned a second and sometimes a third time. We got into our clothes as quickly as possible, and in the dark, for it was strictly forbidden to show a light. The sounding of the air alarm five or six times a day was not an uncommon occurrence. Sometimes they came, sometimes not, but—which was almost as bad—one was always waiting for them.

It was considered a miracle that no priest or nun of the Columban community was killed or wounded during the protracted bombing. Other priests and nuns were less fortunate.

Hankow suffered very severely and is a spectacle of ruins and wreckage [Bishop Galvin wrote]. The Cathedral itself is a sad looking ruin and the Bishop's residence almost a wreck. Across the street from the Cathedral is the Canossian Institute where Italian Sisters of Charity have been working among the poor, the sick and the abandoned for more than 80 years. Bombings reduced the whole place to a pile of shattered bricks; the hospital, orphanage, schools and convent were completely wiped out. Four Sisters and eight nurses were killed in a single night.

Bishop Massi was killed by a fragment of shell which pierced his heart. He fell and died instantly. His death was a terrible shock and a great loss to me. When I was in trouble or in doubt, Monsignor Massi was one of the friends to whom I could always go. He was a kindly, generous man who had a heart and a home for everybody. It did one good to talk to him, for he looked at life with a smile and, no matter how dark things were, he saw a silver lining. But during these last years, when worries came to him thick and fast, that smile was not so evident as it used to be. Shortly before his death I called to see him on business and found him worried and discouraged. I tried to console him, pointing to the work he had done and the merit he had gained during the forty years of his mission life in China. "No, Monsignor," he said. "I have accomplished nothing. My hands are empty. All that I can hope

343

for now, through the mercy of God, is a small place in Paradise." That was not mock humility. It merely reflected the mind of many a missionary who, looking back, cannot see what he has accomplished because of the immense work still to be done.

Columbans in China contended with bombs and hunger; Columbans in other places faced different circumstances.

On November 25, 1943, The Most Reverend James H. Ryan celebrated a Solemn Pontifical Mass at St. Cecilia's Cathedral, Omaha, Nebraska, commemorating the Silver Jubilee of St. Columban's Mission Society. Twenty-five years in existence, the society announced that it now had 360 priest members and more than 250 seminarians. It had seminaries in Ireland and in Australia as well as in the United States, a house of studies in Rome. Its American-born members numbered seventy.

On July 23, 1943, Father Frank Douglas, a young New Zealand Columban, working in the Archdiocese of Manila, the parish of Pililla, was taken prisoner by the Japanese military police. There were Filipino guerrilla units in the hills near his parish and the Japanese had evidence that some of these guerrillas came in to confession to Father Douglas. They tortured the priest for four days in an attempt to force from him information on the location of the guerrilla hiding place. Father Douglas died under torture, holding the seal of confession intact.

On February 10, 1945, Japanese troops entered the Columban rectory in Manila and arrested Fathers John Henaghan, Patrick Kelly, Peter Fallon, Joseph Monaghan and a layman guest of the rectory, John Sullivan. The church, school and rectory were destroyed and the priests were led away. They were never seen again and many stories of their executions were told, but not verified as to detail. February tenth was to be known as the Day of Martyrs.

Three days later Father John Lalor, who had been on duty at the hospital and had, consequently, escaped the fate of the other Columbans in Manila, was killed by an American bomb when the hospital and its outbuildings were bombed. Father Lalor, the veteran of Hanyang who had experienced captivity in the lands of bandits, had had many close brushes with death before the bomb fell in Manila.

In the Catholic Leper Asylum at Mandalay, on March 16, 1945, Father Thomas Murphy, Columban, was killed by an exploding shell while saying Mass.

The bombs smashed and tore and killed and crippled. Then suddenly they ceased to fall and an incredible silence settled upon the shattered world of Hanyang. Tantalizing stories, hardly comprehensible, came through the grapevine about a super bomb of the Americans, a great destroyer of life, which had ended the war.

The 14th Air Force Unit, U.S.A., moved into Hankow on October 2, 1945. Sgt. John McLaughlin, a member of the medical unit, was from Brooklyn, from our Lady of Sorrows parish. Monsignor Fitzpatrick, his pastor, had told him when he was leaving "Listen now, if you should land in China by any chance, inquire around and see if you can locate Bishop Galvin. He was a fine Brooklyn priest in his day and he's a good friend of mine and I would like it if you gave him a greeting from me."

Sgt. McLaughlin remembered his pastor's little speech now that the war was over, and he asked a Franciscan in Hankow if he had ever heard of Bishop Galvin. He was startled to learn that the bishop was across the river from him in Hanyang.

I proceeded the following day to hike to the vicariate of Hanyang [Sgt. McLaughlin wrote]. Standing outside a compound you see the upper third of the church, a beautiful frontal structure of granite with a large Celtic cross. As we approached the Bishop's house, the Bishop . . . came down the steps and as I knelt to kiss his ring, I told him who I was and that I brought him the regards of my pastor. The Bishop was quite taken back and I believe quite happily surprised. He had been looking for someone from our forces who knew anything about his many friends. He was very anxious about his fellow missionaries of the Philippines and the conditions in which the missions had survived the years of war. The Bishop had four years of news to catch up on, so for the first hour or so I talked and talked, telling all the developments which had led to the Japanese surrender.

At 12:30 we went in for lunch. As I sat there, I marveled at the simplicity and humility of this man. All during our talk, not once had he said anything about his last

345

four years under the Japanese. Here I wish to say a few words about the food. I had, as the other men in the China theatre, eaten rice and potatoes and other native dishes, for we lived off the land. At times our food was not too good but we always had a little to supplement the off-the-land food. The food on the Bishop's table was by far the worst we had eaten. They were putting out their best food and it could not equal our worst fare.

The bishop escorted his visitor to the Columban Sisters' convent.

One of the Sisters commented that it was a shame that a young man of my age should have to go through so much hardship and privation. They were all so solicitous that I could not help marveling at their ignoring of the fact that they had been through much more, and even severer, hardships than I. These Sisters, all of whom are Irish, were grand and seemed quite well and happy, even after the ordeal of four years of Japanese occupation.

The next trip was to the Sisters of St. Mary's House, just ten minutes walk. As the twenty odd nuns gathered around us, the Bishop, speaking in Chinese, told them who I was and why I had come to visit them. They immediately became very angry, for they thought that I was responsible for the devastating air raids the Air Force had carried out on Hankow, Hanyang and Wuchang. After the Bishop assured them that I was not responsible, they became very friendly.

From there we proceeded to the American Sisters' house, about three minutes further up the road. I was introduced to the six nuns who were there at the time. The nuns asked me numerous questions about the States and I did my best to answer them. We had a good time just talking about the States. These nuns had sheltered many refugees during the devastating air raids and in the course of such work the convent became infested with the usual lice and bugs which abound in China. Fortunately we were able to give the good Sisters enough D.D.T. to insure the cleaning out of all the pests which had stayed on after the refugees left.

The young American sergeant was not content to send D.D.T. He had seen great need in the bishop's province and he wanted to do something about it. He scrounged around in the manner of sergeants, requisitioning bits and

346

pieces that would never be missed, but they did not add up to very much.

"We had a cook in our outfit," he wrote, "who wasn't too much of a sentimentalist, as most army cooks aren't. . . . If you wanted extra rations you had either to be an officer or a sergeant a grade higher than him to get it. And yet when I explained to him about the Bishop, the cook said that it was a shame the man over there didn't have jams and jellies when we had jams and jellies and butter. He said 'Let's requisition some stuff.' Being a hospital, nobody questioned our requisitions."

It all helped. Food went over, as well as delicacies and medical supplies. To do what he would consider an adequate job, McLaughlin needed cooperation from his commanding officer, "a Protestant who, for all the three years I'd known him, had been anti-Catholic." By some shrewd maneuvering, the sergeant prevailed upon the C.O. to visit the bishop.

I introduced them [he wrote] and I remember this vividly because I was so surprised—the C.O. wasn't the type of man you would put your arm about—but the Bishop put his arm around the C.O. "Let's go for a little walk," he said. "I'll show you around!" When we had dinner, the Bishop sat the C.O. on his right and chatted with him during the meal. The Major, instead of being his usual arrogant self, was like a baby in a kindergarten. Coming back to Hankow in a sampan, the C.O. said to me: "Give that man anything he wants." I almost fell to the bottom of the boat.

The Bishop had given him a piece of embroidery and the C.O. couldn't understand why this man should give him anything, but I felt that he was more moved by the Bishop's personality than by anything he had seen in Hanyang. Anyway, we backed up 6x6 trucks and we loaded them with everything that was available. The Bishop was very surprised and overcome. He didn't know what to say. I can understand how he felt because when you drive in a 6x6 and start unloading, what can you say? They had had nothing for years.

Taking care of the bishop and his flock became a kind of crusade for Sgt. McLaughlin. "I saw the Bishop's bed and he had only one stinky old blanket on it. I don't mean stinky in terms of being dirty, but in terms of being

347

threadbare, and it looked like something that you'd expect a Chinese coolie to be sleeping on." It disturbed Mc-Laughlin that his own quarters at the base were so much better than those of the bishop. Yet the bishop did not want to accept anything that was brought for himself personally. He thought that there were others who needed things more.

As far as he was concerned, he was living pretty good [McLaughlin continued]. I had seen pictures of Catholic Bishops and they were pretty regally dressed. But Bishop Galvin? How shall I put it? It was a cassock, period. It was real threadbare. He didn't particularly worry about these things. And, after I'd searched out before I met him the correct address to use when meeting a Bishop, I knelt down and kissed his ring and said "Your Excellency" and he said "Father." So he'd rather just be a priest and that is the way I addressed him.

The United States was the big reality in Hanyang now; hunger had abated in the compounds, insects were under control and there was medicine in the kits and cabinets. One theory of Bishop Galvin's, however, was a casualty. The mission buildings, the cathedral and the convents stood on a patch of high ground. All around them, forward and back, the land was churned and shattered, littered with tiny fragments of the structures which had formerly stood on it. The bishop had pointed out the incredible destruction which surrounded his small world on the first day he met Sgt. John McLaughlin. He was convinced that the U. S. Air Force had spared him.

"I felt that your airmen, seeing the cross on the church and the mission buildings, would stop bombing as they approached the compound," the bishop said, "and resume their bombing afterward."

McLaughlin could not accept this theory but he didn't feel qualified to reject it, either. He went over and discussed the idea with the B-25 group, temporarily based at Guan-Yi, which had bombed Hankow, Hanyang and Wuchang. The crew members laughed at the theory.

"That bishop is a nice, crazy priest," a bombardier said. "We pattern-bombed the area. That's all there was to it. We bombed at night. When you pattern-bomb, you just

348

lay them all over everything. And who in hell could see a cross down there at night?"

The sergeant persisted until he had interested a pilot who was skeptical but who wanted to see the area. When he saw it, he shook his head. "I can't explain it," he said. "If I wasn't looking at it, I'd say it was impossible. It shouldn't be like this. This island shouldn't be here. The whole area should be flat."

Bishop Galvin heard him. He looked at the rubble, the scarred earth stretching for miles on either side of the spot on which he stood.

"God is very good to us," he said.

30 : : THE BISHOP OF HANYANG

"Letters are just beginning to dribble in here," Bishop Galvin wrote on December 27, 1945. "Communications are bad. Air mail erratic. No Yangtze shipping to talk about. We have a civil war, too. No business. No banks. Nothing. . . . I wrote to Paul Waldron some time ago, just a note which I hoped some American boy would take out, to let him know we pulled through. Regarding the pulling through, nothing startling. Nothing poetic, just dull mission stuff; but if we had an artist, which we haven't, he might make a great story of it."

The letters which "dribbled in" were often confusing because the writers assumed a knowledge of events on the part of the recipients that they did not have. Four years out of action, four years away from the flow of news and the interchange of information, left gaps in one's understanding of current speech and current thought. Much of the news that came in letters was sad.

Bishop Galvin learned for the first time about the martyrs of the Philippines, all men whom he knew. Father John Henaghan, often described as "second only to Galvin as a storyteller" was one of the small group which launched the society. Ned McCarthy, another of those originals, had been on his way back to his mission station

349

in the Philippines when Pearl Harbor was bombed. He put into Burma and was interned there for the duration. He was one of the priests in the church at Mandalay when a bomb fragment killed Father Tom Murphy.

Bishop Galvin's brother, Patrick, had been killed by a truck in 1942. In that same year Father Patrick J. Judge, who had first welcomed him to Omaha, had died, as had Father Pat O'Reilly, one of the original three, the priest who had come out to him in China with Father Joe O'Leary.

"So long ago, God have mercy on them, and I didn't know," the bishop said.

William Henry Cardinal O'Connell, the grand old man of Boston, had died in 1944 and John McCormack of the magic voice had died in Ireland on September 16, 1945.

There were others. The casualties of those cloaked years were many, but the bishop had one in Hanyang after the peace, when it seemed that no war-tested priest should die. Father William (Willie) Holland died of pleurisy and malaria. This was a priest from his own place, from Lissarda, down the road from his sister Kate's home. The bishop felt his going deeply. "I sometimes think that I should never have started the mission," he said to Sister M. Thaddeus, a Columban nun. "It is too hard for men."

He wrote a letter to Ireland, then, one of his peacetime firsts, that was mailed before he wrote to his own family. He addressed it to Dan Holland, the father of the Columban he had lost:

These years have been difficult but the writing of this letter is one of the most difficult, and one of the saddest things I have had to do. My heart goes out to you all. May God console you and may he show you, as you kneel in Kilmurry Church at Mass and when you say your prayers, that He is a kind and merciful Father whose hand is always extended over us, not to hurt but to heal and to bless. The child whom He gave, He has taken to Himself and the young student who walked into the kitchen in Clodagh some twenty years ago to ask me for an introduction to Dalgan, who left home and friends and country for the sake of souls and for the love of God, has received the reward of a great priest and a great missionary.

350

It was difficult to tune in again to personal relationships, to gain any understanding of what had happened during the war. The reality of the atomic explosions which had devastated Hiroshima and Nagasaki was difficult to assimilate. It was more difficult to understand why Communist Russia was permitted to become a full ally and a sharer in victory by declaring war on Japan *after* the first of those bombs fell. News from the north indicated that the Russian Communists were pouring into territory that Japan had held, and as they disarmed the Japanese they had not fought, they were turning the weapons over to Chinese Communists. Such news, even if it should prove only partially true, was not reassuring to men who had contended against communism in China.

Not all the news was grim or frightening or sad. Bishop Galvin had a letter from home for Christmas and his letter of December 28 to his sister Kate proved to be, ultimately, the first letter that had come through to the family in nearly five years.

"I heard . . . Donal was ordained," he wrote. "Of Winnie's marriage I heard before the war. And now I should like to hear . . . how you and Jack have been making out during all these long years of silence and how all the friends are getting on. . . . I am feeling fairly well though bad food over a long period and terrible nervous strain, especially during the last year before the peace . . . was very hard."

The Chinese were trying to rebuild Hanyang and Hankow. The Nationalist Government provided funds and there were a great many men and women at work in the bomb-ploughed fields that had once been city streets. Bishop Galvin wanted to rebuild, too; to establish contact with the Catholics who could not be reached during the Japanese occupation. Several of his priests, overdue for vacations even before the war, had gone home for the rest they badly needed, and the new priests had not yet arrived. There was a shortage of priests, but he was convinced that it was only temporary. The Columban seminaries had been training priests during the long years when missionaries were not able to work. He decided to visit the parishes himself, the parishes with priests and the ones without.

The Chinese Communists were sharing the immense popularity of the Russians in Great Britain and the United

States, with the Red Army lauded as the saving force of China by newspaper correspondents and authors of definitely slanted books. This enthusiasm was not shared by the Columban priests or the Chinese whom they knew best.

> To us, who saw and understood the behavior of the Communists in the comparatively small areas of Hupeh which they dominated [Father McNamara wrote], it has always been a mystery how Western Intelligence, especially the American Intelligence Department who had access to most of unoccupied China during the Japanese war, could be so deceived and hoodwinked by Communist propaganda as to keep continually reporting to their respective Governments that the Chinese Communists were not really Communists in the sense of the term, a la Stalin and Lenin, but that they were some kind of mild agrarian reformers. In Hupeh, their whole system was no less Russian in method and technique than it was in Yenan. . . . They followed the policy which seems to have been the agreed and deliberate policy of the whole Communist Army during the Japanese occupation: that was to avoid any clash whatever with the Japanese army, to conserve their forces and munitions for the proper time when it would be of most use for furthering the Communist cause.

Father John McNamara, who later held the dual position of vicar general-procurator of the Columban Society in Hanyang, had more friends among Chinese businessmen and bankers than any other member of the society and his concern was colored greatly by their expressed concern; but the other priests, with their friends in the ranks of the poor, encountered the same distrust of all Communists and the same fear. When Gen. George C. Marshall, representing the United States, was instrumental in arranging a truce between Chiang Kai-shek and the Communists on January 10, 1946, it was widely believed that Chiang had been compelled to do so, that he would not have consented to a truce voluntarily and that the Communists would break the truce as soon as they received all the Japanese tanks and aircraft which the Russians were sending to them.

The uneasy political situation and the nervousness of the people, who had hoped for time to rebuild, created additional problems for missionaries. The emotional tide was

352

not running with them as it had after natural disasters such as flood and famine.

Bishop Galvin discovered for himself the great change in the Chinese people which had been wrought by World War II and, more particularly, by the presence of large numbers of Americans in China over long periods of time. Americans changed things; they caused things to be changed. Educated Chinese, with whom the bishop exchanged opinions in cities and in towns, told him that there was a great demand for education on the part of the Chinese people. Simple elementary schools would not satisfy that demand. Bishop Galvin after several months of visiting, inspecting and talking to anybody and everybody, returned to Hanyang convinced that there had to be Catholic middle schools and, ultimately, advanced schools of college level. He was delighted to discover on his return that this desire for education had also been manifesting itself in Hanyang.

The Sisters of Loretto, with all else they had to do, had met the request of wounded soldiers for a class in English. Everyone on the staff of the hospital, which had been established in an old Hanyang temple, became interested in the English classes and a group of forty-eight medical students asked for a course. Their need was narrow and specialized. They wanted to learn medical terms so that they could read the American Medical Association Journals.

All of this pleased Bishop Galvin but the great pleasure of his return was finding Father Charlie O'Brien at his old desk. The war had caught the bishop's secretary on leave and had prevented his return. He was back again now and the office was shining, all the tricky equipment repaired, the filing done. Father O'Brien, who could duplicate the bishop's signature with no effort, had even answered all the routine mail.

"Oh, Charlie," the bishop said, "I'm a whole man again."

On April 11, 1946, a papal decree was issued establishing the hierarchy of China. The Apostolic Internuncio, Archbishop Antony Riberi, formally raised the vicariate of Hanyang to the status of a diocese and installed, as its first residential bishop, The Most Reverend Edward J. Galvin.

353

The Bishop of Hanyang! It had a nice ring to it. It was pleasant to say. Bishop Galvin tried to dismiss it as nothing at all, but he was touched. The Roman Catholic Church did not create a diocese casually, and once a diocese was created, it existed forever. It might disappear from the maps, the seas or the sands might cover it, but it existed still. He was, when first raised to ecclesiastical rank in China, the Titular Bishop of Myrina, and Myrina, except in the memory of the Church, was a name forgotten even in Asia Minor. Now Hanyang was a diocese and Edward J. Galvin was its bishop.

The diocese of Hanyang had a population of approximately four million, with fifty thousand Catholics. At the time of its erection it had thirty-seven Columban priests, including five Chinese, on duty; seventeen priests on leave, and one Chinese priest doing post-graduate work in Rome.

One mentally pictured the Bishop of Hanyang as, perhaps, a stern, strong, masterful Occidental touched with a bit of Oriental glamour or mystery. In July of 1946, two young Columbans, Fathers Daniel P. Fitzgerald and Harold B. Watters, reported to him in Hanyang. It was a brutally hot day. They met a tall, straight man with dark, leathery skin, who was wearing a white cotton Chinese shirt with buttons—three quarters unbuttoned—down the front, a pair of black Chinese pants that were like pajamas and a worn leather belt that did not belong to the rest of the costume. His face and chest were sweaty, bubbled with sweat.

The young priests were wearing suits of clerical black, with Roman collars.

"Why are you wearing those things?" the bishop said. "Take them off before you meet your death in this heat!"

He was a good host when he had his guests relaxed. They were the first new priests to reach Hanyang in five years. The bishop asked them questions about their journey. He told them about Hanyang. All the time there was a little play under the surface of his mind. One of these men, Fitzgerald, was from Cork. The bishop hadn't spoken to anyone from Cork in many years and the letters which came to him were unsatisfactory, filled with words but containing little information. Fitzgerald was up to date on the facts and the rumors, the affairs of people, the

354

sound and the sight of home. Bishop Galvin closed a door in his mind; it would not do to show more interest in one priest than in the other. He never mentioned Cork. It was three days before he spoke to Father Fitzgerald alone and he made it seem almost accidental.

"I was hard put to keep up with him," Father Fitz said. "It seemed that he remembered every farm in the whole county of Cork."

The bishop did not tell him then, but one of the things he had done to preserve his sanity in the idle years was re-create Cork. He had drawn road after road, forcing his memory to fill in the houses and the people, remembering who had owned what, the large houses and the small. In the course of the conversation, however, Father Fitzgerald scored on him.

"You spoke in St. Finbarr's South on October 29, 1916," he said softly. "It was when you were raising funds before this society existed."

"Aye. I remember it." The bishop looked puzzled. "But how would you know about that?"

"It was told to me." Dan Fitzgerald said. "You see, I was baptized only four months before in the same church."

"Is that the truth now?"

The Bishop of Hanyang was shaken. He knew of the years and how many they were, but it dramatized them when he looked at this slender, good-looking young priest and was forced to remember that he had been an older young priest himself when this man was born, with Brooklyn and three years of China behind him.

The summer blanketed down, a blazing hot series of days and long, sleepless, humid nights. There was no escape from it, no place in Kuling since the war. Bishop Galvin wrote to his nephew, Father Donal O'Mahony:

"Father Dan Fitzgerald and another young priest arrived three or four days ago. They are fine fellows, looking well, though they had a long, hot voyage. They are resting now in one of our places here on the banks of the Yangtze where it is cool—or, anyhow, it is the coolest place we have. Indeed, no place is cool here at the moment and that is another reason for a brief letter."

Father Fitzgerald was not finding the banks of the Yangtze either cool, comfortable or endurable. He disliked China and its climate and its people. He suffered, as

355

other young priests had suffered before him, from the insatiable curiosity of the Chinese, the utter lack of privacy. He did not believe that he could ever settle into the ways of these people or be any good to them as a missionary. He walked around, postponing a decision, and finally made it. He could imagine the wrath of the bishop but a man had to face his facts. When he saw the bishop he blurted out his entire indictment.

"I made a mistake," he concluded. "I have no vocation as a missionary to China. I'm sure of it. I'd not be feeling like this if I was meant for it."

The bishop leaned back in his chair. "Tell me," he said, "did you have a bad time leaving Ireland?"

"I did, as a matter of fact. Very bad."

The bishop sighed. He looked out the window. "God, isn't it terrible?" he said.

That was all. He ignored the passionately proclaimed lack of vocation and unsuitability for China. "He said it all in that sentence," Father Fitzgerald declared later. "He told me that he knew how I felt and that he had gone every step of the way himself, that he had rebelled as I did, and it was terrible, just plain terrible. He made himself one with me and, oddly enough, I had the feeling right then that I could make it, that it wasn't supposed to be easy and that, in a long lifetime, I probably wouldn't suffer as much as the bishop had."

Father Fitzgerald went back to the river and to the study of Chinese and he became one of the outstanding young Columbans. His experience with the bishop was not unique. Other Columbans had faced him with one problem or another and had had the problem fall apart in the face of an uncomplicated simplicity. On another occasion the bishop said to Fitzgerald: "Dan, never say to any poor fellow, 'Don't worry!' That is not a bit of help to him. We're constitutionally incapable of not worrying."

"The Communists were on the march," Father Leahy wrote. "They were different Communists from those experienced before. Those of 1926 were glorified bandits; this was a new, well-organized army that moved with diabolical efficiency. It was an army that had come to stay. They marched from the North to the South and from Harbin to the sea, consolidating as they advanced, sweeping everything in their path and meeting in that path only feeble opposition."

The Nationalists held the three cities, and the Diocese of Hanyang was relatively peaceful. The Nationalist officers complained that the Communists were receiving steady shipments of war materials from the Russians and that American aid to the anti-Communists had stopped. The political picture, on the whole, was muddy, difficult to comprehend.

In March, 1947, Bishop Galvin wrote to his nephew, Father O'Mahony, who was now in China in the diocese of Bishop Cleary: "I have just returned from five months in the Missions. Most of the time I had neither pen nor paper. I do not want to interrupt your study of Chinese and I do not want you to come to Hanyang during the summer's heat. You are much better off down there. I called at Dan Fitzgerald's place on my way in and found him in great form. Dan is a splendid man."

Father Fitzgerald's parish was Hwan-Chia-Shan where he was assistant to Father John McMullan. One of the bishop's problems on his journey was a priest who appeared to have gone native, to have adopted too fully the Chinese way of life. The man seemed to have more in common with the Chinese of a village than with any of his fellow priests. The two priests of Hwan-Chia-Shan knew about him, of course, but the bishop did not discuss him.

"Any faults he has," he said, "are faults of an apostle."

"I never heard the bishop say a hard word about anyone," Father Fitzgerald said. "One night someone brought up the names of several men who had left the society, one of them a decided failure. The bishop said only, 'Let us always remember, they all contributed something, each and every one of them.' "

In June, 1947, Bishop Galvin went to Nancheng for a conference with Bishop Cleary and a visit with his nephew, Father Donal O'Mahony, a slender, alert young man with the Lordan features and some of the bishop's own manner of speech. The bishop, who had not seen him since 1924, had a difficult time controlling his voice.

"I never expected to meet you in China," he said. "You were pretty small."

"You didn't encourage me to come to China."

357

"I wouldn't. I was afraid you were trying to follow me. I am glad that you are here."

Bishop Galvin rested well in Nancheng. He enjoyed his fellow bishop's fine, cool French-built residence, standing on rising ground outside the city. It was a good house in which to relax, to escape from the familiar worries of his own diocese; but he was restless in it, and after a month insisted upon returning to Hanyang in the gruelling heat.

"Thereby undoing the value of his rest," said Bishop Cleary.

After a brief stop in Hanyang, Bishop Galvin went to Shanghai. He saw the scars of war and he saw people he had known over long years. What he saw and heard made him thoughtful.

Bishop Galvin had been discounting the Communists, while he worked hard on the organization of schools, the manning of parishes, the rebuilding of physical property. He had convinced himself that in due time Chiang Kai-shek, with armament and backing from the great powers, would drive the Communists into a corner again as he had done before. The bishop had not believed that the great powers would permit Russia a free hand in Asia and control of China for Communism.

He came back from his trip, however, with the conviction that Communism was taking over China on a gigantic, carefully executed plan, and that those who were in a position to save China had no intention of doing so. In the areas already taken over, the procedure had been quite simple, quite efficient. Armed and ruthless outlaws, bandits and thieves had moved into a district chosen by the Reds, robbing and terrorizing the people. In a short time the Communist Army—disciplined, well-behaved, under strict orders—appeared and established order. The people were grateful for relief from banditry. Their fears were lulled. In one area the soldiers said cheerfully, "You are all right now. Everything is fine. But when the men in blue come? Oh-ho!"

The men in blue were officials and clerks. They filled out questionnaires on everyone, and most of the questions were absurd. If answers on any two interrogations varied the individual was arrested and questioned relentlessly. The leaders and the educated people, people with a

358

little money, were the primary targets of the men in blue because these were the individuals most apt to prove obstructive to a Communist takeover. The great mass of the ignorant, uneducated people were flattered. They were encouraged by men, who were seemingly sympathetic, to indulge themselves in self-pity; poisoned by self-pity, their anger was easily aroused against classes and individuals. Social conflict, bitterness of class against class, was an essential ingredient of the Communist revolution.

Back in Hanyang, Bishop Galvin wrote to Father O'Mahony: "Leahy left day before yesterday with feelings of regret. His heart is in Chang-toukow with the Catholics he brought into being, and will be till he dies, I think. It will be hard to fill his place and he knows it. Much of the sweat and blood he put into that district may well go for naught. We shall do our best to prevent that, but I cannot say whether we will succeed. . . ."

In Ireland the Society of St. Columban had its first General Chapter since before the war and Dr. Michael O'Dwyer stepped down from the post of superior general in which he had served a total of twenty-three years. According to canon law, he was no longer eligible for re-election; so he laid the burden down. His successor was Rev. Jeremiah Dennehy.

Although there were warning signals of danger all over his diocese—news of swift bandit raids and stories of agitators appearing suddenly in towns to make inflammatory speeches—Bishop Galvin went out again in September, 1947, to visit the parishes, to share the problems of the priests and to confirm any Catholics ready for confirmation. Toward the end of his swing he was in a village some distance from the large, mountain area parish of Sung Ho with Father Jim Donohoe, when the bandits swooped down. The two priests had only a few minutes warning and could not pick their route. The object was to get safely out of town and, after that, to escape capture. There was, of course, no transportation available to them. They walked.

"We were a half hour ahead of them for the first twenty-four hours," the bishop said.

On December 22, at dusk, they reached Hwan-Chia-Shan and were greeted by Fathers McMullan and Fitzgerald. "Both of them were tired," Fitzgerald wrote.

359

"They had one good pair of boots between them and Jim was wearing them! The Bishop saw to that. He himself was wearing a pair of old shoes with the soles practically gone."

After they had dinner, the bishop went to bed early; but he was restless and Father Fitzgerald brought him a hot drink. "He laughingly told me how Jim and himself had slept in a heap of straw in an old Chinese shack," Father Fitz wrote. "One would think that traveling non-stop for 100 miles, the great part of it on foot, was a big joke, even if your feet were blistered and your body stiff and sore, and Red bandits were on your trail."

The bishop decided next morning that he would proceed directly to Hanyang City, thirty miles away. The first ten miles had to be walked and Father Fitzgerald accompanied the bishop and Father Donohoe to the river town where they would embark for Hanyang.

> We walked steadily [he wrote]. It was December but the sun came up as the forenoon advanced. We were all wearing soutanes or overcoats when we set out. As we warmed up, the coats were shed. The Bishop's coat was heavy. After we had gone a few miles, we paused for a break. As we were about to resume our journey I laid my hand on the Bishop's coat, remarking, "I'll carry that for a while, my Lord." He looked at me. "You have one of your own to carry," was all he said. I replied that his would help to balance my own, but he refused. My catechist had come with us, so, in desperation, I said that he would only be honored to be allowed to carry the Bishop's coat. "He has his own bundle to carry," replied the Bishop. "I'll carry this coat." And that finished the matter.

For the bishop, carrying his coat, that trip home was a grim affair. Now that he had seen the bandits again, he knew that they were part of a pattern and there would be no military force ultimately to restrain and contain them. The military would come in as the second stage in a process; then, the "men in blue." There would be no freedom after that; no religion, no security, no decent human pride.

Within two months, on February 4, 1948, Bishop Galvin wrote: "In the Provinces north of us, the country

360

districts are entirely in the hands of the Reds. One of our priests, writing recently from Peking, says that there are 1000 priests in that city from Hopeh, Honan, Shantung, Manchuria, Inner Mongolia (where the Belgians took terrible losses) and Shansi, etc. All mission work throughout those provinces has come to a complete stop and losses are terribly heavy. There has been nothing like it in living memory."

On June 23 he wrote: "Cardinal Spellman and party paid me a visit on my invitation. I met the Cardinal twenty-five years ago when he was a young assistant at the Cathedral in Boston. . . . We had a great reception for him at the Cathedral in Hankow and at the American Consulate. 'Like St. Patrick's Day in New York' as he put it. He is a kindly, good man who makes a great impression on everybody. . . . I met Msgr. John J. Boardman of Brooklyn and Msgr. Fulton Sheen and all the party. Great men."

Writing of this visit, Father Gerry O'Collins said: "Rarely had I seen the Bishop show such signs of exhaustion and fatigue as he did just prior to the visit of Cardinal Spellman. . . . During the four hour stay, the Bishop traveled with the Cardinal in the same car from the aerodrome through Hankow streets lined by Catholic schoolchildren. The zeal and the exhausted condition of this veteran missionary Bishop did not fail to make a deep impression on the Cardinal, as was shown by the talk he gave in Los Angeles a few weeks later. . . ."

Shortly after the visit of Cardinal Spellman, Donal O'Mahony came up to Hanyang to see his uncle. He had been appointed pastor of Chiuliang, replacing Father Dan Lucey, another Kilmurry man, who was going home; but Father O'Mahony developed a duodenal ulcer which put him in a Shanghai hospital. He was being invalided to the United States now and was calling to say good-bye. While he was in Hanyang, word came of the death of Denis, the bishop's brother, erstwhile keeper of the bees at Clodagh. A few days later, Father Jerry Buttimer, who was Father O'Mahony's first pastor in China, died of heat prostration at Lienchu.

In November 1948 the immensely popular Father Patrick Brennan was appointed Prefect Apostolic of Kwangju, Korea.

In February 1949 [Father John McNamara wrote] it was decided to make an attempt to return to the country parishes and live under the Red rule, as by that time it was evident that the Communists had come to stay. They had settled down in all the small towns along the Han River. They allowed boats to pass up and down to Hankow, collected taxes on everything and, except for a certain amount of propaganda, were making no radical changes. . . . Father Vallely and Father Geraghty went to Mo-Wang-Tsui; Fathers Paul Hughes and M. Collins went to Sien-Tao-Chen; Fathers J. Donohue and Peter Chang to Yo-Kow. They were allowed in by the Communists and permitted to settle down. Father Hughes had a Middle School in Sien-Tao-Chen which was more or less self-supporting. The others continued with their ordinary mission work.

Bishop Galvin, writing of this staffing of the mission, said: "We can, I hope, keep the flag flying in Mienyang and move further afield when more help arrives. The wish of the Holy See, and the wish of God's will for us are the only two things about which we are concerned at present. The three communities of American Sisters, and a good many of the priests, have gone from Wuchang but our Sisters want to stay until they are put out."

Despite the quiet and the seeming tolerance of the Communists, there was uneasiness among the priests, fear among the people. There were Communist agents everywhere, asking questions and filling out forms. There was much confusion about money and flat Communist orders that gold, silver and foreign currency in anyone's possession must be turned in and exchanged for Communist Chinese paper money.

On March 4, 1949, Bishop Galvin wrote to his Brooklyn friend, Daisy Hall:

The Communists have control of all the country north of the Yangtze except these three cities and we think they can take them any time they wish. We have no notion how we will fare when they take them. We know from what happened in the north that they have no love for the Church, to put it mildly. On the other hand, it is the wish of the Holy See that priests and Sisters remain at their posts. I do not want to conceal that there is tension. We would not be human if there wasn't. I have, as you know,

362

three Communities of Sisters; one from Kentucky, one from Ireland and twenty-six Chinese Sisters. When I think of the uncertainties of the future, I can't help being worried about them. Keep us in your prayers every day.

On May 4 he wrote again: "The Government has fled from Nanking which is now in the hands of the Communists. They have crossed the Yangtze at several points without opposition and are marching rapidly southward. It looks as if the whole country will be in their hands very soon. They are within thirty miles of us here but have not yet attacked. The priests and Sisters are quite calm. We shall welcome what God is pleased to send and hold out as long as we can. No more now. God bless you."

On May 14 the Red Army marched into Hanyang.

The day following the arrival of the Communists, Bishop Galvin and Father Martin J. Croffy were arrested while walking along the street. They were taken to the temporary police station, questioned and released. It was quite an orderly procedure, almost polite, but the iron fist was there, an integral part of life in Hanyang from now on. There were armed guards on the roads, the gates, the ferry boat piers.

Bishop Galvin made one trip to Hankow with Father Fitzgerald during July, 1949. As they were about to board the ferry boat to cross the Han River to Hanyang on their return, they were stopped by Red soldiers armed with Sten guns. The soldiers searched the two men, turning out their pockets, indifferent to identification. Father Fitzgerald had a small carryall which contained, among other things, a pair of rubber overshoes. A soldier asked him, "What are these things?" Father Fitz could not think of the Chinese word. He looked over toward the bishop who was trying to explain to a soldier that a medal in his pocket was not foreign money.

"Excuse me," Father Fitzgerald said. "But what's the Chinese for overshoes?"

The bishop looked at him startled; then he laughed. He laughed heartily at the inanity of the inquiry in a moment of stress, at the whole preposterous situation. Father Fitzgerald joined him. The two men standing there

363

under the guns continued to laugh and the Communist soldiers thought they were crazy.

"Once Wuhan was occupied, trouble started for the peasants and the small town traders all over the country districts," Father McNamara wrote, "and naturally, for the priests who were there also. Preparation for the re-distribution of land was set afoot and the accusations against 'landlords and reactionaries' began. The priests were restricted in their movements and the general situation for the Church rapidly deteriorated."

The Communist method had been perfected through long practice. Everyone, great or small, had to make an inventory of all he owned for the Government, including even the smallest things; a pencil, so many sheets of paper. Everyone had to fill out full information on his family, names and ages, living and dead, dates of birth and death, lists of friends and business acquaintances, addresses of past residence, names of past employers, record of taxes paid, of travel.

Few men could make such inventories without overlooking items. At the convenience of the Communists, a man was called in and asked the same questions that appeared on any one of several sheets he had filled out. A secretary checked his answers against the sheet and any differences or shade of difference in an answer brought the accusation that he was trying to deceive the Government, not taking his responsibility as a citizen seriously. A man marked for liquidation, because he was obviously not the material from which good party members are made, was constantly harried, questioned, intimidated; as his nerves gave way, he gave answers which were checked against him. The executions did not begin immediately, but they were over the hill of time and ultimately were carried out on a large scale.

On January 6, 1950, Great Britain recognized Communist China one day after breaking diplomatic relations with Chiang Kai-shek's Nationalist Chinese regime. On February 15 Mao Tse-tung arrived in Moscow to sign a treaty of friendship and mutual defense with Stalin.

That June the Korean War began as communism sought to take another stride in the conquest of Asia.

In September and October of 1950 Bishop Galvin had a great many letters from his sisters and brothers in Ireland.

His brother, Jim, had offered Clodagh for sale and everyone in the family opposed his selling it. No one felt financially in a position to buy Clodagh or free to work it, but some of them considered it holy land because of its association with Bishop Galvin.

> Clodagh has been home to all of us [the bishop wrote to Donal O'Mahony] and the associations with the living and the dead are part of it. I know more about its history and its purchase than anyone in the family. I would do anything under heaven to save it, but goodwill in the matter at issue counts for little, and, as you know, I have, like yourself, nothing at all to my name. Had I something of my own, Clodagh would never go to a stranger. I would gladly give all I had if only for the sake of father and mother, and never ask for any return, for I know that, even in their graves, they would thank me. Though its passing from the family is a thorn in my heart, I do not wish to interfere. . . . At this distance, my letters could deal only with generalities, and being away from home so many years, and not having an intimate knowledge of conditions or circumstances, any suggestions of mine to other members of the family would, I fear, have little practical value—like so many things, I leave it in the hands of God.

Clodagh was sold to a "Mrs. O'Keefe" for £3050 in November.

On November 20 the Chinese *Peoples' Press* stated: "The Catholic and Protestant religions must become social activities, completely liberated from foreign protection and belonging to the Chinese themselves."

On February 18, 1951, Bishop Galvin reached one of the saddest decisions of his life. The Chinese nuns of the Order of the Blessed Virgin Mary in Hanyang had been living as nuns under the Communist regime, although dispersed and not daring to wear religious garb or admit their identity as nuns. Bishop Galvin, feeling the Reds closing in more tightly on him day by day, had summoned all the nuns he could reach and requested them to seek dispensation from their religious vows as a precautionary measure. He granted the dispensations on this date. Sisters Justa and Clementia, the only two non-Chinese nuns left in Hanyang, were witnesses. Sister Isabel, Chinese Sister of Loretto, was also dispensed.

On September 7 Father Joseph Seng, known as "the Chinese Father with the Irish brogue," ally and co-worker with the Columbans and the Sisters of Loretto, was arrested by the Communists. He later died "a saintly prison death" in a Shanghai prison at the age of thirty-five.

In October, 1951, Father John McNamara, with Sisters Justa and Clementia, went on trial, charged with selling property of the people. The items involved were an old generator and some gasoline which had once belonged to the school. The trial was extended to November and, inevitably, the three defendants were found guilty. The verdict of the court was "expulsion from China forever." Sister Justa and Sister Clementia were sent out on November 22, Father McNamara on the 24th. No one was allowed to bid them farewell. Bishop Galvin, under house arrest at the time, was, however, permitted to go to the river bank and give his blessing to the two nuns after they were already in the sampan which would take them to Hankow.

As the two sisters crossed the station platform in Hankow to the train for Hong Kong, a slender girl in ordinary civilian attire intercepted them. The two nuns were frightened when they recognized Sister Isabel, but she embraced both of them.

"Sister, you should not be here," Sister Justa said. "You take too great a risk."

The girl straightened, lifting her chin. "You are here," she said. "I, too, am a Sister of Loretto."

On November 2, 1955, Sister Isabel was executed in Hankow with Fathers Paul Chang and John Gao. There were several reports of the triple execution which stated that the prisoners were shot from behind while kneeling. One account said that they were beheaded.

Bishop Galvin was penned up, restricted in his own house, subjected to frequent interrogation, to searches of his house, to a long series of annoyances. His patience, often commented on by his priests, was put to a severe test and survived.

"Always, in this country, one has to learn to hold his patience in his hands," he said once, "to look at it and to remind himself that it is necessary to him."

"He was wonderful when the Reds took over all that he had built," Father John McNamara wrote. "He was good during the Japanese and the bombing troubles, but the Communists brought out the very best in him. He was really magnificent."

Another letter, from Father Dan Fitzgerald to Father Donal O'Mahony, said: "He [the Bishop] is keeping remarkably well, God bless him. As you would expect, a few gray hairs have appeared with the passing of the years and with this and that. I make it my business to call often. We have many a chat about places which still mean a fair deal to him. Anyhow, when you are writing to mid-Cork you can tell them that the great man was never greater. We will leave it at that."

In December Very Rev. Jeremiah Dennehy, superior general of the Columban Fathers, died of cancer. The council of 1952 elected Father Timothy Connolly to succeed him—the same Father Connolly who considered himself temperamentally unfit to be a bursar, who learned about figures and money from a correspondence course and who, in the adding up, was pretty generally considered the closest approach to a financial genius that the society had ever had.

The old superior general passed with the dying year and the new one assumed responsibility in mid-year 1952. The effort to hold on in China was no longer worthwhile. There was too little left. On June 27 Fathers Eugene Spencer, Daniel P. Fitzgerald and Harold B. Watters left. One of them wrote a brief letter and summed it up in a phrase: "Everything is folding up."

Through the summer, two renegade Catholics tried to frighten or persuade Hanyang Catholics to give testimony against Bishop Galvin. Not a man or a woman would accuse him of anything. A general accusation meeting was announced, to be held in the school at the rear of the bishop's house on September 10. No one attended. The people who refused to accuse, and the people who ignored the Communist-sponsored meeting, were inviting reprisals upon themselves and trouble for their families, but the bishop had a special place in their hearts and, Christian or pagan, they would not turn against him.

On September 15 at 7 A.M., just as I was preparing to say Mass [Bishop Galvin wrote] a policeman appeared at the sacristy door with a document summoning me to ap-

367

pear at Police Headquarters in Hankow. Permission to say Mass was refused so, escorted by the policeman, I left Hanyang without breakfast and at nine sharp I was ushered into the presence of the Chief of Police and a number of assistants. Reading a document, he said:

"You have been summoned here to be informed that the Government of China has decided to expel you from the country and you are to leave Wuhan within three days. The charges against you are as follows: You have opposed and obstructed the establishment of an Independent Church in China. You have brought into being a reactionary organization called The Legion of Mary. You have engaged in anti-patriotic propaganda against the Government. You have disobeyed the Government and you have destroyed the property of the people."

After the reading of the order of banishment, the bishop was escorted back to his room by the police. A thorough search of his personal effects began. A sentry was posted at his door. "You are to understand," the policeman in charge said, "that you are a criminal under sentence of expulsion from China. You are to have no communication whatever with anyone in this compound or outside of it."

On the morning of September 17, the man in charge told me that I was to leave Hanyang that day at 1 P.M. [Bishop Galvin wrote]. I need not tell you how I felt. Indeed I could not do so if I tried. I, who had come to Hanyang so many years ago to do my little best there for God and souls, was now leaving it as a criminal. The memories of the past thronged in my mind; the great priests, Brothers and Sisters, who under almost insuperable difficulties, had worked for God throughout the diocese, so zealously and loyally; the high ideals, the grand ideals they had; the mass conversions, the struggle to finance the work, the great hope that in the not distant future the Diocese of Hanyang would be entirely Catholic! Now, the diocese was almost completely deprived of its priests. It was a mass of ruins and the hopes of other days seemed to have vanished like a dream.

With these thoughts in my mind, I was informed that it was time to leave. Guarded by seven policemen, I went down the path by the Cathedral walking on the streets of Hanyang for the last time.

368

The seven policemen and the criminal in their charge walked along the street and suddenly the criminal, having reached a high point, halted. He turned slowly.

"I blessed the Compound," he wrote, "and the Cathedral, the whole diocese; its priests, its Sisters and the people. I put them under the protection of Our Lord and His Blessed Mother and of St. Columban, the patron of the diocese and of the Cathedral. It was all that I could do."

That done, he walked again—his back straight and his head high, looking ahead, not seeing the policemen. It was all over and he was leaving, leaving everything. But he was, now and forever, the Bishop of Hanyang.

31 : : LAST POST

Three Communist policemen escorted Bishop Edward J. Galvin to the Chinese border, a journey of thirty-six hours from the three cities. During those thirty-six hours he had no food and was unable to sleep. He was badly spent, physically, when he stepped onto British soil at Hong Kong.

"Bishop Galvin arrived here last evening, September 19," Sister Gabriel, a Columban Sister wrote. "Thin and worn looking, he was more like a beggar than anything else. Fathers John McNamara and Malachy Murphy were at the border to meet him when he crossed over to freedom. We got word as soon as the three of them got to the Catholic Center in Hong Kong and went immediately."

There was world interest in the Bishop of Hanyang and it was a problem to protect him from press interrogation until he had food and rest. "I'd rather not say anything," he said. "If I said anything that those people didn't like, I might make it difficult for those I had to leave behind."

He was worried about those still in China within reach of the Reds. His Chinese priests were there and his Chinese nuns, released from their vows but still, he was certain, faithful in their vocations. Fathers Joseph Crossan and

369

Paul Hughes were in Hanyang and Father Sands was still in his country parish, Hsin Ti. Nobody had seen Father Sands since the summer of 1949 but word came out occasionally which indicated that he was still functioning.

In Hong Kong, a medical checkup revealed the fact that the years of starvation during the war and the later even more deadly years under the Communists had taken their toll of the bishop. He had leukemia, cancer of the blood. He waved the verdict away, refusing to take it seriously.

"A lot of these Chinese things clear up," he said. "I have medical friends in the States. They'll take care of me."

He was in good humor on October 9, when he wrote to Donal O'Mahony:

> When you read the following cable you will readily grant that the O'Mahony clan must, at least pro tem, take a back seat. I received it yesterday from the head of a Hongkong firm.
> "Please contact Bishop Galvin of the Columban Fathers. Give him one thousand pounds, sterling, for his own personal needs from Australian Galvins. Tell Galvin we will pay all his expenses for holiday wherever he chooses. (Signed) John Galvin, Woodside, California."
> I don't know John Galvin at all, never met him, never wrote to him. But his Hongkong partner, to whom he cabled the above, gave me his address and I shall write, and later call to say how proud I am of the name. Talk about surprises! I was as poor as St. Francis yesterday and I am as rich as a Banker today. If you need any money, you know the Bank to call at. Ask me no more questions. I can't answer except that the Galvin clan is *It*. No secret at all about the above. You may tell it to whom you wish, but you are to keep strictly away from Woodside.

He celebrated the Silver Jubilee of his consecration on November 6 in Hong Kong, with Mass in the Ruttonjee Chapel of the Columban Sisters. "Sister Maureen and her two were there," he wrote. "No others were let in on the secret. We did not want to make a fuss nor to provoke speeches and hot air. I received a letter of congratulations through Father Hanahoe from His Holiness which, I suppose, the poor man, who has so many things on his mind,

370

never saw. It is a gesture of good will and on the diplomatic menu."

On November 23 he was seventy years old. "I can do the sum in my head," he said, "but still it is difficult to believe. There are times when nothing seems long ago. I'm feeling fine except that I'm tired. When I get a rest, I'll be all right."

The bishop left Hong Kong, which he did not consider "quite China," on November 26 aboard the *S. S. President Madison*. "I have always wanted to sail on this ship," he said. "It has a grand Catholic captain."

Bishop Galvin had a good voyage and he had to face the press again when he landed in San Francisco on December 15, 1952. He was able to avoid any statements which would embarrass his people in China because his watch provided a colorful story lead.

> For the past three years, China has not been a place where a wise man keeps a gold watch [*The San Francisco Examiner* stated]. That's why Bishop Edward J. Galvin, 70-year-old founder of the Catholic Columban Fathers and veteran of forty years in China, gave his watch to a returning priest in 1949. Yesterday, Bishop Galvin received his watch back. He arrived from the Orient . . . and was met at the pier by high-ranking Catholic dignitaries and friends. At the pier also was the Very Rev. Peter McPartland. He was the priest to whom Bishop Galvin entrusted his watch. With a smile, the watch was returned.

San Francisco had always been good to Bishop Galvin and the clergy and people celebrated his return with a testimonial banquet at the Fairmount Hotel on the seventeenth.

The Christmas season brought reunions with many old friends, the most cherished, perhaps, being that with Father Joe O'Leary. Long ago, the two men had dreamed of an organization such as the Columbans in China and they had had a third dreamer with them, Father Patrick O'Reilly. On December 12, 1915, Fathers O'Reilly and O'Leary had landed in Shanghai and were met by Father Galvin. Now, thirty-seven years later, the two survivors stood beside the grave of Father O'Reilly in San Diego, California, and had their pictures taken.

Another bit of drama was being played out in China; on December 15, 1952, Bishop Patrick Cleary was expelled. He had been twenty-one years in China without a relief, a vacation, or a trip away. In the United States, on his way to Ireland, one of the first to welcome him was Father Joseph Mullen, who had accompanied him to China in 1931 and who had served twelve years under him in China. Father Mullen had not left China voluntarily, either. He had left because of illness in March, 1943.

In San Francisco the doctors had examined Bishop Galvin and confirmed the diagnosis of leukemia; but the bishop was not conceding to it.

"I have always had a purpose when I came to the United States," he said. "There was always something that I wanted and tried to get. Well, I still want something. I am not just a poor old bishop for the women to make a fuss over."

He set up a difficult project for himself, one that would compare in difficulty with those he had undertaken in his youth. He prepared to visit every bishop in the United States to obtain signatures petitioning Rome to place St. Columban's name on the Universal Calendar of the Church. No saint of the Irish race had yet been included in the Universal Calendar and it would be fitting, the bishop believed, for St. Columban, Ireland's greatest missionary saint, to be the first.

Before he could start on his self-imposed journey, Bishop Galvin had a long distance phone call which he reported in a letter to Father O'Mahony: "Dan Hallahan of Chicago called me last night and said that Margaret Lorden [a maternal cousin] was taken to the hospital and that she is dying of cancer. He said that she was calling for me and I told him to tell her that I would be there as soon as possible."

He flew to Chicago and he was with Margaret Lorden when she died. She bequeathed her large home to Bishop Galvin and he signed it over to the Sisters of St. Columban to be used as a convent. Father Donal O'Mahony came to Chicago from Omaha and had several days with his uncle, who talked of a return to Ireland once his American campaign was concluded, but who did not speak of his illness.

A cable was awaiting Bishop Galvin on his return to

372

San Francisco. Father Hugh Sands, the last Columban missionary of the Diocese of Hanyang, was expelled by the Communists on January 28.

"Thank God he's safe!" the bishop said.

John Galvin, the benefactor who had cabled a thousand pounds to Bishop Galvin in Hong Kong, came to San Francisco and the bishop saw him, as he reported in a letter to Father O'Mahony:

> I met John Galvin, a great man and a great Catholic. His wife expects a baby one of these days and is in a hospital here. She was born in Dublin but left it at the age of three and spent all of her life in the Orient. John met her in Hongkong and he says it was the most fortunate day in his life. She is a real Catholic lady. They have three children and young Sean, who is five, is the white-haired boy; the two others are girls, Patricia (14) and Eileen (3). They are hoping that the little one who is coming will be a boy. John and I had dinner together and a wonderful talk on relationship, then went to see Mrs. Galvin in the hospital. . . . He told me that he was a very wealthy man and wished to give me a London address to which I could apply for cash at any time; whatever you want, he said. I thanked him but refused to take the address. John is a man whose friendship I treasure but it will never be said that I am after his money.

Joseph Stalin died on March 5, 1953, and for a while Bishop Galvin looked hopefully for signs of a Communist breakup which would spread to China. He was probably shrewd enough in his appraisal of Asian affairs to doubt seriously his own hope, but he was firm in his faith that the Church would return to China and that the Columbans, a single one of the Church regiments, would be among the first to go back.

The Far East reported on the gallant campaign which the aging and ill bishop was waging in denial of both age and illness. The magazine quoted a letter of his written from San Diego:

"Arrived here yesterday. On my way from Chicago, I spent a night with the Archbishop of Denver, then on to Pueblo, Santa Fe, El Paso, through Texas, Louisiana, Little Rock, Amarillo, and back through Tucson to San

373

Diego. All the Bishops gave me a great reception; all signed the letter of petition."

The Far East added: "He would spend a month in a hospital, or resting at a Columban house, then hit the road again. Soon he was spending three months laid up and only a few days on the road, but the flow of signatures to Rome continued."

On July 27, 1953, an armistice in the Korean fighting was signed by representatives of the commands of the United Nations and of the Communist armies in Panmunjom.

On September 16 the bishop wrote a letter from Chicago to Daisy Hall, signing it "Father Galvin." He had had a rather bad collapse which put him in the hospital. In his letter he said: "I have been resting here for more than two weeks. For several months I have been interviewing bishops of the South and West, asking that they request the Holy Father to inscribe the Feast of St. Columban on the calendar of the Univeral Church. I did some 10,000 miles by car. It was tiring work. In the Chicago area I did a thousand miles. I was very tired. The Doctor said, after examination, that I was suffering from heat exhaustion and virus pneumonia."

On November 6 the bishop was still in Chicago and he wrote again to Daisy Hall, stating that "in a day or two" he would leave for Loretto, Kentucky, to see the mother general of the Sisters of Loretto. From there he planned to visit more bishops, then go to the Columban college at Silver Creek, New York. After that he would visit Brooklyn and go home to Ireland for Christmas.

His plans did not work out. He visited the Sisters of Loretto, but he had to stop at Buffalo, New York, for a long stay in Mercy Hospital. He wrote to Father Donal O'Mahony from there on February 7, 1954, reporting that he had neuritis from the left hip to the left knee, with a blazing red rash. "The dead ache in my leg cost me two weeks of sleepless nights and days," he wrote. "I am much improved now and the rash is clearing up. But I shall be here for some time yet."

He left the hospital on February 22 and went to the Columban seminary at Silver Creek. He wrote from there on March 10: "I lived on the third floor of the Seminary but the doctor was averse to my climbing stairs, so I am

374

in residence at the stucco house with Fathers Francis Glynn, Tom Tracy and Maurice Quinn. Their kindness to me is really embarrassing."

The reason for the doctor's aversion to stairs, as far as the bishop was concerned, becomes apparent in a letter from Father Martin O'Brien, the bursar at Silver Creek, to Father O'Mahony. "First of all," he wrote, "the Bishop looks better and feels better than he did a few weeks ago. However, the doctors were not too pleased with his last attack. He had a blood clot both in the lung and in the leg. He responded well to treatment but they are afraid of a recurrence, unless he takes plenty of rest. . . . In spite of the doctor's reports, I am convinced that a few months of general rest in Navan will restore the old pep and energy to His Excellency."

Through gains and reverses, ups and downs, Bishop Galvin continued to write letters to people and to answer those which came to him. A letter from Daisy Hall, reporting on a number of illnesses and ailments in her family, brought a prompt reply. "Hospitals and illness are a part of life," he wrote, "but they are lonely things. Let us all try to accept them as a part of God's will."

An attorney wrote to the bishop from Chicago, conveying to him ten thousand dollars from the estate of Margaret Lorden. He turned over nine thousand dollars to Father Martin O'Brien at Silver Creek, and sent a thousand to the Sisters of St. Columban in Chicago. Urged to retain some of the money for his own use, he rejected the idea. He had taken traveling expenses out of gift money from other people and from John Galvin's gift of five thousand dollars, but he had turned over most of his personal gifts intact to society funds. When another priest argued that the John Galvin money was a straight gift to him personally and that the society had no claim on it, he laughed.

"I am nothing personally," he said. "No one would make gifts to me. If I were not the Bishop of Hanyang I would never have been in this good man's home at all, and I'd never have had any money from him."

On May 3, 1954, after a rather vehement argument with his doctors, the bishop flew to Boston. After less than two days there and a visit to the archbishop, he flew on to Brooklyn, to the friends of his parish and the all but obliterated scenes of his young priesthood. He wrote to Father O'Mahony on May 11 from the Columban house at 869 President Street:

Dear Donal,
All the priests are in for lunch, including Vallely and Loftus.
Had a most cordial reception from Cardinal Spellman, Bishop Malloy, Bishop Sheen, Bishop Lane and the Maryknoll Fathers with whom I spent about an hour and a half. I saw Daisy Hall and her clan and spent Sunday with them. I'm all packed and the prelude to lunch is on.
Goodbye, Donal. God bless you.
Find enclosed a spot for anything you fancy.

Always,
Edward.

He had no idea whatever of the impression that he had created in New York. His Eminence Francis J. Cardinal Spellman said of him: "He was a living saint. What more can you say?" The Most Rev. Fulton J. Sheen sought to define his own thought.

"He made an indelible impression on me," he said. "The impression that remains with me is of a man of evangelical simplicity which hid great spiritual power. He was simplicity itself, and humility itself. But while you meet many people who are simple people, you do not meet many who manifest the spiritual power that he did. In himself he was not an impressive man and he wasn't impressive except to those who were interested in spiritual things. He is not a man who can be written great; he has to be seen great. He was the type of man who could be a saint because he wasn't conscious of being saintly. In a bench of bishops he wouldn't be the 'outstanding' bishop because he fools you, as a saint should fool you. There was the same disproportion between the man and the results which he achieved as there is between the hem of Our Lord's garment and the cure that was worked in the woman who touched it. I wonder if anyone in a lifetime has had such spiritual filiation. There are few founders who have had such progeny in their generation."

Bishop Galvin was not aware of how others regarded him outside his tight circle of friends; he gave little

376

thought to impressions or appearances. He still wore collars that were too large for him and shabby shoes, sharply polished. He did not know what he ate or when he ate it. He never, however, forgot anyone who had been his friend.

There were many friends at Idlewild Airport to say their farewells—all of the Columbans and veteran priests in the area, and the old guard of parishioners.

> We all . . . went to Idlewild airport to see him off on his last journey to Ireland [Ava McHale Strenz wrote]. He was so tired that day but so gentle and, as always, considerate of others. . . . I asked him what he would do in Ireland. He said, "I want to walk in the green fields that I walked in as a boy."
> My last picture of him is his coming to the door of the plane and slowly waving his handkerchief. He had gone to the plane and had been settled in his seat when someone in the crowd went to the door of the plane and asked him if he would come out and wave again. Although very visibly weary, he got up and came to the door and waved to us.

The plane took off and they were all left behind. Bishop Galvin knew that he would never see any of them again; that the United States, like China, was gone, a part of his life forever but a part that was over. He was flying to Ireland and he would travel incredibly fast; a drink, a dinner, a nap, and the trip over the ocean would be over. He could remember when the ocean took weeks out of a man's life, and sickened him, and tossed him up on the shore with a weariness of the sea. An airplane deposited a man on a foreign shore before he was ready for it; but when one was old, it was better to reach a destination fast. Few things waited when one was slowed by years.

He had seen television and had learned to take it for granted. When he first went to Omaha he had had one of the early crystal radios with headsets and he had listened to the music which came to him through the air, marveling at it. He had seen gas street lights when he first went to Brooklyn and he had watched the lamplighter on his rounds. He had ridden in horsecars. He could remember a large parish in a big American city when there was only

377

one automobile in the entire parish. A person could not talk over the telephone to cities far away when he was young; now anyone could carry on a conversation with another person practically anywhere in the world. He was flying home to Ireland, with the memory of long boat trips and rough seas.

The bishop landed at Shannon Airport on May 13, 1954. Father Timothy Connolly, the superior general, was there to meet him, and Dr. Maguire; Father Walsh of Cahercon; Father Leahy; three Columban Sisters; the bishop's nephew, Sean O'Mahony, and Sean's wife, Julia. He sat between Sean and Julia, not knowing these young people but paying attention to them.

Sean O'Mahony wrote his account of the landing to his brother, Father Donal: "There was no confusion and I really think that Uncle Edward's plan for a quiet homecoming was the best thing to do."

The bishop rode to Dowdstown House with Father Connolly, and looked at the large, modern seminary that had been erected east of the house and well away from it. Bishop Cleary and Father Blowick, who were living in the seminary, came out to greet him. At Dowdstown House there were China hands, Fathers Lane and Hughes and others.

As always, the bishop was optimistic about his physical condition to the point of making plans which could not be fulfilled. He planned a trip to Cork to visit his brothers and sisters and the other relatives within two weeks, but the time stretched to a month. Priests visited him at Dowdstown House and he had Columbans around him all the time. He was still a storyteller.

There were talks on Ireland and talks on China. One of the Irish priests wanted to know what was the matter with the Government of China that it had not prevented the rise of the Reds by legislation. "You can only legislate for normality," the bishop said. "We never had five years of normality so we didn't know what was normal for China."

On another occasion, he said: "You could exist with the Japs and go on sick calls, but there was no existing with the Commies."

The pattern of the United States was soon repeated in

378

Ireland; gay, confident activity, big plans, then collapse and never a concession from the bishop.

> I came to Dublin on August 24 [he wrote] and feeling tired, I went to see Dr. O'Donovan at his office. He sent me to St. Vincent's and the following morning he found a vein in my left leg inflamed, for which he said there was little remedy except rest in bed. I had no pain or discomfort and spent a pleasant time reading. After a few weeks in the hospital the red blood count was down. I was still enjoying myself reading but the doctor and the Sister took a rather serious view of the blood count and suggested that I be anointed. They gave me a blood transfusion, two pints. I reacted to it very favorably. The blood count went up, to the great delight of the doctor. Some injection of Cortisone helped a good deal, too. I saw no reason for worry. I felt quite happy about passing over the border. I knew that Columban would be there and that I would meet a merciful Lord. For a few nights I had wild dreams of a race across country which I won and in which I was disqualified because I came from Cork.

Bishop Galvin had contended with dreams all of his life. The recurring dream was of a high wall. He walked along a narrow path on top of it and as he wearied, his balance became uncertain and he was in terror of falling. So vivid was this dream, and so constant, that he made a point of visiting any wall that he heard of in the places which he visited. He never found the wall of his dreams.

Father Leahy had a car. When he asked the bishop where he would like to go, the bishop's eyes lighted. "There is just one place," he said. "My pastor in Brooklyn, Monsignor McEnroe, God rest his soul, said that he wanted to come back here to see the sun set again on Loughsheelin. He said it was the loveliest sight in Ireland. He never got back. I would like to look at it for him."

That request, of course, was one to honor. Father Leahy drove him to Monsignor McEnroe's home town of Ballyjamesduff in County Cavan. They saw the lake, but the sky was overcast and there was no sunset. Father Leahy tried it with the bishop several times more with the same result. Father Connolly tried three times and several other priests volunteered; sunset over Loughsheelin eluded them and Bishop Galvin never saw it.

Rita Galvin, the wife of young Seano, became a faithful volunteer and drove the bishop over old trails and to places he remembered. His favorite stopping spots were graveyards. He talked vaguely about writing a book, but he seemed mainly interested in the graves of priests. It was easy to find the priests in Irish cemeteries, even in the large ones. Their headstones did not face in the same direction as the stones of the people; they faced in the opposite direction. In death, as in life, the priest faced the people.

Bishop Galvin found the stones of men he had known, men he remembered. He was interested in those who were veteran priests when he was young and in discovering when they died. But he was more interested in contemporaries who were already gone and he seemed to be wondering how it would have fared with him if he had stayed in Ireland.

"Perhaps I should have been the shepherd of a different flock," he said one day.

He speculated along that line only when he was depressed, which was rarely, haunted by the what-might-have-been of China. Normally he was cheerful, finding nothing gloomy or saddening in a cemetery.

"I'll tell you the best epitaph I ever heard," he said one day to Rita Galvin. "Or, no, I won't. I'll tell you the second best."

He leaned back in the seat of the car, a cigarette between his fingers, and recited softly:

> *Here lie the remains of*
> *It doesn't matter who*
> *He died of*
> *It doesn't matter how*
> *The work he did on earth*
> *Is done much better now.*

The trips to cemeteries were farther apart as the months went along; then they stopped.

In March, 1955, Edward O'Mahony wrote to Father Donal O'Mahony: "Peg, my wife, is the mother of a baby boy . . . born on the morning of March 18. He has been christened Patrick Joseph. Uncle Ned did the job. The

Bishop wanted to do it because the baby was born on the anniversary of Grandmother Galvin's death."

That was the last child baptized by the bishop.

After Christmas of 1955, the bishop could no longer rally his resources to deny that there was anything serious troubling him. He was confined to his room and Mother Finbarr, one of the first Columban nuns, was placed in charge of him. In brief flashes of revolt, the bishop conspired with the housekeeper for some delicacy forbidden in his diet, for some assertion of free will, no matter how brief.

On February 21, when Mother Finbarr was temporarily away, the bishop prevailed upon the housekeeper to let him have one more adventure. He wanted to go down to the front door of Dowdstown House and look out upon the world. With the housekeeper's help he made it, holding himself straight, walking firmly. She had a desperate time, however, helping him back again and the stairs were a slow agony.

It was the final test. He drove his body to meet it and he knew when he finally regained his bed that he would never again leave it.

A letter from one of the Sisters of St. Columban relates the sequel:

> On the afternoon of Wednesday, 22nd, which was a bitterly cold day with frozen snow patches and a harsh wind, Sr. Catherine Laboure noticed a heavy sweat on the Bishop's face and brow. Knowing that the room was not too warm, she became uneasy, especially as she noticed when wiping off the perspiration and trying to ease the weight of clothing, that his lungs seemed to be collapsed and the ribs sunken. Sister called in Father Leahy and others who were near at hand, and a rosary was said very quietly in the room. Just at 4 P.M. Bishop Cleary came on his daily visit to Bishop Galvin and was shocked at the quick change, so unlike the person he had been on the previous day.
>
> Very clearly and quietly Bishop Cleary spoke to him about Nancheng and the care he hoped Bishop Galvin would take of his poor Chinese Catholics and the diocese of Nancheng. In his words and manner, Bishop Cleary conveyed to 'Ned' as he spoke that the parting with life on earth was at hand. Bishop Galvin paused a moment,

381

seeming to ponder the whole message and then said very deliberately, "Yes, I will."

The final absolution, plenary indulgence, and prayers were said, and Bishop Galvin responded every time he was asked to say or do something quite conscious of everything.

Very soon he seemed to revive and lose the ghastly appearance, and in the course of the evening he seemed 'as usual.' Many of the priests were inclined to think it was one of many passing weaknesses. The Sisters were less optimistic and unobtrusively prepared for the imminent death of the Bishop . . . so that Mother M. Finbarr would not have to face a crisis that night, unprepared. Sister Catherine Laboure held out no hope of even a temporary recovery, in spite of the almost normal appearance of the Bishop at 10 P.M., and thanks to her, all preparations were adequately made. The priests were at hand to find all the Bishop's robes, etc., and Father Connolly and Father Thomas Kennedy remained nearby on call for the night. At 1:30 A.M. Mother M. Finbarr called both priests and they said the prayers again, as the Bishop was so weak and his breathing rather laboured. However, once again he rallied and took some liquid, and the breathing got easy.

At 3:30 A.M. Mother M. Finbarr who had been very vigilant, saw that the end was come. Father Connolly and Father Kennedy came back and together the two priests and Mother M. Finbarr helped the brave soul to face into eternity. Quite gently he breathed his last, and the priests read the office together.

The Mass for the dead was sung by Father John Blowick, and "all the fields were covered with snow and the morning was bright and sunny. Thin columns of people walked along the paths after the coffin, the black clothes of the students contrasting with the clear white of the snow."

There was, almost miraculously, a touch of China. Ten Chinese Catholic students of University College, Dublin, journeyed to Navan and brought mourning scrolls for the man who had spent his life for their unfortunate country.

It was all over. Father Timothy Leahy gave the last salute in *The Far East*.

He was [he wrote] a man without fear, born with a spark of high adventure and an illimitable confidence in the Providence of God. Robert W. Service once wrote a poem picturing the Yukon as addressing her future settlers:

> *And I will not be won by weaklings,*
> *Subtle, suave and mild,*
> *But by men with the hearts of Vikings,*
> *And the simple faith of a child.**

Priests who served in China under Bishop Galvin, and who are alive today, will one and all agree how adequately the last two lines epitomize the outstanding characteristics of him whom we were so proud to claim as our leader and our chief.

Messages flowed in from all over the world; cables and notes of condolence, of appreciation, of admiration, of grief. In a short time the flow was slowed and only a few humble, necessary tasks remained to be done. Edward O'Mahony, the bishop's nephew, totaled up his estate. There was, of course, no money.

"I wrote, explaining to the bishop's brother, Sean Galvin," said Edward, "that I was sending one or two things to him of the bishop's personal possessions, but that when I came to dividing the few things he had—some underwear, a few pairs of stockings, a few books, a few cheap pens, an inexpensive watch that he'd had probably all of his life—I found that I had very little to divide. Sean wrote back, thanking me for the little parcel and made the wonderful comment: 'The bishop never had very much that was his own.' "

It was, in a sense, an epitaph.

* From "The Law of the Yukon," *The Collected Poems of Robert Service* (New York: Dodd, Mead & Company).

0-595-26232-5